AF519397

Indian Epic Tradition

Indian Epic Tradition

Professor Tapodhir Bhattacharjee
Vice Chancellor
Assam University, Silchar

AKANSHA PUBLISHING HOUSE
NEW DELHI-110002 (INDIA)

AKANSHA PUBLISHING HOUSE
4649-B/21, Ansari Road
Darya Ganj, New Delhi - 110 002
Ph.: 23263193 / 9811582579 / 09435116718
Fax: 011-23263193
Email: ektabooks@yahoo.com
www.akanshapublishinghouse.com

Indian Epic Tradition

First Edition 2009
ISBN 978-81-8370-186-0

PRINTED IN INDIA

Published by Akansha Publishing House, New Delhi and Printed at Aryan Enterprises, Delhi.

In

Everlasting Fond Memory of

My

Beloved Mother

ARUNA BHATTACHARJEE

'My Teacher and My Maker'

[Inferno : i. 82]

and

Professor Sukumari Bhattacharji

'Who always guides my eyes upward'

[Purgatorio : xxi. 124]

Contents

Acknowledgments

My indebtedness are indeed too numerous to enumerate. I offer my sinceremost obeisance to my illustrious teachers: Late Lakshmikanta Biswas, Late Kulendra Bhattacharya, Late Anima Bhattacharya and Late Gogiraj Basu who sowed in me the seeds of unquenchable love for literature in general and Sanskrit poetry in particular during my studenthood. I can never repay the debt which I owe to my respected teachers: Dr. Sukhamay Bhattacharya, Dr. Rajlakshmi Devi, Shri Gagannath Roychoudhury, Prof Amaresh Dutta and several others. The words of encouragement from my colleagues viz. Dr. Sanjay Roy and Shrimati Nandita Bhattacharya as well as timetested friends like Dr. Debaprasad Kar and Shri Ranabir Purkayastha are my everlasting treasure.

I also fondly remember my grandfather Late Nalini Mohan Ray whose deep interest for learning encouraged me to take up sustained academic studies. The sad memory of my fellow traveller, Dr. Chandidas Bhattacharya makes me nostalgic about some precious moments shared with him.

I am grateful to the staff of National Library, Asiatic Society, Bangiya Sahitya Parishad, North Bengal University library and Cachar College (Silchar) library for their cooperation.

I must here mention late Dr Asim Kumar Dutta who introduced me to Professor Sukumari Bhattacharji and ushered in a new phase in my life.

And, I owe everything to my loving parents for inspiring and guiding me from childhood to take up the challenging academic pursuits; no word can ever sufficiently express my unrepayable debts to them.

Last but not the least, I have overwhelming debts to my wife, Dr. Swapna Bhattacharya, without whose unflinching help no venture is ever possible.

26 Jan. 2009 **Tapodhir Bhattacharjee**

SECTION –I

1
Introduction

The concluding decades of the twentieth century have witnessed unprecedented proclamations of selfannihilation. Death of history has been announced with morbid glee when history is wiped out, traditions and their continuum also evaporate. With the renewed onslaught of postmodernisms and their corollary conceptual anarchism, nothing remain static and dependable. In such a scenario of total decentredness what makes us read Indian epics? Surely we have around us the most uncongenial atmosphere for reading epics which existed in the remotest possible antiquity. Why then are we attempting to read epics in an era which is frankly antagonistic even for an honest academic exercise of reinterpretation? Paul de Man, one of the prominent poststructurlist in the late twentieth century, commented in his famous book entitled *Blindness and Insight*, 'The specificity of literary language resides in the possibility of misreading and misinterpretation. (p. 280)

Basically any reading of epics, whether Indian or Western is rereading. Now we undertake such a project of reading only to reinterprete. First we discover the aporias anew from where our insightful journey commences. While doing so, we question ourselves: what kind of worldview, attitude or philosophy can these epics offer which we might now find elsewhere? Besides what modes of reading we can use to decipher various strata of experiences and insights stored in the epic texts? Several other questions can be framed. But there cannot be singular response to these and similar other queries.

The pertinent point is this: one can embark even now upon the study of Indian epics and the generic continuum. The task is amalgamation of the tough endeavour of both sisyphus and tantalus. Hence such a study never ends; it can only resume time and again.

This fact can hardly be disputed that only total reading can be fruitful. The onus of response indeed rests with the penetrating readers. But a total reading is also not without certain predicaments of its own particularly when its focal point is a literature of the past. Do we have any quest for relevance while we read? Is there any harm if we very rigidly maintain our neutrality with regards to the multipolar experiences of the bygone days? Well, response to such queries cannot be simplistic. Readers are required to negotiate with the varying facets of the epic genre. The dialogics of the continuum and breach in Indian epic tradition promises to be a fascinating study because the collective experiences of several epochs spread over two millennia assumed robust literary form in this solemn genre. The conflicting worldviews emanating from different regions and nourished by heterogeneous people melted into the great couldron of the epic genre as it were to effect the genesis of the lofty art form.

The timeless depth and exquisite beauty of the Sanskrit epics fascinated me in my early student days. Thereafter I took it up as my area of further research. I subscribe to this firm opinion that any literary genre of the ancient time can be meaningfully explored if it is firmly placed in a contemporary perspective. The sequential reading of the Indian epic genre progressed through phases. The conclusion was inevitable that the continuum of the epics in the Indian literatures has been revalidated beyond any doubt. I accept with sincere modesty that any journey into the vastly varied territories of the Sanskrit epics and then its extension to vernacular Bengali literature cannot but be provisional.

It is provisional because the measures of our exploratory responses to the variegated microcosms are intertwined with the multilinear expression of the epic legacy. There are several breaches and renewals through which the continuum has been disrupted time and again yet always reaffirmed. The Indian creative mind has never failed to respond to a timeless schemata though the temporal situation has also cast its shadow over the typical generic manifestation. Even as we are approaching the closure of the first decade after the countdown to the third millennium, those old works continue to fascinate us. The Sanskrit epic genre has great individual works to its credit; but it is its totality that still stretches, widens, heightens, deepens, expands or enriches our understanding and awareness about the imaginative reconstruction of life and nature around. Whatever might have been the opinions of ancient readers, we too have something to speak of the Indian epic sequence that may shed illuminating light on the quintessence of the form and content of the old genre. In fact, the roof and crown of the old literary tradition never lose their power to stretch and stimulate and that is why the immense value of rereading those works can never be lost sight of. Both the great epics are highly interesting since these are most mysterious and perplexing having innumerable exits and entrances into text. Besides, the epics of Aśvaghoṣa, Kālidāsa, Bhāravi and others appeal to us by the expanding frontiers of the genre; the formal structures of their work possess high degree of order and equilibrium. At the same time, the craving of the then cultural milieu for new form, new order, new meaning found creative expression in their own contemplation and execution of the genre. Thus the Sanskrit epic firmament provides a vision ever-renewing and also rich, various and complex world in such a manner that the limited patterns, which the temporal situation sought to freeze into the then reality and human truth, seem irrelevant.

Undoubtedly, the conflict between form and content in the genre remained unresolved to a considerable extent. The epic sequence under question is also far from being homogeneous. Nevertheless, being mutually exclusive, different works of this genre have remained the cynosures of readers through several epochs. Of course, there are wide divergences of opinion, taste and emphasis culminating into basic differences in conclusive appreciation or otherwise. Notwithstanding the unavoidable discrepancies in response and understanding of the unique position of the Sanskrit epic tradition, its study is rewarding for the modern reader. Because, such an endeavour helps us in correctly deciphering the modes of classical literature; besides it shows as to how the individual talents have been productively integrated within tradition. Thus the shades and colours inherent in the warp and woof of the epic continuum are quantified. Under the aegis of a centralised concept of sequential order, the historical, ideological and textual positions are blended together. This also proves the wonderful sagacity of the epic poets who knew the philosophical import of the continuum of tradition; that is, every poetic object is situated dialogically. This also signifies that there is nothing altogether old, nor is there anything absolutely new in the arena of creative literature. It is the poetic skill that ultimately holds the key since though the subjects and words-in-stock may be wellknown, yet the new poem is chiselled out of them. Thus there is the famous saying:

> 'Ta eva padavinyāsāsta evārthavibhuātayahū
> Tathāpi navyamū bhavati kāvyamā grathanakuslāt'.[1]

The word 'Grathana' may be rendered as 'discourse', which has become a very important critical term in recent years. The above-mentioned verse thus signifies that the materials are meant for the community but that novelty lies only with the idiosyncratic use of the talented creative personality. This is where imagination takes command and gives to the airy nothing and also to the long-trodden path a local as well as a new habitation and a name. Vālmīki and Vyāsa turned the disjointed oral materials into two peerless epic wonders while Aśvaghoṣa, Kālidāsa, Bhāravi, Bhaṭṭi, Māgha and others, in their own singular way, explored this legacy of renewing the heritage again and again. In the Indian weltanschauung, Time is infinite and an individual existence is likened to a wave in the endless ocean; neither past nor present is absolute. Yet the link in the great cycle of life has to be affirmed over and over again. The epic genre is unique since it is inseparable from this philosophical position; its subtlety and expansiveness are only two different manifestations of the great cycle of Being. There is no enigma for the Indian epic poets because their creative imagination is expected to illuminate this cosmic truth of being and becoming. It reminds us of a well-known expression of Ānandavardhana:

'Dṛṣṭapūrvā api hyarthāh Kāvyarasaparigrahāt
Sarve navāivābhānti madhumāsa iva drumāh'.[2]

The Sanskrit epic poems do not have a very wide range of theme since they usually fell back upon the known sources. Obviously, their readers did not raise any eyebrow or frown upon the poets because they used to be happy if aesthetic and ethical legacy were reaffirmed. The social control exerted by the power elites over the epic genre was so unassailable that the term 'Siddharasa' came to stay. However, that does not mean that those readers were fond of stereotypes only and failed to attain the coveted status of the connoisseurs. On the contrary, the role of creative imagination was unequivocally recognised in the process of metamorphosing old materials into new aesthetic existence; that is why, Bhattatauta made the oft-repeated pronouncement: 'Prajñā navanavollekhaśālinī pratibhā'.[3] Though the subjectmatter of the epic poems was thoroughly standardised and the elaborate paraphernalia were also dictated by the rhetoricians, the imaginative versifiers could nevertheless display their eagerness for ringing in the new. The dichotomy emanating from the socio-cultural situation was unquestionably imposing yet the poets somehow learned to live with it. As a result, the epic microcosms were built in such a manner that the implicit and explicit dichotomy simultaneously nourished and swamped the genre. Predictably, the rhetoricians could see only the inexhaustible range of poetic themes.e.g.

'Vācaspatisahasrānām sahasrair api yatnatah
nibaddhā sākṣayam naiti prakṛtir-jagatāmiva'.[4]

This indicates that they had totally different notion about the magnitudes, vision, expansiveness of an epic poem; the individual verses were more important than the central scheme of the work. Like the miniature painting, the individual verses were considered separately and, what is significant, creative imagination was thought to be concentrated in depicting some unique moments of existence. Mahimabhaṭṭa hints at the excellence of such 'momentariness' when he observes:

'Rasānugunaśabdārthacintāstimitacetasah
Kṣaṇam svarūpasparṣottha prajñaiva pratibhā kaveh'.[5]

Yet, at another level, the creative mind is aspirant of nothing less than cosmic expansiveness. Thus, none other than Bāṇabhaṭṭa, observes ambitiously:

> 'Kim kavestasya kāvyena sarvavṛttāntagāminī
> katheva bhāratī yasya na vyāpnoti jagattrayam'.[6]

Undoubtedly, therefore, the epic poets too had to operate between these above-mentioned polarities which are difficult to reconcile. In the arena of the epics of art, the standardised dos and donts effectively clipped the wings of the Epic Muse and the whims of patrons were rather too easy to negotiate. Many a poets tried to sail through the Scylla nad the Charybdys but their poetic vessel got stuck in the quicksand of rhetorics. Only an Aśvaghoṣa or Kālidāsa or Bhāravi, to some extent, could successfully find the passage to the zanadu of creativity. Thus their epics bespeak of inimitable synthesis between subtlety and expansiveness, sacredness and profanity, timeless and temporal, mundane and spiritual. In fact, the dialogical imagination is at its very best in their epic microcosms. On the other hand, with the advent and gradual proliferation of rhetorics, the later poets became virtually prisoners of formalism. Yet the vales and meadows, peaks and caverns confirm the existence of reassuring epic sequence. In spite of the changing sociocultural perspective, Indian epic imagination thrived on a plausible unifying principle and, by and large, enjoyed relatively autonomous power that developed according to its own operative laws. The achievements of the great poets of the genre remind us of a comment by an eminent critic: 'The dream (of the strong poet) is not merely a phantasmagoria of endless gratification, but is the greatest of all human illusions, the vision of immortality.'[7]

What does this 'immortality' actually mean? This means, perhaps, that succeeding generations of readers may meaningfully respond to the texts offered by the poets. The study of epic sequence is also no exception; if its texts can be reread and reinterpreted, in that case, these may be said to be endowed with ontological signification. This simply means that, both aesthetically and socially, these exist. Of course, the epic texts have validity epistemologically as well and the quest of knowledge may induce several generations to undertake explorations. Some readers may swear by racial memory but some others might understandably shy away because the texts have lost their immediacy and faded out altogether. Besides, the apparent inadequacies of the generic conventions and their resultant discourse prove to be stumbling block even for the enterprising readers. The very fact of co-existence of Vālmīki and Bhāravi, Kālidāsa and Bhatti, Aśvaghoṣa and Śrīharṣa in the Sanskrit epic sequence posts the signal that multiple variances of dichotomies and nuances are to be expected as 'natural' for the genre. The readers are, therefore, to be prepared for a unique kind of emotional and intellectual transactions which do not occur along singular continuum nor are these in accordance with the dimensions of any homogeneous metaphor. In fact, the sensitive readers are expected to maintain several simultaneous states of liasion and feeling towards a text. Otherwise the true import of the dialogue between mundane and divine, form and content or intellect and emotion would remain beyond total comprehension.

What an eminent western critic spoke about the magnitude of the epic genre may not be equally and wholly applicable to the Sanskrit epic sequence but this definitely holds good about the foremost poets of the genre. Therefore, let us have a closer look at that comment: 'Epic answers man's need to clear away an area he can apprehend, if not dominate; and commonly this area expands to fill the epic universe, to cover the known world and reach between Heaven and Hell. Epic characteristically refuses to be hemmed in, in time as well as in space, it raids the unknown and colonizes it. It is the imagination's manifesto, proclaiming the range of it's grasp, or else it is the dream of the will indulging its fantasies of power.'[8] Thus, the epic genre is particularly marked for its unique handling of time and space by dint of which it unfolds a central metaphorical scheme. In this process, the foremost epic poets proclaim, as it were, an unputdownable manifesto of creative imagination which is always original and yet for ever renewed. The readers are only required to distinguish between the inherent and extraneous, substantial and accidental characteristics of the epic text. Though the Indian epic sequence apparently left no scope for the readers' manoeuvrability, yet we seek to operate from the very foundation of the closed epic microcosm. This is possible if we can correctly decipher the social intention of the epic poet; in fact, even the versifiers who are excessively loyal to the dictum of the rhetoricians, cannot but try to methodically integrate an audience into their experience. The epic hero may have superhuman status but he, too, acts for his community and the state. Indeed, even the rule-abiding Sanskrit epics would not be aesthetically relevant if a potential human habitation cannot be discovered and recognised in an otherwise deliberately prepared valley of the divinities and the titans.

II

It is an undeniable fact that no single factor ever works in isolation in creative literature. Several factors combine, presuppose each other and what matters in the end is the specific quality of each individual work of art. However, this uniqueness can be fully appreciated only when we know perfectly about the traditions and conventions that have been accepted or modified. When we are conscious of an ever-continuing literary tradition, we can really analyse and weigh the success and merits of an individual work of art. The Bengali epics may thus be properly assessed only when we hold the works in the context of a greater literary tradition of the Indian epics.

An analytical account of the Epic sequence as well as the influence of Sanskrit epics on nineteenth century Bengali epic poetry provides the readers with that perspective which allows them to be properly aware of the continuum of literary and cultural traditions. It becomes obvious that the reassuring presence of a wider and richer Sanskrit epic tradition continually surrounded, pressed upon, entered and modified the Bengali epic genre. However, an epic is not simply a recreation of old things; it is altogether a new creation in terms of the old. In fact, epic poetry has been used by various people all over the world and in different ages to artistically voice forth their high seriousness and also to transmit their eagerness to revitalise tradition. It is significant that the epic genre was cultivated at a crucial stage in the history of Bengal when, under the yoke of colonial rule, the Bengalis had to struggle for a national identity and a world of their own.

The very magnitude of the epic form itself which the Bengali mind, being inspired by the emergent nationalism adopted for its national self-expression, became a symbol of national self-realisation and spiritual identity.

The opening decades of the nineteenth century were important as a period of experiment and preparation for greater things to follow. That is why, the second half of the nineteenth century was marked with a rare flourish in almost all the streams of literary activities. In the realm of poetry, the epic genre was practically a craze and in prose, the novel became the darling of the readers. Towards the close of the century, the novel gradually outshone and eclipsed the epic and then finally replaced it.

The Young Bengal movement did not completely anglicize the Bengali intellectuals; rather, the tie with the Indian literary tradition was never altogether snapped. Even during the crazy days of the Young Bengal, the Indologists worked sincerely to explore the legacy of the past. Their activities gradually paved the way towards unveiling the country's past which proved to be an important factor in the national awakening of India. The acceptance of the Epic sequence and also the evolution of the epic genre in Bengali literature is indeed the artistic manifestation of that awakening and its consequent all-pervasive high seriousness. Literature is always tuned with many crosscurrents of thoughts and ideas prevalent in society. The flourish and decay of the literary genres are conditioned by their social perspectives. Towards the close of the nineteenth century, Bengali society was almost clogged in the quicksand of revivalistic tendency and hence the epic genre was impoverished and ultimately became artistically irrelevant.

However, the urge for patriotic heroic poetry in nineteenth century Bengal may be interpreted as an index to the growth and development of nationalism under colonial subjugation. As poetical works of this type were inspired by nationalism, these at the same time inspired nationalism immensely in their turn. The poets had, however, no definite political consciousness as they speak of no particular political goal to be achieved. Yet the political unconscious was the motivating force underneath; a tremendous urge for national upliftment must have worked deeply in their subconscious as is amply testified by the way in which they selected and handled their themes. A study of the heterogeneous epic poems composed during that period shows clearly that, whatever might be the themes chosen by the poets, these had to be substantially transformed to be adjusted to the prevailing conditions and the hopes and aspirations of the nation. This transformation or re-adjustment of the Sanskrit Epic sequence helped the poets to a great extent in making old and retold themes acceptable and attractive to the readers of the nineteenth century.

It is very natural that the achievement of the major poets of the genre is qualitatively different from that of the minor poets of the period. Because the creative emotion of the minor poets is born in a hazy twilight and at a comparatively superficial level in the creative soul. A true poet, however, can easily descend into the depths of life and touch the deepest layers. The poetic sense is the first epiphany of creative intuition in which consists the prime and basic intentional value in the structure of the poem. Creative intuition is indeed the only supreme gift that a poet, in any literary genre whatsoever, ought to seek. But, in order to understand the process of development of the genre, we have to examine the twilight zones as well.

Before the flourish of the midday sun, there always exists a dawn. Likewise, before the Epic Muse attained the pinnacle of glory through Michael Madhusudan Dutta's immortal works, Rangalal Bandyopadhyaya ventured to cultivate the epic possibilities. It is immaterial whether he achieved success or not because we know that he is important not for what he actually achieved but for what he promised for his immediate successors. It is significant that at a particular juncture of time, Rangalal graduated into a versifier of pseudo-epic and narrative poems from his original status of a stray writer of verses and essays. Rangalal was not an artist of a high order, nevertheless, he can claim credit as a pioneer. A new awareness for a spirit of patriotism inspired Rangalal to search for heroic episodes in the annals of our country. Consequently, his *Padminī Upākhyāna* (1858) has been responsible to give rise to the later epics and pseudo-epics. Even his *Karmadevī* (1862), *Sūra Sundarī* (1868), *Kāñcī-Kāverī* (1879) exerted considerable influence on the poetasters of the last quarter of the century.

This new awareness for the legacy of the past has no doubt emanated from the impact of deepening high seriousness among the colonial elites. It is nothing but an unconscious manifestation of the search for psychological compensation for the darkly night that descended on the colonized people. As no light was visible at the end of the tunnel, the poets undertook a reverse journey to an apparently glorious past where the epic genre seemed to be most befitting. Rangalāl was substantially inspired by the Sanskrit historical *mahākāvyas* which perhaps made him conscious of the possibilities of exploring our past history. In fact, the study of these historical *mahākāvyas* leads us to the inevitable conclusion that though the old Indian literature may be said to be deficient in the scientifically written history, it is not entirely unaware of the artistic possibilities of historical episodes. However, the historical themes, besides reflecting the vague nationalistic urge of pride, merely serve as the framework for the display of the poet's subtle art and rhetorical embellishment.

It has already been explained that the authors of the Sanskrit historical mahākāvyas freely used similes, metaphors and other figures of speech and incorporated descriptions of landscape, seasons and such other things, which according to the dictum of the Indian poetics should form integral part of an epic. It has also been noted that the classical Sanskrit poetry had become stereotyped from fairly early times and was bound by certain norms and conditions. Pedantry had also become the characteristic hallmark of the later Sanskrit poetry. These historical mahākāvyas are full of word-play, conceit, rhyme and alliteration and these works strictly follow the rules laid down by the rhetoricians. When Rangalal turned to these poets for inspiration, he could not but imitate their methods of versification which included mannerism as well.

III

After Rangalal, the major poets like Michael Madhusudan Datta and Hemchandra Bandyopadhyaya were busy in finding a golden mean between the repertory of ancient heritage and modern rationalistic approach. The fact remains that the nineteenth century Bengal is remarkable for fostering the spirits of rationalism and humanism. Scientific theories also prompted some of the poets (including Hemchandra) to remodel the classical or Puranic episodes on a scientific basis. But the scientific spirit coupled with the positivistic and utilitarian philosophy, was also indirectly responsible for a rapid decline of the wonder and awe with which the medieval gods and goddesses had been regarded. It began with the introduction of the figures like Niyati (Destiny), Bhāgyadeva (the god of luck), Capalā etc. in the *Vṛtrasamhāra* (1875) and was zealously perpetuated in the repetitive pseudo-epics of the minor poets of the century. At any rate, the most promising feature of the Bengali epic genre was that a tendency became manifest to define divinity in terms of humanity.

However, Madhusudan is the most outstanding poet of the genre who, because of his meteoric rise, was a surprise even to his friends and contemporaries. He dived deep into the territories of the world literature and succeeded in enriching his own literature with the help of the gems he could gather. Madhusudan's most epochmaking contribution was the introduction of the blank verse, the Amitrāksara. Its introduction was no doubt stimulated by a spirit of revolt against the fetters of the conventional pattern of rhyming, but it was also inspired by the demands of a heroic age. It may be regarded as the artistic manifestation of the awakening of our national consciousness on one level. Thus the introduction of the blank verse was immensely significant because it went a great way in rousing the readers from our habituated slumber and had far-reaching effects on poetry and drama.

In the *Tilottamāsambhava*, Madhusudan arrived at the nearest point of success in epic versification. In fact, he was endeavouring to come to terms with his poetic self. The *Meghanādvadha* (1861) is the natural culmination of the process that began with the *Tilottamā Sambhava* (1860). Madhusudan was possessed by the Muse and his poetry was nurtured in the 'great mother' as Yeats called it i.e. in the collective memory of the entire people, in the territories of myths and legends. His much-professed westernism did not make him oblivious of the poetic possibilities of the Indian legacy. That is why he declared in one of his letters, "I love the grand mythology of our ancestors. It is full of poetry."[9]

In spite of the occasional intrusion of the Greek air in the epic narrative, the *Tilottamāsambhava* derives its sustenance more intimately from the *Mahābhārata* and the *Kumārasambhava*. Indeed the creative life of Michael Madhusudan Datta has a symbolical quality; it unfolds the defeat of false promises of the phase of over-westernisation in the history of Bengal. It is significant that he started to write in his mother tongue only three years after the great revolt of 1857. Madhusudan had realised, quite early in our modern period, the futility of the anglicizing tendencies of the renaissance. He has even regretted his homeless wanderings across fanciful foreign seas and in alien ports in one of his famous sonnets. He has poetically proved that our renaissance can be fruitful only through realisation of own background, the life and culture of our entire people from which roots the epic imagination blossoms forth. As the mid-nineteenth century ushered in the awakening of our national consciousness, it naturally brought in its wake a spirit of revolt against foreign subjugation. Rangalal, Madhusudan, Hemchandra and Nabinchandra are practically the harbingers of this new heroic era of nationalism and they have been substantially supported by the contemporary novelists, dramatists and essayists. The themes of the epics or other psuedo-epics of the period prove that these poets fell back upon either the heroic episodes from the annals of the country or the episodes from the great epics or later court epics or from the Purāṇas. The patriotism of the litterateurs of the century, including poets, novelists, dramatists and essayists, is revealed in two ways; first, in the choice of themes and secondly, in the reorientation of the whole theme to conform to the demands of the age. The epic tradition accelerated the pace of this new aesthetic epoch.

Madhusudan endowed the old story of the *Rāmāyaṇa* with new significance to make it relevant to the innermost aspirations of the age. In the *Meghnādvadha* Madhusudan artistically recreates the story of the valiant fight of Meghanād who fell in defence of his homeland. In order to achieve his poetic end, Madhusudan has freely cultivated the storehouse of the Sanskrit epics and with his unmistakable genius, marked the poetic materials with the idiosyncratic stamp of his originality. However, we are aware that poetic intuition can neither be learned nor improved by exercise and discipline, because it depends on a certain natural freedom of the soul and the imaginative faculties and on the natural strength of the intellect. Madhusudan was successful as he had all these qualities essential for a poet of the first order while his successors were not so much equipped.

IV

The *Vṛtra-Samhāra*, which is the representative work of Hemchandra, is a poetic elaboration of the Puranic tradition of the killing of the mightly demon, Vṛtra, by the gods who were once badly defeated and driven away from heaven. The most appealing scene of the poem constitutes of the episode of Dadhīci's self-sacrifice; his bones were fashioned into a bolt with which the demon was killed. Hemachandra made his appearance in the realm of Bengali poetry as an ardent admirer and follower of Madhusudan; but though his theme was perhaps better chosen for the epic purpose, he could not rival the glory of his predecessor because of his unimpressive, prosaic diction and an inherent lack of poetic fervour. Characteristically, the execution of the *Vṛtra-Samhāra* is apt to remind us of the post-Kālidāsa Sanskrit court epics in which the extraneous epic paraphernalia completely drowns their respective themes, though its theme is derived from the *Mahābhārata*, it deviates from the mood of the original to a great extent. In order to turn the meagre materials into a bulky epic,

Hemachandra succeeds in imitating the methods of epic versification, followed commonly by Bhāravi, Māgha, Srīharṣa and others.

Nabinchandra Sen's trilogy, constituting of the *Raivataka* (1886), *Kuruksetra* (1893) and the *Prabhāsa* (1896) centres round the great life of Kṛṣṇa as narrated in the *Mahābhārata* and some of the Purāṇas. But the actual intention of the poet was to put before the people of Bengal, the lofty and ennobling ideal of Kṛṣṇa, the divine redeemer, who is perfect in wisdom, valour and penetrating vision as well as tenderest in love and sympathy. His special mission was to create a great India (*Mahābhārata*) out of the chaos of the shattered political life and a society full of religious controversy, animosity and racial iniquities. Nabinchandra had a wider imagination and a more poetic rhythm than that of Hemchandra but he often suffered from a lamentable lack of the sense of propriety. There is vigour in his descriptions, thrill in the emotional rhapsodies but these are not always sufficient compensation for his total indiscipline in imagination and irretrivable excess in execution. He too took the clues for widening and further expanding the scope of narrative from that of the Sanskrit court-epics, but his excessive ardour has induced him to overdo the customary methods.

Hemchandra, Nabinchandra and other minor poets of nineteenth century Bengal could not appreciate the fact that the Sanskrit court epics flourished in an environment completely different from the situation prevalent in their time. Hence any mechanical imitation of the manners of an age-old tradition cannot be wholly relevant to the changed circumstances of the nineteenth century Bengal. Epic versification is essentially an intellectual activity and hence it is a process of purposive and systematised reflection of reality and its results and the transformation in the sphere of social consciousness. That is why the wholesale transplantation of the mannerisms of Sanskrit epics on nineteenth century Bengali epics cannot be artistically justified.

The emotional world of the poet is, in ultimate analysis, determined by the social milieu in which he lives and the more deeply he reflects the basic trends of society and the more sensitive he is to its processes, the more significant will be his work. Madhusudan's *Meghanādvadha* is the artistic manifestation of different facets of the contemporary social reality and precisely on that point, it is the foremost among the Bengali epics. Madhusudan has borrowed materials from the traditional repertory but he had taken care to organize them in such a way that these have become integral to the epic narrative. In fact, the perusal of Indian Epic sequence which had its regional restructuring and reschematising are vital for understanding the differences between the unthinking epigones, the time-servers in literary history and the genuine artists whose emotions and art are dedicated to their age and society. The imagination of a great literary artist like Madhusudan is deep and linked to the social reality of his times and it helps others to understand the meaning of the epoch.

Hemchandra and Nabinchandra only half-reacted to the aspirations of the age; as a result, their literary products are comparatively inadequate. In order to compensate for their lack of vision, they became more attentive to formal excellence and to the preaching of particular brands of philosophy. They failed to appreciate the fact that the poet's position is situated between objective reality which he must apprehend and the zenith of creative vision which he must unveil. This position in the system of social and intellectual reality determines the uniqueness of the tasks before him and gives rise to the specific structure of the poetic mind. The authors of the minor epics of nineteenth century Bengal had no conception of that poetic reality. Hence they wasted their time in weaving poems around the socially irrelevant themes of 'Samhāra,' 'Vadha,' 'Haraṇa,' 'Jaya' etc. Their over-dependence on the formalism of Sanskrit epics and dicta of rhetoricians only worsened their miserable plight.

It is very interesting to note another important feature of the Bengali epics. Except Madhusudan, all other poets of the genre have some overt purpose, ethical or religious, behind the composition of their poems. Significantly enough, all the poets except Madhusudan have failed to poetically interpret those 'Purposes'. They did their best to explore the Puranic and epic antiquities but their attempts exhaust themselves on a superficial level. We understand that the poet's apprehension of reality is linked precisely with the justification of an artistic validity whose specific nature consists in the emotional authenticity of its reflection of the essential aspects of reality. But revelation of the essence of reality is impossible on the level of emotional reactions alone; it also requires profound rational assimilation of the world. The rational mediation of the poet's emotional structure is seen with particular clarity in his possession of a certain worldview which includes not only an emotional, but also a rational apprehension of the world.

V

The very fact that the Bengali epic poets turned to Sanskrit epics for models or prototypes shows their groping for an adequate receptacle for the new experience and their implied resistance to borrow from Europe or England. There was challenge to find out a worthy genre and by recreating, at least partially, the ancient epics they seemed to proclaim to the world that the legacy of Indian Epic sequence could lend them suitable models. It was a statement of proud self-determination. But the explicit influence of the Western epics was most talked about, because the colonial elites were also emulating these, consciously trying them out, and fashioning a form which would be recognizably an Indian model and yet assimilate the useful traits of the foreign epics.

An epic poem has to reflect its author's attitude to the world because it is the creation of a synthesis of reality and the poet's unique individual traits. Hemchandra and Nabinchandra were practically obsessed with their ethical and philosophical concepts but these did not necessarily ensure the excellence of their poetic endeavours. Madhusudan is superior from this point of view as well. His *Meghanādvadha* unfolds the fact that a successful epic poet is not only the creator of new works but also a powerful reformer of reality itself. But this does not hold good about other poets of the genre.

The study of the widening of the horizon of Indian Epic sequence shows that a true creative poet looks for those which could somehow help him to find his own artistic identity. Because of obvious sociocultural reasons, the Bengali poets found themselves automatically surrounded by a stronger Indian tradition. Madhusudan used it to his advantage while Hemchandra and Nabinchandra also achieved partial success. If a writer wants to become a major artist of his particular genre, he should adopt what is most valuable from his tradition and learn from his predecessors. However, he must know how to transform it into true poetry which has its own aroma and stability. A creative poet has to reach the highest intellectual level from whose heights the world is revealed in all its breadth and depth, its infinite complexities and the resultant chiaroscuro. The generic sequence is established beyond dispute when the readers find that even after the lapse of several centuries and after going through several phases of socio-cultural and linguistic evolution, its relevance gets revalidated. This is the basic foundation on which the preceding epochs positively influence the thoughts of succeeding generations.

In the history of literature, that influence may be called beneficial which never violates the individuality of a poet but helps it to manifest itself more powerfully. From that point of view, the influence of Sanskrit epics was most beneficial for Madhusudan while Hemchandra and Nabinchandra are less fortunate. Thus the emergence and development of a poet's individual identity seems to be a complex process. His success depends on the ability to rediscover the world, renovate traditions and seek out and invent new means and devices for artistic recreation. However, it has been proved that a poet like Madhusudan does not meekly submit to influences but seeks them for his own artistic ends. For this reason we must not think of influence as a passive continuation of a sequence, that is, what has been done by the predecessors. Because, by choosing to accept influence, a creative poet not only unites with his literary predecessors but also stands in opposition to them. A poet of genius like Madhusudan, therefore, constantly tries to stride forward and to make his own discovery of reality.

Being a connoisseur of world literature, Madhusudan was well aware of both the merits and demerits of the Sanskrit epic tradition. He was definitely conscious of the fact that the Sanskrit literary epics were the careful production of trained and experienced specialists. The difficulty of the language as well as its complexity naturally involves prolonged endeavour and practice. It also affords endless opportunity and temptation for astonishing feats of verbal jugglery which perhaps would not be possible in any other language less accommodating than Sanskrit. This tendency is further encouraged by the elaborate rules and definitions of the rhetoricians until inborn poetic fervour is entirely obscured by superficial technicalities of expression. Ultimately it degenerated into a slavish adherence to rules and the effects are found in the limitation of range and outlook and conventionality of themes.

The influence of the formal - i.e. structural, rhetorical and prosodic—aspects on the nineteenth century Bengali epic poets is not uniform. Each poet was influenced differently; some more by the primary epics, others by later courtly and derivative epics. The thematic influence is comparatively negligible; the Bengali writers turned to glorious periods and episodes in the national history presumably because they thought that theirs was also a significant and memorable period. Where they borrowed themes from Sanskrit epics, it was more for the sake of ignoring the explilcit 'frame' of the 'story' which was well-known and therefore could be simply used as a suitable container for their message or ideas. In most cases, the method of restructuring of borrowed themes was more significant than what they actually borrowed; for, the alterations signified the new directions of their attitudes, new trends of their thoughts. The epic genre was considered as an appropriate vehicle for their enhanced national self-respect, hence they turned to it.

The borrowing of formal aspects was creatively justified in a poet like Madhusudan but an unfortunate cumbrous load of extraneous rhetoric in the less talented poets. Many failed to realize that the Bengali language should also be adequately refashioned since the hangovers of wornout habits of the preceding period were still persisting. Besides the colonised mind had blindness of their own; in the midst of self-abnegation, the bridges with tradition were indiscriminately burnt. Yet the search for the roots continued and the colonial contradictions deepened the crisis on the one hand while on the other, sharpened the dialogical perspective which is conducive for kindling the fire of creativity.

Obviously, the Bengali language has a distinct character of its own; hence, unimaginative and uncritical adaptation of the ancient materials cannot be justified. Therefore, when the over-enthusiastic poets were obsessed with the ancient epic sequence, they imitated even the mannerism of the Sanskrit epic poets. It very naturally led to an unhealthy tendency of incorporating irrelevant and commonplace descriptions that clog the course of the narrative. What we expect from an epic poet is the manifestation of a poetic personality which reveals itself in the warmth, movement and integrity of imagination and expression. If this is wanting, we call his work dull, cold or flat and all the philosophical and ethical ideas in the world cannot save a work from being a failure. Particularly, from the poets of nineteenth century Bengal, we expect something more; we want to see how they develop their poetic identities as well as their 'weltanschauung.' For a real poet, there is hardly an armoury of readymade weapons; he forges his own weapons to fight his own particular battles. The study of a generic sequence and its ever renewing influence becomes more meaningful when we are aware of this.

The value of the study of parallels lies in the light they shed on the qualities and merits of the individual works; at the same time, they indicate similarities and differences in our national literary tradition. We further note that the influence of Sanskrit epics on nineteenth century Bengali epic poetry is no mechanical phenomenon and it does not, in any way, diminish the originality of a sensible poet. On the contrary, even the influenced author produces work which is essentially his own. Here it may be affirmatively observed that creative influence is not confined to individual details or images or even sources—though it may include them—but is something pervasive, something organically involved in and presented through artistically significant works.

The widening of the horizon of Indian Epic sequence to include the nineteenth century Bengali epics may be vindicated by the organic qualities of the latter especially in their essential inspiration or artistic presentation which they otherwise would not have had. It has been observed that literary influence appears to be most frequent and most fruitful at the times of emergence of national literatures when these undergo radical change of direction. Nineteenth century Bengal witnessed such a phase in Bengali literature during which the influence of Sanskrit epics proved to be most fruitful. This influence became more significant as it was accompanied by social movements and political upheavals. Thus it added new dimensions to the Bengali epics which gained a meaningful sociocultural context in addition to its literary values.

VI

It is rightly observed that where there is no vision, the people perish. A living community is inspired by the vision of a higher and fuller life. This vision is rooted in the legacy of the past, as modified by the aspirations, ideals and actions of the present. It generates a sense of belonging and a sense of pride among the members of the community. The harbingers of the epic genre in nineteenth century Bengal also felt that their poems were expected to communicate the feeling of what it was aspiring for to be alive at that time. Behind them, they felt the presence of a big multitude of men of whose most serious convictions and dearest habits they acted as champions.

Like their prototypes, the Bengali epic poets probed into the mysteries of life, explored the potentialities and the utmost limits of human nature. In fact, pride in one's own language, country, culture and traditions is natural, desirable and essential. At the same time some of them also felt that it should not degenerate into mere chauvinism or escapism which seeks refuse in a romanticised past or into exclusiveness which remains impervious to the life-bestowing influence from other lands. Unfortunately, this awareness was not of equal magnitude for all the poets of the genre.

The perusal of the expansion of Indian Epic sequence makes us keenly aware of the truth that no great poet participates in a genre without modifying it; in other words, when we speak of epic tradition, we have in mind change as well as continuity. Naturally, it follows that no single epic would exemplify all the norms of the genre. Therefore, the differences of approach envisaged in the works of Madhusudan. Hemchandra and Nabinchandra should not puzzle us any more. Because, in spite of their poetic sincerity, all of them cannot equally justify the hope of discovering new worlds and able to give a fresh lease of life to the old model. Our study of the continuum of the Epic Sequence will be aesthetically valid only if we take into account which tendencies were absorbed, what were transmuted as well as what were rejected by the epic poets of nineteenth century Bengal. We are expected to consider as to what the influenced poet does with what he receives and what effect it has cast upon the finished literary work. What counts in the final analysis is the individual note, the special variation and the fresh nuance.

The nineteenth century Bengali epics brought with them their own forms. Like other creative products, these are to be considered from two points of view: that is, a unit integral in themselves and as part of a culture which is the patrimony of all Indians. The works of the major epic poets transcend experiences of ordinary social life, personal factors and the historical period in which their producers happen to live. They venture to reawaken the wealth of experience dominant in the collective unconscious of the Sanskrit epic firmament. The creative processes, that link nineteenth century with the Indian epic sequence, confer on the Bengali epics an aesthetically symbolic significance. The epic artist's creative zeal facilitates the reemergence of the old archetypes; it induces him to enter into a mystical participation with the ancient repertory of the Sanskrit epics.

Perhaps the Bengali epics flourished in an epoch which is basically not conducive for such a genre. The colonial society cannot vouch for extensive totality of life; on another plane, the generic technicalities, that evolved sequentially in the Sanskrit epics, cannot also be recycled.

The protagonists and their worldviews were entirely different as well; though the Bengali poets had longing for lost heights, they had to attend to the more immediate mundane experiences. Accordingly the Epic sequence was accepted as the mark of aesthetic protest of the colonial elites against trivialities and profanations but the genre was irrevocably denuded of traditional contents and the poets had to negotiate with the unsurpassable feeling of distance as well as an awareness of the abyss of irrelevance over which the essential epic imagination is suspended.

Nevertheless the legacy of the Indian epic sequence has not only been carried forward but also substantially readjusted by the Bengali versifiers in an altogether different historical situation. The genre gradually faded out because the epic microcosm was continually subverted by the temporal predicaments of the rapidly changing socio-cultural milieu. Moreover, the novel was ascending to great heights and the readers' response also was overwhelming in its favour which meant that the wheel had indeed come full circle for the epic genre. The epic sequence became truly a matter of the past and hence no more textual fabrics could be woven out of the given world; the myths and archetypes, metaphors and symbols by then had become denuded of aesthetic meaning. Poetic truth was consequently obscured by heaps of falsehood since the Bengali epics relentlessly repeated the theme of slaying of Yavanas and demons as well as regaining of paradise. Both the mundane and spiritual domains of history and metahistory were distorted ne plus ultra till the Muse got stuck into the quicksand and the point of no return. The epic genre sank to the bottomless pit of oblivion as the true import of the Sanskrit epic sequence remained quartered between shortcomings and excesses.

Whatever might be the fate of the Bengal epic genre, the greater Indian epic sequence unfolds before us the interesting process of paradigmatic encounter between the evolving text and the different generations of readers. The sequential evolution of the epic text undoubtedly offers a bonanza of intellectual and aesthetic feast. The Sanskrit epic sequence has been often misread and only partially interpreted; we may now venture to re-read and understand the genre anew. The sequence has its inherent strength and weakness, its dialogical situation interwoven with excesses and shortcomings. But no human artform can be entirely perfect; likewise, the Sanskrit epics too have their craving for perfection but the mount of sisyphus remained as tantalising as ever. Thus the fact remains that the sequence was built with mists and sunshine; in order to be true to its human schemata, it had its tryst with destiny and negotiated with both trivialities and sublimities. The static and monumental texts of the Indian epic sequence may therefore be read and reread again and again; their closures are only apparent. We are indeed implicated in a matrix of inexhaustible possibilities.

NOTES

1. Quoted by Sreekantiya, T. N. 'Imagination in Indian Poetics', *The Indian Historical Quarterly*, vol. xiii, 1937, p. 73.
2. Dhvanyāloka. iv. 4.
3. Quoted by Masson, J. L. & Patwardhan, M.V. : *Sāntarasa and Abhinavagupta's Philosophy of Aesthetics*, Poona, 1969, p. 18.
4. Dhvanyāloka. iv. 10.
5. Vyaktiviveka. ii. 117.
6. Harṣacarita. i. 9.
7. Bloom, Harold: *The Anxiety of Influence*, Oxford University Press, New York, 1973, p. 9.
8. Greene, Thomas: 'The Norms of Epic' in *Perspectives on Poetry*, ed. by James L. Calderwood and Haròld E. Toliver, Oxford University Press, New York, 1968, p. 195.
9. Madhusudan's letter to Rajnarayan Bose, dated 15th May, 1860; ed. Ksetra Gupta, *Kavi Madhusudan o tnār Patrāvalī*, Granthanilaya, Calcutta, 137, p. 132.

2

Genesis of Indian Epic Poetry

The genesis of epic poetry makes an interesting study as it leads us to remote antiquity when various strata of Vedic literature were taking shape. It seems that the penchant for tales and anecdotes was not quenched in the Vedic hymns; hence the first generations of ancient bards came into existence. They sought to transform the chaotic variety of human records of mythic tales, proto-historical events and allegories into what may be called a cosmos of epic imagination. These records therefore seem to have the quality of emerging from the stream of time itself. It may be recalled here that the interpretation of the human world is said to have evolved through three stages, viz., mythic, epic and historical. The epic stage came in vogue when ancient men developed the concept of a model super-man or culture-hero. Thereafter the floating legends and tales crystallized into a new totality centring around such model man or culture-hero. The primary epics or epics of growth are thus the outcome of a process of prolonged accretions and synthesis. Scattered ballads of various description by and large clustered together to form legend-cycle within a couple of centuries and then these, too, were rechiselled by the final generations of bards having more skill and expertise.

The tendency of telling a story is inherent in human mind from time immemorial and the Vedic Aryans were no exception as well. That is why, the samhitās contain such hymns having elements of ancient ballads which may be regarded as one of the primary sources of epic narrative. These are the Samvāda Sūkta or dialogue hymns of the Ṛgveda which, according to Oldenberg, were archaic ākhyāna or ballads. He thought that oldest form of Indian epics thrived on prose and verse and that the latter, containing dialogues, was fixed and memorised. Thus the Samvāda Sūktas were preserved for the benefit of posterity while the prose portion containing narrative passed into irretrievable oblivion. This view was contested by Max Muller and Levi according to whom the dialogue hymns could have germinated that dramatic genre. Hertel and Von Schroeder were of the opinion that these might have formed the parts of some kind of religious ritual enactments. Winternitz, on the other hand, regarded these dialogue hymns as ancient ballads which might have inspired both the epic and dramatic genres to bloossom.

If we look at the Brāhmaṇas, we would find that the remnants of the narratives from remote antiquity shed illuminating light on the genesis of the chequered development of the epic poetry through almost a millennium. While the role of the Samvāda Sūktas of the Ṛgveda is basically conjectural, the Gāthā Nārāśamsīs (Songs in praise of men), ākhyānas (narratives), itihāsa (legend), purāṇa (ancient lore) etc. had definite roles to play in the formation of epic nucleus. Even though the abovementioned materials were part and parcel of religious rituals, these nevertheless consolidated the impact of the diversified expressions of oral tradition on the creative pursuits of latter centuries. With the passage of time, the simple subjectmatter and brief span of the anecdotes of the Gāthā-nārāśamsīs developed gradually into bulky ballads and heterogeneous cycles of songs with intricate plots. It should also be noted here that while the Vedic literature was sacerdotal in origin and import and always confined within the priestly class, the proto-epic episodes in spite of their sacerdotal association were never meant to be exclusive. Hence, the sūtas as ancient bards took up the responsibility of popularizing those episodes among the masses. They were the first editors as well as compilers; they were the best assessors of the moods of the people and hence might have boldly and unhesitatingly added such details that might sharpen the tale and captivate the attention of the listeners.

At a time when magic had a very prominent role in the life of early men who took recourse to spells and incantations, the bards of oral tradition could not be distinctly separated from priests or magicians performing spells. In the early proto-epic stages, only those episodes seemed to have found favour with the people which had potential magic qualities. The orthodox priests had to swallow them but their disapproval bespeaks of the popular base. The *Taittirīya Brāhmaṇa* (1:3:2:6) says that the impure portion of the Vedas became gāthās and nārāsamsīs. Various other minor genres had found so much favour with the people at large that the Vedic seers could not but recognise them. The rituals had to be percolated to the masses and hence some materials from the oral tradition were accommodated in the periphery of ritual texts. Thus the dialogues between Urvaśī and Pururavas (R.V.X.95), Yama and Yamī (R.V.X.10), Indra Indrānī and Vṛsākapi (R.V.X.86), Saramā and the Panis (R.V.X.108), the Dānastutis of the Ṛgveda, the Vālakhilya hymns (R.V.VIII. 49-50), the Kuntāpa Sūktas, the pāriplava ākhyānas (*Śatapatha Brāhmaṇa* xiii:4:3) have very little to do with the rituals. However, the Vedic authors seemed to have invented myths and legends to justify their sacerdotal practices and custom. They drew heavily from the floating tales and beliefs of the Little Tradition which, as we have already stated, may be regarded as the fountainhead of the epic nucleus.

Here we may also recollect that the word 'pāriplava' in the *Śatapatha Brāhmaṇa* stands for the cyclically recurrent legends which seemed to have been collected by the ancient bards for narrating them every ten days during the sacrificial year. The narrated legends were non-Vedic in import but nevertheless the merits of Vedic studies were to be achieved through such pāriplava sessions. The proto epic-puranic genre might have originated in a nebular form quite earlier but it was crystallizing when the compilatory and editorial activities of the Vedic poets were at the concluding stage and the ballads and legends in the oral tradition were being zealously collected. The epic-puranic formulation gradually distanced itself from the liturgical association and then finally snapped the umbilical cord to flourish independently. We may recall here that between the eighth and fourth centuries B.C.

the Āraṇyakas and Upaniṣads were taking shape to signify the process of transition from the sacrificial religion to the non-sacrificial religious belief with clearly defined metaphysics. That was the time when Buddhism and Jainism originated with new worldviews bringing in their train altogether new concepts and attitudes towards life and consequently effecting the creative process itself.

The gāthā nārāśamsīs and ākhyānas might have been the first progenitors of the proto-epic and proto-puranic poetry. In the initial phase, these were brief and fragmentary, cryptic and straight-forward; their subjectmatter was simple and uncomplicated. There was little embellishment in those nebular compositions. But in course of time these developed into lengthy ballads with the outgrowth of tendencies continuously germinating within an expansive society. Various cycles of tales took shape with intricate plots and everincreasing attempts of formal embellishment. When we think of the two Great epics of India, viz. *Rāmāyaṇa and Mahābhārata* we detect unique dynamism and impelling wholeness in their formative processes. The sūtas or the charioteers were the professional bards, who being close witnesses of many an upheavals of the then society, took up the task of popularizing the archaic forms of epic poetry among the masses. While transmitting the ancient sagas of valour and magnificence, such sūtas recited and edited older materials as well as compiled and authored new details to usher in new vigour in the oral tradition. The nucleus of the two great epics of India were formed by these bards which soon became distinct from praises of deities, eulogy of sacrificial details and metaphysical speculations. In the preliminary inceptive phase, the proto-epics might have been confined to the chosen power elites but soon these percolated to the people who, on their turn, influenced the process of new crystallization. The wandering singers of tales i.e. the Kuśīlavas seemed to have played very crucial role in the formative centuries of both the *Rāmāyaṇa* and the *Mahābhārata*. The existence of professional singers of tales in ancient India may be proved by the references to 'Aitihāsikas' and 'Paurāṇikas'. Some scholars even thought of the presence of a 'proto'(Ur) 'Itihāsapurāṇa' text in remote antiquity. But this does not seem to be very plausible.

Nevertheless, Indian tradition has time and again referred to the great epics as 'Itithāsa or 'ākhyāna' emphasising thereby on the considerable honour associated with such generic names. The *Rāmāyaṇa* has been described as an 'ākhyāna' in the beginning of the epic text itself signifying the emphasis on narrating the interesting story of the illustrious dynasty of Raghu.[1]

The *Mahābhārata* is designated as 'Itihāsa'; however, the great epic itself makes it a point to declare that it is a 'Kāvya'. It seems that the generic names like 'Akhyāna' and 'Itihāsa' enjoyed much prestige because of their Vedic connection. Hence, the bards of the *Mahābhārata* relished its coveted position as the fifth 'ākhyāna' or 'Itihāsa' besides the four Vedas.[2] Even in their formative stages, the cycles of fragmentary bardic poetry seemed to have been granted elevated status in the Vedic firmament. Thus the *Atharva Veda*, *Taittirīya Āraṇyaka, Bṛhadāraṇyaka Upaniṣad, Chāndogya Upaniṣad* and the *Nirukta* refer to them approvingly.[3]

From the floating mass of various legends emanating from diverse popular tradition, the two great epics came into being through successive stages. The growth of the epic genre, as envisaged in the *Rāmāyaṇa* and *Mahābhārata,* shows that it has constantly made and unmade its own rules. As time rolled on, new generations of bards felt it imperative to structure their own experience in a different way while entrenched beliefs were questioned and readjusted. Each generation tried to forge new associations to break the spell of monotony. Sometimes new legends and episodes were successfully synchronized into unfolding structure while sometimes symmetry and order were lacking. Modern analysis has sought to locate the extrinsic materials which were continuously accumulated in the manifold textures of two great epics. Through the process of constant renewal, the unageing, archaic elements have not only been preserved in the epic genre but also have been contemporized. Both cultural transformation and miscegenation have been heralded by constant shifts in artistic values inherent in the complex pattern of the progressive development of the epic genre. The two great epics have unmistakably proved that this genre is unique because it is old and new simultaneously. It is reborn and renewed at every new stage in the process of gradual development and is therefore always the same and yet not the same. Likewise, the two great epics also have many elements in common yet they differ from each other substantially.

The great poets like Vālmīki or Vyāsa do not ever flourish in vacuum; their emergence is the logical culmination of variegated processes of the cultural history of the people. Even if there were several individual poets beneath the magic names of Vālmīki or Vyāsa, nevertheless the fact remains that they treated the epic genre as basically a cultural phenomenon of importance in dynamic interrelationship with the social and moral existence of the Indian people. They had developed the method of communication not out of any sudden flush of inspiration even though the posterity might have concocted such fanciful stories. The consummate artistry of the epic poets and the resultant formal excellence cannot be the outcome of chance or whim. The progress of the two great epics through various phases may be regarded as the unique creative reflection of the historical destiny of the Indian people who searched for the meaning of human existence in a rapidly changing society. However, the sublimity and greatness inherent in epic imagination have been recognized in no uncertain terms. It has been emphatically stated that a poet with genuine gift of talent is known by his intuitive capacity to create the objects anew time and again.[4] Epic poetry is not only good but also great and its foremost quality is expansiveness. The benedictory verse of the *Kāvya Prakāśa* clearly formulates that the excellence of poetic creation elevates it to an exalted status.[5] Of the two great epics, the *Rāmāyaṇa* is undoubtedly much more organized as a finished work in the epic genre.

II

The popular term, 'Mahākāvya', first appears in the colophons of the *Buddhacarita* and the *Saundarananda* which, being the works of Aśvaghoṣa, must have been in vogue in the first century of the Christian era. The term, 'Mahākāvya', is also found in the colophons of the *Kumāra-sambhava* and *Raghuvamśa* of Kālidāsa as well as the

Setuvandha or *Rāvanavadha* of Pravarasena. However, doubts persist about the authority of such colophons. In the seventh century, Māgha makes a straightforward reference to the genre of Mahākāvya in his *Śiśupālavadha*.[6] In course of time, another generic name was suggested for such compositions, viz., 'Sargavandha' which was extensively used by the rhetoricians in their pursuit for apt definition of epic poems. While the older term, 'mahākāvya' connotes sublimity, expansiveness and uniqueness, the latter term, 'sargavandha' accurately signifies the formal or structural arrangement. It may be noted here that the *Rāmāyaṇa,* commonly acclaimed as the Ādikāvya' or first poem of the literary firmament, is arranged in different sargas (i.e. cantos) and thus seems to have provided the clue for the rhetoricians. But nowhere it has described itself as 'Mahākāvya' or 'Sargavandha'. As we have already noted, it preferred to be designated as 'ākhyāna' in accordance with the ancient oral tradition. At any rate, in one of the latest interpolations, the qualifying epithet 'mahat' has been used to describe a special type of 'Kāvya'.[7] Indeed it is a reference to the *Rāmāyaṇa* itself.

According to Indian rhetoricians, the non-dramatic poetic compositions are the Śravya-Kāvyas which are thus suggested to be the scions of the ever-renewing oral tradition. Dandin significantly remarks in his *Kāvyādarśa*[8] that 'Muktaka' (stray verse), 'Kulaka' (cluster of verses), 'Koṣa' (compilation), 'Sanghāta' (larger collection) etc. are basically ripples of a great wave. These minor genres are all derived from the genus of '*Mahākāvya*' or 'Sargavandha'; therefore the former varieties do not deserve any special treatment in poetics. It has also to be noted that Indian rhetoricians considered the two great epics as the fountainhead of the poetic compositions. They believed that those monumental works were inspired by the heavenly Muses; besides, being the relics of the ancient 'Itihāsa' literature, these great epics were considered too sacred to be profaned by including them in the discussions about the epic poems composed by mortal poets. In the meantime, a supramundane halo had completely engulfed the figures of Vālmīki and Vyāsa as a result of which their creations were also thoroughly mystified. Therefore, when Indian rhetoricians sought to establish a workable definition of the epic, they excluded the two great epics and instead concentrated on the brilliant examples of epic of art or court epics or secondary epics composed by Aśvaghoṣa, Kālidāsa, Bhāravi and Māgha. Of all the Indian rhetoricians, Bhāmaha came up first with the definition of 'Mahākāvya'.[9] If we analyse the gradual development of the definition, we would find that Bhāmaha laid the foundation of such attempts of the succeeding rhetoricians. Hence, for all practical purposes, Bhāmaha's definition has become classical. The later authors of poetics have mainly sustained on him and adopted his view with slight variation and improvement. We may as well say that the *Kāvyādarśa* of Daṇḍin, the *Agni Purāṇa*, the *Kāvyānuśāsana* of Hemacandra, the Pratāparudra-*Yaśobhuṣaṇa* of Vidyānātha, the *Sāhityadarpaṇa* of Viśvanātha and the *Śṛngāraprakāśa* of Bhoja, have more or less reiterated the view of their illustrious predecessor. However, Rudraṭa seems to have taken an independent stance regarding some details of compositional technique.[10]

We may have a closer look at these definitions. Bhāmaha has a very simple formulation according to which the poems arranged in sargas or cantos may be regarded as 'mahākāvyas'. Daṇḍin observes that these cantos should not be very lengthy; almost all the later rhetoricians share this view. Viśvanātha has sought to regulate the lowest limit of the number of cantos; he has precisely stated that there should be more than eight cantos in mahākāvya.[11] According to him, these cantos should neither be too lengthy nor too brief. On the other hand, the *Īśānasamhitā* observes that the highest limit of the number of cantos in a mahākāvya should not exceed thirty. In his commentary on the Kāvyādarśa (chapter I), Rangācārya tried to explain that the particular word 'Anatibistirṇaih' did not refer to the length of a canto, it hinted only at the number of cantos in an epic poem. The rhetoricians did not try to regulate the number of verses in a canto because they had before them contradictory examples of the *Kirātārjunīya* and the *Śiśupāla Vadha*. Thus there are only 38 verses in the fourth canto of the *Kirātārjunīya* while the second and nineteenth canto of the *Śiśupāla Vadha* have 118 and 120 verses respectively. In the post-Bhāravi Sanskrit court epics, the absence of a clear dictum regarding the number of verses to be set in a canto was exploited to the brim. Hence, we find that the *Naiṣadhīyacarita* has as much as 221 verses in its seventeenth canto. But the poets were busy only in extrinsic verbosity while heaps of unnecessary details were tirelessly accumulated. The circumference of subject-matter was so much predetermined that it hardly allowed any elbow room for creative imagination. Excessive details succeeded in choking the forward movement of the story itself and even the sparks of quality were extinguished. The accumulated mechanical norms of the rhetoricians had no room for genuine feeling and experiences of life.

Though Viśvanātha has the opinion that each canto should suggest the subjectmatter of the succeeding canto in its concluding portion, it hardly helps either the poet or the reader. Because the barrenness and artificiality of courtly life are so evident that no amount of exaggerated embellishment can redeem such work. But the rhetoricians were too busy in framing formulations for court epics to recognize the validity of a distinctive worldview. Being alienated from the living society, the poet-laureates could not but be deprived of the pulsating experiences. Naturally they had no story to tell and no feeling to communicate. Instead, they were busy in manufacturing an art of abstractions distant from the real world. They had to produce court epics of formal experiments without any viable content and interpretation of life so that these may not displease the power elites. Therefore Viśvanātha and other rhetoricians tried merely to establish the semblance of a story preferably from the storehouse of tradition. They thought only about the customary details and structural arrangement. There was no elucidation of the links between man and his social milieu, nor there was any recognition of the poet's creative individuality. Viśvanātha was only eager to determine the name of a particular sarga (canto) with the help of meagre story contained therein. Undoubtedly, the emphasis is on the maintenance of extrinsic structure in a well-defined manner.

Hemacandra refers to the various names of cantos in Sanskrit, Prākṛta, Apabhramśa and Grāmyabhāsā as sarga, Āśvāsa, Sandhi and Avaskandha respectively. Bhoja proposes to place the *Mahābhārata* into a different category known as 'Parva-vandha' because its major divisions are arranged under the name of 'parvan'. Likewise the 'Kāṇḍa-vandha' type has been specially made to accommodate the *Rāmāyaṇa*. Obviously, such categorization does not help the readers at all in understanding the inherent greatness and uniqueness of the two great epics. Moreover, the concentration on the names of the division of narration inadvertently equates all compositions arranged in cantos. But we know that even the *Rāmāyaṇa* and *Mahābhārata* are miles apart; even among the court epics, there are distinctive differences in the worldview and execution of the genre. But the rhetoricians do not seem to recognize this adequately. It did not occur to them that the compositional principles of a poetic work are basically manifestation of a poet's view of life. On the contrary, individual idiosyncrasies have not been allowed in framing the rules for the epics of art; the poets are only expected to faithfully shadow the dictums of rhetoricians.

Aśvaghoṣa and Kālidāsa flourished in a comparatively stable and expansive society agog with activities in various spheres. They drew their inspiration directly from the spiritual life and the continuing legacy; besides, they were not chained by the do's and don'ts of the rhetoricians. They had no need to coerce themselves to write on well-defined subjects nor they had any inclination to violate their frontiers. But by the times Bhāravi appeared in the horizon of epic poetry, poetic art was fast degenerating into being a luxury article which had little to do with the experiences of life. The post-Bhāravi court epics were prepared for the consumption of the feudal aristocrats only who sought amusements for the leisure hours and did not like to be bothered with any unpleasant truth. That was the time when the rhetoricians directed their attention to formalism with monotonous accuracy. Therefore, it is but natural that the later rhetoricians like Bhoja would spare little time in searching for new idea or new artistic form which might be alloy of the social and the aesthetic. Interestingly he borrowed Daṇḍin's long discourse about mahākāvya in toto. However, he tried to arrive at a new definition for Sargavandha. Indeed no rhetorician considered that the poet should draw upon the fullness of life, and not from any idealised and abstract universality of norms.

With the increasing negation of the external reality, the subject matter was continuously on the wane and hence the aroma and colour of the story also evaporated gradually. But nevertheless a distinctive story was required on the basis of which the warp and woof of the epic fabric might be woven. All the rhetoricians had therefore something to comment upon the epic narrative. Bhāmaha said that the narrative of a mahākāvya should present the account of a noble personality and contain details regarding counsel, embassy, march of army, battle and above all, the worth and prosperity of the protagonist. The epic narrative would unfold a successful martial exploit of the central figure against the antagonist. Daṇḍin and almost all the later rhetoricians agree with Bhāmaha in this respect. Such a plot should consist of five sandhis or junctures. It is further observed that four ends of life (i.e. caturvarga) should be depicted in general and the attainment of material prosperity in particular. Viśvanātha suggests that any one of these four aims may be developed in a māhākāvya. Daṇḍin, however, emphasises on the historicity of the plot.

The concept of protagonist is also immensely important. The central figure of Sanskrit court epics cannot be an average man; he is, on the contrary, the roof and crown of beings. Being the epitome of all possible virtues, he cannot but transcend particular social and personal environments. Bhāmaha and other rhetoricians never thought of a real man with flesh and blood; they had to serve the interest of the feudal lords and aristocrats who liked phantasmal and idealized figures of abstraction. So any temporal sequence in the plot was overlooked and instead, the charismatic culture-heroes were preferred as the protagonists. According to Bhāmaha, the protagonist should be introduced in the beginning of the epic text along with appropriate description of his illustrious family, his prowess and learning. His exploits should be depicted prominently throughout. Daṇḍin observes that the protagonist should be wise, noble and sublime. Rudraṭa says that he should be of royal lineage and may be either real or imaginary or partly real and partly imaginary.[12] One cannot but feel that under the aegis of exaltation of the central figure of court epics, isolation from life has actually been validated.

Indian rhetoricians further held that the protagonist should be attached to the three aims of life, viz., 'dharma' (duty in accordance with one's varṇa), 'Artha' (attainment of material prosperity) and 'Kāma (love). He should be powerful, meritorious, enthusiastic and resourceful to conquer his opponent. Viśvanātha adds that the protagonist may be a divine figure or a Ksatriya of a noble family. He further says that there may be several protagonists in a single poem. Understandably he has the *Raghuvamśa* before him. When every minor detail has to be accounted for, no quarter was given for creative imagination. Hence Kālidāsa's uniqueness has also been interpreted mechanically. The rhetoricians did not consider the antagonist an average person as well. He is also stated to be virtuous and scion of a respectable family with no less valour and learning. It is simply because no ordinary man can challenge the protagonist. It might remind us of the famous expression in the *Rāmāyaṇa*: 'The battle between Rāma and Rāvaṇa can only take place between Rāma and Rāvaṇa.'[13] Thus the excellence of the antagonist has been exhibited in the court epics with the sole aim of enhancing the glory of the protagonist.

In fact, the protagonist is something more than a central figure of a particular genre; he is the emblem of moral values. The frontiers of literature and ethics being obliterated in a fragmented and fossilised society, the protagonists had to act as the torch-bearers as well. This trend was set by Rāma, who was essentially an excellent human being in Vālmīki's schemata of imagination ('naracandramā') but with the advent of the puranic Brāhmanism, the theory of incarnation had thoroughly brought about a metamorphosis in the conception of Rāma. He became a god in the early phase of feudalism; hence the rhetoricians could not but observe: 'One should follow the path of Rāma and avoid that of Rāvaṇa'.[14] The *Īśānasamhitā* says, 'Mahākāvyam prayoktavyam mahāpuruṣakīrtiyuk'. It seems that the rhetoricians put a premium on the normative ethical essence of the epic narrative and the personalities depicted thereby. This reminds us of a famous saying in the *Gītā* according to which 'Common people generally follow the path set by the noble persons.'[15]

Daṇḍin holds that the treatment of the subjectmatter should not be brief in a mahākāvya. Bhāmaha sounds a note of caution as it were when he says that the details of description may be in abundance but these should not be over-exhaustive. He seems to have realised that exhaustive details leave little room for the suggestive sense and the creative imagination is neutralized. In fact, excessive interference under the pretext of guidance only inexorably leads to the debasement of epic art. This has been proved time and again in the post-Bhāravi court epics. At any rate, the genre is particularly fed by inexhaustible details of description. Though Bhāmaha has enumerated some elements, it seems that Daṇḍin was much more aware about their place in the mahākāvya. He prepared a list of such details whose numbers went on increasing at the time of later rhetoricians as if almost *ad infinitum*. Daṇḍin mentions the following: city, ocean, mountain, season, sun-rise, moon-rise, sports in garden and lake, drinking and frivolous festivities, separation, marriage, birth of a son, counsel, march of army, sending of messenger, battle etc. Rudrāta has made observations regarding the development of plot and use of descriptive details. It may be presented here as follows.

The description of the city of the protagonist should be followed by an account of his family. He is then to be introduced as busy in guiding the destiny of his nation. Thereafter, the seasons are to be described. The readers may then be informed about the activities of the antagonist through some messenger to the royal protagonist and the latter's customary excitement and wrath. Next comes the protagonist's counsel with his ministers; after that, he sends a messenger to his rival or initiates the march of army against him. As the army rolls on, the following details may be introduced while the dominant technique of formalistic description takes command: the citizens, different provinces, mountains, forests, lakes, desert, ocean, island, tracts of land, camping, youthful sports, sun-rise, sun-set, night, rendezvous of young men and women, music, drinking and adornment of body. Undoubtedly action remains suspended or virtually smothered under the heaps of descriptive materials. This descriptive method is emphatically mechanical and lacks human warmth and flare of imagination. The penchant for detailed description suceeds only in denuding the materials of significance as a result of which poetic vitality is altogether lost. These details do not interpenetrate or reciprocally effect each other and consequently remain dispensably extrinsic to the epic narrative.

After the descriptions are over, the epic poet should depict the siege of the city of the antagonist. In the previous night before the battle, the young soldiers meet their spouses with the terrible news of participation in the battle on the following day. Thereafter a fierce battle is described in which the protagonist comes out victorious. The fall of the antagonist is expected to prove for the umpteenth time that the virtuous is for ever the vanquisher of all evil forces. Thus Viśvanātha and Hemacandra hold that the wicked should be denounced and the virtuous be praised in a mahākāvya.

The rhetoricians have generally spoken about the emotive nature of communication. The genre of mahākāvya should sustain on all the varieties of emotion. Viśvanātha, however, recommends that the principal emotion (angīrasa) should be any one of the following: love, heroism and tranquillity. However, the poets were too busy in following the conventions entrenched in scholastic formalism and hence 'authentic' expression of emotion was much more important than arousing genuine feeling. They wrote to amuse their royal patrons, aristocrats of the court and the elegant and sophisticated nāgaraka. If we remember the testimony of Vātsyāyana, we may say that it was a society thriving on surplus and abundance. The privileged few in the higher echelon of society had nothing to do with the common people. In a settled agricultural community, supplemented by prosperity through foreign trade and expanding commerce, the nāgarakas used to spend their endless leisure in gay abandon. The women gradually lost social mobility and freedom which they had been enjoying before. They became objects of enjoyment for men. This typical world of the nāgarakas recognised no depth but frivolous excesses of exhibitionism; there were explicit refinement and heightened moments but no stirring of the soul. It had profound influence on the worldview of the composers of post-Bhāravi court epics and the thoughts of the rhetoricians as well. The display of heroism was also according to the dreary habits and traditional conventions. In spite of earnestness, occasional subtlety, power of observation, decent elaboration and skilful treatment, we come across only disjointed memorable verses which had little or no relevance with the epic narrative.

The contemporary connoisseurs might have more exacting demands to the poets than the frolicking nāgarakas, but they too were satisfied by noticing technical correctness of expressions. They were more fond of intellectual vigour than rare poetic insight.[16] Even the never-ending display of dogmatic formalism and monotonously inflated rhetoric were no occasion for raising eye-brows. Naturally the poets were equally eager to prove their imaginative power (Śakti), erudition (byutpatti) and practice (abhyāsa). Indeed, Māgha seemed to have opened a floodgate with his *Śiśupālavadha*. Several manuals for training the budding poets came into existence which furnish the readers with elaborate lists of conventions (Kavisamaya) to be followed by the poets. These manuals also deal in details with the subject and method of description. These works discuss the processes of constructing different metres and various devices of verbal ingenuity which include skilful display of words, double meaning, conundrums, riddles, alliteration etc.

Rājaśekhara, an eminent rhetorician, zealously advocated for an elaborate training of the poets who should have well-defined duties to perform everyday. Such poets are regarded as no ordinary persons but men of fashion and enriched in purity of body, mind and speech; moreover, they are to be assiduous and hardworking in their respective occupations. As poetry became more an object of learned pursuit than a spontaneous outgrowth of inspiration, the poets were required to be proficient in different branches of knowledge. That is why, the instances of Māgha and Bhatti inspired the rhetoricians to furnish long list of arts and sciences for the consumption of the poets. Such lists are found in the works of Bhāmaha,[17] Rudrata[18] and Vāmana.[19] While the enumerations of the first two authors are quite alike, the latter dealt with these in details.[20] The attitude revealed here is particularly interesting.

The rhetoricians thought a great deal about the poetic diction of the mahākāvya. Bhāmaha said that it should be highly polished with an embellished and magnificent style bedecked with appropriate rhetorical devices. He observed that metres should be judicious and melodious. Daṇḍin, Hemacandra and Viśvanātha held that the metre employed in a canto should be changed at its end. According to the rhetoricians, one particular metre should usually be used throughout a canto. But Viśvanātha observed that some cantos might have different metres for the sake of variety. It may be noted here that the change of metre at the end of a canto seems to be the continuation of the legacy of the oral tradition. Because when poetry was orally transmitted to the listeners around, the bards used to indicate the beginning of a new episode or a temporary break by dint of changing a prolonged pattern in rhyme. Though the phases of oral poems were long over, the succeeding court epics nevertheless adopted this useful technical device. There is no hard and fast rule about the use of any particular metre in a mahākāvya. The Subṛttatilaka has, however, put forward the view that the Anuṣṭubh metre should be employed at the beginning of an epic.

When all-absorbing tendencies towards abstraction threaten to banish mundane reality from the domain of poetry and over-indulgence to idealisation tends to make human existence irrelevant, the poetic diction cannot but degenerate. The Sanskrit court epics validated this observation time and again. Being isolated from the vital struggles of life and thereby from varied experiences, those poets missed the basic warmth of humanity as a result of which their works thrived on abstractions. Instead of being mirrors of experience and feeling, their language became fossilized and soon transformed into fortified cages. No stream of life can ever flow through dry and stony basin repleted with heaps of dead words. The tendencies of attempting description with those materials only exposed the inherent inhumanity and aesthetic incongruity of the conception of the epic composition. Because of this the characters portrayed mostly became superficial and shadowy abstractions. The mechanistic use of musical cadence, pictorial effect as well as atrocious word-play and incredible witticism only make the ornate language farther from spontaneity, sensitiveness and natural ease. The difficulties and complexities multiply and poetic diction becomes synonymous with verbal jugglery. Bhāravi and Māgha were indeed the pioneers of clever verbal tricks; they took it to such an absurd extent that the lesser poets repeated these ad nauseam.

Being encouraged by the rhetoricians, the glory-hunting decadent poets went on twisting the language of the power elites as much as they could. There was, in fact, a bon homie atmosphere; a feast for the intellect as it were at the courts of the feudal lords. At that time, popular dialects were evolving in the shape of regional Prākṛtas and variant Apabhramśas. Actually, the last phase of the Sanskrit court epics were concomitant with the emergence of modern Indian vernacular languages. New dawn was ushering in fresh hopes, aspirations and possibilities at the different horizons of vernacular literature because these were initiated and shaped by the people. But, on the other hand, the patrons of Sanskrit literature in general and the court epics in particular refused to listen to the tune of the time; instead, they preferred to shut their windows to commonplace experience. Therefore, the poetasters ignored the opportunity of a regeneration by transfusing fresh blood into the worn out veins of the decaying genre. On the contrary, the exuberance of fancy and intellectual gymnastics continued uninterruptedly while taste, feeling and judgement were dispensed with. As decadence further set in, the poetic diction was entirely obscured by multitudes of so-called 'Kavisamayas'. While content and theme became progressively irrelevant, the catalogue of customary descriptions swelled along with grandiloquent diction. As we have already explained, the innate poetic imagination could not but have been entirely obscured by abundant technicalities of expression. It was but natural that none other than the learned would appreciate involved construction, recondite vocabulary, laboured embellishment, strained expression, constant search after conceits, double meanings and metaphors. But these did not continue for long; when language ceases to act as the unerring mirror of life, it ceases to exist as well. With the arrival of vernacular literature, the days of these decadent court epics became numbered. The epic genre flourished in a bang but ended with a whimper.

The poets like Aśvaghoṣa and Kālidāsa had totality of conception and therefore, in spite of their wonderful display of creative imagination in individual verses, neither of them lost sight of the necessity of a continuous narrative. The story of the epic composition is neatly presented; moreover, the innate theme bespeaks of a deep poetic vision. The intricate symmetry of art is well maintained in the works of the above-mentioned maestroes of the epic Muse. But the requisite balance had tilted towards opposite direction in Bhāravi's court epic. Thereafter, the epic narrative was relegated to the secondary position and the theme was given no importance at all. The poets chose to ignore the continuity of story and instead, zealously directed their attention and creative ability exclusively towards constructing individual verses. From Māgha onwards, the Sanskrit court epics, therefore, turned out to be heterogeneous collections of loosely woven miniature poems in which each verse is a separate unit.

This phenomenon reminds us of the rich legacy of Indian miniature painting, existing beside the genre of mural painting since remote antiquity. In fact, the fine arts constituted part of the syllabi for education of the sons and daughters of the nobility during the age of the Upaniṣads.[21] The *Mahābhārata* speaks of the expertise of the painters.[22] Rāvaṇa seemed to have a gallery of painting in his palace at Lankā. The Buddhist texts like *Ummāga Jātaka*, *Mahāvamśa* etc. bear testimony to the existence of various forms of painting in ancient India. Kālidāsa himself referred time and again to unique specimens of painting. Śūdraka, Bhavabhūti, Dandin and Harṣa too mentioned paintings of various categories. These instances bespeak of generous patronage of the royal courts.

Vātsyāyana placed painting in the fourth place but the *Viṣṇudharmottara*, a text belonging to the genre of minor purāṇas and written between fourth and seventh centuries A.D., placed painting at the top. Being contemporary with the world-famous frescos at the caves of Ajantā, it explains the techniques of artists in details. It declares the prominence of painting in no uncertain terms.[23] All these facts undoubtedly prove that the power elites of ancient India had not only patronized the composers of court epics but also caused the exponents of various genres of fine arts to flourish simultaneously. This objective condition must have been ideal for mutual illumination of arts. The impact was very deep and fundamental; the painters thrived on the literary tradition on the one hand and the poets were stirred in the fathomless depths of their creative imagination. The category of miniature painting might have cast a spell on the poets with its microscopic precision and vivacious poignancy. Obviously, the genre of lyric poetry absorbed this influence most fundamentally and hencc each verse in the lyric works tended to become delightful piece of miniature painting. But, the epic genre too was effected to a great extent. Till Kālidāsa, a delicate balance was maintained but afterwards this influence seemed to have changed the complexion as well as the basic character of the epic genre altogether. Instead of being mutual illumination, it came to be an one-way-traffic and consequently the genre succumbed to the developing pressure from both within and without.

Neither the poets nor the rhetoricians were aware of the depth of the problem. Because of the constant degeneration of the poets' relationship with the pulsating life around, they could not confront the exacting requirements for a new epic of creativity. On the contrary, the poets were compelled to share the illusion of the feudal epoch solely controlled by their aristrocratic patrons. The latter had the stratified and hierarchical Indian society at their disposal and the poets were nothing but parasites sustaining on their mercy. Hence, they had only to echo the ideology of the power elites. As all access to life was denied, the artificially built poetic microcosm was polarised into uncomplicated opposites like good and evil, bright and dark, sublime and trivial etc. Therefore the rhetoricians like Hemacandra and Viśvanātha were satisfied to note that the mahākāvya should denounce the wicked and eulogise the righteous.

Viśvanātha tried to formulate the method of naming a mahākāvya. According to him, the names of author or protagonist or theme might be used for the purpose. Thus we may cite the *Bhaṭṭikāvya, Kirātārjunīya* and *Kumārasambhava* as respective examples.

Along with Daṇḍin, Viśvanātha was attentive of the epic paraphernalia viz., they pointed out that the mahākāvya should begin with benedictory verses or salutation or indication of the subject matter. As we have already stated, the subjectmatter was always centred around gods and demons or kings and aristocrats. Though the rhetoricians ignored the claim of spiritual personalities, the instances of the *Buddhacarita* and the *Soundarananda* prove otherwise. With a view to propitiating the patronizing feudal lords, it was ordained that the protagonist should be a very powerful king as well as a great conqueror. But Buddha and Nanda, the protagonists of two epics mentioned above, cannot be regarded as such. Perhaps Aśvaghoṣa was ignored by the rhetoricians for his Buddhist countenance. Likewise, the description of battle is generally regarded as the central motif of all epic narratives. But the *Buddhacarita* and *Śaundarananda* of Aśvaghoṣa and the *Naiṣadhīyacarita* of Śrīharṣa are conspicuous by the absence of battle. Moreover the protagonist in the *Buddhacarita* is utterly passive which is an anathema for heroic spirit. Even if Māra is taken as the antagonist, this humanized figure of lust is no Satan of the *Paradise Lost*. Although Buddha had to confront with the devilish tricks of Māra, he remained absolutely serene and unconcerned. He did not even utter a single word to express his annoyance; such a figure was never seen again in the later court epics. Māra's figure also was metaphorical on the basis of which a more poetic figure of Kāma was later contemplated by Kālidāsa for his *Kumārasambhava*.

Love and battle alternate in a regular interval, as we have observed earlier, with monotonous accuracy. In the firmament of court epics, love is almost always conventional; it blossoms strictly according to a predetermined pattern. There are abundant details of physical charm and frank descriptions of tireless infatuation of men for women. Love is nothing but lust that lacks depth and even minimum decency and sagacity. There are of course some exceptions but the common trend is undoubtedly centred around the traditional Indian conception of women as objects of sexual enjoyment. Obviously, love is possible only between two independent, selfreliant persons. In the *Ṛgveda*, the women did not go down the ladder of the society and hence they could choose their own spouses.[24] Even during the age of the *Taittirīya Brāhmaṇa*, a loving lady could rejoice with her beloved.[25] But gradually women were looked down upon and ultimately they were denied even basic human rights and became equated with domestic commodities.

As time passed on, women came to be regarded as necessary evil and basically impure.[26] If any wife failed to give birth to a son, she could be left forthwith in the cold.[27] Several Vedic texts had articulated their blithering observations about women to equate them with dogs, mares, black bird, cattle, land, horse, elephant, chariot, vulture etc.[28] Such texts bluntly declared that the women are meant only for enjoyment.[29] In such a situation where women were not entitled to even semblance of independence,[30] they must only surrender to the lust of men. The question of choice and love did not arise since there was no scope for human feeling. Hence, the model of a beloved lady had to be obtained from Vātsyāyana's *Kāmasūtra* about which we have spoken earlier. When education was denied to the women members of the family, the courtesans were expected to be proficient in all the varieties of fine arts and various branches of knowledge. Since the sophisticated nāgarakas could not satisfy their intellectual yearnings at home, they sought compensation elsewhere. Naturally poetry too endowed them with another sort of imaginative compensation by depicting a polished and idealised world. The court epics likewise unveiled such utopian microcosms where poetic art mirrors only the inverted versions of reality.

NOTES

1. 'Iksvākūnāmidam tesām rājnāmvamśe mahatmanām Mahadutpannamākhyānamrāmāyanamiti Śrutam' (*Rāmāyaṇa*, 1.5.3,) also, vi. 131. 119 & vii. 3.26.
2. *Mahābhārata* iii. 44. 8; iii. 55. 9; vii. 9. 31, viii. 91. 44 *Atharva Veda* xvi. 6. 11-12, *Taittirīya āraṇyaka* ii. 9
3. *Bṛhadāraṇyaka Upaniṣad* ii. 4. 10, *Chāndogya Upaniṣad* vii. 2, *Nirukta* xi. 25.
4. cf 'Prajnā nabanabonmesaśālinī pratibhā matā', also, 'Kāvyamtu jāyate jātu kasyacit pratibhāvatah' (*Kāvyālamkāra*, 1.5.) also, 'Naratvam

durlabham loke vidyā tatra sudurlabhā/Kavitvam durlabham tatra Saktistatra Sudurlabhā.' (*Agni Purāṇa*, 1.74. 3-4)

5. 'Niyatikrta-niyamarahitām hlādaikamayimananyaparatantrām Navarasarucirām nirmitimādadhatī bhāratīkaverjayati.'

6. 'visamam sarbatobhadra-cakra-gomūtrikādibhih Slokairiva mahākāvyam byuhaistadabhavadbalam' (*Sisupālavadha*. xix. 41)

7. 'Kim pramānamidam Kāvyam kā pratisthā mahātmanah Karttā Kāvyasya mahatah Kvacāsau munipungabah, (*Rāmāyaṇa*, vii. 94. 23)

8. i. 13.

9. Kāvyālamkāra, i. 18-23.

10. xvi. 5-18.

11. cf. 'Nātisvalpānātidīrghāh sargā astādhikāiha'

12. cf. 'Kalpitayuktotpattim nāyakamapi kutracit Kuryāt'.

13. cf. 'Rāmarāvanayoryuddhah rāmarāvaṇayoriva'

14. cf. 'Rāmādivat pravarttitavyam na tu rāvaṇādivat.'

15. 'Yadyadācarati Śresthastattadevetaro janah sa yat Pramānam Kurute lokastadanuvarttate.' (*Gītā*, iii. 21)

16. cf. 'Vyākhyāgamyamidam Kāvyam Utsavah suddhiyāmalam Hata durmedhasascāsmin vidvat-priyatayā mayā.' (*Bhattikāvya*, xxii. 34)

17. 1.9.

18. 1.18.

19. 1.20-21.

20. The longest list includes the following items: Grammar, lexicon, Metrics, Rhetoric, Arts, Dramaturgy, Ethics, Erotics, Politics, Law, Logic, Legends and Myth, Religion, Philosophy, Medicine, Botany, Mineralogy, elephant-lore, Veterinary science, Martial Arts, Knowledge of weapons, Magic, Gambling, Astrology, Astronomy, Knowledge of Vedic rituals and various ways of the world. Such a list is indeed self-explanatory.

21. cf. *Chāndogya Upaniṣad*, vii. 1.

22. cf. 'Kusalaih silpibhirnyastam pate citramivādbhutam' (*Mahābhārata*, vii. 158. 43)

23. cf. 'Kalānām pravaram citram dharma-kāmārtha-mokṣadam Mangalyam prathamam Vaitad gṛhe yatra pratisthitam' (iii. 45. 38.)

24. cf, 'Svyam sā mitram vṛnute jane cit' (*Ṛgveda*, 10.27. 12)
25. *Taittīrīya Brāhmaṇa*, 2.4.6.56.
26. *Maitrāyanīsamhitā*, 3.8.3; *Taittirīya samhitā*, 6.5.8.2.
27. *e.g.*, *Āpastamba Dharmasūtra*, 1. 10. 51-53; 2. 5. 11-14. *Baudhāyana Dharmasūtra*, 2.4.6. *Manu Samhitā*. 9.4. *Vaśiṣtha Dharmasūtra*, 28. 2-3. *Śatapatha Brāhmaṇa*, 5.2.3. 13.
28. *Sānkhāyana Srauta Sūtra*, 12. 29. 21; 14. 11. 31. *Satapatha Brāhmaṇa*, 3.2.4. 6. *Āpastamba Dharmasūtra*, 1.9.23.45.
29. 'Tasmādu ha striyo bhogameva hārayante' (*Taittirīya Samhitā*, 2.3.10.7.) Pasubhūmistrīnāmanātibhogah', (*Gautama Dharma Sūtra*, 12.39)
30. cf, 'Pitā raksati Kaumāre, Bhartā raksati Yauvane, Raksanti Sthavire putrā, Na strī Svātantryamarhati', (*Vaśiṣtha Dharmasūtra*, 5. 1-2)

3

Epics of Growth

Like all other great works of art in ancient languages, the Sanskrit epics too have the quality of emerging from the stream of time. These are exceptional vehicles of communication which intend to transmit aesthetic, cultural and historical concepts to every generation for reemphasizing the validity of their inherent recreative aspect. The readers are always affected by mainly three constituents of such works, viz., materialized form, thematic idea and content. When we talk of realisation of aesthetic experience, we actually expect the unity of these three elements. By virtue of affirmation of their recreative functions, the two great epics viz. the *Rāmāyaṇa* and the *Mahābhārata* continued to positively influence the course of later court epics. A closer look at the evolution of the epic genre in the Sanskrit literary firmament unmistakably proves that constant forward movement of a genre never means slavish submission of a later generation to habitual practices of the predecessors. Because a true genius is endowed with an instinctual and unerring ability to extract from the granaries of past just what he needed.

There cannot be any doubt that the new creative perspectives in literature do not eliminate achievements of earlier masters or minimize their active role. Each true poet brings his own contribution into the treasury of human culture. In fact, the specific contribution of a poet exists in dynamic relationship with the works of his predecessors, contemporaries and successors. Thus Vālmīki is a never-ending source of inspiration for Aśvaghoṣa and Kālidāsa; but this has only elucidated the particular qualities of the borrowers. A study of such creative influence reveals what is infinitely more important than the fact of influence. That is the turning points at which Aśvaghoṣa and Kālidāsa free themselves of the influence and find their originality. Likewise, Aśvaghoṣa too had influenced Kālidāsa to a considerable extent but the latter could build his own microcosm in an unparalleled way. Kālidāsa also cast his spell over Kumāradāsa and Bhatti but the result was not quite encouraging. This reminds us of a pertinent comment of T.S. Eliot:

> "Tradition is a matter of much wider significance. It cannot be inherited, and if you want it you must obtain it by great labour,...what is to be insisted upon is that the poet must develop or procure the consciousness of the past and that he should continue to develop this consciousness through his career."[1]

Kālidāsa seems to be the decisive watershed of Sanskrit epic poetry. The process of creative influence ceased to exist thereafter. When old habits become tiresome burden, it impairs the growth of the epic genre and the concept of influence degenerates into mechanical adherence. Bhāravi and Māgha could not find any meaning rendering stimulus in the creativity of their illustrious predecessors because historical compulsion blinded them altogether. Instead, they became the fountainheads of negative influence when the poets of lesser eminence zealously imitated them without recognizing the true import of originality. The chequered evolution of the Sanskrit epics through the ages makes us aware that originality applies to creative innovations in form or content as well as reinterpretations and combinations of ingredients borrowed from diverse models. In fact, the reception of the past is not entirely governed by some expansive force immanent in it but rather by attempts of the later generations to find in the past that stimulus which would help them to discover the best possible, if not tangible, solutions to their typical problems.

We have already noted that the great poets like Vyāsa and Vālmīki did not originate in vacuum; they absorbed the long and varied legacy of the bardic oral literature and then gave new lease of life to the creatively restructured materials. That is why, the two great epics even now possess the same ageless sparkles with which hundreds of generations had been dazzled. Both these great masters seemed to have inspired the later poets to come to terms with the ever present tradition on the one hand and their contemporary time and community on the other. However, we should also note that the history of Sanskrit epics unfolds regular pattern of breach and continuity of tradition. Almost all the prominent poets are tossed between Scylla and Charybdis of originality and influence of the predecessors, mechanical convention and unique innovation, conscious adaptation and spontaneous transmutation. While Aśvaghoṣa and Kālidāsa provide us with a rewarding invitation, from Bhāravi onwards, the process tends to become dreary and inconsequential. Though the literary influence has different manifestations, it cannot be measured quantitatively. We are only to note whether the poetic art of a particular composer is significantly directed by the past masters; at the same time, it has also to be scaled if the ageold tradition is noticeably altered or readjusted by that particular poet.

Undoubtedly the collective impact of the continuously renewing creative influence of Indian cultural legacy on the Sanskrit court epics can never be denied. However, it is important to take into account not only the resemblances between the physical and aesthetic properties of the poems but also the intentions of their creators as well as the volume and span of various traditions at that juncture of time. And, above all, according to an eminent critic, "The original author is not necessarily innovator or the most inventive, but rather the one who succeeds in making all his own, in subordinating what he takes from others to the new complex of his own artistic work.... Influence, to be meaningful, must be manifested in an intrinsic form, upon or within the literary works themselves. It may be shown in style, images, characters, themes, mannerisms, and it may also be shown in content, thought, ideas, the general 'weltanschauung' presented by particular works."[2] Such meaningful manifestation of the continuity of ancestral legacy through 'intrinsic form' of an epic is best demonstrated by Kālidāsa's *Raghuvamśa*. Kālidāsa made excellent use of what already existed in the *Rāmāyaṇa* and then modified it in such a brilliant manner that the traditional theme was thoroughly revitalized. But this cannot be said about Bhāravi's *Kirātārjunīya* vis-a-vis the *Mahābhārata.*

Let us assert here once again that the discovery of the literary debts of a particular poet does not diminish his originality in any way. If a particular court epic moves the readers aesthetically and produces a new and independent artistic effect, in that case, it may be regarded as significant. Bhāravi and Māgha may not provoke the readers any longer, but their 'independent' poetic effect to a considerable extent cannot be denied. Even Bhaṭṭi has an interesting treatment to fall upon with which he has proposed a typical reinterpretation of the *Rāmāyaṇa*. He may not have been an enthusiastic innovator but nevertheless he has succeeded in making the traditional materials all his own. But the same observation is not possible with regard to Kumāradāsa's *Jānakīharaṇa* or Śrīharṣa's *Naiṣadhiyacarita*. This proves that a poet's readiness to establish significant contact with the works of his famous predecessors and to allow them to affect his own creative pursuits must have depended on a feeling of kinship or fascinated hostility. Such feeling is always conditioned by the prevalent sociocultural environment. Besides, there is the individual capacity of assimilation or synthesis which, for obvious reasons, controls the final success or otherwise of the poetic work.

It has been rightly observed that creativity is not simply originality and unlimited freedom, there is much more to it than that. That creativity also imposes restrictions has not been correctly appreciated in the post-Kālidāsa epoch of Sanskrit epics. Otherwise Bhāravi and Māgha would not have extracted the lifeforce of language itself under the pretext of sharpening poetic diction with the razor of intellect. In fact, they had done away with all 'creative restriction' in such a way that, for the succeeding generations, the arena of epic poetry was made free for all sorts of odd verbal gymnastics. There is no doubt that the works of the predecessors remain present in the memories of creative poets as pieces of living reality. Whether perfect or imperfect, great, mediocre or poor—these inevitably turn into relevant raw materials whenever a new work of art takes shape. Before we attempt an analysis of the Sanskrit epics evolved through different phases, we may summarise that a particular epic poem excels only when it is able to absorb the legacy of the past according to a scheme of its own. Indeed, the innate strength of a successful poetic creation lies there. But most of the post-Bhāravi court epics do not seem to have a well-designed and neatly organised scheme of composition of their own because of which they remain superficial and uncommunicative.

When we speak of significant literary influence absorbed by the prominent poets of the epic genre, we do not mean to say that it operates mechanically. In fact, it is not mechanically confined to individual details pertaining to use of figures of speech or images or diction. Nor can we refer to the monotonously repetitive use of stock expressions known as 'Kavisamaya'. Rather, it is something basic and pervasive ingredient, organically involved in and presented through a literary work. Moreover a poet is generally not influenced by an eminent predecessor in entirety. Now if we want to determine as to what a great creative personality seeks to transmit to the younger generations, we find that sometimes it is stylistic device, sometimes a tone, sometimes a structural detail or sometimes a reflection of value beneath the norms of character portrayal. Many a seeds from various strata of human experiences may be collected but nevertheless only those for which the soil is prepared will germinate. Even thereafter care and nourishment will determine as to which among these sprouts will finally blossom. In the study of Sanskrit epics also, as in the cases of other artistic expressions, 'ripeness is all' that matters ultimately.

II

There can be no two opinion about the multifarious importance of the two great monuments of Indian epic poetry, viz., the *Rāmāyaṇa* and the *Mahābhārata.* In the later phase of Sanskrit epics, these appeared not only to be most remote but also inaccessible to mortal poets.

Their impact was impossible to deny; but being deified thoroughly, they turned out to be the sources of unintended aesthetic and philosophical predicament as well. Since the Muse who smiled at Vālmīki and Vyāsa was thought to be unattainable in a profaned world, the *Rāmāyaṇa* and the *Mahābhārata* were unquestionably accepted as the products of transcendent imagination. But the composers of court epics were mortal beings and as such they could not but tread a different path altogether. The sacred halo around the seer-poets deepened with time which could never be penetrated. This suggests that their greatness is due to 'the greatest of all human illusions, the vision of immortality.'[3] The epic genre was indeed the supreme manifestation of the strength of this 'vision' which reminds us of a famous expression of Theophile Gautier in his poem entitled 'L' art':

"Time passes, only
Strong Art is eternal."

At any rate, the later poets and critics could not accept the two great epics only as literary monuments; on the contrary, the deified works were interpreted as the sources of ethical, theological and metaphysical wisdom. Naturally the poets were aware of the ever present illuminating impact of these great works, but because of their historically conditioned attitude and respectable but cold distance, the aesthetic significance of such illumination could not but be limited in the long run. But nevertheless the ageless sparkles of the *Rāmāyaṇa* and the *Mahābhārata* have remained intact and both continue to exert their very deep presence even on the most modern genres. T.S. Eliot said correctly:

> "Surely the great poet is, among other things, one who not merely restores a tradition which has been in abeyance, but one who in his poetry retwines as many straying of tradition as possible."[4]

There is no other great epics in the world which can be placed in the same rank with the *Rāmāyaṇa* and the *Mahābhārata*. Of course, there are the *Iliad* and the *Odyssey* composed by Homer of which the former is universally acclaimed as the best flower of epic genius.

There cannot be any dispute about the artistic excellence of the *Iliad*: but in spite of its being a perennial source of inspiration for several later generations of poets and dramatists, it cannot be equated with either the *Rāmāyaṇa* or the *Mahābhārata*. Terence, one of the greatest poets and playwrights of ancient Rome, articulated the famous expression: '*Homo sum; humani nil a me alienum puto*' (i.e. I am a man; nothing human is alien to me). Such anthropocentrism reminds us of an emphatic statement in the *Mahābhārata*: 'nothing is more sublime than man.'[5] No other epic demonstrates this fact so competently, effectively and pervasively as the *Mahābhārata* does. In the very beginning, the great epic declares confidently: 'This is the body, truth and nectar of India'.[6] Even it does not hestitate to claim: 'Whatever is not found here cannot exist elsewhere.'[7] But neither the *Iliad* nor the *Odyssey* can possibly make such declaration. In fact, the *Mahābhārata* is not merely an epic, it is the whole literature. The *Rāmāyaṇa,* too, is unique in many respects; hence, its impact on the ethos of the Indian people has been absolutely unfathomable for over two millennia. The epic rightly declares, 'The episodes of the *Rāmāyaṇa* will continue to nourish the peoples' mind so long there are mountains and rivers on the earth.'[8] Therefore the comments of Monier Williams, one of the most famous pioneers of Indological research, seem quite logical to us:

> "To compare these vast compositions with the *Iliad* and the *Odyssey* is to compare the Indus and the Ganges, rising in the snows of the world's most colossal ranges, swollen by numerous tributaries, spreading into vast shallows of branching into deep divergent channels with the streams of Attica or the mountain torrents of Thessalay."[9]

The western world can justifiably boast of Homer and a few other luminaries in the galaxy of epic poetry. We have already spoken of two distinctive categories viz. Epic of Growth or Primary Epic and Epic of Art or Secondary Epic. Besides Homer's *Iliad* and *Odyssey*, the following epics belong to the former category: *Beowulf* (English), *Song of Roland* (French), *Nibelungenleid* (German), *Kalevala* (Finnish), *Epic of Gilgamesh* (Babylonian) and a few Eddas of

Scandanavia. The second category is led by Virgil's *Aeneid* (Latin), Dante's *Divina Comedia* (Italian), Milton's *Paradise Lost* (English); besides there are host of epic poems of which Tasso's *Gerusalemme Liberata* (Italian), Camoens' *Os Lusiads* (Portuguese), Ariosto's *Orlando Furioso* etc, are more prominent. It will suffice to observe here that the categorization does not seem to answer all the queries of the readers satisfactorily and that the frontiers of two groups often overlap. Even among the works belonging to a particular category, there are wide disagreements. The superior genius always revolts at the perpetuity of hegemony of rules and therefore, he tends to break the spell of monotony and chooses his own form to suit the new conceptual frame. However, all the prominent epics have surpassed the dimensions of realism.

None of the western epics of growth is comparable to either of the two great Indian epics. In more ways than one, those scions of oral tradition belong to the mysterious twilight provinces of eternal childhood and, to some extent, adolescence of humanity. But the great work of Vālmīki and Vyāsa captivate the readers with maturity in approach towards life and enlightenment of very high order. Both the great epics gradually evolved out of the school of bardic poetry; but, in the final stage, both of them outstepped the limits of the oral epic tradition. Homer, the supreme genius in the history of the western epics of growth, gave a final and artistically the most coherent shape to the floating legends about ancient heroes of Greece. These legends must have been continuously rearranged and new details incorporated to them by the enterprising singers of tales of every succeeding generation. While Homer acted as the final editor cum composer of the bardic legacy, at that time the mode of writing was fast emerging beside oral art. This fact is indelibly imprinted on the structure and language of both the Homeric epics. The other European epics of growth were not benefitted by the service of any second Homer; hence these continue to fascinate us as the uncut diamonds of epic poetry. Their legends and beliefs do not have any particular poet to rely on; instead, these seem to have emerged from the unilluminated depth of the racial consciousness.

In the earlier stages of the evolution of the two great Indian epics, these might have been nearer to the western primary epics. But, as finished products, these seem to have been born to outshine the prevalent normative systems of poetic craftsmanship and rule over others only by the boundless power of imagination. As we have already stated, the *Rāmāyaṇa* and the *Mahābhārata* are the unique relics of ancient Itihāsa literature and, as such, the 'Parthenon' of Indian culture. While the figure of Vyāsa seems to be shadowy because of his overtly mythical associations, Vālmīki is comparatively entrenched on a more secured ground. Many a scholars thought Vyāsa not to be an individual poet but the name seemed to have the connotation of the clan of redactors. According to them, Vyāsa was perhaps never an individual poet; probably several generations of bards used to sing the traditional tales and in the process, they might have collected, edited and reorganised the epic nucleus. When the later generations of listeners became inquisitive about the identity of the poet, this brief but ambiguous name, which is practically a generic name or perhaps an epithet, was chosen. With the popularity of the great epic, the name of the supposed author was also mystified ne plus ultra. That there must be several poets or redactors in the *Mahābhārata* is evident from its overtly heterogeneous character attained through multiple stages of development.

III

But, in spite of mythical association of Vālmīki, the *Rāmāyaṇa* proves beyond doubt that barring the commonly recognized interpolated portions, it is a masterpiece of an individual poet. Though the poet's name can be interpreted metaphorically, the final version of the great epic does not hint at any major textual engima due to heterogeneity except, of course, in the interpolated first and seventh book. Vālmīki wielded his pen not to eulogise a god or justify his ways to men: on the contrary, the events and persons narrated by him enhance our belief in the worth of human achievement and in the dignity and nobility of man through weal and woe. Vālmīki's Rāma.is definitely not an incarnation of Viṣṇu because such theory did not get currency in his time. His Rāma is a wonderful man, having extraordinary qualities, but he is no god; the poet says, Rāma is 'Naracandramā' i.e. 'The moon among men.' However, in the spurious first and seventh book, the then Brahmanic ideology brought about a metamorphosis in the conception of the protagonist. As a result, Rāma became a cult figure receiving devotion from the worshippers. But we shall deal with it in details later. It may suffice here to note that Vālmīki's Rāma is a culture-hero who is the consummation of dreams and aspirations of an entire epoch. In that age of remote antiquity, when the gods were believed to be cohabitants of this world with the human being, Rāma outshined the divinities. Nārada, the divine sage, tells Vālmīki unequivocally that, 'There is none even in the pantheon of gods who is endowed with so much qualities (like Rāma).'[10]

The *Rāmāyaṇa* is unique because of this anthropocentrism. In a world dominated by gods and titans, Vālmīki searched for a human alternative and through a very difficult terrain of ascents and descents, he sought to establish albeit poetically a human centre as well as a human circumference of the wonderful narrative. The great poet tried to answer not only the queries of ancient men but also felt the basic human essence relevant for the posterity as well. His poetic art did not expend itself in narrating an interesting story admirably, but it also built up a microcosm of allegorical import in an unprecedented way. Vālmīki seems to have furnished us with a manifesto of the poetic imagination which seeks to raid the domain of possibilities and colonize it. Rabindranath Tagore observed, "It will not suffice if we describe the *Rāmāyana* and the *Mahābhārata* simply as epics; these are chronicles of history but not of some events alone; because ordinary history thrives on the temporality while these two unveil the eternal history of India. Ordinary chronicles have undergone transformation many a times but this will never change. The variegated history of the multiple endeavours, penances and earnest promises of the Indian people have been established on the eternal throne placed in these two great poetic palaces."[11]

Vālmīki composed his great epic from the floating legends about Rāma which, as we have already stated, was continuously rearranged and recomposed by several generations of bards. In its present form, the *Rāmāyaṇa* consists of 24,000 verses arranged in seven books or Kāṇdas. According to the scholars, many cantos of the first and the entire seventh book are later interpolations in which Rāma has been described as the incarnation of Viṣṇu. Besides there is abundance of loosely woven episodes fraught with supernatural elements. According to some scholars, the great epic came into being by judiciously amalgamating various episodes, related to Rāma, sung by different groups of bards. Such episodes may have been the following: (a) The palace intrigue culminating in the banishment of the protagonist, (b) The abduction of Sītā, (c) The battle between Rāma and Rāvaṇa and (d) the folk-tales and legends about the worship of Monkey as totem god by a non-Aryan cave-dwelling race in South India. Of these, only the first might have some historical basis.

Many a reputed western scholars have enriched the Rāmāyana studies of whom Lassen was an important figure. He thought that the great epic had evolved in four distinct stages and that the work might be regarded as the allegorical representation of the conquest of Deccan by the Aryans. He argued that the original epic nucleus dealt only with the incidents culminating in Rāma's banishment who was accompanied by Sīta and Laksmaṇa. However, Rāma went to the Himalayas instead of the Dandaka forest. In the second phase, the narrative was revised to locate the place of banishment to the land adjacent to the Godāvarī river where the protagonist protected the hermits from the intruding uncivilized races. In the third phase, the accounts of conflicts with the local inhabitants were incorporated in which the uncommon heroic spirit of the protagonist came to the fore. In the fourth and the final revision, further amplifications of the epic narrative took place and the great battle between Rāma and Rāvaṇa, the monarch of Lankā, became the focal point.

Weber made significant contributions to the study of the *Rāmāyaṇa*. However, his conclusions were contradicted by later scholars. For example, it was pointed out that the *Daśaratha Jātaka* could not be the source of the *Rāmāyaṇa* since the former took shape from the Ceylonese oral tradition, a couple of centuries after Vālmīki's epic nucleus came into existence. Besides, the Jātaka does not refer to the most important episode of Sīta's abduction and the fierce battle thereafter. Secondly, Vālmīki's alleged indebtedness to Homer was also contested on several grounds.

Jacobi's analysis seems to us to be much comprehensive and systematic. He noted that the great epic is a unique combination of historical and allegorical elements. He tried to trace the genesis of the conflict between Rāma and Rāvaṇa in the Ṛgvedic antiquity. The mythic struggle between Indra and Vṛtra might have been poetically recreated by Vālmīki.

Among the Indian scholars, C.V. Vaidya, Telang, Dinesh Chandra Sen, Suniti Kumar Chattopadhyay and Sukumar Sen made significant contributions in the study of the *Rāmāyaṇa*. In the wake of the famous controversy in the mid-seventies, Suniti Kumar had a crucial role to play in enhancing a rational, unbiased and scientific attitude to the *Rāmāyaṇa*. Dinesh Chandra Sen spoke of three different sources of the great epic while Sukumar Sen made an in-depth analysis of the genesis of the great epic from diverse sources and through distinctive phases. When the epic nucleus was gradually taking shape as a result of the collective efforts of the singers of tales of several generations, it must have been in a diluvial state. The Sūtas, while orally transmitting the floating mass of materials to the curious listeners, did not hesitate to incorporate additional materials or restructure the older details for making them more interesting and also perhaps more representative. It may easily be conjectured that the popular taste and attitude might also have inspired the bards to shift the areas of emphasis which, in its turn, culminated into sharper readjustments in the narrative style, characterisation and thematic arrangement.

As the Bhārgava interpolations have brought about very significant realignments to transform the 'Bhārata' nucleus into the fullfledged *Mahābhārata,* likewise, it is argued, the redactors belonging to the illustrious Bhārgava clan might have incorporated didactic, ethical, philosophical, political materials as well as Purānic legends in the *Rāmāyaṇa* also to endow it with encyclopaedic traits. The bulk of the first and the entire seventh book was added to the main corpus in this way. Besides, the genuine portion of the great epic is also interspersed with such materials of which the 'Kaccit-Sarga' or the canto depicting the famous conversation of Jābāli, the philosopher of Lokāyata school, with Rāma is particularly important.

The famous critical edition of the *Rāmāyaṇa*, prepared by the M.S. University of Baroda, sheds illuminating light on the textual study. It is now well-known that the *Rāmāyaṇa* has been preserved in two recensions, viz., the northern and the southern, each of which is further sub-divided. Thus the northern recension has the northeastern, the north-western and the western variation while the southern recension has the Telugu, the Grantha and the Malayalam version. The variant versions of text in the northern recension are noted for the abundance of peculiarities but the texts preserved in various forms of the southern recension do not differ substantially among themselves. In spite of much differences between the two major recensions, the preservation of common text has also to be noted carefully. This commonness has been interpreted by some scholars as unfailing evidence of the existence of archaic nucleus of Rāma-epic (also termed as the Ur-Rāmāyaṇa) in the initial phase of composition. Even when the major redactional activities ceased, many a regional scribes seemed to have continued to make enthusiastic interferences to accommodate their pithy reflections on a variety of subjects. Such processes might have been responsible for even further divisions of the north-eastern and north-western versions of the northern recension. Let us conclude this discussion with the comment that such preponderance of variant texts bear undoubted testimony to the phenomenal popularity of the *Rāmāyana* and its unfathomable impact on the Indian cultural milieu for hundreds of generations.

Vālmīki is the roof and crown of Indian epic poets; that is why, he is traditionally accepted as the first poet. His style is graceful but uncomplicated, elegant but simple, precise but spontaneous; his similes and metaphors are wonderful gems of Sanskrit poetry which had cast very deep spell on none other than Kālidāsa. Aśvaghoṣa was also considerably influenced by Vālmīki in respect of stylistic devices. The similes and metaphors are based on the ingredients of nature and the animal world as a result of which these are endowed with pulsating freshness of life. Aśvaghoṣa and Kālidāsa took the cue from their great predecessor but the act of transplantation in a thoroughly changed social situation could not but produce a different result. While the ingredients adopted from nature sound convincingly primitive in Vālmīki's poetic language as well as in his conception of characters, these appear to be basically figurative in the realm of the court epics. Vālmīki flourished in an age of agricultural prosperity but at that time the process of urbanisation did not quite take place. The dense forests were not cleared by the intruding men, the settlements in a few towns were encircled by those forests which were the habitats of wild animals and various aborigines. In that juncture of time, the poetic worldview could not but reflect the contemporary reality. But, in the age of the imperialist expansion of the Kusāṇas and the Guptas, there were fundamental changes in the social experiences and consequently the attitude to life could not but be different. Both Aśvaghoṣa and Kālidāsa substantiate this observation through their creative reconstruction of Vālmīki's poetic materials. A few examples may be cited here.

Vālmīki had always referred to the animal world to describe tense emotional situation; his similes and metaphors are collected from the domain of nature; thus we find:

(a) "Tadā tu vaddhā bhrukutīm bhrubormadhye nararsabhah
Nisasvāsa mahāsarpo vilasthaiva rositah'.[12]

Here, angry Laksmaṇa, a bull among men, is compared to an enraged big serpent in a cave.

The same expression is repeated on several occasions. The angry heroes are described as 'Nisvasan iva pannagah'. Laksmaṇa, in another occasion, is said to be angry like a sighing elephant:

'Avravīllaksmanah kruddho ruddho nāgaiva svasan.'.[13]

(b) A dead Daśaratha, lying on the ground, is said to be like a trunk of Sāla tree felled by an axe:

'Tamārtaṁ devasankāsam samīksya patitam bhuvi
Nikṛttamiva sālasya skandham parasunā vane.'[14]

(c) Rāma and Laksmaṇa are again and again likened to mountain lions:

'Parvatādiva niskramya simho giriguhāsayah'[15]
and 'Tatastu tasmin vijane mahāvalau
Mahāvane rāghava-vamśa-vardhanau
Natau bhayam sambhramamabhyupeyatur
Yathaiva simhau girisānugocarau.'[16]

(d) Sītā is compared to the spouse of the lord of elephants on several occasions:

'Tatrainām tarjanairghoraih punah Sāntvaisca maithilīm
ānayadhvam vasam sarvā Vanyām gajavadhūmiva'.[17]
and 'Gṛhītām lāditām stambe yūthapena vinākṛtām
Nisvasantīm suduhkhārtām gajarājavadhūmiva'.[18]
Sītā is also likened to a female antelope among the tigresses:
'Sātu Sokaparītāngī maithilī janakātmajā
Rāksasīvasamāpannā Vyāghrīnām harinī yathā.'[19]

(e) Vālmīki compares a dejected Rāma searching in vain for Sītā to a sad elephant trapped in mud:

'Pankamāsādya vipulam sīdantamivakunjaram'.[20]

Such expression is also found in the following places:

'Uvāca rāmam sampreksya pankalagna iva dvipah'[21]
and 'Ayuktacāram durdarsamasvādhīnam narādhipam
Varjayanti narā dūrānnadīpankamivadvipāh'[22]

It seems that Aśvaghoṣa has echoed Vālmīki's simile verbatim in the *Buddhacarita*:

'Bharatah Sīdati me ceto nadīpanka iva dvipah'[23]

(f) Vālmīki's society being predominantly agricultural thriving on the wealth of cattle, it was but natural that his similes and metaphors would emerge in good numbers from that reality. Thus we come across the following:

Daśaratha compares Rāma to the cloud fraught with rains since he is eager for the prosperity of the people with philanthropic attitude to all:

'Vṛddhikāmo hi lokasya sarvabhūtānukampakah
Mattah priyataro loke parjaṇya iva vṛṣtimān'[24]

Without Rāma, the kingdom is paddy bereaved of water:

'Śasyam Vā salilam vinā'.[25]

Sītā tells Hanumat, the emissary of Rāma, that she is happy to see him as the earth with half-grown paddy is delighted to have the rains:

'Tvāmdṛstvā priyavaktāram samprahṛsyāmi vānara
Ardhasanjāta Sasyeva vṛṣtim prāpya vasundharā.'[26]

Agricultural fact is reflected in nicely constructed metaphor when Rāvaṇa speaks to Mārica:

'Vāk vam nisphalamatyartham Vījamuptami vokhare'.[27]

There are abundant uses of similes based on bull and cow since cattle were source of prosperity and security at that time. Daśaratha tells Kaikeyī:

'Yathā hyapātāh pasavo yathāsenāhy anāyakāh
Yathā·candram vinā rātriryathā gāvo vinā vṛṣam
Evam hi bharitā rāstram yatra rājā na dṛṣyate.'[28]

When Rāma went on exile, all the queen mothers appeared like cows devoid of calves:[29] Sarvā mahisyastā vivatsā iva dhenavah'. Kauśalyā told Rāma that she would follow him as a cow goes after her calf:

'Katham hi dhenuh svavatsam gacchantamanugacchati.
Aham tvānugamisyāmi yatra vatsa gamisyasi'.[30]

This simile is also used by Aśvaghoṣa in his *Buddhacarita:* 'Tatah Savāspā mahisī mahīpateh pranastavatsa mahisīva vatsalā.[31]

As the cattle was an integral part of the family units at the time of Vālmīki (probably around fifth century B.C.), the highest ideal of relationship was expressed in terms of relevant experience. That is why, Kauśalyā speaks of her son, Rāma and daughter-in-law, Sīta in terms of bull and its spouse:

'Kadāyodhyām mahāvāhuh purīm vīrah praveksyati
Puraskṛtya rathe sītāvāhuh govadhūmiva.'[32]

It may suffice here to say that such similes recur again and again in the *Rāmāyaṇa*. Let us conclude this discussion with citation of some more examples:

(i) When Vāli was killed by Rāṃa:

'Hate tu Vīre plavagādhipe tadā
Vanecarāstatra na sarma lebhire
Vanecarāh simhayute mahāvane
Yathāhi gāvo nihate gavāmpatau.'[33]
'Ahaṃ puttrasahāyā tvāmupāse gatacetanam
Simhena pātitaṃ sadyo gauḥ savatseva govṛsa.'[34]

Such expression is also echoed in Aśvaghoṣa's *Buddhacarita.*:

'Vivarnavaktrā rurudurvarānganā
Vanāntare gāva ivarsabhojhitāh'.[35]

(ii) While describing the autumnal beauty, Vālmīki observes its impact on the bulls which speaks volumes about the typical weltanschauung of that cattle-rearing society:

'Saradgunāpyāyita-rūpasobhāhPraharsitāh
pāmsv-samutthitāngāh
Madotkatāh samprati yuddhalubdhā
Vṛṣa gavām madhyagatā nadanti'.[36]

(iii) Even in the description of a moonlit night, the favourite simile is employed with untiring zeal:

'Tatah sa madhyamgatamamsumantam
Jyotṣnāvitānam muhurudvamantam
Dadarsa dhīmān bhuvi bhānumantam
Gosthe vṛṣam mattamiva bhramantam'.[37]

(iv) Vālmīki uses this recurrent simile rather indiscriminately to describe the heroism of even a minor Rāksasa warrior, Gavāksa, who is said to be:

'Gavām dṛpta ivarsabhah'.[38]

(v) When Rāma returns to Ayodhyā, Bharata hands over the charge with these words:

'Dhīramekākinā nyastāmvṛṣabhena valīyasā
Kisoravad gurum bhāram na bodhumahamutsahe.'[39]

We have already noted that Aśvaghoṣa did not hesitate to imbibe Vālmīki's similes but the wonder associated with creative reconstruction can be experienced only in Kālidāsa's court epics. The great poet was sensitively aware of the grand heritage of the ancestors in which Vālmīki's *Rāmāyaṇa* had a very prominent place. Kālidāsa wrote in the beginning of the *Raghuvamśa*:

'Athavā Kṛtavāgdvāre vamśe'smin pūrbasūribhih.
Manau vajrasamutkīrne sūtrasyevāsti me gatih'.[40]

In comparison Vālmīki's non-urbanised primitive agricultural society in which the culturally dominating Aryans and the forest-dwelling totem-worshipping non-Aryan rustic tribes co-existed with the aggressive inhabitants of prosperous city-states, Kālidāsa flourished in the heyday of the Imperial Guptas when Indian society was reaping the harvest of stability. As a result the material position of the aristocrats was secure and they became the patronising doyens of literature and arts that thrived in their sophisticated courts. Kālidāsa was the brightest star among the luminaries of that age. But, because of the reasons stated above, the spontaneity, directness, rustic vivacity and deep association with the primitive nature, as reflected in Vālmīki's poetic art, was replaced by a deliberately cultivated poetic style developed by Kālidāsa. This new style is remarkable for its elegance, urban sophistication, multiplicity and elasticity. In spite of his indebtedness to Vālmīki, Kālidāsa could nevertheless usher in a new phase of creativity. We may use his famous expression to state that the rustic beauty of Vālmīki's grand style was outshined by cultivated urbanity of Kālidāsa's poetic art: 'Dūrīkṛtāh Khalu gunairudyānalatā vanalatābhih.'[41]

Unlike Vālmīki, Kālidāsa wielded his pen in an ossified and hierarchical society in which the aristocratic Rājanyas used to rule in perfect collaboration with the priestly class. At that juncture of time, nobody dared to violate the prohibitory frontiers prescribed by various scriptures. According to Kālidāsa's own testimony-

> 'Rekhāmātramapi ksunādāmanor bartmānah param
> Na vyatīyuh prajāstasya niyanturnemivṛttayah.'[42]

Undoubtedly Vālmīki's society was totally different and hence his world-view and the concomitant creative devices could not but differ widely from that of Kālidāsa. That is why, the similes and metaphors based on animal world in the *Rāmāyaṇa* underwent significant metamorphosis in Kālidāsa's epic poems. Thus the cattle-metaphors were divested of their direct mundane appeal and were endowed instead with symbolic propensities centring around abstraction and idealisation. A few examples may be cited here to show that in spite of their genesis in the Vālmīki's poetic microcosm, these typical usage of Kālidāsa became independent and remote from their source in the ultimate analysis:

(a) About Vaśiṣtha's sacred cow protected by king Dilīpa:

(i) Patyodharībhūta-catuhsamudrām
gugopa Gorūpadharāmivorvīm'.[43]

(ii) 'Sancārapūtāni digantarāni
Kṛtvā dinānte nilayāya gantum
Pracakrame Pallavarāgatāmrā
Prabhā Patangasya munescadhenuh'.[44]

(iii) 'Babhau ca sātena satām matena,
Sraddheva sāksād vidhinopapannā'.[45]

(b) About the sacred cow placed between king Dilīpa and Queen Sudaksinā:

> 'Tadantare sā virarāja dhenu
> Dinaksapāmadhyagateva Sandhyā.'[46]

The impact of the *Rāmāyaṇa* can be detected on several counts. Kālidāsa's elaborate description of Rāma's aerial journey, from Lankā to Ayodhyā along with Sītā, in the thirteenth canto of the *Raghuvamśa*, is a fine display of his creative imagination. The poet seems to have taken his cue from a very brief interlude in the *Rāmāyaṇa*.[47] Besides, in some places, one can detect close resemblances in language as well.[48] The description of king Dilīpa and his royal administration in the first canto of the *Raghuvamśa* seems to have been modelled on Vālmīki's description of Dasaratha and Ayodhyā under his rule in the first book of the *Rāmāyaṇa*. Moreover, the description of the approach of the gods—tormented by Tāraka, the lord of demons, to Brahman with a prayer to get rid of the demon seems to have been fashioned on a similar description in the *Rāmāyaṇa*[49] where Brahman was implored by a deputation of the gods, gandharvas, siddhas and sages to devise means for killing Rāvaṇa. In fact, Kālidāsa seems to have followed the description ascribed to Vālmīki very closely. Even the title of the epic i.e. *Kumārasambhava* appears to have been coined from the *Rāmāyaṇa*.[50] Some other details in the narrative of the *Kumārasambhava* might have been construed from the great epic. For example, in the *Rāmāyaṇa* Indra sent Rambhā, a celestial nymph, to disrupt the penance of the famous sage, Viśvāmitra. Indra's words of encouragement to Rambhā bear close resemblance to the former's coaxing words to Madana in the *Kumārasambhava*.[51] We may also refer to the description of the birthday of Umā[52] in which the paraphernalia of details seems to have been incorporated from the description of Rāma's wedding day in the *Rāmāyaṇa*.[53]

However, the deepest and most farfetched creative influence exerted by Vālmīki on Kālidāsa must have been in the sphere of the latter's attitude to nature. Vālmīki not only felt the nature around to be pulsating with life, he regarded the flora and fauna as the extension of human existence. The great epic bespeaks of a unique kinship of the human beings with the animal world; that is why, human emotions are not simply imposed on the animals from without. On the contrary, these animals and birds participate in the ever unfolding drama of human life and even arouse elevating feelings in their human cohabitants. The myth of composing first poem by Vālmīki may be cited as an example. Kālidāsa recognised this metaphysics of creativity when he writes in the *Raghuvamśa*:

> 'Nisādabiddhāndajadarsanotthah
> Slokatvamāpadyata yasya Sokah.'[54]

In the *Rāmāyaṇa* Rāma and Sītā have been described time and again to be integral parts of the great family of nature. A few examples will suffice:

(a) When Rāma, Laksmaṇa and Sītā proceeded towards the forest, the trees and birds as well as the river Tamasā seemed to have implored them to return:

> 'Anugantumasaktāstvām mūlairuddhataveginah
> Unnatā vāyuvegena vikrosantīva pādapāh
> Niscestāhārasancāravrk saikasthānaniscitāh.
> Paksino' pi prayācante sarvabhūtānukampanam'
> Evam vikrosatām tesāmdvijāti\īnām Nivartane
> Dadṛse tamasā tatra vārayantīva rāghavam'[55]

(b) When Rāma went on exile, the inhabitants of Ayodhyā consoled themselves with the thought that the natural phenomena would soothe the former's hardship during his forest-sojourn with their abundant presence:

> 'Sobhayisyanti Kākutsthamatavyoramyakānaneh
> Apagāsca mahānūpāh Sānumantascaparvatāh
> Kānanam Vāpi Sailam vāyam rāmo'nugamisyati
> Priyātithimiva prāptam nainam saksyanty anarcitum
> Vicitrakusumāpīdhābahumanjarīdhārinah
> Rāghavaṃdarsayisyanti nagābhramarasālinah
> Akālecāpi mukhyāni puspāni ca phalāni ca
> Darsayisyantyanukrosād-girayorāmamāgatam
> Prasravisyanti toyānibimalāni mahīdharāh
> Vidarsayanto vividhān bhuyascitrāmsca nirjharām
> Pādapāh Parvatāgresu ramayisyanti rāghavam'[56]

(c) When Sītā was abducted by Rāvaṇa, she asked the flora and fauna around beseechingly to inform Rāma about her misfortune.[57]

The natural objects were struck with grief and expressed their protests against such heinous act.[58] When Rāma searched feverishly for his beloved, he, too, turned to the flora and fauna around for obtaining information about Sītā. The situation was as follows:

> 'Dadarsa parnasālānca sītayārahitām tadā
> Sriyā virahitām dhvastām hemante padminimiva
> Rudantamiva Vṛksaisca mlānapuspa-mṛgadvijām
> Sriyā vihīnam vidhvastam santyaktam vanadaivataih'[60]

The impact of such expressions was indeed great and far reaching for the succeeding poets in general and Kālidāsa in particular. A couple of examples may be cited here:

(i) 'Tvam raksasā bhīru yato'panītā
Tam mārgametāh kṛpayālatā me
Adarsayan vaktumasaknuvatyah
Sākhābhirāvarjita-pallavābhih
Mrgyasca darbhānkuranirvyapeksā-
stavāgatijnam samavodhayanmām-
vyāpārayantyodisi daksinasyām-
Utpaksmarājini Vilocanāni.'[61]

(ii) 'Tato' bhisangānila-viprabiddhā
Prabhrasyamānābharanaprasūnā
Svamūrte-lābhaprakrtim dharitrīm
Lateva Sītā Sahasā jagāma
Nrtyam mayūrāh Kusumāni vrksā
Darbhānupāttān vijahurharinyah
Tasyāh prapanne samaduhkhabhāvam
Atyantamāsīdruditam vane' pi'[62]

It may also be noted that Vālmīki's Sītā wept like 'Kurarīva dīnā' on several occasions,[63] likewise Kālidāsa's Sītā, too, shed tears in the same manner:

'Sāmuktakantham vyasanātibhārāc-
cakranda bignā kurarīvabhūyah.'[64]

It may be mentioned here that Aśvaghoṣa also took the cue from Vālmīki to write:

(i) 'Sā cakravākīva bhṛsah cukūja.'[65]
(ii) 'Bisāda-pāriplava-locanātatah
pranastapotā Kurarīvaduhkhitā.'[66]

(d) Vālmīki's wonderful display of poetic imagination in the subtle descriptions of various seasons and their unique effects on human emotions inspired Kālidāsa to the greatest possible extent. Particularly the first, twenty eighth, twenty ninth and thirtieth cantos of the Kiskindhyā Kānda of the *Rāmāyaṇa* seem to contain the brightest specimens of creative imagination. Besides Kālidāsa, Aśvaghoṣa and Bhatti[67] tried to absorb Vālmīki's grandiloquent craftsmanship as best as they could.

The abiding influence of the *Rāmāyaṇa* on the later phases of Indian literature and culture is astounding. The great epic was never meant to be confined within the elites and aristocrats. No scale has yet been invented to scale its impact on the Indian people continuing for over two millennia. Being the real Vedas for the masses, the great epic was adopted by various creeds and schools of thought. In the final stage of redaction, the *Mahābhārata* included an abridged account of Vālmīki's great epic (known as '*Rāmopākhyāna*) in the Vana Parvan which interestingly does not refer to the fire ordeal of Sītā and the events narrated in the last book.

The popularity of the great epic was so tremendous that the exponents of religious creeds considered it rewarding to preach their philosophy under the pretext of restructuring the *Rāmāyaṇa*. Among such works, the following deserve mention: the *Adhyātma Rāmāyaṇa,* the Yogavāśiṣtha *Rāmāyaṇa,* the Ānanda *Rāmāyana* and the Adbhuta *Rāmāyaṇa.* A few minor Upaniṣads were also based on the Rāma-cult, e.g., the *Rāma-Pūrva-Tāpanīya Upaniṣad*, the *Rāmottaratāpanīya Upaniṣad* and the *Rāmarahasya Upaniṣad*. Several Purāṇas and Upapurānas had also faithfully narrated the Rāma-story.

The impact of the *Rāmāyaṇa* on the various branches of classical Sanskrit literature has been of far reaching consequence. We have already noted that Aśvaghoṣa (1st century A.D.) absorbed Vālmīki's influence in his both the court epics (The *Buddhacarita* and the *Saundarananda*) in the spheres of diction, style and poetic imagery. However, Kālidāsa, the supreme genius of Sanskrit literature, was the most consistent, spontaneous and significant recipient of the creative influence exerted by the great master. Beside his two court epics viz. the *Kumārasambhava* and the *Raghuvamśa*, the profound influence is discernible also in both the lyric poems (The *Ṛtusamhāra* and the *Meghadūta)* and most of the dramatic works (the *Vikramorvasiya* and the *Abhijñāna Sakuntala*). Kālidāsa absorbed the essence of Vālmīki's creative art in a unique way which could have been done only by him. We have already spoken of the positive influence on the various aspects of craftsmanship; we may also add here that Kālidāsa's penetrative insight in depicting characters as well as graceful unfoldment of plots have been modelled on the *Rāmāyaṇa.*

Vālmīki's great epic also inspired Bhatti, the grammarian poet of the sixth century A.D., to compose his *Rāvaṇavadha* (commonly known as the Bhattikavya), in twenty two cantos. Kumāradāsa (probably fifth century A.D.) wrote the *Jānakīharaṇa*, a court epic consisting of twenty cantos, to celebrate the Rāma-epic in his own ornate way. Their indebtedness to Vālmīki is quite obvious.

Even when decadence set in the arena of Sanskrit court epics, the *Rāmāyaṇa* continued to cast its magic spell on the poetasters. But the story of the great epic has not been presented with precision and aesthetic congruity. As Vālmīki's lofty imagination was beyond comprehension of these ambitious versifiers subsisting on the spoils of courtly life, they tried to make up for their deficiency by dint of gymnastics of formalism ad absurdum. Various sub-genres came into existence as a result of such endeavours in which Vālmīki and his

Rāmāyaṇa seem to be intruders. These works include: (a) Abhinanda's *Rāmacarita* in which the story begins with Sītā's abduction and ends with the death of Kumbha and Nikumbha; (b) Sākalyamalla's (also known as Kavimalla or Mallācārya) *Udāra Rāghava*; only a fragment of this highly artificial work is available; (c) Venkatesvara's *Citrabandha-Rāmāyaṇa* which is composed in a very difficult style, artificial to the degree of being absurd. That the epic narrative is practically redundant has been emphatically demonstrated by the employment of citrabandha style with which verses are composed diagrammatically in the form of sword, cross, wheel etc.; (d) The *Rāmacandrodaya,* written in thirty cantos in 1635 A.D.; (e) Venkatesa's *Rāmayamakārnava,* composed in 1656 A.D. in which the Rāma-epic is not an end in itself; because these verses are constructed in such a twisted way that the words therein might have two different meanings; (f) Ksemendra's *Rāmāyaṇa Mañjarī,* written in eleventh century A.D.

When vernacular literatures were flourishing in India, the writers of court epics tried to infuse fresh blood in the dying genre by emphasising on the variety of formalistic devices. However, the all-enveloping decadent traits of feudal society had blunted such strategems. Hence, as we have hinted earlier, even the great epic like the *Rāmāyaṇa* could not resuscitate the degenerating literary pursuits. Nevertheless it is interesting to note that the exponents of the sub-genre called 'Śleṣa-Kāvya' (in which each verse has double meanings) also turned to Vālmīki for a ready flow of story. This category has a few works to reckon with: (a) Sandhyākara Nandi's *Rāma-carita*, written in eleventh century A.D., in which two separate stories are narrated simultaneously. One is, of course, about Rāma while the other is about Rāmapāladeva, the younger brother of king Mahīpāla II of Vārendra: (b) Dhananjaya's *Rāghava Pāṇdavīya* written in the twelfth century A.D.; the poet belonged to the order of Digambara Jaina; (c) Kavirāja's *Rāghava Pāṇdavīya*, written in the same century. Both the abovementioned works deal ambitiously with the incidents of two great Indian epics simultaneously; (d) Haradatta Sūri's *Rāghava-Naisadhīya* which narrate the stories of Rāma and Nala at the same time; (e) Venkatādhvarin's *Yādava-Rāghavīya*, written in the seventeenth century A.D., with a view to dealing with the stories of the *Rāmāyaṇa* and the *Bhāgavata Purāṇa* simultaneously, and (f) Cidambara's *Rāghava-Pāndava-yādavīya*, composed in late sixteenth or early seventeenth century A.D., to narrate the stories of the *Rāmāyaṇa,* the *Mahābhārata* and the *Bhāgavata Purāṇa*. Obviously, the tendency of furnishing double meanings was not considered enough and the elasticity of the sub-genre was taken to the frontiers of endurance. As a consequence of this, the true import of Vālmīki's great epic was lost to the readers of such verbal gymnastics.

Besides these works, there is another semi-independent genre called 'campū', which is a mixed product of verse and prose. Vālmīki's unabating influence was felt there as well, the famous *Rāmāyaṇa Campū,* a work of twelfth century and ascribed to king Bhoja, shows that the impact of the great epic was indeed far reaching.

There are some works which dealt with a few chosen episodes of the *Rāmāyaṇa.* For example, there is the *Rāvanārjunīya* of Bhatta Bhīma (also known as Bhauma or Bhaumaka), which dealt with Rāvana's battle with Kārtavīryārjuna. But it has another novelty for which it can be compared to the *Bhattikāvya*. Bhatta Bhīma used the story of the great epic to illustrate certain rules of grammar.

Vālmīki's unflinching influence percolated to the Buddhist and Jaina literature as well. But while the Buddhist Jātakas, e.g. Dasaratha (No. 461), Jayaddisa (No. 518), Vessantara (No. 547), Sāma (No. 540) etc. provide us with an opportunity to study the parallel developments of the Rāma-epic at the initial stage of oral tradition, the Jaina Rāmāyaṇas unfold before us a spectrum of totally reorganised poetic work. Because of thoroughly sectarian approach, the restructured works have practically nothing to do with the original story and instead, these have undergone complete metamorphosis to be the vehicles of indoctrination by the Jaina monks. Let us refer to some of them: (a) Vimala Sūri's *Pauma-cariya* (or *Padma carita*), consisting of 118 cantos in Jaina Mahārāstrī Prākṛta, is regarded as the earliest work in this category. Its differences with the *Rāmāyaṇa* are pronounced in many respects. All the later Jaina *Rāmāyaṇa* have been modelled on the *Paumacariya*. (b) Ravisena wrote the *Padma Purāṇa* in 678 A.D. which is known as merely a slightly extended version in Sanskrit of Vimala Sūri's work. Besides these two, other works have also been attempted on the model of the Rāma-epic in order to preach Jaina doctrines in an interesting way. However, none of these has any literary merit whatsoever.

It is well known that the *Rāmāyaṇa* has inspired several lyric poems and plays in Sanskrit literature. But this is beyond the scope of our book. Likewise, all the modern Indian languages have sought to imbibe the great impact of Vālmīki's unique work of art in their respective literatures. Many a translations have been executed and in medieval age even all the modern genres have been enriched by the never-ending presence of the metaphors, allegories and archetypes deduced from the *Rāmāyaṇa*. This presence is total and dynamic—always felt, accepted and renewed by each succeeding generation.

IV

The *Mahābhārata* is an unparallelled encyclopaedia of Indian culture and that is why, it cannot be merely regarded as an epic. According to a well-known comment, it is not simply an individual work of creativity belonging to a particular genre; rather it is a whole literature. In its present form of 'Satasāhasrī Samhitā i.e. one hundred thousand verses, the *Mahābhārata* is the consummation of the multidimensional experience and realisation, mundane thought and metaphysical pursuit, ideological conflict and creative imagination of the Indian people for over almost a millennium. Therefore as we have already noted, the authorship ascribed to Vyāsa is nothing but symbolic. Vyāsa, in fact, stands for those innumerable generations of compilers and redactors of this encyclopaedic work whose tireless endeavours made the epic nucleus evolve as well as attain bulk through three distinct stages known as 'Jaya', 'Bhārata' and 'Mahābhārata'. The work rightly introduces itself to the readers in the very beginning of the epic narrative: This is the body, truth and nectar of India.[68]

As we have discussed earlier, the primary materials of the great epic crystallized in the presentation of the bards presumably in the prolonged sacrificial sessions and community gatherings. Those bards used to be direct witnesses of heroic battles and adventures of various nature. For all practical purposes, they were the custodians of the collective memory as well as the conscience keepers of the tribes they served; undoubtedly there had been professional bards as well. Many a folk-tales, legends, myths and ballads must have been nourished by those singers which floated parallel to the Great Tradition of the Vedic Aryans. According to the scholars, the epic nucleus had begun to formulate around sixth century B.C. Opinions differ as to whether any battle was ever actually fought at Kurukṣetra: even if such incident occured in reality, it might have happened in the ninth century B.C. It can easily be conjectured that the contemporary bards sang their own versions of that battle as a result of which new cycles of ballads and legends came into existence. With the passage of time, more mythic and semi-historic details were incorporated which, in their turn, amalgamated with the floating cycles of gāthās and proto-ākhyānas to form clusters of poetic compositions. During sixth and fifth centuries B.C., such oral tradition was used with certain modifications and additions by the Buddhist, Jaina and Brahmanic litterateurs to their respective advantage.

If we are to recognize the individual role of any talented redactor in crystallizing chaotic mass of oral materials into the cosmos of an epic, it may be imagined in relation to the initial phase of the great epic, known as 'Jaya'. Being basically a story of battle, it may also be described as the legacy of the Ksatriyas. Undoubtedly, the 'Jaya' was remarkable for primitive expression of heroism, love, hatred and zeal for life. This phase seems to have been complete within fourth century B.C. By that time, the interesting story of conflict between the Kauravas and Pāṇdavas had attained enormous popularity. So the epic nucleus became a magnetic centre, as it were, for gradually accumulating various tales and anecdotes in the periphery. These were sharpened and reorganized in the second phase of redaction known as 'Bhārata'. The earliest recension of the great epic i.e. 'Jaya' seems to have been a small text consisting of, perhaps, less than ten thousand verses. In the initial phase, the conflict of the Kauravas and Pāṇdavas might have been recorded as nothing more than a typical tribal battle.

When the wandering minstrels sang as well as edited the 'Jaya' text for their own benefit, the points of emphasis began to shift gradually. During that period, Indian society had to negotiate with the mutually exclusive tendencies of decadent sacrificial religion, tenets of Buddhism, Ajivakism and Jainism, metaphysics of the Upaniṣads and preachings of the monks of various schools of thought. Besides, several foreign invasions brought about strange beliefs, attitudes and norms of life. The nucleus of the 'Ksatriya epic' had by then decisively yielded to the Brahmanic elites who sought to regain lost ground by turning the 'Jaya' text into compendium of moral philosophy. A good number of episodes euologising kindness, forgiveness, non-violence, hospitality, truthfulness, self-restraint etc. were incorporated into the 'Ksatriya epic'. Consequently there was a thorough metamorphosis both in the texture of the epic narrative and the values underneath. With the addition of the new materials, the epic nucleus was turned motivatedly into a medium of mass education. It may be presumed that the archaic ballad-cycles about tribal conflicts assumed the shape and character of an epic around first century B.C. This is the second phase of the great epic, known as 'Bhārata', probably containing not more than twenty four thousand verses. Though the episodes preaching various ethical norms were incorporated in the phase, these slowly brought about an interesting transformation in the epicentre of the narrative. The acrimonious battle between two neighbouring tribes turned into a fratricidal conflict fraught with great ethical and allegorical import. Therefore, the 'Bhārata' text was undoubtedly enriched with unique human appeal that surpassed the barriers of the temporal existence related to class, community and region.

We may also reasonably conjecture that the 'Jaya' text was concerned mainly with an uncomplicated account of the battle. But, under the changed circumstances, the 'Bhārata-text' could not confine itself within the older frontiers of the story. The singers of the new compilation thought it imperative to account for the origin of the fratricidal feud, which in all probability, necessitated the existence of two vast armies as well. According to the Vedic legacy, the 'Bhārata-jana' was a very ancient tribe; the redactors of the 'Bhārata text' had to take up the responsibility of narrating a series of internal strife and tension in that famous clan for a couple of generations. The great battle at Kurukṣetra, effecting the Indian sub-continent, does not seem to have been depicted at this stage. But nevertheless the 'Bhārata' seems to have prepared the background of that bloody war which ultimately assumed enormous proportion in the final phase of the '*Mahābhārata*' recension.

The Brāhmanic interpolations continued unabatedly till fourth century A.D. The final phase of enlargement is believed to have been caused by the bards belonging to the famous clan of the Bhārgavas. Hence, this phase of 'Mahābhārata' is said to be the outcome of a systematic process of interpolation initiated by the scions of Bhṛgu. They undertook the task of elevating the 'Bhārata epic' to an enormous encyclopedia of Indian wisdom. Therefore innumerable narratives, episodes, fables, legends with little merit were added which seldom had any relation with the epic narrative. Likewise many a discourses on didactic, philosophical, theological, political and mythical subjects were incorporated which had no pretension of relevance with the central text. Such addition did not altogether cease around fourth century A.D.; as a result, we come across much difference among various recensions of the great epic. For example, the northern recension has 82,136 verses while the southern version contains 95,586 verses. According to the famous critical edition of the *Mahābhārata* prepared by the Bhandarkar Oriental Research Institute, Poona, the great epic has more than eighty five thousand verses.

The regional versions of the great epic retained several thousand spurious verses because of which the well-known legacy of hundred thousand verses gained currency. We may refer to the Khoha inscription of king Sarvanātha at Bagelkhand recorded in 214 Gupta era, that is, 533 A.D. There the *Mahābhārata* is described as 'Sātasāhasrī Samhitā'. If we analyse the bulk minutely, we would find that the episodes related to battle and the didactic anecdotes together constitute only about one-third of the complete great epic whereas the Brahmanic (i.e. Bhārgava) interpolations account for the remaining portion, that is, more than two-thirds of the prevalent text. In the latest phase, we can locate some of the unageing legendary stories: e.g., Ruru and Pramadvāra, Nala and Damayantī, Sāvitrī and Satyavat, Rāma and Sītā, Duśyanta and Sakuntalā etc. These narratives seem to have been composed by some experienced bards with rare poetic insight and craftsmanship. That is why, these have proved to be perennial sources of inspiration for later poets and dramatists. But quantitatively such episodes, embellished with creative fervour, do not constitute the major portion of Brāhmanical interpolation. On the other hand, the overwhelming majority of the Bhārgava redaction deals with loosely constructed and incompetently handled stories about superiority of a sectarian god, importance of pilgrimage to holy places, performance of various duties according to one's status in the system of 'varnāsrama', vows and penances, duties of women to their husbands, cheap philosophising, theories of destiny, action and rebirth, supremacy of the Brahmins etc. From the literary point of view, these are utterly devoid of merit. However, if we analyse this section of the great epic along with the evolution of the purānas, our endeavours may be fruitful.

It is interesting to note that the *Mahābhārata* has never put forward its claim as an epic though only once it has described itself as a 'supremely venerated poem.'[69] It has preferred to accord various terms to itself perhaps with a view to emphasising its multidimensional character. We may have a look at those terms here: (i) Arthaśāstra, Dharmaśāstra, Moksaśāstra;[70] (ii) Purāṇa,[71] (iii) Itihāsa[72] (iv) Samhitā and holy book capable of dispelling fear of sin;[73] (v) Veda;[74] (vi) Upaniṣad[75] and (vii) Ākhyāna.[76] Obviously no single work of the epic genre, flourishing anywhere in the world, could ever claim so much for itself. The *Mahābhārata* seems to be not only created by the primeval nature itself, but also it aspires to become the literary correlative of nature or perhaps even usurp its role, as it were, to the greatest possible extent. The great epic sought to provide us, therefore, with an etymological explanation of its name: 'Mahattvāt bhārabattvācca mahābhāratamucyate'[77]: 'The *Mahābhārata* is so called because of its sublimity and great essence.' There cannot be any two opinions about the unfathomable depth of the central episode, the unscalable heights of several epic personalities, the symbolicity of the rise and fall of a great dynasty spread over many generations, amalgamation of multifarious subjectmatters. These are sufficient for placing the *Mahābhārata* at the highest peak of the epic range of the world.

The *Mahābhārata* has referred to three opening points of the epic narrative,[78] but there is doubt as to whether these indicate the beginning of the 'Jaya', the 'Bhārata', and the 'Mahābhārata' about which we have already made some observations. Here we may add that the 'Jaya' recension might have emerged in the later Vedic period and that the 'Bhārata' version did not exist in the early phase of Buddhism. Actually, one cannot be certain about the structure and character of the 'Jaya' recension. However, there is indication about its antiquity in the *Mahābhārata* where the world 'Itihāsa' must have been used in a restrictive sense.[79] At that stage, the narrative might have had a volume manageable for the wandering minstrels. The *Āsvalāyana Gṛhyasūtra* refers to two distinct works known as the 'Bhārata' and the 'Mahābhārata'. It means that the 'Jaya' recension has been by that time (i.e. around third century B.C.) restructured thoroughly; besides the enhanced text has already obtained the approval of the power elites. But the reference to 'Mahābhārata' is misleading because the phase of Bhārgava redaction could not have commenced during Āsvalāyana's time. It may therefore be conjectured that both the names (Bhārata and Mahābhārata) were in vogue and used indiscriminately. At any rate it is very difficult to fix the dates of the compositions of these three recensions authoritatively. Winternitz was of course right when he commented that 'one date of the *Mahābhārata* does not exist at all.'

Modern scholars have sought to analyse the historicity of the division of the great epic into eighteen parvans. It seems quite plausible that no such division existed at the initial 'Jaya' recension. Because, the present Ādiparvan, containing almost ten thousand verses, seems to have been equal in volume with the 'Jaya' text. But, being the nucleus of a Ksatriya-epic, the most relevant portions of the narrative leading to the battle and its immediate impact must have constituted that recension. When some didactic episodes were incorporated, the nucleus graduated into a regular epic through which the attempts to rationalise both the form and the content began. The bards were confident about immense possibilities of the Bhārata-epic. Hence we find a boastful utterance:

> 'Yathā samudra bhagavān yathā ca himavān girih
> Khyātāvubhau ratnanidhī tathā bhāratamucyate'.[80]

We cannot say whether the parvan type of division has been introduced in that stage. But, a text of nearly twenty five thousand verses cannot but become unwieldy and chaotic if it is not arranged systematically into separate units, according to different phases in the development of the narrative. Probably the Bhārata-text had developed the original nucleus upto the level of the present 'Strīparvan' except the materials belonging to the Smṛti and Purāṇic sources. We may also add the preliminary structure of the Sānti Parvan to that second recension.

The final phase of the great epic underwent constant revision and realignment probably till fifth century A.D. The eighteen parvans must have come into vogue at a very late date. Moreover, the huge supplement of 'Khila' called *Harivamśa* was added in the colophon of the epic corpus even later when the Purāṇas were assuming their final shape. Hence the materials of the supplement were deduced heavily from the Viṣṇu, Bhāgavata and Bhavisya Purāṇas. The 'Khila'. divided into three subparvans called the Harivamsa parvan, the Viṣṇuparvan and the Bhavisyaparvan which together have three hundred seveteen chapters and more than sixteen thousand verses. The context of the supplement clearly shows that it had no literary pretension whatsoever; even it had nothing to do with the basic scheme of the great epic. The 'Khila' only tried to secure its passage to posterity by way of forging an association with the great epic.

Presumably at the end of the redactional activities centring around the final 'Mahābhārata' recension, the arrangement of parvans had to be decided once for all. This was felt to be more imperative because presumably the earlier division made into the 'Bhārata' text became reduntant by then and moreover, the tendencies of adding supplement to the sacrosanct epic corpus had to be counteracted so that the frontiers could be distinctively demarcated. But due to the heterogeneous character of interpolations in the last phase of redaction continuing for almost five centuries, the arrangement of parvans could not but be difficult. Besides, the earlier parvans must have swelled beyond all proportions and consequently the older points of demarcation as well as those of beginning and closure of various episodes must have shifted continuously and ultimately went beyond recognition.

Therefore the parvans had to be rearranged but even then the topsyturvy and multilinear text proved to be the mount of Sisyphus for the last generation of redactors. As a result, the Ādi, Vana and Śānti parvans emerged with over ten thousand verses each while the Mahāprasthānika parvan constituted of only one hundred and twenty verses. The Śānti parvan has over fourteen thousand verses and the Anusāsana has almost seven thousand verses.

As all of us are aware, the twin parvans i.e. the Śānti and the Anusāsana constitute the didactic fables and metaphysical discourses incorporated by the Bhārgavas. Significantly, these two books taken together, comprise almost one-sixth of the great epic. The Bhīṣma parvan is particularly important because it contains the most important didactic interpolation in the *Mahābhārata* that is, the celebrated *Bhagavad-Gītā.* The very inclusion of such a lucid philosophical discourse at the impending hours of a fierce battle is impregnated with allegorical meaning. The scholars, both Indian and Western, as well as ancient and modern, have never felt tired in attempting varying interpretations of the *Gītā* for over a millennium. It may suffice here to say that poetic excellence of the Gītā is one of the redeeming features of the great epic, otherwise impaired by excessively monotonous bulk of dry materials. The Brāhmanic redactors were never particularly attentive towards maintaining literary merit. On the contrary, the predominantly anthropocentric traits of the Jaya-recension were relegated to background and instead, theocentric world-view took command. This is also evident in the conception of 'eighteen' parvans of the great epic. Like many other ancient people, Indians too seemed to have developed numerological belief in the concluding centuries of the first millennium B.C. when foreign contacts opened up new vistas of thought. But this could not have been reflected in the arrangement of the epic corpus before the Bhārgavas initiated their redactional activities. With the progress of the last phase of recension, numerological bias spread firm roots; the *Gītā* was arranged in eighteen chapters and the great battle was fought for eighteen days by eighteen 'aksauhiṇī' of soldiers. Thus the recitation of the *Mahābhārata* was expected to be a religious ritual assuring a berth in the heaven. It was therefore equated with the four Vedas.[81]

There is one verse in the Ādiparvan which seeks to establish the authorship of Vyāsa and attempts to rationalise the bulk of the great epic as well: The great sage called Kṛṣṇadvaipāyana composed this excellent *Mahābhārata* by working relentlessly for three years.[82] Obviously this claim was put forward on behalf of the Bhārgavas to authenticate the entire text so that the posterity cannot dare to profane a work sanctified by a sage like Vyāsa. Presumably Vyāsa was already deified and a halo had developed around his mystified personality. In order to justify the unwieldy bulk, the Bhārgavas introduced the interesting myth of Ganapati as scribe. Thus one can detect a tacit acceptance of the genesis of the epic corpus in the oral tradition of the common people in that cleverly disguised myth. Besides there are enough indications of the evolution of various recensions of the epic text in the Ādiparvan. We may refer to the following verse:

> 'Manvādibhāratam kecidāstīkāditathāpare
> Tathoparicarādanye Viprāh samyagadhīyate'[83]

According to this, one text began with the episode of Manu, another with that of Āstika while the third with that of Uparicara. We may note here that in the present Ādiparvan, these are found in the first, thirteenth and fifty sixth chapters respectively. According to the testimony of the great epic itself, Vyāsa (obviously the original bard) composed a primary epic called 'Jaya' on the basis of materials pertaining to a bloody battle which consisted of about ten thousand verses. He recited those verses to four disciples of whom Vaiśampāyana was his most favourite since the latter probably had phenomenal memory and also fairly good expertise in singing the bardic tales to the community gatherings. That might be the reason for his invitation to the venue of 'Snake-sacrifice' by king Janmejaya where Śuka Vaiśampāyana narrated the new recension to the assembly of sages, priests and nobility.

In the mythic paradigms, the temporal time-scheme has hardly any significance; even distinct phases of cultural history constitute a few moments of eternity. The sequence of persons and events is not construed logically; hence the presence of Vaiśampāyana, the favourite disciple of Vyāsa, in the sacrificial session of king Janmejaya, the great grandson of the Pāṇdavas, should not be interpreted too literally. For us, the mythic account has profound symbolic or allegorical value from which we may deduce some clues about the composition of the great epic in different phases. Several centuries must have intervened between the chief redactors of the Jaya and Bhārata recension, represented above by Vyāsa and Vaisampāyana. Therefore the latter could have been the disciple of the former only in the sense that they were the two arch priests of the legacy of oral tradition. When some other bards of a much later generation recollected the contribution of these great stalwarts with gratitude, the tendency of mystification had already set in the Indian society in which the role of the spiritual preceptors was an accomplished fact. Likewise, the reference to a bard named Ugrasrava, son of Lomaharśana and scion of Sūta, who is said to have listened to the recital of Vaiśampāyana's Bhārata text, should also be interpreted in this way. It has been stated that Ugrasrava was requested by the assembled people to recite the great epic while the 'Satra' (Sacrifice to Soma), organised by Śaunaka had been continuing for twelve years. Obviously the epic corpus referred to here is the final recension called 'Mahābhārata'.

V

As we have already noted, various scholars have sought to interprete and comment on the *Mahābhārata* in accordance with their own preference. The traditional schools like to emphasise on the propagation of moral values in the great epic. They argue that the objective of the ancient narrative is to make its readers aware of the four cardinal principles of human life (i.e. dharma, artha, kāma and mokṣa) in general and the supreme excellence of righteousness (dharma) in particular. Understandably such view was the culmination of socio-cultural trends in post-Gupta India when art and literature were not regarded as end in themselves.

Opinions cannot but vary about a work of such heterogeneity and magnitude. We have already noted that no definition is adequate for the *Mahābhārata*. Indeed it is a unique story of several noble and extraordinary personalities; it has innumerable episodes on almost infinite varieties of human situation that invoke equally multifiarious emotional responses. Occasionally we come across wonderful imagery, elegant use of poetic language with simple and dignified metres and captivating figures of speech. But we are equally baffled to see dreary and monotonous expression with little poetic merit. In fact, the *Mahābhārata* leads us to the epicentre of its microcosm through mountains and marshy tracts, dense forest bedecked with mystifying flora and fauna and prolonged barren desert with no sign of respite. Therefore an overview of totality is an essential prerequisite for a study of the great epic. It is neither only a chronicle of ethics nor a guide to metaphysics; likewise it is neither simply an allegory on the struggle between good and evil nor an account of mythicized history. Those who accept the *Mahābhārata* at its basic generic category of a literary work, may have to reconcile with the inadequacy of definition.

The great epic seems to have several enigmatic contradictions. The foremost of them is the seemingly unjustified victory of the deceitful Pāndavas over the more deserving Kauravas. This has generated a lot of speculative interpretations by the European scholars. Adolf Holtzmann, Lassen, Winternitz, Meyer, Von Schroeder and

Grierson shared the view that the Kauravas were the actual winners in the Jaya recension. But with the rise of Brahmanism, the late redactors could not ignore the dictum of the power elites who were the ideologues of the then Indian society. Consequently the Kauravas were depicted as unrighteous while the Pāṇdavas were declared victorious. This necessitated successive revisions of the epic narrative in which the original positions of the two contending sides interchanged. This 'inversion' theory was contradicted by Barth, Levi, Pischel, Jacobi, Oldenberg and Hopkins. However, we need not deal with it further since the Bhārgava interpolations have made all such speculations irrelevant. V.S. Sukthankar, the famous expert on the great epic, commented rightly: 'The Bhṛgus have to all appearances swallowed up the epic nucelus such as it was, and digested it completely, and it would be a hazardous venture now to reconstruct the lost Ksatriya ballad of love and war.'[84]

Though more than two third of the epic corpus having little poetic value is regarded as extraneous to the main narrative, yet the great epic is unsurmountable even on the basis of remaining one-third replete with excellent expressions of creative imagination. We should again observe here that the *Mahābhārata* is placed at the zenith of epic poetry not for any isolated moment of superb craftsmanship in narrative technique or descriptive art or characterisation or brilliant imagery or portrayal of human emotions; rather it is the totality of poetic vision that counts. The ancient bards had spontaneously collected the ingredients of description from the nature around because they used to interact with the natural objects practically at every step of life. Therefore there is not only an abundance of the description of nature, but the epic personalities are also portrayed in terms of epithets chosen unabatingly from nature. This tendency is seen everywhere; particularly the innumerable dramatic moments of the epic narrative are always heightened by the assiduous usage of epithets drawn from nature. Let us cite a few examples here:

(a) While describing the fascinating physical beauty of Draupadī, Yudhiṣthira refers to blue lotus again and again:

'Naiva hrasvā na mahatī na kṛsā nātirohinī
Nīla Kuncitakeśī ca...........
Sāradotpalapatrāksyā sāradotpalagandhayā
Sārdotpalāse vinyā rūpena srīsamānayā.'[85]

The recurrence of stock-epithets is an interesting feature of the great epic. Thus Draupadī has been describ.d earlier in an identical manner:

'Syāmāpadmapalāśāksī Nīlakuncitamūrdhajā
Nīlotpalasamo gandho Yasyāh Krośāt pravāyati'.[86]

Even in the heavenly abode, Draupadī continues to have that feature; that is why Yudhiṣthira could find her as 'Kamalotpalamālinī'.

Likewise all the important characters have some special features concomitant with natural phenomena. It may also be noted that this method of description cast a deep spell on the Sanskrit court epics. But due to the prevalent artificial environment in the ossified society in general and the royal courts in particular, these stock responses soon degenerated into cliches.

(b) In the descriptions of fierce battle, individual heroism and great calamity, the bards look back unhesitatingly to the infinite reservoir of nature for sustenance. Instances are plenty; we may choose a few for examples:

(i) Being struck by Arjuna's endless arrows, the Kaurava army is massacred like beasts trapped in a forest fire:

'Mahāvane mṛgaganā dāvāgnitrāsitā Yathā'.[87]

or, the army is destroyed like the burning bamboo-forest in mountain at night:

'Mahāgirau venuvanam nisi Prajvalitam Yathā
Tathā tava Mahāsainyam prasphutachharapīditam'[88]

(ii) Kṛpa explains to Karṇa that the impertinence of waging battle with the Pāṇdavas may be compared to a suicidal attempt like extracting poisonous tooth from the mouth of a snake:

'Āśībiṣasya Kruddhasya Pāṇimudyamya dakṣinam
Avamucya pradesinyā damṣṭrādātumicchasi.'[89]

This expression has amazing resemblance with one verse of the *Rāmāyaṇa* where Sītā rebukes Rāvaṇa for the latter's licentious advances:

'Āśiviṣasya vadanād damstrāmādātumicchasi
Mandāram parvataśreṣṭham pāṇinā hartumicchasi
Kālakūtam viṣam pītvā svastimān gantumicchasi'.[90]

(iii) When a Ksatriya warrior goes down fighting heroically, some unique metaphors are evoked. While describing the death of Vṛṣasena (Karṇa's son), the poet observes:

'Sa Pārthavānābhihatah papāta rathādvirāhurvisirā dharāyām
Supuspito vṛksavaro' tikāyo vāteritah sālaivādrisṛngāt'[91]

The description of Karṇa's death is perfectly poetic as well:

'Tadudyadād-ādityasamānavarcasam
Sarannabho-madhyaga bhāskaropamam
Varāngamūrvyām-apataccamūpate divākaro'
Stādiva raktamandalah'[92]

also,

'Yathā Kadambakusumam Keśaraih sarvatovṛtam
Citam Śaraśataih Karṇam dharmarājo dadarsa sah'.[93]

(iv) While describing the warriors engrossed in fighting or depicting anxious moments at the battle, the poetic imagery based on natural phenomena comes to the fore. Thus Droṇa burns like smokeless fire in the battlefield:

'rarāja sa mahārāja vidhūmo' gniriva jvalan'.[94]

While fighting with each other, Bhīma and Duryodhana look like two flowering Kimśuka trees in the Himalayas:

'Dadṛśate himavati puṣpitau kimśukāviva.'[95]

Being tormented by Droṇa's incessant flow of arrows, the Pāṇḍavas trembled like emaciated cows in the winter:

'Śiśire Kampamānā vai kṛśā gāva iva prabho.'[96]

When Karṇa arrived at the battlefield as the commander of the Kaurava army, they were relieved to see him as people inflicted with winter look at the sun:

'Śītārtāiva bhāskaram.'[97]

While recognizing the piercing arrows shot at him by Arjuna from behind Śikhaṇḍī, Bhīṣma articulates his agony with the help of a simile based on splendid observation of insectile behaviour:

'Arjunasya ime Vānā neme Vānāh śikhandinah
Kṛntanti mama gātrāṇi māgamam segavā iva.'[98]

The above reflection occurred to Bhīṣma when he was lying on his bed of arrows. But there is another unique expression when Arjuna was striking him with arrows; it is particularly remarkable for the suggestion underneath:

'Smayamānastu gāngeyastān jagṛhe tadā
Uṣṇārto hi naro Yadvajjaladhārāh praticchati
Tathā jagrāha gāngeyah śaradhārāh śikhandinah'.

Along with those brilliantly innovative expressions, there are abundant examples of repetitive usage which, in later court epics, became tiresome cliches. A couple of instances will suffice:

(i) Arjuna makes this jibe at Karṇa:
'Sṛgālo' pi vane karṇa śaśaih parivṛto vasan
Manyate simhamātmānam yāvat simham na paśyati'.[100]

(ii) Vidūrā says this to her son, Sañjaya, while rebuking him for lack of enterprise:

'Alātam tindukasyeva muhūmāyasva jijivisuh'.[101]

Indeed it is proved beyond doubt that the similes and metaphors of the great epic are solidly grounded in nature which is the secret spring of the poetic vision. Everything in nature that the poets of the *Mahābhārata* encountered, came to life and became incarnation of some aspect of their human experience. In the last phase of composition, the poetic vision was explicitly narrated which seemed to have been firmly embedded in pantheistic philosophy. The verses quoted hereafter would remind us of the famous Indian attitude about nature: 'Antahsamjñā bhavantyete sukhaduhkha-Samanvitāh!' One of the philosopher poets belonging to the Bhārgava school of redactors observed thus:

'Sukhaduhkhayosca grahaṇācchinnasya ca virohanāt
jīvam paśyāmi Vṛksāṇām acaitanyam na vidyate
Usmato malāyate varṇam tvakphalam puspameva vā
Mlāyate caiva sītena sparsastenātra vidyate
Vāyyagnyasani-nispesaih phalam visiryate
Śrotreṇa gṛhyate śabdastasmācchṛṇvanti pādapāh'[102] etc.

The *Mahābhārata* shows time and again that the creative poets operating in different phases of its composition had a mysterious sense of correspondence with nature and knew the secret to decipher the metaphorical essence of the natural phenomena. The court epics remained artistically relevant so long their poets could maintain this attitude to nature. Particularly a poet like Kālidāsa competently demonstrated that everything which lived, grew, suffered, moved or crystallized in the human world also existed in nature.

Let us now look at a few recurrent allegories of the *Mahabhārata*. Their prominence in the epic narrative illuminates the process of mutual interaction of human world and natural phenomena; it might be surmised that those visionary poets of the great epic had chosen their own structure of language carefully to suit the thematic requirements. Their language could be fascinatingly evocative, thought-provoking and multi-dimensional if the situation in the epic narrative had so warranted. With the help of metaphors and allegories effortlessly chiselled out from the domain of nature as well as social history, the poetic texture of the great epic did not remain confined to the dreary language of common description but was elevated to a new heightened status which transcended the limits of appearances. That is why such expressions of the great epic have crossed all temporal frontiers to be relevant even to the modern readers.

It seems that the allegory of burning fire has very deep and hence fundamental involvement in the unfoldment of the thematic scheme of the great epic. In other words, such episodes are endowed with archetypal significance. The *Mahābhārata* has depicted three principal episodes of burning fire, the first of which is the burning of waxhouse at Bāranāvat. Duryodhana tried to trap the Pāṇdavas along with Kuntī inside that inflammable palace. The Pāṇdavas could manage to escape but a family of hunters perished in that fire. The second episode is the burning of Khāṇḍava forest in which all the inmates of that forest died helplessly being unable to escape the destructive zeal of Kṛṣṇa and Arjuna. This episode might have been a mythicized version of the extermination of the indigenous population, mostly consisting of the worshippers of Nāga totem by the expansionist Aryans. The third episode is the forest-fire to which Dhṛtarāṣtra, Gāndhāri and Kuntī succumbed. But all these seem extraneous to a more fundamental scheme of baptism by fire manifested through that all-annihilating battle at Kuruksetra. Thus it seems to be one of the basic ingredients of the essence of the *Mahābhārata*.

The circumference of the allegory of fire may indeed be widened to a great extent. The archetypal fire had practically swallowed all the major personalities; each of them proved to be a burning ember in smouldering fire of passion. That fire did not spare anybody in the long run; both the victorious and the vanquished were therefore its indiscriminated victims. It is interesting that the great warriors and their weapons described again and again as fire and its combustible fuel. The immense significance of this recurrent metaphor is finally established when a tearful Yudhiṣthira tells dying Duryodhana:

> 'Nātmānuśocanīyaste ślāghyomṛtyustavādhunā
> Vayamevādhunā śocyāh sarvāvasthāsu Kaurava'[103]

Therefore, the wheel comes full circle when Yudhiṣthira asks Indra in the concluding parvan: 'Juhuvurye Śarīrāni ranavahnau mahārathāth'[104]: Where are those great warriors who offered their bodies to the fire of battle?

There are many episodes in the *Mahābhārata*, enriched with metaphorical import which unfold a unique schemata of creative imagination. For example, the famous game of dice may be regarded as an event with far reaching consequences for both the winners and losers, ultimately culminating in the battle of Kurukṣetra where the colossal allegorical significance of that game became clearly evident for all. Yudhiṣthira, the incarnation of righteousness, became an easy prey to the enticements of dice while Duryodhana, being allured by the possibility of easy victory through dice, only paved the way for total annihilation of the Kauravas. Thus the game ultimately turns out to be a cruel stratagem of fate to set the wheel of destruction of all the players involved in the game into motion.

Another episode is the annihilation of the Yādavas narrated in the Mausala Parvan. Neither Gāndhārī's curse nor the infantile joke was actually responsible for such wanton self-destruction. The iron pestle was indeed symbolic; it is the accumulated corruption, jealousy, hatred and sensuousness of the Yādavas that culminated in their terrible internecine feuds. In fact, the *Mahābhārata* has tried to prove that the fratricidal conflicts are condemned to end only in total disaster. The curses inflicted by Gāndhārī or the ridiculed sages were nothing but poetic attempts of having mythical rationalisation of the destruction of a great race. The innate symbolicity of the episode becomes crystal clear from the very pattern of using details; e.g. the blades of reeds turned into swords and spears in the hands of the fighting Yādavas. We feel that though the abovementioned episode is only cursorily connected with the central narrative, nevertheless the essence of the great epic has been further elaborated here.

If we have a closer look at the narrative details, we would undoubtedly find that many of them are impregnated with metaphoric truth having relevance to readers of all ages. The great epic is particularly remarkable for its unquenchable inquisitiveness regarding the meaning of human life; through various phases, it has always renewed its interpretation of human essence—sometimes suggested and sometimes overtly stated. There are innumerable instances of poetic expressions that emanated from very deep realisation of life and hence are apt to be regarded as everlasting gems of Indian literature. It is well nigh impossible to make a representative selection of such verses since the depth of philosophic vision and the expanse of wisdom can hardly be measured. Therefore we are only making reference to a few verses collected at random:

(i) 'Apriyasya hi pathyasya vaktā śrotā ca durlabhah.'[105]

(ii) 'Ekah sampannamaśnāti vaste vasasca śobhanam
Yo samvibhajya bhṛtyebhyah kah nrsamsatarastatah.'[106]

(iii) 'Pṛthivyām pṛthivīhetoh prthivīpatayo hatāh
Pṛthivīmupa-gṛhyāngaih suptāh Kāntāmiva priyām.'[107]

(iv) 'Yathā varāhasya sunasca yudhyato-
Stayorabhāve svapācasya lābhah.'[108]

(v) 'āturasya kuto nidrā narasyāmarsitasya ca
Arthamscintayatascāpi Kāmayānasya vā punah.'[109]

(vi) 'Yatra nāsti Saraih Kāryam na mitrairna ca vandhubhih
ātmanaikena yoddhavyam tatte yuddham samāyātam
Etajjitvā mahārāja Krtakrtyo bhavisyasi.'[110]

(vii) 'Yathā Kāsthanca Kāsthanca samāyātam mahādadhan
Sametya ca vyapeyātām, tadradbhūtasamāgamah.'[111]

(viii) 'Na samsayamanāruhya naro bhadrāni pasyati
Samsayam punarāruhya yadi jīvati pasyati.'[112]

(ix) 'Puspānīva vicinvantamanyatra gatamānasam
Vṛkīvoranamāsādya mrtyurādāya gacchati.'[113]

(x) 'ātmaiva hyātmano bandhurātmaiva ripurātmanah
ātmaiva hyātmanah Sāksī Kṛtasyāpya Kṛtasya ca.'[114]

(xi) 'Jīyanti Jīryatah Kesā dantā jīryanti Jīryatāh
caksuh-srotre ca jīryete tṛsnaikā na tu Jīryate.'[115]

Even a bird's eyeview of the above quoted verses makes one aware of their universal appeal. In spite of its basic position and overwhelming emphasis on the heroic episodes culminating in the great battle, the *Mahābhārata* has cautiously built up a treasure house of human wisdom on the strong foundation of experience and realisation of life. Those verses, being unique articulation of pithy thoughts strewn over a millennium, bear evidences of the multilinear growth of the great epic. Whatever might be our primary understanding about the loud and sharp portrayal of heroism, war, love, hatred and suffering in the *Mahābhārata*, we are required to ultimately confront with an all-enveloping barrenness and morose void without form and contour. Everything is extraneous to this great epic except the cosmic struggle between good and evil as well as craving for ethical excellence and hedonistic ambition. On another plane, it is emphatically a human world inspite of the presence of gods and demons. Otherwise, the mortality of Kṛṣṇa would not have been depicted in the Mausala Parvan. As we have noted earlier, the great epic declares unambiguously:

> 'Gūhyam brahma yadidam te Vravīmi na
> mānusācchresthataram hi Kincit'.[116]

It is therefore significant that Ānandavardhana held the 'Śānta rasa' (feeling of tranquillity) to be the 'Angīrasa' (Principal sentiment) of the *Mahābhārata*. One may perhaps be taken aback by this comment since the great epic seems to be overwhelmed by violent exhibition of heroic spirit and nerve-shattering battles. But, as we have already explained, the central allegory of a more fundamental spiritual battle has, in the long run, outshined the bloody feuds on the mundane level. As the great epic comes nearer to closure, human feeling is glorified even in the vicinity of heaven because Yudhiṣṭhira refuses to part with a dog and says: 'Mā me Śriyā samgamanamantu, Yasyāh kṛte bhaktajanam tyajeyam.'[117] All passions have been finally spent and the feeling of tranquillity took over. Hence Yudhisthira tells a sneering Indra that he likes to meet his departed brethren in their heavenly abode. He retains his human feeling and declares unhesitatingly that withoug his near and dear ones, he will not prefer to stay even in heaven. Let us, therefore, conclude this discussion with the firm opinion that no other epic in the world could ever attain such an unscalable height of human vision.

VI

Quite expectedly, the *Mahābhārata* has exerted tremendous influence not only on the later court epics but also on other genres of Sanskrit literature. Its impact is equally discernible in the Buddhist and Jaina literature as well as on various vernacular literatures in India. We have already discussed the meaning of creative influence in details. Therefore, it may suffice here to refer to a relevant opinion of Ānandavardhana. According to him:

> 'Samvādāste bhavantyeva bāhulyena sumedhasām
> Naikarūpatayā sarvete manatā vipasitā.[118]

He told about three types of literary influence viz. ālekhyapraḳhya, Prativimbatulya and Tulyadehivat. Of these, the first category results into non-creative mechanical imitation while the second is marginally better. ānandavardhana recognised the third type as valid in literary creativity that promotes the process of magic synthesis. However, the court epics could absorb only a few beams of the colossal cluster of rays, that is, the *Mahābhārata*.

In the initial phase of the court epics, several poets might have wielded their pens to build the primary foundation of the genre. But except the monumental works of two stalwarts in that simmering phase of creativity (i.e. Aśvaghoṣa and Kālidāsa) all other works of apprenticeship have sunk in irretrievable oblivion. We can only conjecture that the apprentices of the epic genre might have found their ideal models in the two great epics. The *Hayagrīvavadha*, written by Mentha or Bhartṛmentha in the fifth century A.D., seems to be the most prominent among the extinct works. That is why, many anthologies and rhetorical works of later period have profusely quoted from its text. Except one incomplete manuscript which has been recorded in the catalogue of Sanskrit manuscripts preserved in the library of the Punjab University, there does not seem to have any second edition of the work. Mentha might have faithfully followed the stylistic traits of the evolving genre; otherwise he would not have been lavishly praised by the rhetoricians. The *Hayagrīvavadha* might have been a compendium of seemingly disjointed mythical episodes about a secondary incarnation of Viṣṇu. The poet seems to have borrowed his subjectmatter from the *Mahābhārata* on the one hand and the Padma, Bhāgavata and Agni Purāṇa on the other.

Of all the court epics fashioned on the great epic, Bhāravi's *Kirātārjunīya* occupies the foremost position on several counts. It is regarded as one of the trend setters in the genre. Bhāravi, who flourished in the sixth century A.D., composed this ornate epic in eighteen cantos to describe one of the episodes of the Vanaparvan. The poet mainly dealt with Arjuna's penance in the Himalayas to win the favour of Siva for having divine weapons. Except this simple structure of the subjectmatter, Bhāravi became independent of the *Mahābhārata* and crowded his poem with host of unnecessary details.

Māgha, who lived in the latter part of the seventh century A.D., enjoyed much repute for his *Śiśupālavadha*. As the title clearly states, it is a court epic in twenty cantos to describe the killing of Śiśupāla by Kṛṣṇa. This episode has been taken from the Sabhāparvan where it does not occupy much space. But Māgha, about whom the traditional commentators seemed to have been crazy (e.g. 'Māghah *Śi* *ś*upālam Vidadhat Kavimadavadham Vidhatte'), concocted several prolonged descriptions engraved with scholastic details with a view to constructing an elistist court epic.

The great impact of the *Mahābhārata* on various aspects of Indian life was not properly transcreated in the court epics precisely because of tendencies of decadence. After Māgha, the Sanskrit court epics degenerated progressively as the poets completely turned their deaf ears to the rhythm of life. Besides, the social institutions were also betraying the unmistakable signals of exhaustion and decay coupled with benumbing elitism. In such a situation, the human essence of the *Mahābhārata* was lost to the poetasters. They searched for stereotyped ethical and religious guidance along with the readymade elements of entertainment; the court epics were regarded as popular medium for reproduction of the old stories from the great epics and purānas in a predetermined manner. Thus Vāsudeva, a contemporary of king Kulaśekhara-varman of Kerala in the ninth century A.D., wrote the *Yudhisthiravijaya*, a Yamaka-kāvya, in which the principal incidents of the great epic have been retold in an artificial and monotonous manner. This futile exercise in epic composition, however, shows that the *Mahābhārata* has, by that time, attained the status of a holy book. This also marks the beginning of the Kṛṣṇa-cycle in Indian literature. We may refer to two works of such category which seem to have some relevance with our discussion. Lolimbarāja wrote the *Harivilāsa* in the eleventh century A.D. which accepted the epic paraphernalia to a certain extent but unfortunately it has no recognizable merit in it. We may next speak of Kavirāja Sūri's *Pārijāta Haraṇa* which is based on an episode of the *Mahābhārata*. This work is replete with devotional feelings, romantic lyricism and penchant for figures of speech; but the poet's lack of inspiration is too much evident throughout the work.

Śrīharṣa composed the *Naisadhīyacarita* in the latter half of the twelfth century A.D.This work deals with the famous episode of Nala and Damayantī in twenty two cantos. It is one of the most popular episodes of the *Mahābhārata* remarkable for its intense romanticism and heart rending pathos. While Srīharsa dealt with only a part of the episode of Nala, Kṛṣṇānanda made use of the entire story in his court epic, the *sahrdayānanda*, complete in fifteen cantos. He might have flourished in Orissa in late thirteenth century A.D. The Nala-episode had also been dealt with by Vāmanabhatta Bāna in his *Nalābhyudaya* in eight cantos. He was a court poet of prince Vema at the juncture of fourteenth and fifteenth century A.D.

Vastupāla, a poet of thirteenth century A.D., wrote the *Naranārāyanānanda* in sixteen cantos to narrate the famous friendship of Kṛṣṇa and Arjuna as well as the latter's romantic love with Subhadrā culminating in marriage. Viśāladeva, who flourished in Gujarat in the same century, composed his *Bālabhārata* in nineteen cantos with a view to preparing a faithful summary of the great epic.

The impact of the great epic was felt expectedly in various genres and subgenres of the Sanskrit literature. Thus we find that Kṣemendra, the famous writer of Kashmir, attempted an abridgement of the great epic in verse entitled the *Mahābhārata Mañjarī* in eleventh century A.D.

The composite genre called Campū was also substantially influenced by the great epic. For example, Anantabhaṭṭa composed the *Bhārata campū* in twelve stavakas or chapters in order to retell the popular story in a new method. The famous episode of Nala has been dealt with by Trivikrama Bhaṭṭa, a poet of tenth century A.D., in the *Nala-Campū* or *Damayantī Kathā*. But only a small portion of the story has been covered in its seven ucchvāsas.

As scholastic formalism continued unabated in that decadent phase of Sanskrit literature, the sub-genres called Yamaka Kāvya and Śleṣa Kāvya found favour with the poetasters. We have already spoken of Vāsudeva, an author of Yamaka Kāvya from Kerala in ninth century A.D. In fact, he wrote two Yamaka Kāvyas of which one is the *Yudhisthira Vijaya* and the other is the *Nalodaya* based on the popular story of Nala. Nītivarman, who lived somewhere in eastern India before eleventh century A.D., composed a Yamaka-Kāvya entitled the *Kīcakavadha* to narrate the slaying of Kīcaka by Bhīma.

In the sub-genre of Śleṣakāvya, there are a few works structured on the *Mahābhārata*, some of which have already been discussed earlier in the section pertaining to the *Rāmāyaṇa* e.g., Dhananjaya's *Rāghava-pāṇdavīya*, Haradatta Sūri's *Rāghava-Naiṣadhīya*, Cidambara's *Rāghava-Pāṇḍava-Yādavīya Nala-yādava-rāghava-Pāṇḍaviya* composed by Lakṣmīdhara in which he tried to narrate as many as four stories simultaneously, two of which owe their origin to the *Mahābhārata*. It may also be noted here that Laksmīdhara fashioned another poem on the episode of Nala. viz., the *Nala-Varṇana Kāvya*.

The *Mahābhārata* has inspired many a playwrights to compose on the basis of its various episodes. Bhāsa, Kālidāsa, Bhattanārāyana and Rājaśekhara are the most prominent among them. But we refrain from discussing them in details as the dramatic genre is beyond our jurisdiction.

Both the Buddhist and Jaina literature have absorbed the influence of the *Mahābhārata* to a considerable extent. Several Pāḷi texts bear its evidence in the treatment of narrative details, delineation of character and presentation of certain episodes of the great epic though these have been renovated by the Buddhist authors in accordance with their own scheme of composition.[119]

In the domain of Jaina literature, we come across the category of 'Harivamsa', which should not be confused with the famous 'Khila' of the great epic. The aforesaid work is a Jaina version of the *Mahābhārata* replete with the characteristics of that religious school of thought. Thus the Jaina doctrines and sermons are interspersed throughout the work and even the Pāṇdavas and Kauravas are portrayed as converted to Jainism. In this work, Kṛṣṇa or Vāsudeva is the chief protagonist and Balarāma is next in importance while Jarāsandha is the antagonist or prativāsudeva. Aristanemi, the dominant Tīrthankara of that period, has been depicted as a cousin of Vāsudeva; hence the Jaina ingredients are blended indiscriminately with the narrative of the great epic. The aforesaid 'Harivamśa' has been treated differently by the two principal sects i.e the Śvetāmbaras and the Digambaras. Thus the Śvetāmbara version of the work has virtually excluded the account of the great battle but the Digambara version chooses to follow the original as closely as possible.

The earliest extant work of this category entitled '*Harivamśa Purāṇa*' was completed by Jinasena, in sixty six chapters belonging to the Digambara sect, in 783 A.D. The following works also deal with the central narrative of the *Mahābhārata*:

(i) Gunabhadra's *Uttara Purāṇa*, composed in ninth century A.D., which is actually a part of the Trisati-laksana-Mahāpurāna.

(ii) Subhacandra's *Pāṇḍava Purāṇa or Jaina Mahābhārata*, written in 1551 A.D.

(iii) Maladhārin Devaprabha Sūri's *Pāṇḍava Carita*, consisting of eighteen cantos (sarga) composed probably in the beginning of the thirteenth century A.D. which is in fact a remodelled but concise account of the entire great epic.

(iv) Asaga's *Pāṇḍava Purāṇa*, a Digambara version of the great epic, written in the eleventh century A.D.

(v) Sīlācārya's *Caupanna-mahāpurisacariya* composed in 868

A.D. in Prakrit prose in which the story of the great epic has been retold in an independent manner.

(vi) Puspadanta's *Tisatthi-mahāpurisa Janalankara* written in Apabhramsa in 965 A.D.

(vii) Somaprabha's *Kumārapāla-patibodha*, written in twelfth century A.D. deals with the popular story of Nala to impress upon the readers about the great calamities caused by gambling.

(viii) Subhasīla Ganin's *Pancasatī-Prabodha-Sambandha*, written in 1464 A.D., is an interesting collection of multifarious stories which includes some episodes about Draupadī and Kuntī as well. The author also composed the *Bharatādi Kathā* in which the incidents of the great epic have been retold.

Besides the tenth to twelfith cantos of the *Satrunjayamāhātmya* deal with the story of the great epic. There is also the sixteenth chapter of the *Nāyā-Dhammakahāo* in which the story of Dovaī (i.e. Draupadī) has been presented in connection with an ingenious composition about a Jaina version of rebirth. We may also refer to the last book of the *Kathā Kosa* which has been described as a curious Jainistic adaptation and extension of the Nala episode of the *Mahābhārata*.'

Because of close association with the Kṛṣṇa cult from a very early period, the Jaina texts have incorporated many legends from that legacy. Sanghadāsa Ganin and Jinadāsa, who might have flourished in sixth or seventh century A.D., wrote *Vāsudeva-hindī* in Prakrit which partially dealt with the legend of Vāsudeva Kṛṣṇa. By that time the Kṛṣṇa-cycle of legends and myths were firmly entrenched in the final recension of the epic corpus along with some Vaiśṇava purānas.

The impact of the *Mahābhārata* on the different vernacular literatures has been astounding. It is not confined within the genres of medieval period; it has been proved time and again that the modern genres in Indian literature even now discover subtle and deep methods of resuscitation from the perennial source of the great epic. The court epics were the principal beneficiaries; nevertheless there was the dramatic genre always showing great concern for the two great epics as these were the eternal granaries for value-loaded themes as well as models of human essence. It is not only true for various other genres and subgenres of Sanskrit literature, but also for the comparatively modern genres of vernacular literature. The resurrection of the epic genre in nineteenth century Bengali literature, for example, shows that it discovers itself to be a generative power that not only engenders tradition but is also part of a generative scheme that extends far back into the past in which the two great epics outshine all other temporal objects and epitomize the timeless schemata of human imagination.

NOTES

1. Eliot, T.S.: 'Tradition and Individual Talent,' *The Sacred Wood*, Methuen, London, 1969 (1920), pp. 49, 52
2. Shaw, J.T.: 'Literary indebtedness and comparative literary Studies,' *Comparative Literature: Method and Perspective*, ed. Newton P Stallknecht and Horst Frenz, revised edition, Southern Illinois University Press, 1971, pp. 86, 92-93.
3. cf. Bloom, Harold: *The Anxiety of Influence,* Oxford University Press, New York, 1973, p. 9
4. Eliot, T.S. : *The Use of Poetry and the Use of Criticism*, Faber & Faber, London, 1945, p. 85.
5. cf. 'Na Mānusāt sresthataram hi kincit' (*Mahābhārata*, xii. 238. 20)
6. cf. 'Bhāratasya vapurhyetat satyancāmrtameva ca', (ibid. i. 1. 201.)
7. cf. 'Yadihāsti tadanyatra yad nehāsti na tad kvacit.'
8. cf. 'Yāvat sthāsyanti girayah saritasca mahītale Tāvatrāmāyanakathā lokesu pracarisyati'
9. Williams, Monier : *Indian Wisdom*, p. 306
10. cf. 'Devesvapi na pasyāmi Kascitebhirgunaih yutam Sruyatām tu gunairebhiryo yukto naracandrama.'
11. Tagore, Rabindranath: 'Rāmāyana', *Prācīn Sāhitya*, Rabīndra Racanāvalī, Vol. xiii, birth centenary edition, Calcutta, 1961, p. 662 (4).
12. *Rāmāyana*. ii. 23. 2.

13. *ibid.* iii. 2.22.
14. *ibid.* ii. 72. 22.
15. *ibid.* ii. 16.26.
16. *ibid.* ii. 53. 35.
17. *ibid.* iii. 56. 31.
18. *ibid.* v. 19. 18.
19. *ibid.* iii. 56. 34.
20. *ibid.* iii. 1. 13.
21. *ibid.* iv. 18. 51.
22. *ibid.* iii. 33. 5.
23. *Buddhacarita*. vi. 26.
24. *Rāmāyaṇa*. ii. 1. 38.
25. *Rāmāyaṇa*. ii. 12. 13.
26. *ibid.* v. 40. 2.
27. *ibid.* iii. 40. 3.
28. *ibid.* ii. 14. 54-55
29. *ibid.* ii. 20.6.
30. *ibid.* ii. 24. 9.
31. *Buddhacarita*. viii. 24.
32. *Rāmāyaṇa*. ii. 43. 12
33. *ibid.* iv. 22. 31
34. *ibid.* iv. 23. 26.
35. *Buddhacarita*. viii. 23.
36. *Rāmāyaṇa*. iv. 30. 38.
37. *ibid.* v. 5.3.
38. *ibid.* vi. 4. 15.
39. *ibid.* vi. 128. 3.
40. *Raghuvamśa*. i.4.
41. *Abhijñāna Sakuntala*. i. 16.
42. *Raghuvamśa*. i. 17.
43. *ibid.* ii. 3.

44. *ibid.* ii. 15.
45. *ibid.* ii. 16.
46. *ibid.* ii. 20.
47. *Rāmāyaṇa*. vi. 123 (Āryasāstra edition).
48. cf. (a) 'Esa seturmayā vaddhah sāgare lavanārnave', (*Rāmāyaṇa*. vi. 123. 16.) and 'Vaidehi pasyāmalayādvibhaktam, Matsetunā phenilamamburāsim', (*Raghuvamśa*. xiii .2.)

    (b) 'Pasya sāgaramaksobhyam vaidehi varunālayam Apāramiva garjantam sankhasuktisamākulam', (*Rāmāyana*. vi. 123. 17-18) and 'Urdhvānkura-protamukham kathancit, Klesādapkrāmati sankhayütham.....Ete vayam saikatabhinnasukti, Paryastamuktāpatalam payodheh', (*Raghuvamsa*. xiii. 13, 17.)

    (c) 'Esā sā dṛśyate pampā nalinī citrakānanā, Tvayā vihīno yatrāham vilalāpa suduhkhitah', (*Rāmāyana*. vi. 123. 40-41) and 'Dürāvatīnā pivatīva khedād Amüni pampāsalilāni dṛṣtih Atrāviyuktāni rathānganāmnām Anyonya-dattotpalakesarāni Dvandvāni dürāntaravartināte Mayā priye saspṛhamīksitāni.' (*Raghuvamśa*. xiii. 30-31.)
49. *Rāmāyaṇa*. i. 15.5.-11.
50. cf. 'Esa te rāma gangāyāh vistaro' bhihito mayā Kumārasambhavascaiva dhanyah punyastathaiva ca.' (ibid. i. 37. 31)
51. *Kumārasambhava*. iii. 12-21. *Rāmāyaṇa*. i. 64. 1. 6-7
52. 'Prasannadik pamsuviviktavātam, sankhasvanānantara-puspavrstih Sarīrinām sthāvarajangamānām. Sukhāya tajjanmadinam vabhüva', (*Kumārasambhava*. i. 23)
53. 'Puspavṛṣtirmahatyāsīd-antariksāt subhāsvarā Divya-dundubhinirghosair-gītavāditra-nisvanaih, Nanrtuscāpsarah sanghā gandharvāsca jaguh kalam, Vivāhe raghumukhyānām tadadbhūtamadṛṣyata' (*Rāmāyaṇa*. i. 73. 37-38)
54. *Raghuvamśa*, xiv. 70.
55. *Rāmāyaṇa*. ii. 45. 30-32.
56. *ibid.* ii. 48. 9-15.
57. *ibid.* iii.49. 30-34.
58. *ibid.* iii. 52. 34-40.
59. *ibid.* iii. 60. 12-25, iii. 63. 16-17, iii. 64. 15-18.

60. *ibid.* iii.. 60.5-6.
61. *Raghuvamśa.* xiii. 24-25.
62. *ibid.* xiv. 55. 69.
63. *Rāmāyaṇa*, iii. 63. 11. iv. 19. 28.
64. *Raghuvamśa.* xiv. 68.
65. *Saundarananda.* vi. 30.
66. *Buddhacarita.* viii. 51.
67. *Bhaṭṭikāvya*, ii, 1-19; vii. 1-13.
68. cf. 'Bhāratasya vapurhyetat satyancāmrtameva ca' (*Mahābhārata.* i.201.)
69. cf. 'Kāvyam paramapüjitam' (*Mahābhārata.* i. 1. 61.)
70 cf. 'Arthasāstramidam punyam dharmasāstramidam param Moksasāstramidam proktam vyāsenāmitabuddhinā' (*ibid.* i. 56. 21.)
71. cf. 'Dvaipāyanena yat proktam purānam paramarsinā'. (*ibid.* i. 1. 15.)
72. cf. 'Bharatasyetihāsasya punyam granthārthasamyutam' (*ibid.* i. 1. 17.) also, 'Itihāsamimam cakre punyam satyavatisutah' (*ibid.* i. 1. 52.)
73. cf. 'Sanhitām srotumichhāmo dharmyām pāpabhayāpahām' (*ibid.* iii. 1.19.)
74. cf. 'Kārsnam Vedamimam vidvān' (ibid. i. 1. 205.)
75. cf. 'Atropanisadam punyām krsnadvaipāyano' vravit' (*ibid.* i. 1.191)
76. cf. 'Yovidyāccaturo vedān sāngopanisadā na dvijah Na cāckhyānamimam vidvānnaiva sa syādvicasksanah' (*ibid.* i. 1. 235.) also, 'Idam sarvaih kavivarairākhyānam-upajīvyate' (*ibid.* i.1. 241.)
77. *ibid.* i.1. 209.
78. *ibid.* i.1. 50.
79. cf. 'Jayo nāmetihāso' yam srotavyo bijigīsunā' (*ibid.*i. 56. 19)
80. *ibid.* i. 56. 27.
81. cf, 'Catvāra ekato vedā bhāratam caivamekatah' (*ibid.* i. 1. 208.)
82. cf, 'Tribhirbarsaih sadotthāyīkrsna-dvaipāyana munih Mahābhāratamākhyānam krtavānidamuttamam' (*ibid.* i. 56. 32.)
83. *ibid.* i. 1. 50.
84. Sukthankar, V.S. *On the Meaning of the Mahābhārata*, Asiatic Society, Bombay, 1957, p. 110.

85. *Mahābhārata.* ii. 65. 33-34.

86. *ibid.* i. 155. 42, 43

87. *ibid.* viii. 80. 19.

88. *ibid.* viii. 80. 80.

89. *ibid.* iv. 49. 13.

90. *Rāmāyaṇa.* iii. 47. 39-40.

91. *Mahābhārata.* viii. 85. 36 (Vangavāsī edition)

92. *ibid.* viii. 67. 24.

93. *ibid.* viii. 96. 33. (Vangavāsī edition)

94. *ibid.* viii. 19. 35.

95. *ibid.* ix. 57. 31.

96. *ibid.* vii. 130. 6.

97. *ibid.* viii. 22. 14.

98. *ibid.* xii. 119. 65. (Vangavāsī edition)

99. *ibid.* vi. 117. 23-24.

100. *ibid.* viii. 27. 45.

101. *ibid.* v. 126. 18.

102. *ibid.* xii. 172. 10-12 (Vangavāsī edition)

103. *ibid.* ix. 59. 27 (Vangavāsī edition)

104. *ibid.* xviii. 2. 2.

105. *ibid.* ii. 64. 17. (Vangavāsī edition)

106. *ibid.* v. 33. 45.

107. *ibid.* vii. 146. 47.

108. *ibid.* vii. 180.8.

109. *ibid.* x. 4. 21.

110. *ibid.* xii. 16. 21-22.

111. *ibid.* xii. 28. 36.

112. *ibid.* xii. 138. 34.

113. *ibid.* xii. 175. 13. (Vangavāsī edition)

114. *ibid.* xiii. 20. 21. (Vangavāsī edition)

115. *ibid.* xii. 288. 20.

116. *ibid.* xvii. 3. 9.

117. *Dhvanyāloka*. iv. 11.
118. *Samyutta Nikāya*. x. 12.

Jātaka No. 495 & 545 (Vidhura-Pandita Jātaka: Vidura and Yudhiṣṭhira)

Jātaka No. 355 (Ghata Jātaka: legend of Kṛṣṇa)

Jātaka No. 444 (episode of Māndavya)

Kunāla Jātaka (distorted account of Draupudī in an episode of Kṛṣṇa)

etc.

4

Epics of Art: The Zenith

In the earlier phases of the evolution of the oral poetry, the bards thrived in the company of patronising nobles and chieftains. At that time, they might have been very close to each other and in the community gatherings, the singers of tales narrated their experiences in an uncomplicated and straightforward manner. As the singers and listeners were also participants both in the event and in the process of narration, there must have been innumerable revisions and readjustments. In spite of an understandable tendency of glorification of the patrons, the narrative was marked for its untarnished freshness. Because of the basic requirements of oral poetry, those bards untiringly used stock epithets and depicted stock responses to certain predetermined situations. All the characters, events and details of narrative retained their preordained identities and paradigms which the very nature of oral composition compelled them to keep intact.

But the succeeding generations of bards could not maintain that straightforwardness or freshness for long since they were no longer participants or direct witnesses of the events described. With the passage of time, Indian society had also gone through varying experiences of strife and tension, acceptance and refusal, synthesis and regeneration bringing about far-reaching modification in the system of values. The new bards had to respond to the new conditions which summoned new creative abilities to survey altered scenes as well as to cater to the requirements of the leisurely power elites. But eventually that altered situation brought about a metamorphosis in the personality of the bards. In the meantime, two epic corpuses were also simultaneously graduating into a new kind of literary monument setting the tune thereby for the succeeding generations of poets. Besides the redactors around those two epic corpuses, some other poets must have wielded their pens under the imposing and chequered shades and hence, their art must have been shaped in various poetic campaigns.

In the changed circumstances community gathering decisively took the shape of selective conglomerations at the courts where carefree bards were replaced by learned artisans.

By that time, many a legends about ancient warriors and amorous heroes had accumulated on the one hand and the language replete with stock expressions and limited vocabulary had also undergone crucial change on the other. Each singer of tale had added new details or slightly modified the stock responses in every generation which ultimately laid the foundation of the epic corpus. As long as the bards composed from memorized elements, there was recurrence of established patterns with which the listeners were well acquainted. But as the wandering minstrels had to sing to different gatherings, they had to constantly make minor adjustments and renovations in their art. The singing of tales was basically a lively creative process in which the functional element of oral style was predominant. But when the learned artisans gradually evolved from the banquet songs and heroic ballads, they looked back to antiquity for appropriate subject matter with cool scholasticism. Their accounts of battles and various exploits were naturally divorced from directness and warmth; they could not depend on the recurrence of memorized elements. Metrical words and expressions had to be substituted by elaborate procedures and invention of new motifs.

The royal and aristocratic patrons wanted soothing enjoyments for their leisurely life; therefore, the old ties existing between the singers and their listeners as mutually assisting participants were snapped. Instead the poets churned out materials selectively and then tried to improve upon the traditional paradigm by sharpening the elegance of form and inventing new pretexts for erudition. Rather than stilling the hearts of patrons, the poets of the new order tried to thrill. The impact of the great epics, as we have noted earlier, was impossible to deny; but the reality of changing time demanded an altogether new awareness from the poets. They could nevertheless deduce valuable clues from those literary monuments regarding subject matter, narrative art, characters etc. But as the changes envisaged in time and temperament dictated new values, the poets had to usher in an era of conscious and ordering thought expressed appropriately in new schemes and sequences. The bardic composition was thus replaced by an elaborate literary style which, unlike the spontaneous oral style, was basically self-conscious and hence selective as well as elusive.

As we have already discussed, the first seeds of the epic of art sprouted in the domains of the *Rāmāyaṇa* and the *Mahābhārata* when their oral texts were undergoing transformation into more elaborate epic corpus. The new poets seemed to have been particularly inspired by Vālmīkī's unique display of creative imagination. We may as well conjecture that the supra-mundane attitude reflected in the contemporary Buddhist literary genres might also have necessitated the crystallization of the budding poets under the fold of Brahmanic society. The proto-Purānas and the floating ballads were not enough for quenching the thirst for creative literature. In spite of great treasures underneath, neither the contemporary recensions of the great epic nor the Buddhist tales and legends could entirely satisfy the aspirant poets. They were constantly developing firm grip on the stylistic devices while searching for elaboration of new scheme of thematic structure as well as manipulation of sequences. At that time Indian society was in transition; both the Brahmanic metaphysics and the Buddhist pessimism were being effectively countered by the emerging literary genres with a more accommodating and syncretic worldview. Unlike the great epics and various commendable works of Buddhist literature, the new literature frankly offered recreation and entertainment which were sources of its strength and weakness at the same time. The proclaimed preference was for elegant craftsmanship and neat formalism.

The new genre, therefore, could not have come into existence all on a sudden. Besides creative literature, many other works were composed in Sanskrit, Pāli and Prākṛta which have lasting value in their respective spheres. In the concluding five centuries of the first millennium B.C., the last phase of Vedic literature was enriched with the Upaniṣads and Sūtras. The basic texts of the various schools of Indian philosophy were composed; the initial nucleus of the Puranic texts was formed. The *Gītā* and *Manusamhitā*, the *Aṣṭādhyāyī* and *Mahābhāṣya*, the *Kāmasūtra* and *Arthaṣāstra* were composed. Besides there were the *Jātakas*, the *Lalita Vistāra* and *Mahāvastu*, the *Bṛhatkathā* etc. Thus it is obvious that the concluding centuries of the first millennium B.C. were remarkable for great flourish of multidimensional processes of composition - both literary as well as non-literary. As a result, the principal beneficiary was the Sanskrit language whose elasticity, veracity and capability of taking on new loads were enhanced to a great extent. Thus significant metamorphic changes took place in the domain of Sanskrit literature, particularly through the genesis of new genres, which were directly correlated to the progressive maturity of Sanskrit language. Literary genres noted and assimilated these manifest as well as subtle changes. In course of time, they developed their own system of communication for conveying the new models of experience and interpretation expressed dialectically through the evolving form and content.

The emergence of Aśvaghoṣa as an accomplished poet of the new genre (i.e. secondary epics) is therefore neither accidental nor without objective correlative. As we have noted earlier, several poets must have wielded their pens but unfortunately such works were completely shadowed by the overwhelming popular response to the evolving epic nucleus as well as other non-literary compositions. But those nameless poets undoubtedly paved the way for a more competent poet like Aśvaghoṣa. Though Vālmīki was perennial source of inspiration for him, nevertheless those minor poets seemed to have maintained a living link of continuity between two epochs. Their works have passed into irretrievable oblivion but some names have somehow been retained. Jalhana's *Sūktimuktāvalī* informs us that Pāṇinī, the great grammarian of fourth century B.C., composed the *Jāmbavatījaya.* According to some, he had also authored the *Pātālavijaya.* But we can hardly arrive at a tangible conclusion regarding these works; even their generic status is uncertain. Patañjali, another eminent grammarian of second century B.C., has told us that Vararuci too composed a poetical work. Moreover in course of his discussion, Patanjalī had made such observations which could not but have been based on a good number of earlier as well as contemporary poetic compositions. One such comment is: 'Chandovat Kavayah Kurvanti'. Likewise we may refer to Pingala's *Chandahsūtra* which enumerated many a metres presumably on the basis of which several poems might have been composed in the concluding centuries of the first millennium B.C. Besides there are the evidences of several inscriptions which bespeak of a commendable though not yet completely mature style of composition. Thus Aśvaghoṣa did not plunge into creative writing to obliterate any total void; rather his emergence as a poet seems to be the logical outcome of the process of sincere absorption of all unique legacies of the past.

II

Aśvaghoṣa, the first important poet of the Sanskrit secondary epics, is said to be a contemporary of Kaniṣka, the famous emperor of the Kuṣāṇa dynasty in the second half of the first century A.D. At that time the Mahāyāna Buddhism was emerging with its distinctive characteristics. It is said that Aśvaghoṣa had a prominent role to play in the famous Jalandhara council of Kaniṣka in which, according to one tradition, as many as five hundred Bodhisattvas took part. It is interesting to note that Aśvaghoṣa is called a 'Bodhisattva' in the Chinese *Samyukta-ratnapitaka-sūtra.*[1] This fits in well with the poet's untiring zeal for proselytizing Buddhist tenets to the masses. Such reference to the presence of a distinctive category of monks called Bodhisattvas in the council held during Kaniṣka's reign may be regarded as significant since the *Divyāvadāna* also tells us of the Bodhisattva-jātaka class of monks who did not find favour with the followers of the Hīnayāna school. However, Tārānātha, the well known expert, had doubts about the presence of such monks in the council.[2]

In fact, Aśvaghoṣa lived at a time when, on the one hand, the conflict between the adherents of the Hīnayāna and the Mahāyāna school continued; while on the other, there were relentless efforts for systematizing the Mahāyāna doctrines. The following Buddhist texts bear unmistakable evidences of that strife for ascendancy: the Prajñāpāramitās, Saddharma Puṇdarika, Lankāvatāra *Daśābhūmikāsūtra* and *Gaṇḍavyūha*. It is generally believed that the famous ideologues like Nāgārjuna and Āryadeva were Aśvaghoṣa's contemporaries. The evidences deduced from the Chinese and Tibetan treatise confirm that the poet was the spiritual counsellor while Caraka was the royal physician of King Kaniṣka. It is a pity that we know very little about his life. Kumārajīva translated purely legendary biography of the poet into Chinese between 401 and 409 A.D. Some modern Indologists like Sylvan Levi, T. Suzuki, Sten Konow, Eliot, Rhys Davids, H. Zuders, Nalinaksha Dutta, B.N. Mukhopadhyaya etc. have however helped us a great deal in understanding the socio-cultural perspective of that period when both Buddhism and Hinduism were in transition. The very fact that Aśvaghoṣa was born in a Brahmin family and was thoroughly educated in the traditional Brahmanic school of thought but was later converted to Buddhism, seems to us to be of great significance.

It means that his creative faculties were decisively sharpened by the symbiosis of two different worldviews as a result of which the budding genre of secondary epics went forward to graduate into the final phase of maturity.

The name of Aśvaghoṣa's father has not come down to us; however his mother's name is Suvarnāksī. He is said to have been born in Sāketa which was renamed as Ayodhyā during the reign of the imperial Guptas. According to the Tibetan biographer, Aśvaghoṣa was a scholar *per se* and he could subdue his opponents in the scholastic debates 'as frequently as a strong wind breaks rotten trees.' He was also an excellent musician who travelled to far off places in the company of singers. His melodious compositions on various Buddhist tenets used to captivate the listeners and won them over to his religious fold. I-tsing, the famous Chinese scholar who travelled extensively through India in the last quarter of the seventh century A.D., also bears testimony to such wandering monks who successfully resisted the heretics and preached Buddhism to the masses. According to him, Aśvaghoṣa was one of such respectable monks who had compiled a few sacred texts. I-tsing spoke of the collections of such texts in different Buddhist sanctuaries, some portion of which were regularly chanted even at his time. According to him, besides being composer of songs. Aśvaghoṣa also wrote the *Buddhacarita* and the *Sūtrālamkāra*.

We come across a schedule of Buddhist patriarchs arranged chronologically from the Chinese sources which placed Aśvaghoṣa after Pāsva and Punyayasas but before Nāgārjuna and Āryadeva. The first two names are alternatively mentioned as his teacher. We have already stated that Aśvaghoṣa was widely acclaimed as one of the exponents of the Mahāyāna school. That is why the authorship of the *Mahāyāna-Sraddhotpāda* might have been attributed to him. In fact, at least eight works of different genres have been attributed to him; viz., the *Buddhacarita, Saundarananda, Sāriputra-prakarana, Gandīstotragāthā, Vajrasūcī, Sūtrālamkāra, Mahāyāna Sraddhotpāda* and *Kalpanāmanditikā*. Of these, the first four works are accepted as the compositions of Aśvaghoṣa while the remaining four do not seem to have been authored by him. The last work is now ascribed to Kumāralāta. a younger contemporary of Aśvaghoṣa and the founder of the Sautrāntika school. Tārānātha held that Mātrceta, the author of doxological works like *Satapancāsatika* or *Prasādapratibhodbhava* and *Catuhsatakastotra* (as well as the *Kaliyugaparikathā* and *Mahārājakaniskalekha* found only in their Tibetan version) was none other than Aśvaghoṣa. But this view has now been proved as untenable.

It seems that Aśvaghoṣa might have associated himself with the Sarvāstivāda school at the outset but nevertheless he was very much aware of the contemporary religious tendencies in general and the creed of devotionalism in particular. We have noted already that Aśvaghoṣa flourished when both Buddhism and Hinduism were in transition. The Mahāyāna school was in the initial stage of evolution while the conception of 'pūjā' was gradually attaining momentum in Brahmanism. The icons of various Brahmanic deities were assuming definite shape and character; simultaneously the typified images of Buddha were also gaining currency. At that time the Bhārgava redactors were busy in interpolating the portions related to community worship (Pūjā) of deities as well as the doxological hymns to three principal gods i.e. Brahmā, Viṣṇu and Śiva in the *Mahābhārata*. Such tendency had obviously switched on an increasing mutual competition among the worshippers of Brahmanic deities and that of Buddha for establishing the supremacy of their respective cult-figure. A closer analysis of the evolution of Buddhism from a predominantly monastic and intellectual phase to a frankly popular facet of later Buddhism undoubtedly proves that the folk mind and the monk mind were at variance in their approach to religion. It may suffice here to note that the practice of the worship of stūpa (i.e. an artificially constructed mound of earth and stone) was introduced by the common people to Buddhism. In the beginning the practice was basically private and individualistic but in course of time it assumed the character of a regular large scale congregational ceremony. On the one hand, it hastened the blossoming of a distinctive architectural tradition and on the other, it paved the way for the emergence of devotionalism (bhakti) as the decisive trend in religious belief.

The concept of 'Three Refuge' or 'Trisarana' seems to be the logical outcome of such tendencies. When popular enthusiasm could no longer be ignored, ecclesiastical sanction had to be arranged and appropriate legends were invented. The elite monks felt afterwards that it was imperative for them to render canonical support for what had been originally uncanonical. As the popular facet of Buddhism became dominant around third century B.C., the monks had to shirk off their earlier apathy not only to recognize what had already been spontaneously evolved but also to invest them with due sanctity and scriptural sanction. But with the passage of time, disagreement between scriptural legends and their scriptural rendering became evident; it has been interpreted by the scholars as subtle suggestion about new approaches to Buddhism in general and different attitude towards the concept of Buddha as well as his great life and personality in particular. For a pretty long time, the essence of the legends had been suggested through numerous symbols and emblems. The penchant for symbolic reduction of Buddha's holy life resulted in the mystery of 'Unseen Buddha'. The artists did not hesitate to depict a 'Bodhisattva' but they carefully refrained from drawing or sculpting a figure of Buddha even when it was required to do so. This reticence was obviously deliberate and self-restrained since at that time the supramundane concept of the eternal, immutable and unalterable Buddha completely shadowed all speculations about his human personality. As long as the Buddha-concept was thought beyond the attribute of form and hence above the reach of plastic art, any attempt to depict him in human image was dismissed as 'unreal' and 'imaginary'. But the wheel came full circle with the gradual impact of devotionalism and the theory of incarnation. The Enlightened Lord became the compassionate Saviour; thus we come across two distinct Buddha-concepts thereafter, viz. Sammā-Sambuddha and Pacceka-Sambuddha. This new situation brought about a qualitative change in art and literature; the human figure of the Buddha was chiselled out which, in its turn, restored human relations as well as relations of time and space.

All sceptic doubts about the actual human existence of the Buddha had to be finally dispelled. This yearning resulted in the invention of an appropriate human image of the Buddha which seems to have appeared in the beginning of the first century A.D. Because in a sculpture of the Mathura school, we find a seated image in which the Buddha is shown in the form of celibate with the physiognomical marks of superman. But the worship of symbols persisted for some more time even after the emergence of the humanised image. The preliminary works of the Mathura school were later substantially modified by the formidable impact of Indo-Hellenistic art. In fact, the

Indo-Hellenistic Buddha was ultimately standardised and eventually accepted by several Asian countries. It is now well known that the earliest Indian Buddha images evolved in two different schools of sculpture, viz., the Gandhara and Mathura. On the basis of archaeological evidences, some scholars have argued that the Buddha image appeared at Mathura almost a century earlier. When the cult of Bhakti became prominent in the vicinity of Mathura, a concrete image of the Buddha was much sought for. The Gandhara school absorbed the Hellenistic traits profusely and gradually cast its spell on the icons of the Mathura school.

When great metamorphic changes were ushered in by the sculptors, it was natural that the Buddha legends would also be reinterpreted in new light. It seems that each school had its own version of the life of the Buddha which was tuned essentially with its approved Buddha- concept. We may refer to here a complete legend on Buddha's life, extant both in Chinese and Tibetan, whose title has been reconstructed as 'Abhiniskramana sūtra' i.e. 'The table of the Renunciation.' The author of this late work has referred to five versions of the life of the Buddha existing in five different schools. These are as follows: (a) The *Mahāvastu* in the school of the Mahāsanghikas, (b) The *Lalitavistara* of the Sarvāstivādins; (c) The *Avadāna* by the Kāsyapīyas; (d) The *Buddhacarita* by the Dharmaguptas and (e) The *Vinayapitakamūda* by the Mahīsāsakas. Whether the *Buddhacarita* referred to above is identical with Aśvaghoṣa's epic, it is difficult to ascertain conclusively. However, we can surmise that the conceptual Buddha of the earlier cults had gradually become a real human personality who inspired the Buddhist literature to launch ambitious poetic works around the noble life of the founder of a new religious order. This bespeaks of a tacit recognition by the legend-makers that he who was the Buddha or Bhagavā or Superman was also at the same time a renowned personality named Gotama, respected by the common people for his innate compassion and holiness. It seems quite plausible that cycles of ballads and folk-tales were prevalent among the common people regarding Gotama; these might have been invoked in the personal reminiscences of the direct disciples. Thus the famous formulaic phrase, 'Evam me sutam' (i.e. so have I heard) provides us with an interesting clue regarding the earliest foundation of legends about the life of Buddha. But thereafter these were entirely restructured by the monks whose legends succeeded in transfiguring Gotama the man to the mahāpurisa or superman, the object of Buddha-cult.

All sects and schools of Buddhism inherited the conventional form invented by monks for the casting of Buddha legend. The transmutation of materials from folk tradition to monkish legends was total. But somehow the dichotomy between the traditional memory of a unique human being and a thoroughly metaphysical Buddha-concept could not be eliminated. When Aśvaghoṣa flourished in the later half of first century A.D., he seemed to have negotiated with an essentially dynamic concept of the Buddha. Because of certain imposing sociocultural trends enumerated earlier, the stereotyped monkish worldview had to yield considerably to the revisionists. Undoubtedly the Buddha was beyond mundane and celestial existence; his sublimity and uniqueness as a 'Mahāpurisa' was an unassailable fact. Yet nevertheless he seemed to have been consummated by a process of becoming, which was conceived as having been accomplished in a human career on the mundane world. Though the docetists rigidly proclaimed that the Buddha never lived in this world, the followers of the Theravāda school had put forward some pointed questions regarding the historicity of some wellknown incidents at Lumbinī, Uruvelā, Vesāli, Kusinārā, Pātaligāma etc.[4] When the bhakti-cult brought about the emergence of the supremely compassionate Buddha, a poet like Aśvaghoṣa must have been aware of the trends of different schools of Buddhism. The growing syncretism inspired him to reconstruct the image of the Buddha to poetically validate, as it were, a unique Indian Divine comedy. Aśvaghoṣa seems to have been most competent monk at that juncture of time to judge the intricacies of canonical texts as well as the nuances of various traditions. According to Vasubandhu, he is supposed to have assisted Kātyāyanīputra in preparing a commentary on the Abhidharma. It is interesting to note here that Paramārtha, an Indian monk settled in China, did not think that the Buddhist Council was organised by Kaniṣka. According to the record prepared by him, it was actually organised by Kātyāyanīputra, a monk of the Sarvāstivāda school, in which Aśvaghoṣa played a very crucial role in rearranging the scriptures into appropriate literary forms and composing new commentaries thereon.

Whatever might be the fact, Aśvaghoṣa seemed to have been successful in finding out the golden mean between a temporal and human Buddha on the one hand and an eternal supra-mundane Buddha, transfigured in faith, on the other. The reconciliation had become meaningful because the poet could make brilliant creative use of a literary mode in the making. The new mode of epic poetry, being the scion of folk imagination thoroughly impregnated with various traits of continuing legacy, reenacted the living image of a reoriented Buddha, who is not only the manifestation of an impersonal and immutable cosmic order but also an excellent human being and the first protagonist of a budding genre. Aśvaghoṣa must have been considerably influenced by the *Lalitavistara* of the Sarvāstivāda school in which the Buddha-legends were arranged in the manner of an epic narrative. It is believed that it was originally composed by a single author who might have been a monk well acquainted with Kapilāvastu but subsequently the work was extensively remoulded to suit the needs of developing Mahāyāna doctrines. The narrative commences from the Buddha's prenatal existence in blissful heaven and ends with his attainment of 'Sammāsambodhi'.

Though the enumerated legends are claimed as real (cf. 'Tāni ca tathāgatasya mitrāni bhūtavādina na mṛsāvādinah'), this reality is qualified. The title signifies that it represented the divine sport of the Buddha: 'Lalitavistaronāma dharmaparyāyasūtrānto mahā vaipulya Bodhisattva-Vikrīdhitah'. This central idea has manifested itself insinuatingly throughout the epic-like narrative, particularly through its imagery and romantic extravaganza. However the protagonist of the *Lalitavistara*, unlike the earlier Pāli legends, does not unfold a human career of a developing personality whose character evolves through living experience. The Buddha's happy youthful days in princely luxury, spiritual crisis culminating in renunciation of mundane life, attainment of the enlightenment, propagation of the new faith and foundation of the new order and ultimately his passing away at Kusinārā—all these bespeak of a unique human drama of gradual ascendance to the zenith of blissful perfection. But the protagonist of the *Lalita Vistara* remains a static and immutable personality throughout; everything he does becomes the 'sport' of the eternal being.

While the followers of the Theravāda strongly believed that no Buddha could be conceived with the human and earthly relations, the docetic traits in the *Kathāvatthu* on the other hand declared unequivocally that Buddha never existed in the world of men: 'no vottabham Buddho Bhagavā manussaloke addhāsiti.'[5] The Theravāda school put emphasis on the literal truth of the Buddha legends. But, in course of time, these legends could no longer remain simple and uncomplicated; because the inevitable changes in the socio-cultural milieu stuffed the older materials with metaphysics and mysticism. The Buddha-concept, as we have already noted, had undergone several changes. That was a continuing process of which the *Lalitavistara* was prominent milestone and undoubtedly a great source of inspiration for Aśvaghoṣa. Another important work of this category was the *Mahāvastu* or *Mahāvastu Avadāna* (composed in second century B.C.) belonging to the sect of Lokottaravāda under the school of the Mahāsānghikas. In accordance with the Avadāna tradition, the biography of Buddha had been presented as a miracle story, which did not substantially differ from the Pāli canonical texts. However its important difference with the *Lalitavistara* lies in the fact that, unlike the latter, it had little literary value. It is basically 'a labyrinth in which one can discover the thread of a connected story of the life of the Buddha only with great difficulty.' In fact the *Mahāvastu* exhibits no principle of arrangement in its text; there is no uniformity in language and style. There is not even a vague attempt of establishing workable connection among the loosely woven heterogenous materials. Some scholars have detected remnants of the antiquarian style of ancient ballads which were not fortunate enough to procure the redactional service of contemporary epic bards. At any rate, Aśvaghoṣa must have been aware of the special value of the *Mahāvastu* as treasure house of legends connected with Buddha's life and his doctrines.

Though Aśvaghoṣa was conversant about the rich tradition of Buddha-biography, it seems that the poet in him was most indebted to the *Lalitavistara*. It might not be regarded as regular Buddha epic but nevertheless it bore some unmistakable evidences of containing strong generic resemblances. We have already noted that Aśvaghoṣa flourished in a critical juncture of Indian cultural history when art and literature were illuminating each other on the one hand while foreign impact was ushering in a new phase of creativity on the other. The poet had no dearth of materials for an epic poem on the life of Buddha; the great epics in the making were also there as guiding polestars. The vast Buddhist literature allowed the poet to pick and choose his required details; he did not even have to grope for an appropriate form. Because both the Brahmanic and Buddhistic traditions provided him with enough clues to build his poetic edifice. The great epics in the making were wonderful treasuries; the Buddhist tradition replete with legends, ballads, Gāthās in the Jātakas, Avadānas and Buddha biographies—also proved to be invaluable for the innovating poet, who tried successfully to fill the lacunae of legacy by virtue of his insight. Aśvaghoṣa must have been substantially inspired by competent use of various metres, polished language and poetic observation in the older Pāli and Sanskrit (both chaste and hybrid variation) literature. A consummate scholar like him could not but have been aware of varying forms envisaged in the canonical texts while the perceptive poet in him must have simultaneously observed the specific roles of 'Sūta-kavi' (bard), Patibhāna kavi' (improviser poet), 'Attha-Kavi' (didactic poet) and 'Cintākavi' (reflective poet) in the domain of Pāli literature.

While choosing his own forte, Aśvaghoṣa might have closely analysed the contributions of the older Buddhist poets like Vāgīsa whose compositions (found in the *Theragāthā/Samyutta Nikāya* and the *Suttanipāta*) bespeak of his ability in constructing simple but striking similes and metaphors as well as graceful metres like Vaitālīya and Vaktra. We also come across some praiseworthy verses composed by famous monks like Sāriputta, Mahākassapa, Moggallāna and also by some lesser known monks like Godhika, Sunīta and Pārāpariya as well as nuns like Subhā and Dantikā. There are traces of commendable craftsmanship in the use of both old and new metres like tristubh, anustubh, vaktra, aupacchandasika etc. as well as in the judicious employment of poetic diction and fascinating descriptions. It seems that the contemporary Sanskrit bardic poetry had considerably influenced the Buddhist poets who chose to imbibe the popular poetic style of their epoch in depicting brief episodes of the life of the Buddha. It is quite plausible that the earliest Pāli poetry drew inspiration from the floating mass of epic materials being constantly sharpened by folk imagination. The early Buddhist poets were consciously emulating these in enhancing the appeal of their religious subjects. When, in course of time, further development took place in metrical schemes and poetic vocabulary, the evolving generic features became prominent in Pāli texts as well. The Jātakas bespeak of such reorganisation; besides the *Suttanipāta* and the *Dhammapada* also bear evidences of new tendencies. From the third century B.C. onwards the increased use of a variety of metres and more elaborate poetic vocabulary ushered in a phase of fusion of different literary traditions. Let us say, this fusion laid the foundation of that process through which Asvaghosa emerged as the first champion of the genre of secondary epics a couple of centuries later.

III

Aśvaghoṣa was fortunate to have Vālmīki as his great predecessor whom he lauded as the first composer in verse.[6] Though he was aware of the talented Buddhist poets, the coveted status of the 'first poet' was awarded to none other than Vālmīki because the latter's stupendous contribution towards chiselling out the accumulated bardic materials into the monumental epic genre had indeed relegated all other poets to semi-oblivion. That is why not more than twenty verses of an epic called the *Jāmbavatījaya* by Pāṇini (probably not identical with the great grammarian of the fourth century B.C.) and simply the name of the *Pātālavijaya* of the same poet were preserved for posterity. Besides Kautilya referred to Biographies known as Ākhāyikās.'[7]

Vararuci (also known as Kātyāyana), author of the supplement called *Vārttika* and probably a junior contemporary of Pānini, also referred to biographies.[8] Patanjali (2nd century B.C.) went a step further and named three biographies, viz., *Vāsavadattā*, *Sumanottarā* and *Bhaimarathī*.[9] Patañjali also alluded to a poem composed by Vararuci;[10] he seemed to have become legendary figure in the Indian poetic tradition quite early but nevertheless this work did not survive. Patanjali did not furnish any details about Vararuci's poem but much later, Rājasekhara names it as the *Kanthābharana*.[11] If the assumption of scholars about its generic classification (i.e. Citrakāvya) is correct, in that case we will have to conclude that the Sanskrit poetic tradition had developed the tendencies towards verbal music and linguistic virtuosity before third century B.C. This would prove undoubtedly that the ascension of Vālmīki to the sublime pinnacle of poetic creativity was no accident at all. Thus Vararuci is believed to have composed several poems which include the *Cārumatī* belonging to the genre of either biography or romance.

But evidences are so meagre that we cannot arrive at a definite conclusion about the status of Sanskrit poetry, not to speak of the epic genre in the concluding centuries of the first millennium B.C. We can therefore only collect the disjointed threads and then attempt a conjectural reconstruction of the poetic texture. Likewise we come across the name of a poet called Subandhu who was a minister of Bindusāra, the emperor, in the first half of third century B.C.

However, he was a poet only in somewhat extended sense; he seemed to have been a playwright or a dramatic theorist. Subandhu's play was probably known as *Vāsavadattā Nātyadhārā* which was apparently obsolete before the text of the present *Nātyaśāstra* was finalised. This only shows that various popular traditions furnished the litteratures with literary ingredients when the early genres were gradually crystallizing. Patañjali's evidence bespeaks of the use of prominent myths by the ancient poets and dramatists as their central motif. The grammarian also helps us a great deal in forming opinion about the gradually maturing stylistic devices of the early poets which include metres, figures of speech and suggestive expression. Thus it seems certain that Aśvaghoṣa did not flourish in literary vacuum; on the contrary, he had a fairly strong tradition, both Buddhistic and Brahmanic, to work upon.

In the *Kāvyamīmānṣā*, Rājaśekhara spoke about some ancient patrons of arts who might have been instrumental in providing the objective conditions for the genesis of court epics. Of them, Śīśunāga, a king of Magadha in the late fifth and early fourth century B.C., seems to us to be the earliest. But except an interesting anecdote, we do not have any details. There were also the following royal patrons: Sātakarnī I and Gautamīputra Sātakarnī, belonging to the dynasty of the Sātavāhanas (3rd &2nd centuries B.C.) Vāsudeva Kāṇva (1st century B.C.) of Magadha and Kuvinda of Sūrasena. It seems that the imperial court of Magadha might have set the trend in patronising arts in general and refined courtly poems in particular. The well-established control over ancient trade routes ushered in an age of great prosperity which brought about a sense of calm security, stability and permanence. This seems to have provided the composers of occasional verses that much-desired fillip in going for more ambitious poetic venture. The accumulated materials by the bards of the floating epic nuclei were readily available for such poets to pick and choose their subjectmatter as well as the standardised metres, diction and figures of speech. They brought about a reorientation of bardic poetry to quickly shoot into fame by being acceptable to the aristocratic listeners of the imperial court and sophisticated city-life. The poetic endeavours were presumably tuned to propagate predetermined ideals and also to please the scholars with increasing tact, subtlety and formalism. These necessitated the emergence of an altogether new poetic genre viz., the court epic under the protective care of those enthusiastic royal patrons.

Aśvaghoṣa might have settled in the prosperous Kusāṇa empire since it was propitious for Buddhism as well as for pursuit of creative activities. As we are aware, he had composed two epics viz. the

Buddhacarita and the *Saundarananda*. He had himself spoken of his didactic purpose in the latter poem where he frankly told that due to the attractiveness and popularity of the new poetic genre, he had made its use as a vehicle for propagation of Buddhist ideals.[12] However he had also been careful to maintain conformity with the compositional principles of the budding genre and, in the process, added his own innovative contribution. He had, in fact, laid the foundation of a typical tendency in court epics when he absorbed various intricate theories regarding poetics, erotics, poetic diction and elitist discussion of contending philosophical doctrines quite consciously and successfully. He had thus set the wheel in motion which came full circle in the epics of Bhāravi, Māgha, Bhatti and Śrīharṣa. But the essential difference between v and his successors lies in the fact that unlike the latter he did not write to exhibit his scholarship or in the fun of enjoying multifarious compositions, nor he was detached from the creative process and object of creation. The poet seemed to have consciously lived through the conflicts of human existence and composed from intense personal experience. Aśvaghoṣa's poems are woven with poignant spiritual tension; he seems to have brought about a unity of two opposites viz. aesthetic pleasure in depicting the fascinating mundane existence and liberation from the illusion of reality with a view to attaining spiritual bliss.

Aśvaghoṣa's *Buddhacarita* consisted of twenty eight cantos of which seventeen cantos have been preserved in the available edition in Sanskrit, covering the events upto Buddha's first sermon at Varanasi. But even there the first thirteen cantos and half of the fourtheenth are said to be the genuine composition of Aśvaghoṣa. However, we are in a position to have an idea of the original epic from its complete translations preserved in Chinese and Tibetan sources.

The famous account of I-tsing, the Chinese traveller, also helps us in this respect; he tells about the *Buddhacarita*: "this extensive work .... relates the Tathāgata's chief doctrines and works during his life, from the period when he was still in the royal palace till his last hour under the avenue of Sāla trees". However, intensive research has revealed that the Chinese translation by Dharmaraksa between

414 and 421 A.D., (entitled *Fo-sho-hing-tsan-king*) did not seem to have faithfully followed the original text; on the other hand, the Tibetan translation of the 7th or 8th century might have been more accurate and dependable except the first canto. Whatever it was according to the testimony of I-tsing, its popularity was spread far and wide that included India and the countries of south-east Asia. The traveller also commented upon the poetic merit of the *Buddhacarita* which, according to him, was a source of untiring joy for the connoisseurs. The poet's command over his craft had succeeded in maintaining economy of words while extracting manifold meanings from the context.

Though the *Buddhacarita* is available to us only as a torso, its claims as an artistic presentation of the noble life and doctrines of the Buddha can be easily established. It calls itself a 'mahākāvya' which shows that Aśvaghoṣa was quite sure about his distinctive technique of composition and thereby he also proclaims his affinity with the continuously evolving Indian epic tradition. Therefore his creativity did not exhaust itself in mere proselytism and dry propagation of religious doctrines. Like the *Lalitavistara* and the *Mahāvastu*, the *Buddhacarita* was also based on the floating myths and legends about Buddha in the folk and monkish traditions; but unlike the two former works, it attained the coveted status of an actual Buddha-epic by virtue of its classical literary traits manifested in artistic delineation of events, narrative details, characterisation and diction. Aśvaghoṣa was very much careful about the truthful presentation of the exalted figure of the noble and compassionate Buddha: but at the same time he was keenly conscious about his unique position as an imaginative poet of a budding genre. His language was chaste but archaic, embellished without being artificial, simple but subtle and sensible. As we have already stated, Aśvaghoṣa was much indebted to Vālmīki and a host of other unnamed poets of the oral tradition while he was himself a constant source of inspiration for Kālidāsa and Bhāravi.[14]

Aśvaghoṣa made judicious use of the materials made available to him by the ealier Buddhist texts and legends; but he could imprint the stamp of his individual genius by creating a cosmos as it were out of disorderly mass of chaos. He was therefore able to successfully plan and artistically arrange a new Buddha-epic which erected a lasting bridge between two contrastive worlds. It was possible because Aśvaghoṣa could sensibly exercise his free option as a creative personality and could demonstrate for posterity those important turning points at which a thoroughly traditional poet should free himself and choose to step into the space of new possibilities. The *Buddhacarita*, therefore, proved its distinctive character in relation to the *Lalita Vistara* and the *Mahāvastu* on the one hand and the *Rāmāyaṇa* and other epic nuclei on the other. The episodes related to the famous three excursions of the prince bespeak of the poet's imagination and skill; some of the narrative details turned out to be indispensable ingredients for the later court epics.[15] The description of a unique battle of Buddha with Māra and his train[16] also became a prototype for the later poets. Inspite of his unmistakable religious passion, Aśvaghoṣa did not lose sight of his primary responsibilities as a poet. Because of his earnestness of feeling, he was able to infuse spontaneity and forcefulness, freshness and directness in his poem. His scholarship and religious preference did not impede the readers' enjoyment of the inherent aesthetic qualities of the work.

Aśvaghoṣa's passionate faith was a direct offshoot of the contemporary trends of 'Buddha-bhakti'; this has also transformed the earlier doctrinaire image of Lord Buddha. The protagonist of the *Buddhacarita* is basically a new personality who has scaled hitherto unattained heights of human dignity. Aśvaghoṣa seems to have closely studied the protagonist of Vālmīki's great epic i.e. Rāma, the 'maryādāpuruṣottama' with a view to determining the quintessence of heroic idealism. The poet has however added new dimensions to the concept of an epic protagonist. Vālmīki's Rāma relinquished royal happiness and accepted exile for fourteen years to be true to his obligations towards father as a son. His sacrifice was indeed of great magnitude but nevertheless behind such act there was no inspiration of spiritual quest. On the contrary, Buddha gave up all mundane bonds, including his youthful wife and son, on his own with the nobler mission to discover the meaning of human existence. He had to tread alone in the difficult path chosen by himself and fraught with unprecedented struggles within. The spiritual turmoil experienced by Buddha constitutes the much-discussed epic struggle in which the antagonist i.e. Māra along with his scheming lieutenants have left no stones unturned to thwart the noble voyage of the protagonist to the sublime enlightenment. However, ultimately Buddha reached his unique goal. Rāma was accompanied by Laksmaṇa and Sītā and assisted by a galaxy of warriors leading the monkey army in his most difficult hours while Buddha had to carry on his spiritual struggle alone and thus his dignified solitude had rendered rare depth to human endeavour. The *Buddhacarita* is the first Sanskrit epic which has been woven around a historical personality since the protagonists of neither the *Rāmāyaṇa* nor the *Mahābhārata* were drawn from clearly recognizable historical chronicles.

The *Buddhacarita* has been described as 'an exactly proportioned epic' in which there are four distinct parts of equal length that correspond to the four stages of the life of the protagonist. Each quarter of the epic consists of seven cantos the first of which deals with the birth and youthful days of the protagonist till his renunciation of the mundane life. It is followed by the second stage in which Buddha attains enlightenment after prolonged quest and a great spiritual struggle with Māra. In the third quarter, the great proselytizing mission of the Buddha is described that puts the martial conquests of the emperors into shade. In the last quarter, the poet seems to transcend the ordinary limits of the description of a life since the events after the Parinirvāna have also been zealously recorded. It is interesting to note that the narration ends with the redistribution of the holy ashes in eighty thousand stūpas by Asoka, the emperor in third century B.C. We may do well to remind us of the fact that the *Buddhacarita* was completed by a Nepalese scholar named Amṛtānanda in 1830 A.D. According to whose own submission, he wrote a few additional cantos because he was unable to trace out a complete manuscript.

The *Saundarananda* is the second court epic composed by Aśvaghoṣa in eighteen cantos all of which, unlike the *Buddhacarita*, have been preserved in Sanskrit. However its concluding verses seem to suggest that the *Saundarananda* was composed first and then the *Buddhacarita* was executed. This epic was discovered and edited by Haraprasad Sastri in 1910. A critical edition was later prepared by E.H. Johnston in 1928. Several European scholars have sought to shed new light on various aspects of the *Saundarananda* as a work connected with the noble life of the Buddha, However, Asvaghosa has been careful to deal with particularly on those aspects and episodes of Buddha's life which were not covered in the *Buddhacarita.* This epic has been woven around the humourous story of Nanda, the love-lorn half-brother of Buddha, found in the *Vinayapitaka* and the *Nidānakathā*[17] The Buddhist texts furnished the poet with the basic facts that Nanda was ordained as a monk against his will by Buddha. Besides, the poet seems to have been aware of other legends as well. For example, there was the legend about Nanda's ascent to heaven and his yearning for the celestial nymphs.[18] The wide prevalence of such legends about Nanda is further corroborated by the exponents of the Greco-Buddhist school of art since some relevant episodes have been depicted by them in reliefs.

Aśvaghoṣa wrote in the *Buddhacarita* about Buddha's supramundane life culminating into the exalted state of enlightenment as a result of his own sustained pursuit of perfection. His next venture in the *Saundarananda* seems to have been undertaken to narrate the proselytizing skill of Buddha by dint of which he could induce an extremely worldly person like Nanda to become a monk. This might seem to be extrinsic episode of Buddha's life but actually the portrayal of his excellent success as a preacher was equally important for a poet like Aśvaghoṣa who was himself a rare synthesis of a poet and a preacher. None of these two tendencies has impaired his spontaneity or even surpassed each other. Though the *Buddhacarita* is generally regarded as richer in content and more appealing as a finished poem, E.H. Johnston thought that the handling of the *Saundarananda* is altogether more mature and assured than that of the *Buddhacarita.* Aśvaghoṣa chose such legends from Buddhist text which, by themselves, were not at all sufficient to support an elaborate structure of court epic. Therefore the poet made use of various extrinsic materials at his disposal. The first six cantos of the poem are more relevant and contain the pertinent narrative details. The poet could skilfully extend the territory of his subject matter by describing the mythical foundation of Kapilāvastu, the king, the birth of Buddha and Nanda.

These descriptions are followed by the depiction of Nanda's intense love for Sundarī and Buddha's begging of alms from Nanda when the latter was assisting his spouse in her toilet. Buddha performs a miracle and draws his half-brother to a monastery. Nanda is totally averse to the life of a monk but he is forcibly converted which leads to a great conflict of feelings. As Sundarī laments for her lost husband, Nanda, too, grieves for his beloved wife.

In the remaining twelve cantos, the poet has little story to build upon; therefore he tries to compensate with the abundant use of his religious ideas and convictions as well as miracles under the brunt of which the epic narrative is choked. We find that the monks try in vain to cheer up a dejected Nanda. When Buddha's soothing words also fail to rouse him, the Lord performs another miracle and ascends to heaven along with his half-brother. Buddha aska Nanda to compare Sundarī's beauty first with an ugly one-eyed female ape in the Himalayas and then with the celestial nymphs in the heaven. On his return to earth, Nanda undertakes the ascetic practices of the Buddhist community with great devotion and seriousness with a view to attaining the heavenly nymphs. After he has made splendid progress in the rigorous training of celibacy, ānanda makes him aware of the absurdity of his self-contradictory position. When he is convinced of his totally incongruous aim since even the heavenly pleasures are futile and hollow, he is redirected towards true happiness by the delighted Buddha. The Lord's preaching of the salient features of his doctrines has consumed several cantos. Here the preacher in Aśvaghoṣa has pushed the poet in him to background; hence he devotes the entire space to the detailed exposition of the Buddhist conceptions about futility of the zest for pleasure, evils of pride and lust, voids of the mundane aspects of life and bliss of enlightenment. There cannot be any two opinions about Aśvaghoṣa's involvement in such presentations because his religious passion was never dimmed by his poetic temperament.

In the concluding phase of the epic, Nanda takes refuge in forest to practise the four prescribed meditations and eventually attains the status of an Arhat. He pays obeisance to Buddha who now instructs him to preach the doctrines to the common people to make their liberation possible. There are two interesting points to note here; first, Aśvaghoṣa unambiguously declares that he has composed this epic with the clear intention to proselytize. The particular literary form has been chosen carefully to win over non-Buddhist readers to the fold of Buddhism. The noble doctrine of liberation and perfect peace has been propagated under the pretext of presenting a story through a newly developing genre. The basic idea was to make the doctrines palatable to the common readers, 'just as one mixes a bitter medicine with honey to make it drinkable'. Secondly, the emphasis on the bliss of solitude and meditation in this epic proves its adherence to the school of Hīnayāna. It is clearly discernible when Nanda pays homage to Buddha, who dissuades the former from doing so since, worship is due to Dharma only, not to him.[19] However, the scholars have found some traces of the Mahāyāna concepts in the poem; as similar tendencies have also been detected in the *Buddhacarita*, it has been concluded that Aśvaghoṣa flourished in an age of transition when the Mahāyāna concepts were in the initial phase of their evolution. Hence in spite of his belonging to the Hīnayāna faith, he could not ignore some of the new traits. Likewise his several allusions to a good number of Brahmanical legends and materials drawn from the nuclei of the two great epics unmistakably prove that the poet did not altogether disown his ancestral heritage as well.

Aśvaghoṣa had the rare ability to maintain a delicate balance between his innate poetic sensibility and deep religious conviction. He was a scholar per se but at the same time he could retain his elementary simplicity. We have already discussed about the poet's use of extrinsic materials in order to fill up the void in the narrative. That way Aśvaghoṣa seems to be a distant forerunner of the post-Kālidāsa court epics. It appears that the poet might have been aware of the epic paraphernalia in the making. Thus he made use of the following descriptive details in the *Buddhacarita*:

(a) birth of a son: Canto I & II

(b) display of learning in medicine, astronomy, architecture, painting, grammar etc.: Canto II

(c) Youth, marriage, lovemaking, royal palace, women folk in frivolous mood: Canto II, III & IV.

(d) hermitage: Canto VII

(e) Counsel, political consultation, intrigue and sending of emissary: Canto IX, X & XI.

(f) battle, siege: Canto XIII & XXVIII.

(g) lexicography, philosophy: Canto IX, XII, XIV, XVI, XVIII, XXVI.

Unlike the later court epics, these descriptive details are always kept in check and these are generally never used for pedantic exhibition.

In the *Saundarananda*, Aśvaghoṣa used the following details:

(a) Hermitage, City: Canto I

(b) King: Canto II

(c) Lovemaking: Canto IV.

(d) Spring: Canto VII.

(e) The Himalayas: Canto X

(f) Internal battle: Canto XVII.

It is not without justification that Aśvaghoṣa was regarded by the later rhetoricians as a grammatical poet who excelled in displaying his command over nouns and verbs. The poet's speciality lies particularly in his unique ability to extract undiscovered delight from the seemingly dry arena of grammar. Obviously, this is where Aśvaghoṣa seems to have cast his spell on a few illustrious successors of whom Bhatti is the most prominent name. Aśvaghoṣa appeals to us as a poet of ideas; likewise Bhāravi's epic is also noteworthy for its emphasis on skilful delineation of ideas. While Aśvaghoṣa could retain his basic simplicity inspite of his explicit philosophical preference and grammatical bias, Bhāravi's scholasticity often impairs the development of the epic narrative and grammatical complexities do not always augur well with the enjoyment of the poem. Nevertheless Bhāravi's treatment of ideas is distinctive and generally the modes of expression are well integrated with the subjectmatter. Even then Aśvaghoṣa seems to be comparatively more disciplined in his approach to the epic narrative, though on some occasions he, too, indulges in humourous linguistic games. On another plane, he excels in the portrayal of emotion and paves the way for the poets to come. Moreover his powerful characterisation, psychological penetration as well as polished and figurative description based on well-chosen poetic vocabulary laid the foundation for the later improvising poets, particularly Kālidāsa.

IV

In the first four centuries of the Christian era, Indian civilization entered a new phase as a result of intense intellectual activities in several regions since, with the fading out of political centralisation, there was no longer cultural hegemony of particular city. The well-established literary forms were cultivated earnestly in different regions in their respective vernaculars as well as in Sanskrit, the idealised pan-Indian language. With the ossification of a leisurely society, the experiences gained from such literary activities had to be consolidated further. As Sanskrit showed a tendency of quick assimilation of regional linguistic traits, it was felt to be the ideal vehicle for cultural unification. Consequently it was more encouraged by different patrons among the ruling elites with a view to protecting their historically evolved interests. Besides, innumerable texts were coming out in Sanskrit in the different schools of Brahmanism and Buddhism. Naturally, as a literary language, Sanskrit went from strength to strength; its phenomenal popularity ultimately eliminated the barriers of regional dialects and gradually an edifice of pan-Indian culture and civilization was firmly established. The soil was thus prepared for the blossoming of the finest flower of Sanskrit poetry during the reign of the Gupta dynasty.

Between Aśvaghoṣa and Kālidāsa, the creative legacy of the Sanskrit language was enriched by the litteratures like Mātṛceta, Sūra (or Āryasūra). Bhāsa, Īsvaradatta and Śūdraka. It is interesting to note that a veil of mystery has set around each of them. At any rate their collective contribution to Sanskrit literature in general and to the evolution of the secondary epic genre in particular must have been considerably great. The strong legacy of the 'Kathā' genre in Prākṛta should also be kept in mind which flowed parallel to the greater literary tradition and also interacted with it presumably from the second century B.C. till the emergence of the primary recensions of different Purānic texts. The above-mentioned genre seemed to have close connection with the Pāli literary tradition as well. The basic syncretic tendencies were active at every level which could not but have been creatively synchronised by the litterateur of Great tradition. Around second century A.D., excellent lyric poems were composed in Mahārāstrī, nearest to Sanskrit of all the Prākrtas. It was adored by the connoisseurs belonging to the upper strata of the then society. Sanskrit was the choicest language for social communication though Sūrasenī was in vogue. But due to deep-rooted bias of the Aryans against the inhabitants of the eastern country, Māgadhī Prākrta was looked down upon.

Besides occasional lyric poems and songs often composed by women poets belonging to the unsophisticated peasantry, Mahārāṣtrī was used for epic composition as well. A Jaina poet named Vimala or Vimalasūri, one of the earliest pioneers of literature in Mahārāṣtrī Prākṛta flourishing around second century A.D., is said to have composed Jaina versions of two great epics of which only the work on the *Rāmāyaṇa* has come down to us. This is known as the *Paumacariya* since Rāma is called Pauma by the Jainas according to whom the prevalent text of the great epic was badly tampered by false doctrines and therefore, the true story known by the omniscient Jina Mahāvīra has to be restored. The *Paumacariya* is a huge epic consisting of as much as 118 cantos. This makes us aware of the following: (a) The aversion of the Jainas to the established epic corpus of Vālmīki and also their attempts to furnish an alternative version seem to suggest that the *Rāmāyaṇa* was undergoing major redactional alterations even then; (b) The Jaina preachers could not ignore the popularity of the great epic and might have undertaken to prepare their own version much earlier that might suit their proselytizing programmes; (c) The ethical and religious intentions have clearly subdued and even eclipsed the aesthetic purposes in the *Paumacariya*. Inspite of occasional poetic flourish, the work is nearer to the puranic genre than to the epic; (d) In more ways than one, Vimala was nearer to Vālmīki rather than to Aśvaghoṣa though the latter was almost a contemporary as well as alienated from the Brahmanic society.

Thus the post-Aśvaghoṣa scenario in Sanskrit literature was complex but vibrant with multifarious activities through which the creative personalities of those centuries sought to come to terms with themselves, with the cross-currents of their society and time as well as with the heterogeneity of the cultural milieu. The evolution of various genres and literary styles during the period also makes an interesting study. All these facts taken together shed illuminating light on the objective factors towards the emergence of Kālidāsa, the supreme genius and consummate artist of Sanskrit literature. This period also witnessed a great flourish in architecture and sculpture. The earlier phase marked the beginning of the great schools of Indian art, particularly the inception and gradual development of the Buddhist iconography and the assimilation of foreign influence with indigenous elements. In spite of the exclusively Buddhist character of such artistic creation, we notice in them a sincere effort to faithfully express the life and temperament of the Indian people. Though some of the early architectures were inspired by Brahmanism and Jainism, the genre was predominantly controlled by Buddhist artists who added new depths to form and content by way of exhibiting simple dignity, vivacity, directness, strong feeling for narrative, concern for precise rendering of details and a tendency towards stylisation.

It is indeed interesting to note that the above-mentioned features are also discernible in the literary genres as well, specially in the court epics. We have already referred to the tendencies in the sculpture and architecture of Aśvaghoṣa's time. It seems that the sculptors and architects were making steady progress. The sculptural technique bespeaks of more pronounced reliefs, more elaborate perspective and more orderly composition. The products of Gāndhāra school around second century A.D. exhibit Indian form and subjectmatter though traces of earlier Hellenistic style can still be detected. The images of Bodhisattva bear clear evidences of the formulation of Mahāyāna Buddhism. Likewise the products of the schools of Mathurā and Amarāvatī draw our attention to the evergrowing tendencies of syncretism in Indian art. On the one hand, the oriental and hellenistic features are intermingled; while on the other, there is deep yearning for discovering the soul of Indian art. In fact, the three dominant schools have common elements in the architectural forms and the features of sculpture and painting. Thus, in spite of variations, the art of this period shows a strong emphasis on unity. There is diversity in the sculptural products of those three schools because of the size and variety of the materials used as well as due to difference in creative consciousness. However the sculptors could attain true perfection in their artistic execution since the genre had absorbed aesthetic and technical traits from several sources in course of time. The sculptures and narrative reliefs, therefore, fascinate us by subtlety of composition, calculated elegance, emphasis on individuality, marvellous understanding of balance of form and harmony of line, blending of grace and vitality. In relation to the succeeding classical age of art in the Gupta Era, the first three centuries of the Christian Era may be regarded as the period of transition. Because, being rich in unique achievements and various experimentation, it improved upon its inheritance from the past legacy and initiated the process of final ascent to perfection on the one hand while on the other it paved the way for the full blossoming in the Gupta era.

The Gupta dynasty emerged in 320 A.D. in Magadha; Candragupta I was the founder of his dynasty but the Gupta empire was practically the culmination of the successful martial exploits of Samudragupta (C. 350-375 A.D.). But the Guptas reached the zenith of splendour during the rule of Candragupta II (C 375-414 A.D.) and Kumāragupta I (C. 414-455 A.D.). Though immediately thereafter the Gupta power began to erode in the wake of a continuing invasion of the White Huns from Bactria, the great flourish in various realms of culture persisted even long after the dynasty had withered away. In this brilliant phase of cultural history (from fourth to sixth century A.D.), earlier gains were consolidated and new dimensions were discovered in various forms of art. A remarkable unity of style and excellent refinement was achieved in different genres which had by then become standardised classical forms and pastimes for the elites. This period witnessed a unique blossoming of literature and philosophy as well. Kālidāsa was indeed the best representative of that fertile time.

That age was unique because of the prevalence of a reasonably broad religious tolerance due to which all sects could freely pursue their own ways. All the religions were inclined towards mysticism and growing syncretism. All the prominent Brahmanic philosophical systems were enthusiastically elaborated while the great Buddhist philosophers like Asanga and Vasubandhu built the edifice of Mahāyāna Buddhism with their works. In the backdrop of such colossal transformations of ideological worldview, the intellectual and artistic manifestations of the Gupta era assumed an altogether new character. The intrinsic styles of various genres were deduced from past experiences but nevertheless bore expressions of new preoccupations. Human form was idealised to an unprecedented extent; the artists of the Gupta era used the human figure as their principal subject in sculpture and painting. The tranquil detachment inspired by Buddhism was expressed in a majestic way. There are two types of icons; viz., the Buddha which continues to be shaped according to established legacy and the Bodhisattva and Brahmanic deities whose princely and minutely detailed adornments contrast with the simplicity of the Buddha.

In this period many a Brahmanic temples built of durable materials and generally small in size, came into existence. At the same time earlier form was revived in the rock-cut architectures which remained fashionable for a few more centuries though these were adorned with a multitude of sculpted or painted decorative details. It is well known that from ancient times sculpture has formed an integral and prominent part of architecture and that there is interpenetration of the sacred and the profane element throughout. The works of art of each religion are basically expressive of their own particular spirituality. There is continuity of earlier tradition as well as conformity to canonical regulations. The rock-cut sanctuaries of both the Brahmanic and the Buddhist religions reveal wellorchestrated tendency towards detailed ornamentation not only on the walls but also on the pillars. In spite of a general flourish in the realm of artistic creativity, the Buddhist bas-reliefs seem to have already lost their former qualities even in the Gupta era. The earlier narrative details were replaced by more stereotyped compositions having architectural character. However, the Brahmanic bas-reliefs of this period offered studies in contrast as these were presented with dynamic qualities. Some of the frescos in the caves at Ajanta were executed by the Buddhist artists in this period. Their technical mastery, selection and application of colour, execution of decorative details and purity of line and form undoubtedly prove that these artists were of the very first order.

In the concluding decade of the sixth century, all the genres exhibited the tendencies of following the canonical rules too scrupulously and too mechanically. As a result of such increasing adherence to formalism, the works of art gradually became impersonal and stylised. It is particularly interesting to note that the figures of Buddha appeared to be much fleshier and the Bodhisattvas and Brahmanic deities were bedecked with elaborate jewellery. These bespeak of the symptoms of the weakening of inherent strength concomitant with the compensatory cultivation of extrinsic features. In the midst of the fluctuations of taste and fashion, Indian art retained its basic concern for continuity by a process of juxtaposing old and new elements. From a careful analysis of the salient features of the artistic genres discussed above, we understand that the contemporary literary genres absorbed those features to a great extent. This reminds us of the famous theory of mutual illumination of creative arts. According to this theory, a continuous sharpening and curious expansion of the areas of creative expressions takes place in the generic categories as a result of their interaction and interpenetration inspired mainly by historically conditioned attitude, proximity and convergence of different ingredients. It is indeed very significant that the literature of the period under consideration is replete with innumerable details of icons, temples, sanctuaries, cities, pleasure gardens, flora and fauna and many other items which time and again remind us of contemporary painting, sculpture and architecture. The penchant for stylised decorative details as well as standardised thematic schemes is equally recognisable in the literary and artistic genres which include music as well.

The phase of classicism in Sanskrit poetry was a natural corollary of material prosperity attained during the reign of the Gupta dynasty. Poetics had already developed and hence Kālidāsa, the greatest poet of this age, must have been familiar with the tenets of poetics in general and the *Nātyaśāstra* of Bharata in particular though his genius transcended the frontiers of mechanical dictum. The great poet was conversant with all sorts of poetic expressions which include the lesser known poems of the inscriptions. The famous controversy about the age of Kālidāsa has kept the literary historians occupied for long. According to well-established tradition, he was patronised by Vikramāditya i.e. Candragupta II (375-414 A.D.). But this coveted title was assumed by many Indian rulers; the problem is further compounded by several popular mythical tales in which 'Vikrama or 'Vikramāditya' figures prominently. Besides this title was assumed by two emperors of the Gupta dynasty, viz. Candragupta II and Skanda gupta (455-467 A.D.) It has been argued that the title of his play, *Vikramorvaśīya* alludes to Vikramāditya who might have been the patron of the great poet. According to a well-known legend, Kālidāsa was one of the nine jewels shining in the court of Vikrama, a king of Ujjayinī. Even if this ostensible tradition is dismissed as having no validity, the fact remains that the poet flourished during the reign of Vikramāditya whose capital was the city of Ujjayinī, depicted with glowing colours in the *Meghadūta*. Candragupta II was a great warrior who had ousted the Śakas from Ujjayinī around 395 A.D. Abhinanda, the author of the *Rāmacarita* (9th century A.D.), associated Kālidāsa with 'Sākārāti', a title appended to Candragupta II. It has also been assumed that diverse oblique references have been made in the *Raghuvamśa*.

The title of the *Kumārasambhava* is also said to have been designed to contain suggestion of Kumāragupta (Mahendrāditya: 414-455) or to Skandagupta (another Vikramāditya: 455-467 A.D.). In the Hindu pantheon, Skanda is another name for the god, Kumāra. As Skandagupta saved India from the menacing invasion of the mighty Huns, likewise Skanda, the god, too, saved heaven from Tāraka, the lord of demons. The parallelism might have been construed with an obvious intention to please the patron emperor; such topical allusiveness is not rare in Sanskrit literature. It has been conjectured that Kālidāsa might have enjoyed an unusually long life and that his literary activity began during the reign of Candragupta II and continued well after the expedition of Skandagupta against the Huns. This means that the great poet might have lived between 380 and 465 A.D.[20] At this juncture one can take note of two important points. First, there is the evidence of an inscription dated 473 A.D., discovered in a temple of Sūrya at Mandasor, according to which a poetaster named Vatsabhaṭṭi seemed to have imitated the great poet very closely. This strongly suggests that already Kālidāsa had become a celebrity and that Vatsabhaṭṭi might have been a younger contemporary of the great poet. Secondly, Kālidāsa seems to have been conversant with Greek astrology (vide a few astrological statements in his epics) which reached India in the middle of the fourth century A.D. through Firmicus Maternus.

Besides Kālidāsa refers to his predecessors viz. Saumilla and Bhāsa; the latter had cast his spell over the great poet to a considerable extent. However, his reference to Vālmīki, in the *Raghuvamśa*, is particularly noteworthy. It seems that several centuries must have intervened between Vālmīki and Kālidāsa; hence the latter describes the former, the poet of the *Rāmāyaṇa* as the mythical sage of a distant epoch. If all these facts are taken together, the most plausible conclusion about Kālidāsa's time may be thus put forward: the great poet was creative between the last decade of the fourth century and the first half of the fifth century A.D. This assumption is further supported by the commentary entitled '*Rāmasetu*' on the *Setubandha*, an epic poem composed by Pravarasena II, the Vākātaka emperor (410-440 A.D.); according to this, Kālidāsa's date cannot possibly be brought down to the sixth century though some scholars tried to prove such hypothesis. It is obvious that the great poet had become very famous before the beginning of the seventh century. He was highly praised by Bānabhatta and mentioned with great reverence in the Aihole inscription dated 634 A.D. and another inscription at far off Cambodia (dated early seventh century A.D.). The poet of inscriptions seemed to have been familiar with the *Raghuvamśa*. Such wide popularity suggests that considerable time (may be two centuries) must have elapsed after the death of Kālidāsa.

As the question of the age of the great poet has triggered off much controversy, the problems of the genuine authorship of the work has also engaged the attention of the critics for a long time. The problem has been complicated by a few usurpers who tried to book their easy passage to eternity by assuming the magic name of Kālidāsa. Thus we come across the following: Nava-Kālidāsa, Abhinava Kālidāsa. etc. It has now been almost universally accepted that Kālidāsa's creative monument constitutes of the following: the *Kumārasambhava*, the *Raghuvamśa* (both court epics), the *Mālavikāgnimitra*, the *Vikramorvaśīya*, the *Abhijñāna Śākuntala* (all plays), the *Ṛtusamhāra* and the *Meghadūta* (lyric poems). Though all these works do not have equal merit, yet the connoisseurs have traced the essential features of a genius either in the making or in its full blossoming. He has been considered as the model poet by the later rhetoricians. This reminds us of the following anonymous verse in the anthology entitled *Harihārāvalī*.

> 'Purā Kavīnām gananāprasange
> Kaniṣthikādhisthita-Kālidāsā
> Adyāpi tattulyakaverabhāvād
> Anāmikā sārthavatī Vabhūva'

We can easily ignore the fantastic anecdotes created by popular imagination regarding the life and salient turning points in the career of the great poet since these lead us nowhere. We have already noted that Kālidāsa seemed to have been an inhabitant of Ujjayinī but there are different opinions as well. For example, Haraprasad Sastri thought that Kālidāsa was born in Dasapur of Mālava while Kasmir and Vidarbha are also named as his place of residence. Daṇḍin might have hinted at Vidarbha as Kālidāsa's place of origin in the *Avantīsundarīkathā*: 'Liptā madhudravenāsan Yasya nirvivasā girah/ Tenedam vartma vaidarbham Kālidāsena Śodhitam'.

It is interesting to note here that Kālidāsa's style evolved in the Vaidarbha school in which Sūra, Sarvasena and Mentha were the pioneer exponents. Kālidāsa added new dimensions to this school of style by incorporating the quality of sweetness, suggestiveness, more refined delicacy, glowing fancy and sophistication. Whatever might be the opinions of some rhetoricians like Mammata and traditional critics of the modern period regarding blemishes in his poetry, Kālidāsa's supreme genius has left its indelible print everywhere. The brightest star in the firmament of Indian poetry has surpassed all his predecessors both in depth and subtlety, imaginative vision and conscious craftsmanship. It was definitely not without sufficient reason that Bāṇabhatta eulogised Kālidāsa in the following manner:

> 'Nirgatāsu na vā kasya Kālidāsasya Sūktim,
> Prītirmadhurasādrāsu mañjarīṣviva jāyate'

The uniqueness of his style rests on the innate lyricism and specially on the very conception and execution of the poetic schemata. The great poet had Vālmīki, Aśvaghoṣa, Bhāsa, Mentha and presumably some other illustrious predecessors before him who had furnished various models which were constantly improved upon and readjusted. Because a true genius can never remain confined within the well-defined limits of convention. Therefore the emphasis on lyricism in the epics and plays cannot be regarded as aesthetically incongruous. Contrary to the apprehension expressed by some critics, Kālidāsa did not reduce all literary genres to unnecessary lyric poetry; nor did he substantially eliminate the essential narrative element from the epic text in order to favour occasional lyrics in individual verses. Likewise he did not entirely concentrate on the depiction of emotions in lieu of much sought for dramatic action. Kālidāsa had, in fact, tried to determine through creatively organised experiments as to whether the frontiers of various genres were independent of each other or whether these actually overlapped and interacted with each other in the works of art of a genius. The great poet did not visualise consummate artist in chains. He felt that being a man with creative disposition, he can do no more than to build up his own universe—a symbolic microcosm that enables him to understand and interprete, to articulate and organise, to synthesize and universalize his human experience.

Kālidāsa proved his extraordinary skill and artistic sensibility in both the court epics, viz. the *Kumārasambhava* and the *Raghuvamśa* whose materials have been derived from the great epics and the Puranic tradition. The critics are of the opinion that both these have been apparently left incomplete by the great poet. There is however difference of opinion regarding the order of composition: A.K. Warder prefers to treat the *Kumārasambhava* as the last work of Kālidāsa while Winternitz, Sushil Kumar De and Sukumari Bhattacharji consider it as the poet's earlier work. The *Kumārasambhava* i.e. the birth of Kumāra (or Skanda, the war-god) was admirably conceived in which a mythological theme has commissioned an excellent poetic vision to unfold itself. The myth of the birth of Kumāra has been differently delineated in the great epics and Purāṇas.[21] The origin of this myth might be traced to a remoter past; the *Śatapatha Brāhmana* seems to contain a highly symbolic as well as primarily metaphysical version of the birth of Kumāra.[22] Thus it is certain that Kālidāsa had a very rich and ever-renewing tradition to work upon; presumably it was he who gave a new lease of life to the myth by interpreting it with newly sharpened sensibilities of the age. The poet might have derived his material from an extant Ur-purāṇa corpus from which the earlier Purāna texts might also have drawn heavily. But the later texts seem to have been primarily inspired by Kālidāsa's epic to which their authors of course freely added typical Brahmanic textual details. The myth of an ever young Kumāra might have carried a special appeal for Kālidāsa when he could feel the innermost urge of his age for a culture hero who could provide security on the wake of a foreign invasion. Apart from this subtle political undertone, Kālidāsa might also have been animated by deeply aesthetic and metaphysical considerations in depicting the unique blissful bond of love between Puruṣa and Prakṛti, the Primeval couple, in which physical charm and lust are rebuffed. When love is purified through penance, bliss transcends the mundane existence and the genesis of the evil-destroyer i.e. Kumāra is assured.

According to orthodox opinion, the *Kumārasambhava* had seventeen cantos but it is now generally admitted that only the first eight cantos are geniune. However, for a long time, the eighth canto was the subject of hot debate among the scholars since it frankly depicted the amorous love sport of the newly married divine couple in accordance with the provisions of the *Kāmaśāstra*. The fact that only the first eight cantos were commented upon by Mallinātha and Arunagiri, is particularly noteworthy. Moreover the extreme rarity of the manuscripts of the remaining nine cantos should also be taken into account as a significant fact. It has been argued that the innate promise of the title regarding the depiction of Kumāra's birth remains unfulfilled if the epic ends with the eighth canto. Besides, the number of cantos cannot but seem to be inadequate, though it adheres to the prescribed minimum. Those who sought to justify the inclusion of the latter nine cantos in the epic corpus, have also argued that the staple theme of the birth of Kumāra has matured only in this portion. Kālidāsa's intention in undertaking the poem was to propagate a lofty philosophy of life; he seemed to have a definite scheme which was not finally manifested in the first half. The first eight cantos record a series of events, conceived with superb imagination, which paved the way for the grand occurrence keenly awaited by the inhabitants of the three world in general and the gods in particular. Hence the latter half of the epic cannot be summarily dismissed as spurious.

But these arguments have been effectively countered by those critics who think that Kālidāsa could not have composed the latter half. The unproportionate grotesque manner of the birth of Kumāra smacks of Purānic extravaganza and it is highly improbable that a consummate artist like Kālidāsa, having uncommon sensibility, sophisticated skill and penchant for suggestiveness could have indulged in such overtly uncharacteristic compositions. Though a critic like Sūryakānta discovered 'the very core and the nerves of the poem' in the latter half, he could not satisfactorily explain the abundance of the grammatical and metrical aberrations in this section. It is not only that here the subject-matter is less conducive to poetry and provides less scope for creative imagination (because of which the poet could hardly prove his natural ability in producing lyric ecstasy), but there are fundamental facts to ponder over. Thus the intrinsic evidences of taste, style and treatment positively show that the sequel displays an art far below the well-defined standard of Kālidāsa's natural grace. It is not without merit but the lack of subtlety and spontaneity is surely unkālidāsian. It has been ignored by the early critics, rhetoricians and commentators; therefore it seems to have been composed by a fairly recent poet presumably well-versed in the techniques of later court epics. The traits of decadent poetry are discernible in lack of cohesion in narrative details as well as noticeable absence of precision, suggestive connotation, characteristic poetic diction and sense of control and proportion. Otherwise the love-sport of the divine couple, already described in erotic details in the eighth canto, would not have been repeated to lead the narrative to a grotesque extreme. The chain of odd events culminating into the birth of Kumāra might not cause any eyebrow to rise among the readers of a Puranic text but an epic ascribed to none other than Kālidāsa can ill-afford such wanton expressions of bad taste. The poet of the sequel wielded his pen zealously and did not stop at the birth of Kumāra; he went on to describe the victory of the protagonist over Tāraka, the demon, in order to bring out the motive of that birth. Thus the genuine eight cantos offer us an interesting study in contrast with the sequel; because while the former is fraught with poetic suggestions of very high order, the latter is emphatically explicit and diluted and also clearly oriented to present a story, giving no quarters to the sensibility of the readers.

The genuineness of the eighth canto has been questioned by many a rhetoricians and scholars who seem to have been swayed away by religious conservatism. Mammata's objection has already been referred to; he observed in the *Kāvyaprakāsa* (vii) that love of the metadeities in the shape of erotic ẹnjoyment should not be described since it is as improper as witnessing the erotic delineation of one's parents:

> 'Ratisambhogaṣṛṇgārarūpā Uttamadevatāvisayā na varṇanīyā Tadvarnanam pitroh Sambhoga- Varṇanamiva atyantamanucitam.'

Such religious bias made the critics oblivious of the literary criterion and therefore several manuscripts did not include the eighth canto which allegedly threatened to profane the sacred. However there was Ānandavardhana as well who thought otherwise. He clearly stated that even the great poets have depicted erotic passion among gods but, on that count, impropriety does not vex the reader as vulgar since it has been disguised by the poet's genius:

> 'Mahākavīnam apyuttamadevatāvisayaprasiddhasam bhogas rngāra nibandhanādanaucityam Saktitiraskrtam Grāmyatvena na pratibhāsate yathā Kumārasambhave devīsambhogavarnanam'.[22] Indeed no one can willingly part with this canto which represents the poetic consummation of the innate epic scheme ensuring the genesis of Kumāra i.e. the youthful vigour and heroic spirit as the outcome of the grand union of the female incarnation of beauty and love with the great ascetic, the eternal symbol of bliss—perfectly poised yet disenchanted, meditative yet reciprocating to procreative passion. It is therefore futile to speculate as to whether the hostile criticism of the conservatives compelled Kālidāsa to abandon his work abruptly or whether the sensitive poet in him decided emphatically to not to elaborate the delicate suggestions contained in the eighth canto since even any minor elaboration thereafter would prove to be redundant. According to a recent opinion, the epic has been designed to narrate the unique life of Umā from her birth to marriage. The poet seems to put much emphasis on Umā's winning of husband through asceticism after the external agencies,

symbolised by Kāma and his train, were rudely punished. She felt humiliated as physical charm was proved irrelevant. But she came to terms with herself and practised austere penance to ultimately win over Śiva. Kāma is revived at the auspicious hour of Umā's marriage and the primeval couple rejoices in uninhibited enjoyment. But it is certain that in the schemata of Kālidāsa's imagination, even the outline stated above is nothing more than a foundation to erect an artistic edifice upon it.

The extrinsic structure of the *Kumārasambhava* may be arranged in three distinct phases. The cosmic drama inherent in the theme unfolds itself through these phases. The preparatory phase constitutes of first four cantos while the central phase is manifested in the fifth canto; likewise the concluding phase constitutes of the remaining three cantos. The first canto describes the Himālaya and the birth as well as the youthful beauty of his daughter, Umā, who is the predestined spouse of Śiva. She waits upon Śiva with unflinching devotion but the great ascetic, engrossed in deep meditation, takes no cognizance of her. The second canto narrated how the helpless gods, being tormented by Tāraka, the demon, supplicate to Brahmā for redressal. Brahmā himself cannot do anything against his own creation; so he advises Indra to disturb the penance of Śiva because only his son can destroy Tāraka. Therefore Indra decides to commission the service of Kāma, the god of love. In the third canto, Indra cajoles Kāma to proceed to the penance grove of Śiva for interrupting the latter's meditation. As Kāma arrives with his friend Vasanta (i.e. spring) and consort Rati (i.e. lust), the entire panorama undergoes a metamorphosis. Along with men and gods, even animals, plants and insects are stirred with desire under the impact of the untimely spring. This is one of the most memorable specimens of Sanskrit poetry. A couple of verses may be cited here as example:

(i) 'Madhu dvirephah Kusumaikapātre papau priyām svāmanuvarttamānah.

Sṛngena ca sparsanimīlitākṣīm mṛgīmakandūyata Kṛṣṇasārah.'[23]

(ii) 'Paryāptapuṣpa-stavakastanābhyah sphuratpravālostha manoharābhyah

Latāvadhūbhyastaravopyavāpurvinamrasākhā bhujaban dhanāni.'[24]

But Kāma becomes apprehensive at the sight of Śiva's awe-inspiring meditative figure which has been elegantly described by the poet. At that juncture Umā appears there to offer her daily obeisance to the Lord. Kāma takes it as an opportune moment to strike Śiva with his arrow of enchantment. The lord's passion is aroused momentarily but he regains control; looking around he catches sight of Kāma and burns him down with the flame emanated from the third eye. Śiva disappears and a bashful Umā returns home while Rati falls into a swoon.

The fourth canto contains brilliant lyrical exuberance as Rati wails pathetically over the ashes of her husband. As she contemplates to commit suicide, a divine proclamation intervenes to assure her of the restoration of Kāma's physical form in future. The fifth canto unfolds the severe penance of Umā, dressed in the attire of an ascetic and progressively relinquishing all mundane bond with the worldly existence for winning Śiva as her husband. At last Śiva responds to her austerities and unflinching devotion but nevertheless tests her sincerity under the guise of a celibate. In the sixth canto, the sages act as the emissaries of Śiva and go to Himālaya with the proposal of marriage. A delighted Himālaya readily agrees and the preparations for the ceremony begin. The seventh canto contains the description of the wedding in great details. A series of rites are performed significantly in the manner of a human wedding. Some narrative details shed interesting light on the continuity of epic legacy. One can refer to the depiction of the rush of eager onlookers to the windows for having a glimpse of Śiva entering as bridegroom in the capital of the kingdom of Himalaya.[25] This situation cannot but remind us of a similar occasion in Aśvaghoṣa's epic.[26] It seems to have become a stock situation even for an imaginative poet like Kālidāsa; otherwise he would not have repeated it in the *Raghuvamśa*.[27]

A happy viva restores Kāma's physical frame magnanimously. Then the eighth canto unfolds the very intimate love-sports of the newly married divine couple who pay their visit to Gandhamādana. The epic narrative closes with the information that Śiva enjoyed one hundred fifty seasons in amorous sports yet the span of time seemed to him to be a single time. As the fathomless waters of ocean are unable to extinguish submarine fire, likewise Śiva's craving for love remained as undimed as ever. The canto is bedecked with splendours of excellent images throughout.

As we consider the poetic scheme minutely, the cosmic significance of the epic narrative becomes clearer. We understand that the narrative details set in different backdrops or manifestations of phenomenal existence have in-built symbolism. The natural panorama presents great variety; its perimeter is spread far and wide and includes the Himalayas (Canto I), Heaven (II) and Earth (III & IV). Kālidāsa's unique imagination has added new dimensions to creativity; his craftsmanship is delicately balanced and always inspired by artistic sensibility. There are two full-length descriptions in the epic viz., the Himālaya (i), untimely spring (iii); like the variant notations of music, the poet gives vent to his descriptive power in brief spells as well. The description of Pārvatī's penance (v), discussion of the proposal of marriage (vi), wedding celebrations (vii) may be cited as examples. But the most noteworthy feature of the *Kumārasambhava* is the delineation of a unique conception of love in which both the sacred and profane dimensions are mingled wonderfully. The courtly poetry in Sanskrit developed a love-mysticism in which different tendencies existed simultaneously. Sacred and profaned love were treated as homologous but the process of differentiation was not lost sight of. Kālidāsa seems to have been aware of the cross-currents of thoughts in Indian mind. He could discover a cosmic paradigm in the humanized love of the divine couple. The *Kumārasambhava* unfolds a unique love-symbolism in which asceticism and sexuality are inextricably related. Wendy O'Flaherty writes in an article entitled 'Asceticism and Sexuality in the Mythology of Siva': 'Tapas' (asceticism) and Kāma' (desire) are not diametrically opposed.....

They are in fact two forms of heat, 'tapas' being the potentially destructive or creative fire that the ascetic generates within himself... 'Kāma' is the heat of desire. Thus they are closely related in human terms.'[28] The divine lovers have been humanized through the delightful description of their love play.

It may be conjectured that Kālidāsa got the clue of the title of his epic from the following verse in the first book of the *Rāmāyaṇa*:

> 'Esa te rāma gangāyāh vistāro'bhihito mayā
> Kumārasambhavascaiva dhanyah punyastathaiva ca'

Kālidāsa was deeply conscious about the enlivening legacy to which he was a willing supplicant. However, he had always made it a point to creatively reconstruct those ingredients in accordance with his own artistic formulation. He is therefore adored as the most original poet in Sanskrit literature who has succeeded in making all the materials his own and in subordinating what he took from the continuing cultural tradition to the new complex of his own work. A few instances may be cited here. In the third canto of the *Kumārasambhava*, Kālidāsa wrote 'Paryankavandhasthirapūrvakāyam'[29] while describing the ascetic posture of Śiva; this cannot but remind us of Aśvaghoṣa's following description of a meditating Buddha:

'Tatah sa paryamkam-akampyamuttamam vavandha.'[30] Likewise Kālidāsa's depiction of the great impact of Nandi's silent command- 'Niskampa-vrksam nibhrtadvirepham. mūkāndajam sāntamrgapracāram'[31] echoes a similar expression of Aśvaghoṣa: 'Vavāsire mrgaganā na paksinah/na sasvanurbanataravo' nilāhatāh,'[32] In course of her lament, Kālidāsa's Rati exclaims: 'Tadidam gatamīdrsīm dasām/na vidīrye kathināh khalu striyah';[33] this might have been inspired by the wailing of Aśvaghoṣa's Yasodharā: 'Mamāpi Kāmam hrdayam sudārunam—banam gate bhartari yanna dīryate.'[34] In the *Kumārasambhava*, Rati expresses rather jealously: 'Ahametya patangavartmanā punaramkāsrayāni bhavāmi te/caturaih surakāminījanaih priya/Yāvanna vilobhyase divi'.[35] This is almost a verbatim echo of Aśvaghoṣa's poem where Yasodharā exclaims: 'Māmapahāya rosanām mahendraloke' Psaraso Jighṛkṣati..... Kīdṛsam tu tā vapurgunam vibhratiratra yositah.'[36]

Kālidāsa's poetic language was also built on the foundation prepared by his predecessors. Many more examples may be coined from both the *Kumārasambhava* and the *Raghuvamśa* to illustrate this. In the previous chapter, the impact of the great epics was considered in the context of the continuing renewal of tradition. It may suffice here to note that the poetic diction mirrored the volume and depth of inspiration absorbed as well as the dynamics of changing frontiers of the creative process. The *Raghuvamśa*, a wonderful epic consisting of nineteen cantos, is a unique example of the meaningful continnum of tradition. The uncommon lives and achievements of Raghu and his descendants have been narrated with great skill and artistic flourish. According to many a scholars, it is the best product of the magic genius and no Sanskrit court epic has more diversified and extensive theme than the *Raghuvamśa*. Its popularity among the connoisseurs is proved by the fact that it has many protagonists; in fact, viewed collectively, the epic seems to have the unique feature of depicting 'Time' as the real protagonist. The rise and fall of the dynasty of Raghu is intertwined with the wheel of time coming full circle.

Undoubtedly Kālidāsa put emphasis on Rāma, the roof and crown of the famous dynasty. Indeed the poet did not conceal that Vālmīki, the first among poets, was the unflinching source of his inspiration.[37] It seems that the great composer of the *Rāmāyaṇa* was far away from Kālidāsa's time. He had other sources as well but there can be no two opinion about his indebtedness to the great epic. In the first nine cantos of the *Raghuvamśa*, the poet describes the achievements of four immediate predecessors of Rāma, viz., Dilīpa, Raghu, Aja and Daśaratha. The next seven cantos i.e. from tenth to sixteenth, are devoted to Rāma. Kālidāsa has demonstrated his extraordinary skill in this section where the entire story of the great epic has been abridged with precision and dexterity. In the seventeenth canto, the poet describes the reign of Kuśa (Rāma's son) followed by that of Atithi. We have brief descriptions of a series of twenty kings after Atithi in the next canto who might be inconsequential but nevertheless worthy descendants of Raghu. Then the poet depicts the unusual career of Sudarśana who ascended the throne at the age of six and performed his royal duties efficiently. Among the minor kings in the scions of

Raghu, he was lucky to obtain maximum attention of the poet. The nineteenth canto unfolds the dissolute reign of Agnivarṇa who spent his life in wanton pleasure and consequently died prematuredly of consumption. However Kālidāsa did not conclude his epic with a melancholic note. One of the queens of Agnivarṇa was found pregnant and thus the fear of extinction of the great dynasty could be overcome. That queen was consecrated and thereafter she was guided by the elder ministers in prosecuting the royal administration according to the scriptural dictum while she awaited the birth of her progeny.

It is conjectured that the *Raghuvamśa* might have been inspired by a special kind of epics, designated as 'Samhitā' or 'collection' by Bhoja. According to him, this sub-genre does not narrate the achievement of a single protagonist, rather there are episodes pertaining to a series of protagonists.[38] Bhoja alludes to two poems entitled '*Yaduvamśa*' and *Dilīpavamśa*' but both of them are lost for ever. Likewise we are told of another untraceable work named '*Asmakavāmsa*' which might have been a source of Kālidāsa's work but obviosuly no opinion whatsoever can be formed without any valid evidence. However, an epic like the *Raghuvamśa* is a unique specimen of creative imagination which can go beyond the mechanical dictums of the rhetoricians and discover hitherto unknown dimensions in the genre. Outwardly an epic of this kind lacks unity though a series of episodes are woven around several protagonists belonging to the same dynasty. The general view about epic poetry puts emphasis on the unity of action engineered by a single protagonist and the story reaches its culminating point in accordance with a predetermined plan. But an in-depth analysis of the *Raghuvamśa* shows that its thematic unity is of a different order altogether and it is integrally related to the aesthetic and philosophic vision of the poet. Therefore it is immaterial whether Kālidāsa had a typical subgenre to rely upon or whether he had only poeticized the legendary materials of an Ur-Purāṇa and also creatively reconstructed the wellknown episodes of the *Rāmāyaṇa*.

Inspite of the episodic nature of the *Raghuvamśa*, it can hardly be surmised that the epic is incomplete and that it could be extended indefinitely. Such supposition ignores the innovative traits of a genius (cf. 'prajnā nava-nava-unmesa Sālinī pratibhā matā') who always thrives on originality and gives a new lease of life to both form and content. In fact, Kālidāsa's poetic vision about the basic significance and dignity of human life was remarkably unfolded through a well executed schemata of imagination. The collective impact of the lives and achievements of various kings of the dynasty of Raghu has to be taken into account in its proper perspective. Each protagonist is a unit in the multilinear development of the theme and hence there is no abruptness or discordant note in the sad end of Agnivarṇa and the immediately following event. Indeed the wheel has come full circle in the nineteenth canto of the epic; any more elaboration would have been artistically incongruous. Kālidāsa was aware of the Purāṇic account of the solar dynasty; there were almost a hundred generations of kings from Manu Vaivasvata to the time of great battle at Kurukṣetra in which the seventh king after Agnivarṇa was killed by Abhimanyu. However the solar dynasty is said to have continued even after the battle; the dynasty was finally extinct with Sumitra who came after thirty generations.

Kālidāsa had no reason to repeat a Purāṇic chronicle in toto; so he picked up his threads to weave the epic story at the time of Dilīpa, the sixtieth king of the solar dynasty. The historic reality of the emergence of Brahmanism as dominant ideology of the power elites during the reign of the imperial Guptas had a decisive impact on the poet. It is not without reason that at the very outset of the epic, Dilīpa is described as a rigorous upholder of Brahmanic norms.[39] Of the four cardinal principles of life (i.e. caturvarga constituting of virtue, wealth, pleasure and emancipation), the first three seem to have been proportionately cultivated by Dilīpa and his illustrious successors; however, the first principle i.e. virtue was always the summum bonum of their life. As Agnivarṇa was disproportionately tilted towards propagation of pleasure, he was the most untypical king of the dynasty and brought about his own untimely demise. After going through the epic, the readers cannot but be aware of a recurring pattern of ideal kingship whose primary requirement is irreversible foundation of virtue.

Kālidāsa has obviously depicted the idealised figures of kings in tune with the firmly rooted Brahmanic concept of 'Caturāśrama' or four distinct stages of life. Thus the kings of the *Raghuvamśa* spend their childhood to the study of different branches of knowledge while their youth is devoted to the pursuit of mundane successes. They feel dutybound to protect the social order and act strictly in accordance with the prescribed norms. They are generally good administrators as well as indomitable warriors. Raghu's famous expeditions for establishing his command over the four quarters are particularly noteworthy. After attaining old age, they relinquish the mundane world and retire into forest for pursuing sylvan life like pious hermits. Kālidāsa creates a Utopian wonderland, as it were, when he portrays king Dilīpa as the prototype of supreme excellence:'Ekātapatram jagatah prabhutvam navam vayah Kāntamidam Bapuśca.' The poet expresses the uncommon qualities of his protagonist as a king with the help of a brilliant characteristic simile:

> 'Prajānāmeva bhūtyartham sa tābhyo balim agrahīt
> Sahasragunam utsrastum ādatte hi rasam ravih'.[40]

This bespeaks of the ascendance of contemporary Brahmanic systems of thought in the cultural milieu. The trend is further corroborated by the poet's skilful use of metaphors based on sacrifice presumably because the age-old practice was regenerated by the Gupta kings and which thus became the hallmark of royal prestige.

In the very beginning of the epic, Kālidāsa refers to the ideal king of the dynasty of Raghu as 'Yathābidhihutāgnīnām.'[41] Such a king milks earth for sacrifice just as Indra milks sky for harvest: 'Dudoha gām sa yajnāya /Śasyāya maghavā divam.'[42] This metaphoric expression unfolds a regular pattern when Queen Sudaksinā is described as Adhvarasyeva dakṣinā.[43] The metaphor is not used as an individual epithet; the scions of the illustrious dynasty are basically purified by sacrifice- 'Ijyābiśuddhātmā.'[44] As Raghu performs the Visvajit sacrifice, likewise Daśaratha is said to have performed many a Vedic sacrifices for the sages and the gods:

> 'Ṛṣidevagaṇāsvadhābhupjām śrutayāgaprasavaih sa pārthivah.'[45]

Even Atithi, the son of Kuśa, is also described as performer of several sacrifices.[46] Rāma's eventful Aśvamedha sacrifice is a well-known episode which, however, has been narrated in the last book of the *Rāmāyaṇa*.

The *Raghuvamśa* is regarded by many as Kālidāsa's greatest work because it is the best representative of the poet's craftsmanship, range of imagination, depth of feeling and inheritance of Indian cultural tradition. The epic is undoubtedly a unique gallery of fascinating pictures but at the same time the thematic unity has been maintained with great care. No canto is artistically irrelevant or stylistically lacking in uniformity. Unlike the later composers of court epics, Kālidāsa did not ignore the intrinsic interest of the narrative for the sake of mere adherence to the extrinsic formalism. His text is never impaired with dull monotony which generally plagues the later court epics; he is always absolutely in control of the conception and execution of the form and content of the epic. The microcosm unveiled by Kālidāsa is not merely made of dreamy abstractions; though the poet drew heavily from the seemingly make-belief world of legends, he could manage to retain distinctive individuality of the better known protagonists. Significantly, Kālidāsa was nearer to his epoch in delineating those materials; this also bespeaks of his inimitable capacity of impersonal modelling of life as well as imaginative assimilation of the world.

In the first canto, the greatness of the dynasty is impressed upon through an interesting account of Dilīpa, a perfect king of the solar race. Because of a small omission in one of his daily rituals, he remained childless for a considerable time. Then his preceptor said that the king forgot to circumambulate Surabhi, the sacred cow, and hence he had committed a sin unwittingly. Along with his queen, Sudaksinā, king Dilīpa is therefore required to expiate that sin by tending Nandinī, Surabhi's daughter and Vaśistha's sacred cow, for a period of one year. In the second canto, we find the royal couple humbly performing the vows and austerities. The sincerity of Dilīpa is submitted to a test, in the episode of illusory lion, from which he comes out with flying colours. He is granted the boon of having son who would be the founder of an illustrious dynasty. The third canto records the birth of Raghu and his youth. Thereafter his great martial exploits are narrated. The poet describes with gusto the battle of young Raghu with Indra while the former was in charge of the sacrificial horse of his father. After Dilīpa retires to forest, Raghu's accession takes place followed by his triumphant progress as a conqueror. The critics are of the opinion that Kālidāsa was substantially inspired by the martial exploits of the Gupta emperors while composing these episodes. The fourth canto narrates, with admirable skill and precision, Raghu's splendid career of conquest in the four directions.

His generosity knew no bounds as he gave away everything he had in the Visvajit rite.[47] Therefore, when a young scholar asks for money to pay his preceptor's fees, an impoverished Raghu is in a fix since it is unthinkable that a deserving suppliant would return with empty hand. In order to salvage his prestige, he decides to invade the domain of Kuvera, the god of wealth[48] because all human rulers have already been plundered. In order to avoid embarrassment, an apprehensive Kuvera showers a huge quantity of gold from the sky to fill Raghu's treasury. In the sixth canto, Aja, who resembled the god of love in appearance, succeeds Raghu. Kālidāsa portrays his career with a delicate personal touch since he has the opportunity to create an image of flamboyant lover by making best use of spontaneous artistic skill and tender imagination. The stately ceremony of svayamvara or self-choice has been delightfully described in which Indumatī, sister of the king of Vidarbha, chooses Aja as her husband from amongst an assembly of royal suitors. There is a wonderful verse here in which Indumatī has been compared with the glimmer of a lamp which earned for the poet the epithet 'Dīpaśikhā-kālidāsa':

> 'Sancārinī dīpasikheva rātrau
> yāmyām vyatiyāya patimvara sā
> Narendramārgāttaiva prapede
> Vivarnabhāvam sa sa bhūmipālah'[49]

The seventh canto is noteworthy on different counts. On his way, Aja is attacked by the disappointed suitors and a bloody battle takes place which offers an opportunity to the poet to exhibit his skill in depicting heroic moments. The wedding celebrations are also described colourfully, followed by poetic depiction of Aja's coronation, happy family life, ideal administration and the birth of his son, Daśaratha. But the eighth canto narrates the mysterious premature death of Indumatī and the heart-rending lamentation of Aja on the sudden demise of his beloved spouse.[50] Kālidāsa obviously makes use of traditional mythic motif as it is revealed that Indumatī is actually a celestial nymph cursed by a sage to be temporarily condemned to assume human form.[51] But in spite of such presence of overtly supernatural elements, the overwhelming emphasis is on the human dimension of sorrow intensely felt by a loving husband on the bereavement of his beloved wife. This is also one of the most beautiful specimens of poetic art which has hardly been surpassed by any other poet in Sanskrit literature. The poet is indeed at his very best as the following examples will sufficiently prove:

(i) 'Pratiyojayitavya-vallakīsamāvasthāmatha sattvaviplavāt sa nināyanitāntavatsalah parigrhyocitamankamanganām.'[52]

(ii) 'Kusumānyapi gātrasamgamāt prabhavantyāyurapohitumyadi Na bhavisyati hanta sādhanam kimivānyatpraharisyāto vidheh.'[53]

(iii) 'Gṛhiṇī sacivah sakhı mithah priyaśiṣya lalite kalavidhau karunāvimukhena mṛtyunā haratā tvam vada kim na me hṛtam.'[54]

No amount of consolation could relieve Aja of his excruciating pain; he decides to live further only for the sake of his minor son, Daśaratha. When Daśaratha becomes capable to relieve his father of the regal responsibilities, the latter fasts to death to be reunited with his beloved in the heaven. In the ninth canto, Kālidāsa portrays the exploits of Daśaratha with skill and insight; it seems that the poet has hinted at the deviations of the king from the elevated standard of virtuosity established by his illustrious predecessors.[55] The poet generally follows the *Rāmāyaṇa* from this canto to the fifteenth though he adds some new details as well. The most important of such innovations is the portrayal of Rāma as an incarnation of Viṣṇu. Vālmīki's protagonist, as we have already noted, was an exceptional person, moon among men and the embodiment of highest limits of perfection but never a divinity. Owing to Brahmanic impact during the inception of Purāṇic values, a major portion of the first and the entire last book were added to the original epic corpus of the *Rāmāyaṇa*. In the meantime, the theory of incarnation was deeply embedded in the Indian psyche; the rise of the Guptas further consolidated the metamorphic change in the value-system. As a result, the culture hero of the new Brahmanic epoch has to be an ideal king and protector of the social order as well as an incarnation of one of the metadeities. Hence Kālidāsa's Rāma is none other than Viṣṇu who agrees to assume human form in order to rescue the gods from the oppression of Rāvaṇa, the chief of Rākṣasas. This conception of Rāma as the upholder of cosmic and moral order of the universe is, in fact, literary correlative of the famous saying in the Gītā[56] regarding the divine purpose of incarnation. Even Rāma's three other brothers (i.e. Bharata, Laksmaṇa and Śatrughna) have been described as partial incarnations of Viṣṇu.[57]

As stated earlier, Kālidāsa has closely followed Vālmīki while narrating the events of the life of Rāma. Rāma's youth has been portrayed quite sensibly in the eleventh canto which sheds illuminating light on the unique personality of the protagonist. The events related to Rāma's exile which include Daśaratha's granting of two boons earlier promised to Kaikeyī[58] and the death of the lamenting king are followed in quick succession by abduction of Sītā, fierce battle with Rāvana and victory of Rāma. The poet has exhibited his remarkable skill in condensing the central incidents of the great epic within a single canto. The inherent reality of Kālidāsa's epoch becomes explicit in a significant change of narrative detail. Śurpaṇakhā is said to have felt terrible insult by Sītā's scornful laugh at her rejection by Rāma.[60] An infuriated Śūrpaṇakhā goes to Rāvana for help who abducts Sītā as an act of vengeance. It is thus emphatically implied that Sītā was herself responsible for the sufferings that followed. This departure from Vālmīki's intention stems actually from the changed attitude of an ossified society to the women folk since the evolving smrti codes have already begun to treat the women with contempt and declared them as the source of all evils.

In the beginning of the thirteenth canto, there is an excellent poetic description of the aerial journey undertaken by Rāma and his companions from Lankā to Ayodhyā. Kālidāsa's creative imagination is in full flow. A couple of examples will suffice:

(i) 'Dūrādayaścakra nibhasya tanvī
Tamālatālīvanarājinīlā
ābhāti belā lavanāmburāśer
Dhārānibaddheva Kalankarekhā'[61]

(ii) 'Saisā sthalī yatra vicinvatā tvām
Bhrastam mayā nūpuramekamurvyām
Adṛśyata taccaranārabinda
Visleṣa-duhkhādiva baddhamaunam.'[62]

Rāma's reinstatement to the throne follows these descriptions. The fourteenth and fifteenth cantos are based on the last book of the great epic. The fourteenth canto depicts Rāma's exceptionally virtuous kingship; the episode of Sītā's abandonment has been narrated in a subtle and sensitive manner. Rāma is well aware of Sītā's faultlessness[63] but he does not think there is any alternative on the wake of harsh criticism of the citizens. Kālidāsa generally conforms to the story of the *Rāmāyana* but it seems that he suggests his own disapproval of Rāma's action through the spirited words of Sītā. She does not hesitate to question the propriety and rationale of Rāma's hasty decision:

'Bācyastvayā madvacanād sa rājā vahnau viśōuddhāmapi yat samaksam
Māmlokavādasravanādahāsīh Śrutasya kimtad Sadṛśam Kulasya'[64]

Here Sītā is nearer to her prototype in Vālmīki's great epic.

However Kālidāsa's brilliance is best exhibited in the following verse replete with fathomless depth of human feeling:

'Sāhamtapah sūryanivista-dṛṣtirūrdhvam prasūteścaritum yatisye Bhūyo yathā me janānantare'pi tvameva bhartā na ca viprayogah'.[65]

When the poet makes Vālmīki express his anger and displeasure at Rāma's tainted (Kaluṣa) action,[66] we understand that the poet has not been swayed by extraliterary (i.e. religious) considerations. He shows that even an incarnation of Viṣṇu is susceptible to human frailty. This is indeed an additional proof of Kālidāsa's excellence since, as time rolled on, the composers of court epic became increasingly inclined towards stereotypes and the indefatigable human dimension went beyond their reach. Their predetermined limited world was sharply divided between two opposite poles of good and evil.

Kālidāsa narrates the birth of Lava and Kuśa as well as other events leading to Sītā's return to Earth and Rāma's ascent to heaven in accordance with the *Rāmāyaṇa*. The poet has been able to endow Sītā with a distinct personality based on his own interpretation. Thus his Sītā does not forgive Rāma at the end for his uncalled for cruelty and refuses to bear the burden of insult any more; she prefers to take her final refuge in Earth with a view to keeping her feminine dignity and self-respect untarnished.[67] The next four cantos are entirely the products of Kālidāsa's imagination in which the poet exhibits his expertise on various branches of human knowledge. It seems that the poet extended the frontiers of the epic genre on the one hand and gave demonstration of the creative and proportionate absorption of Ethics, Civics, Aesthetics, Theology and Erotics on the other. Kuśa's enjoyment of pleasure,[68] Atithi's attempt of maintaining a balance among three cardinal principles of life,[69] Sudarśana's command over complex situations,[70] Agnivarṇa's voluptuous wantonness[71] have been depicted with great skill.

There were speculations among the scholars as to whether the seemingly tragic end of the epic was consistent with the norms of Indian poetics. Some of them spoke of the probability of the existence of another set of five or six cantos. Winternitz wondered if a few verses at the end of the nineteenth canto were lost. But we should not venture beyond the existing format of the epic since the evidence of more than twenty different commentaries cannot be ignored. Therefore the alleged incompleteness has to be interpreted in the right perspective of the poet's worldview as well as in accordance with the suggestions in the manifold strata of the epic narrative. The poet's splendid imagination is self-justifying and totally sovereign; nevertheless it is also not entirely unrelated with contemporary reality. Thus it may be argued that Kālidāsa has either Kumāragupta or Skandagupta (Vikramāditya II) in his mind when he compares Atithi with Kumāra under the title 'Sanmukh-Vikrama.'[72] Likewise it has been observed that Agnivarna is none other than Devabhūmi of the Sunga dynasty whom the poet knew from historical tradition. The splendour of the Gupta era, as it has been already noted, has formed the basis of the wonderful descriptions of the pomp and flourish of the dynasty of Raghu since it was directly experienced by the poet. Kālidāsa's society betrayed the sign of the beginning of the process of ossification because: 'Rekhāmātrampi kșunādāmanovartmanah param/Na Vyatiyuh prajāstasya niyanturnemivrttayah'. It is but natural that such a society would inspire the poet to prepare thoroughly idealised portraits of the royal protagonists:

'Sarvātiriktasārena sarvatejo 'bhibhāvinā
Sthitah sarvonnatenorvīmkrāntvāmerurivātmanā
Ākārasadrśaprajnah prajnayā sadṛśāgamah
Āgamaih sadṛśārambha ārambhasadṛśodayah.'[73]

Kālidāsa could add new dynamism to the continuing epic tradition since both of his epics reflected the essences of his time while presenting, at the same attempt, two time/less schema of creative imagination. Life at his disposal provided him with raw materials upon which his creativity, steeped in cultural legacy, imposed an artistic form. What Kālidāsa observed elsewhere-'Chāyā na mūrchati malopahataprade'śe/Śūddhe tu darpanatale sulabhāvakāśā,'[74] has been appropriately given effect to.

VI

Before we proceed further to discuss Bhāravi's *Kirātārjunīya*, the next milestone in Sanskrit court epics, we may talk about some other evidences of epic composition which seem to have been contemporary of Kālidāsa. Presumbaly from the third century A.D., the process of the extensive rewriting of the Purāṇas began while a new system of hereditary vassal rulers was gaining ground under the disintegrating empires. The changes in social reality brought about corresponding readjustments in ideological framework which, in its turn, resulted into a new worldview for the litteratures. They had their own criterion for literature and pursued them freely under various patrons. The existence of several literary centres is proved by the genesis of Vaidarbhī style which flourished under the encouragement of the Vākataka rulers. The themes were deduced from standardised cultural tradition which did not deny the secular tendencies of their legitimate importance. The fact that literary Prakrit was considered suitable for the epic genre is significant.

It is also to be noted that Kālidāsa had a predecessor in king Sarvasena, son of Pravarasena I belonging to the Vākataka clan, who wrote the epic named *Harivijaya* in Mahārāṣtrī Prākrit in the first half of the fourth century A.D. As the work is lost, we have to rely entirely on the observations of the critics like Bhoja, Ānandavardhana, Abhinavagupta, Kuntaka, Hemacandra etc. It may be concluded that the *Harivijaya* was a popular epic; otherwise it would not have generated so much enthusiasm among the critics. Sarvasena's epic seems to have been fashioned on the Puranic episode about Kṛṣṇa's carrying off the legendary Pārijāta tree from the heavenly garden for placating Satyabhāmā's jealous anger. It also depicts Kṛṣṇa's victorious battle with Indra. Because of its Puranic foundation, Bhoja refers to it with great care while he chooses to ignore Aśvaghoṣa's epics altogether. The poet of the *Harivijaya* seems to have been particularly conscious about form. Thus the Vaidarbhī style might have attained maturity in his epic; he was perhaps the first poet to apply 'Rasa' in its proper perspective. Besides, he seems to have inaugurated the structural arrangement called 'Skandhakabandha' and 'āsvāsabandha' which means that the entire epic is composed in the 'Skandhaka' metre and that the epic is arranged into 'āsvāsas' or chapters instead of 'sarga's or cantos. Thus the common features of the Sanskrit epics have been discarded by Sarvasena. However the customary descriptive details of court epics seem to have been used freely. Sarvasena is said to be an innovative poet and, along with Kālidāsa, a representative of the 'Sukumāra' (i.e. delicate) variety of style, marked by simplicity, freshness, elegance and emotionality. It may therefore be surmised that Kālidāsa had flourished in a living tradition in which Sarvasena, too, had an important role to play.

Mentha or Bhartṛmentha, a contemporary of Kālidāsa, composed an epic entitled the *Hayagrīvavadha* but unfortunately this is also lost for ever.[73] Lavish praise was showered on the poet by later poets and critics; he has been ranked among the greatest poets and dramatists. Mentha is described as 'a painter in poetry' who cultivated the Vaidarbhī style like the blade of a sword. On the basis of his verses quoted by many rhetorical authorities and anthologists, we can form fairly dependable opinion about Mentha's characteristic style. He does not seem to have been an exponent of lyricism but nevertheless his expertise in framing 'Vakrokti' was commendable. Besides the poet made delightful use of figurative speeches; several critics have taken note of his praise for the antagonist which, according to them, enhanced the dignity of the protagonist since he could vanquish even a formidable enemy.

Latest scholarship has revealed that Mentha completed the *Hayagrīvavadha* in 412 A.D. under the patronage of king Mātṛgupta of Kashmir, a litterateur and contemporary of Vikramāditya I. As the name of the poet means 'elephant keeper', it has led to further speculations as to whether he was somehow connected with Vikramāditya. Whatever might be his connection with two royal courts, this may be accepted as enough hint towards his proximity with two famous centres of creative activity of that time. The subject-matter of the *Hayagrīvavadha* was derived from the *Mahābhārata* and earlier versions of some puranic texts. The poet seems to have elaborated the myth of the slaying of a demon named Hayagrīva by Viṣṇu in his incarnation of Fish. The demon was slain for stealing the Vedas from the mouth of sleeping Brahmā and then the sacred texts were recovered. The epic connects this myth with the famous legend of Great Flood while the seventh Manu Vaivasvata, was preparing to inaugurate the next aeonic cycle. The remarkable subjectmatter provided Mentha with a wonderful opportunity of exhibiting his range of imagination and skill in craftsmanship. The available verses of the epic, as preserved by the admiring rhetoricians, clearly hint that the poet might have been a seasoned campaigner of the Vaidarbhī style. While depicting the emotions of love and heroism, he is always at his best. His descriptions seem to be of high order while the narrative also unveils epic compactness, richness of meaning and feeling of a sustained force. Some scholars have even ventured to reconstruct the outlines of the epic with hints to its accompanying paraphernalia. One may, therefore, conclude with a good amount of conviction that Mentha's *Hayagrīvavadha* doubly confirms the process of continuous renewal as well as enrichment of the epic tradition; it also proves that Kālidāsa was no soliltary star twinkling with hypnotic glow over a dark horizon.

Pravarasena II, the Vākataka emperor who reigned for c 410A.D. to 440A.D., composed the *Setubandha* also known as *Rāvanavaha* or *Dasamuhavaha*) in Mahārāṣtrī Prakrit. This younger contemporary of Kālidāsa might have completed his epic in the earlier phase of his reign. A very late tradition seeks to establish close connection between the great poet and Pravarasena but it is untenable on various counts. In the realm of poetic fancy and compositional technique, they are in fact miles apart from each other. However Pravarasena has his own redeeming features; for example, his descriptions are fascinating and endowed with elegance. Instead of Kālidāsa, he chose Sarvasena as his mentor. As the word 'Uchhāha' meaning 'energy' was used by Sarvasena at the end of each canto of his *Harivijaya* indicating the principal thematic design, likewise Pravarasena also used the word 'anurāa' at the end of each canto of the *Setubandha* to mark his intention. Bhoja explained it as 'Prabandhālamkāra' which is manifested as devotion in Pravarasena's epic. Rāma's expedition against Rāvaṇa for rescuing Sītā has been presented in its fifteen cantos in a new way, that is, by extracting the essence of the narrative as devotion, love and friendship. The poet picks up the warp and woof of his epic from almost the middle of the *Rāmāyaṇa*. He begins after Sugrīva has been installed as the king of Kiṣkindhyā and conclude with Rāma's return to Ayodhyā along with Sītā and Lakṣmaṇa preceded by the slaying of Rāvaṇa. Unlike the *Paūmacariya*, an epic in Mahārāstrī Prakrit discussed earlier, Pravarasena follows Vālmīki's narrative details quite faithfully.

Though Pravarasena and Kālidāsa lived in the same age, they were temperamentally of different cultural epoch and hence their epics basically represented mutually exclusive attitudes and creative processes. Being an unquestioning champion of the established cultural legacy, Pravarasena treats the great epic as sacrosanct and does not show any inclination towards creative freedom as Kālidāsa does. On another plane, his source of inspiration is Sarvasena; it is evident in his use of 'Skandhaka' metre. Thirdly, Pravarasena seems to be some what nearer to Aśvaghoṣa's archaic epic form. Kālidāsa's subtle and sophisticated style bespeaks of a new phase of development of the epic genre which is clearly wanting in the *Setuvandha*. Pravarasena could not add new dimension to his composition inspite of his success in certain limited spheres e.g. description and portrayal of principal characters. His style has notable affectations and traits of artificiality but nevertheless its penchant for perfection is commendable. That is why the rhetoricians like Daṇḍin, Ānandavardhana and Bhoja as well as creative personality like Bāṇa regarded Pravarasena as a poet of high order. Because of his repeated use of long compounds, puns, farfetched similes, alliterations and fondness of exaggeration, he is said to be nearer to the Gaudīya school of style. In fact, his remoteness from thc Vaidarbhī school might have been deliberate; the poet adhered to Mahārāstri Prakrit as the appropriate medium of communication for a wider section of the reading public. But nevertheless the imposing pressure from Sanskrit, the language of the overwhelming majority of the power elites, was so unputdownable that Pravarasena had to imbibe some liguistic and stylistic traits of Sanskrit into literary Prakrit more as a regenerative than a compromising exercise. Thus the onward movement of creative tradition has been multilinear as well as operative at different levels.

The magic name of Kālidāsa has been associated with a few works for securing their easy passage to posterity. Naturally the attention of the literary historians is drawn to those works of which the *Nalodaya* is an epicling consisting of four cantos. It deals with the legend of Nala and Damayantī in an artificial manner and stylistically it is as remote from Kālidāsa's masterpieces as Hyperion is to Satyr. A great poet like Kālidāsa could not have exhibited such vulgar fascination for rhyming and alliterations. Winternitz speculated whether Ravideva was the poet but could not decide about his age and creative traits. But Keith expressed doubt about the authorship of Ravideva and instead wondered if it was composed by a poet named Vasudeva. However, such speculations are futile since the *Nalodaya* only proves the extent of the diffusion of the epic tradition.

NOTES

1. No. 1329. vol. vi.
2. Accordting to Buddhist tradition, a monk used to become Bodhisattva after passing through a special ordination prescribed in the Brahmajāla sütra and which had to be performed two or three days after the first ordination.
3. cf. "The image of the Buddha seems to have made its appearance simultaneously in Gāndhāra and Mathurā; it appeared in Amarāvatī a little later. It is possible that the idea was Greek and that the image itself was created by Greco-Roman artists from Western Asia.... In the socalled Greco-Buddhist school of Gāndhāra, the figure of the Buddha possesses from the start all the usual Hellenistic characteristics, blended with a few more specifically Eastern features. He is represented as a young man of Apollonian type, with a straight nose continuing the line of the forehead and a firmly drawn mouth, but with heavy eyelids half obscuring the very protruding eyes; a fleshy face with the lobes of the ears lengthened by the weight of jewels. He bears the distinctive signs of his sacred nature; between his eyes is the 'urnā' or coil of hair and he holds in the palms of his hands the 'cakra', the sacred wheel that symbolises the progression of the Buddhist law. His evenly waved hair is gathered at the top of his head in a tight knot secured by a gold cord. The knot was later misunderstood and came to be represented by a cranial protuberance (Uṣṇīṣa), which has been included in all the images of the Buddha throughout Asia down to our time. He wears the monastic robe and cloak of flowing drapery. The school of Mathurā also had this Apollonian type of Buddha, but there was also a very different type, quite peculiar to this school. He has a round head and a smiling, doll-like expression. On his shaven head he wears a skullcap that hides the topknot. His monastic dress is

of a finer material than at Gāndhāra; it clings closely to the body and the light relief is rendered by parallel folds bordered by a faint double outline; the right shoulder is left uncovered.

He is fairly heavily built and makes simple gestures that were later to become the ritual gestures or 'mudrā'. This Buddha is close to the image of 'Yakṣa' of the previous period and belongs entirely to Indian tradition." in *Asian Art*, Hamlyn, London, 1988, pp. 91-93.

4. *Kathāvatthu*. xviii.
5. *ibid*. xviii. 1.
6. *Buddhacarita*. i. 43.
7. *Arthaśāstra*. i. 5.
8. *Vārttika*. iv. 2. 60; iv. 3. 87.
9. *Mahābhāṣya*. iv. 2. 60; xxiv. 3. 87.
10. *ibid*. iv. 3. 101.
11. Jalhana, *Sūktimuktāvalī*. iv. 46
12. *Saundarananda*. xviii. 63, 64.
13. Haraprasad Sastri discovered a manuscript of the *Buddhacarita* in which the text is available only upto the middle of canto xiv. vide *Journal of Asiatic Society of Bengal*, N. S, Vol. V, 1909, p. 47. ff.
14. The colourful description of the night scene at royal seraglio (v. 48-62) cannot but remind us of a similar situation in the *Rāmāyaṇa* (v. 9. 11). On the other hand, the famous description of the curious ladies of the city jostling one another to catch a glimpse of the prince driving out in his chariot (iii. 12-24) seems to have influenced Kālidāsa in depicting a similar situation in the *Raghuvamśa* (vii. 5-12). In fact, the recurrence of such description in the succeeding court epics only shows to what extent Aśvaghoṣa's stylistic device was adopted by the later poets.
15. *Buddhacarita* iv. 24-53; iv. 62-82 etc.
16. *ibid*. xiii
17. *Mahāvagga* i. 54.
18. *Udāna* iii. 2; *Dhammapada*, Commentary 1. 9.
19. *Saundarananda*. xviii. 22.
20. A. Berriedale Keith observes: 'His complete acceptance of the Brahmanical system, the sense of sharing in a world of prosperity and power, the mention of the horse-sacrifice in the *Mālavikāgnimitra*, Raghu's conquest in the *Raghuvamśa*, seem best explicable as the outcome of the enjoyment of the protection of a great Gupta ruler and we must remember that Candragupta II had the style of Vikramāditya,

with whose name tradition consistently connects Kālidāsa. (*A History of Sanskrit Literature*, Oxford University Press, Delhi, 1973, p. 80).

21. e.g.
 Rāmāyaṇa. i. 36-37.
 Mahābhārata. iii. 223-231.
 Skanda Purāna, Avantya Khanda, 39; Nāgarakhanda, 70-71 and Hātakesvaramāhātmya, 245-247, 264; Māhesvarakhanda. 20-30.
 Vāyu Purāṇa, Srāddhakalpa, 11.
 Brahma Purāṇa, Gautama Māhātmya, 2,3,12,32-316.
 Brahmānda Purāṇa, Ganapati Khanda, 1-14.
 Vāmana Purāṇa. 50-58.
 Varāha Purāṇa. 22, 25.
 Matsya Purāṇa. 154-160.
 Śiva Purāṇa. 9-21.
 Viṣṇudharmottara Purāṇa. 228, 229.
 Bṛhaddharmottara Purāṇa, 33-53.
22. *Śatapatha Brāhmana*. vi. 1.3.7-20.
 (also), *Dhvanyāloka*. iii. 6.
23. *Kumārasambhava* iii. 36.
24. *ibid*. iii. 39.
25. *ibid*. vii. 56-69.
26. *Buddhacarita*. iii. 13-24.
27. *Raghuvamśa*. vi.. 5-16.
28. Pt. I, History of Religions, viii, No. 4., May 1969, (pp. 300-337), p. 301.
29. *Kumārasambhava*. iii. 45.
30. *Buddhacarita*. xii. 120.
31. *Kumārasambhava*. iii. 42.
32. *Buddhacarita*. xii. 121.
33. *Kumārasambhava*. iv. 5.
34. *Buddhacarita*. viii. 61.
35. *Kumārasambhava*. iv. 20.
36. *Buddhacarita*. viii. 64-65.
37. *Raghuvamśa*. xi. 41.
38. *Sṛṅgāraprakāśa*. ii. 470.
39. *Raghuvamśa*. i. 25-26.
40. *ibid*. i. 18.
41. *ibid*. i. 6.
42. *ibid*. i. 26
43. *ibid*. i. 39.

44. *ibid.* ii. 75.
45. *ibid.* viii. 30.
46. *ibid.* xvii. 17.
47. *ibid.* iv. 86.
48. *ibid.* v. 26-28
49. *ibid.* vi. 67.
50. *ibid.* viii. 44-69
51. *ibid.* viii. 79-82
52. *ibid.* viii. 14.
53. *ibid.* viii. 44.
54. *ibid.* viii. 66.
55. *ibid.* ix. 48-49, 74, 82.
56. *Gītā.* iv. 7-8
57. *Raghuvamśa.* x. 84.
58. *ibid.* xii. 5-6
59. *ibid.* xii. 10.
60. *ibid.* xii. 36
61. *ibid.* xii. 15.
62. *ibid.* xiii. 23.
63. *ibid.* xiv. 40.
64. *ibid.* xiv. 61.
65. *ibid.* xiv. 66.
66. *ibid.* xiv. 73.
67. *ibid.* xv. 81-84.
68. *ibid.* xvi. 43-71.
69. *ibid.* xvii. 57.
70. *ibid.* xviii. 44-50.
71. *ibid.* xix. 5-47.
72. *ibid.* xvii. 67.
73. *ibid.* i. 14-15.
74. *Abhijñāna-Śakuntala.* vii. 32.
75. According to the *Catalogue of the Sanskrit Manuscripts* in the Punjab University Library (vol. ii. 1941, p. 271) that library at Lahore possessed incomplete manuscript of the epic in Malayalam script. No other manuscript has since been discovered.

5

Epics of Intellect

The epic genre rose to the pinnacle of artistic perfection in Kālidāsa's poems. Those two epics were chiselled out from the very depths of Time and hence formed a distinctive category by themselves. Therefore the epic poets in the post-Kālidāsa phases did not venture to scale that unsurmountable height; instead the later poets tried their best to compensate for lack of creative originality by way of perfectionizing the methods of deliberate construction. Practically a new beginning was made and a new phase of epic composition was ushered in by the later generations of poets. These poets were more remote from Kālidāsa than the great poet himself was from Aśvaghoṣa. But it does not mean that there was a breach in epic tradition; on the contrary the continuum remained uninterrupted while a new lease of life was granted to the reinvigorated genre. Bhāravi was the first as well as the foremost poet of the new order who must have flourished much before 634 A.D., since he was admiringly mentioned along with Kālidāsa in the Aihole inscription of Pulakesin II bearing that date. From the evidence of inscriptions it may be further observed that king Durvinīta of the Gāngeya dynasty, who ruled in Southern Karnātaka in the second half of the sixth century A.D., wrote a commentary on the fifteenth canto of the *Kirātārjunīya*. Therefore Bhāravi should be placed not later than the first half of the sixth century. Besides, in the *Avantīsundarīkathā*, Daṇḍin mentioned Bhāravi as a friend of his great grandfather, Dāmodara who was a writer. Bhāravi might have introduced his friend to a feudatory king under the imperial Guptas, named Viṣṇuvardhana also known as Yasodharman whose capital was at Daśapura in Avantī and who had assumed independence after inflicting a stunning defeat on the invading Huns. According to inscriptional evidences, Viṣṇuvardhana flourshed in the first half of the sixth century A.D. Therefore Bhāravi's date may ultimately be fixed not later than that.

Bhāravi is renowned for his epic entitled the *Kirātārjunīya* consisting of eighteen cantos. It is based on an episode of the *Mahābhārata*,[1] which narrates the battle of Arjuna, the protagonist with Śiva who assumed the form of a kirāta in order to test the courage and heroism of the former before granting him the divine weapons. The decline of the martial and political powers hitherto controlled by the Guptas and the Vākatakas meant that things were falling apart since the centre could not hold them any more. As the material conditions of a historical epoch determine the prominent traits of consciousness and consequently the contemporary artistic correlative, both the form and content of the *Kirātārjunīya* contain subtle suggestion of the inherent uncertainty, hollowness and superfluity of an unproductive epoch. The very fact that Bhāravi chose the episode of Arjuna's procurement of divine weapons as the subject-matter of his epic is fraught with social meaning. With the first signs of degeneration of the society, the extrinsic subjectmatter of the epic poems engaged the attention of the poets while the content was relegated to background. Form was no longer considered as innate, integrated and a natural concomitant of theme; the tendency of exhibitionism turned it into a variegated mask. Bhāravi was the first epic poet to treat subjectmatter as opposed to content which has to be paraded instead of waiting for spontaneous manifestation of the latter. Bhāravi's epic should not therefore be regarded as only a specimen of idiosyncratic talent; rather the basic attitude of an epoch, an elite class, a cultural persuasion was reflected and condensed into one work. A formidable foe with apparent political and martial supremacy has to be vanquished but the task seems to be near impossible without divine dispensation. No reader can probably overlook this new overtone of historical reality in the *Kirātārjunīya*.

Bhāravi was a perfectionist; he sought to develop an altogether new conception of poetic language. While Kālidāsa's style rests emphatically on the evocative traits of suggested meaning, Bhāravi tried to draw the attention of the readers to the possibilities of reorientation in poetic language by way of making it a highly patterned and organized mode of verbal expression. His originality lies in effecting greater force of expression because of which he is regarded as the champion of 'arthagaurava'. But Bhāravi's distinctive poetic language is no accidental phenomenon since the penchant for perfection in poetic expression can be detected in its nascent form in Aśvaghoṣa's epics. He attempted to attain the most possible conciseness in poetic language by exploiting the nuances of grammatical norms. However he concentrated more on the profound import of the epic narrative and did not forsake his content in the name of formalism. Nevertheless he had hinted at the necessity of creative reorientation of language; it was taken to its culminating point by Bhāravi, proving thereby the uninterrupted continuity of the literary legacy. Besides an analysis of the fragments of Mentha's *Hayagrīvavadha* shows that he, too, thought a great deal about extracting vigour from the typical usage of chequered language. As a result Mentha's expressions tended to become figurative but ambiguous though he could manage to retain linguistic simplicity as well as humour and subtlety to a considerable extent. Bhāravi probably had Mentha in his mind as well but he had a more distinctive interpretation of his own about the essence and heightening process of poetic language. The *Kirātārjunīya* decisively proves that its poet has been exceptionally selective about the application of words in heavily loaded expressions. Indeed Bhāravi thoroughly intellectualised the epic form; the first sparks of that possibility were kindled by the scholar poet of the *Buddhacarita* but the *Kirātārjunīya* marked their consummation in a creative fire.

The secret of the maintenance of the intricate symmetry of a living poetic form was known to Bhāravi. But the later poets could not penetrate beyond the exterior of that heightened poetic language. As a result, the creative fire was lost under the embers of empty intellectualism; the idiosyncratic tendencies were imitated more assiduously because the contemporary socio-cultural milieu was not congenial for a new search or a fresh beginning. In this context, Bhāravi's unique position among the exponents of the epic genre becomes clearly evident. He had presented a creative reconstruction of a small episode of the great epic as an intellectual feast for the connoisseurs. The details of the original narrative have not been changed substantially though new details have been incorporated along with the remodelling of the epic action. Bhāravi's famous preference for 'arthagaurava' or 'weighted meaning' has transformed the complexion of the epic narrative to a great extent in which the emphasis on profundity of expression, elaborate conceits, astonishing feats of verbal jugglery enagage the attention of the readers rather disproportionately. This is a significant departure from the epic legacy hitherto cultivated and taken to its zenith by the sensitive poets like Aśvaghoṣa and Kālidāsa. While attempting an embellished expansion of a small episode of the *Mahābhārata* into a court epic of eighteen cantos, Bhāravi undoubtedly adhered to the outlines of the story but the narration did not seem to have been of any particular importance whatsoever. He chose to fill the inevitable vacuum with heaps of such matters which are completely extrinsic to the unfolding theme.

It was Bhāravi's intention to enrich the content of the epic as well as to widen its scope by elaborating the philosophical and mythical overtones of the cultural tradition. He ushered in a new era in epic composition by introducing verbal gymnastics because he no longer depended on spontaneity of imagination and instead usurped the role of an acrobat. Bhāravi was however never unmindful towards his primary task of unfolding the epic narrative; in fact, the poet's conscious elaboration of a thematic design cannot escape our notice. The significant use of the word 'Śrī (i.e. fortune or sovereignty) reminds the readers of a similar use in Pravarasena's *Setuvandha* in which the word 'Anurāga' (i.e. devotion) had a specific purpose in elucidating the areas of emphasis in that epic. Bhāravi seems to have taken note of that convention of 'Prabandhālamkāra' (which means preliminary statement of purpose in the beginning of an epic) and hints skilfully at the schemata of epic composition. Though the use of an auspicious word ('Śrī') at the very beginning of the epic narrative is customary, Bhāravi has loaded it with much more weight than which is generally allowed to a mere rhetorical device. The *Kirātārjunīya* is introduced to the readers with the information that the Pāndavas are deprived of their royal fortune and the antagonist Kauravas are gradually consolidating their firm grip on fortune. It cannot be restored to the Pāndavas without divine dispensation; hence Arjuna undertakes the mission to regain royal fortune through extreme self-restraint, penance and courage. When the protagonist ultimately propitiates Śiva and the coveted divine weapons are granted to him, the victory of the Pāndavas is virtually assured. This signifies the restoration of lost fortune and hence Bhāravi uses the synonym of 'Śrī' i.e. 'Laksmī' in the concluding verse of the epic with a view to indicating the consummation of the epic scheme.[2] The primacy of fortune has also been stressed upon in the course of Arjuna's conversation with Indra just before the epic narrative ascends to its climax.[3]

The wheel of epic narrative sets into motion with the very first verse of the first canto which tells us about the return of Yudhiṣthira's secret agent with a detailed report about Duryodhana's efficient and prosperous administration. This report consumes major portion of the first canto and thereby posts the unmistakable signal of the advent of a new order of epic poetry. Being a master of cultivated expression, the poet takes the opportunity to present the report of the secret agent as a model of good speech. It may also be regarded as a fine example of Bhāravi's awareness of human psychology as well as his elaborate knowledge of statecraft. After the departure of the secret agent, Yudhiṣthira appraises Draupadī and four Pāndavas of the facts about Duryodhana's consolidation of rule. An enraged Draupadī rebukes her husband for his lack of initiative in avenging the mortifying humiliation inflicted on them by the Kauravas. In a very forceful manner, she earnestly requests him to give up the posture, unworthy for a kṣatriya king, and plunge into appropriate action immediately for salvaging the honour of the Pāṇdavas.

In the second canto, Bhīma extends his support to the view expressed by Draupadī in favour of disregarding agreement with the enemy. In a lengthy speech, he requests the eldest Pāndava to opt for fighting without any delay since Duryodhana may otherwise consolidate his position further. Besides, no self-respecting Kṣatriya can accept gift of kingdom from the unscrupulous enemies. In his reply, Yudhiṣṭhira makes a slightly longer speech and opposes any impetuous action. He urges upon his brothers to correctly understand the value of discrimination and endurance. The epithets used by him in praising the speech of Bhīma are revealing since these hint at the poet's opinion about perfect poetic diction:

> 'Apavarjita biplabe śucauhṛdayagrāhinī mangalāspade
> Vimalā tava vistare girām matirādarśa ivābhidṛśyate'[4]

The canto ends with the arrival of the great sage Dvaipāyana.

In the third canto, Yudhiṣṭhira greets the sage who, in his turn, makes a short speech to impress upon the Pāṇdavas about the immediate necessity of acquiring Divine weapons. As the Kauravas have several invincible warriors among their ranks, the stronger enemy can only be subdued by superior weapons obtainable through austere penance. He tells Yudhisthira to not to rely on the crafty enemy and instead be firm about regaining the lost kingdom by valour. Yudhisthira advises Arjuna to act according to the instruction of the sage who then inspires the third Pāndava to be prepared for undertaking penance in the Himalayas where a Yakṣa i.e. a sprite will lead him. Dvaipāyana disappears and the sprite comes there in no time. Draupadī reminds Arjuna of her terrible insult at the court of the Kauravas as the latter prepares to leave for the Himalayas along with the Yakṣa.

The fourth canto has no action whatsoever as it is entirely engulfed by the elaborate description of autumn, in the course of which Arjuna arrives in the vicinity of the Himalayas.

In the fifth canto, the Himalayas is described customarily in which various mythological details are also dealt with. Then the sprite describes Mount Indrakīla and refers to the mythic account of Arjuna's birth. After advising Arjuna to practise penance in that mountain and expressing his good wishes, the Yakṣa leaves. Because of a celebrated though somewhat far-fetched simile in a particular verse of this canto,[5] Bhāravi was acclaimed as 'ātapatrabhāravi' i.e. 'Sun-shade Bhāravi':

> 'Utphulla-sthalanalinī vanā damusmā duddhū tah sarasijasambhavah parāgah.
>
> Vātyābhirviyati Vivartitah samantādādhatte Kanakamayātapatralakṣmīm'.

The sixth canto unfolds Arjuna's ascent to the Mount Indrakīla; he chooses a secluded grove near the summit for practising penance. The poet tries to compensate for lack of action with naturalistic description of the beauty of that mountain. After sometime, the agents of Indra, dwelling there, become apprehensive and report Arjuna's penance to the lord of gods. The poet resorts to the traditional mythic motifs about the austerities of demons for winning heaven and the consequent tension among the gods and other celestial beings. However here Indra is well aware of Arjuna's intentions but nevertheless he decides to test Arjuna's integrity and sincerity. Therefore, in the true Purāṇic way, he commissions the service of celestial nymphs i.e. Apsaras and heavenly musicians i.e. Gandharvas to disturb the penance of Arjuna.

In the seventh canto, the celestial band is described as moving through the heavens to their destination at the mount Indrakīla. This has provided the poet with an opportunity to exhibit his varying fancy as well as penchant for various modes of expression. The arrival of the celestial band at the summit of the Indrakīla is compared to the descent of heavenly river. The epic narrative continues to remain frozen while the poet indulges in the description of the elephants of the celestial bands as well as the beautiful trees against which the exhausted nymphs take rest.

The eighth canto, too, has no relevance with the epic narrative because the poet seems to betray here a Narcissistic pleasure in describing with gusto the frolicking activities of the nymphs. They make mansions on the mountain, enjoy their sojourn in the forest and take their bath in the heavenly river. The depiction of bathing in particular is fascinating.[6] But in spite of the calm and refined dignity of these isolated moments of poetic brilliance, these add nothing to the matrix of the epic narrative.

The ninth canto also continues in the same manner where the poet undertakes to describe various phenomena of nature with unconcealed zeal which were thereafter standardized as the conventional source of inspiration for all the later epic poets. These include the descriptions of daybreak, evening, sunset, night, moonrise, sending of messenger, love-making, dawn etc. among which there are some commendable specimens of poetic expression. A couple of examples may be cited below:[7]

> 'Amsupānibhiratīva-pipāsuh padmajam madhu bhṛśam rasayitvā
> ksībatāmiva gatah kṣitimesy amllohitam vapuruvāhapatangah'
> 'Śam vidhātumabhisekamudāse manmathasya lasadamsujalaughah.
> Yāminivanitayā tatacihnah sotpalorajatakumbha ivenduh'.

But such extravaganza could not instil any movement to the already immobile epic narrative.

In the tenth canto, the celestial nymphs leave no stones unturned to distract Arjuna's penance but they fail to make any impression. The poet has described the seductive beauty of six seasons in glowing colours. A rare literary feast of flower, music, dance and amorous advances has been unfolded in this canto. The nymphs concede defeat as they themselves become enamoured for Arjuna but even their appeal fall on deaf ears.

In the eleventh canto, Indra comes to Arjuna in the guise of an old sage and an interesting conversation takes place between them. At the outset Indra praises Arjuna for practising penance since the fourth cardinal aim of life i.e. mokṣa or liberation can be attained only through such act. But as Arjuna's Kṣatriya attire suggests an altogether different intention, Indra asks him to practise forbearance since quest for victory and wealth begets unhappiness. Moreover fortune is transitory and pleasures are illusory like dream; therefore battles are to be renounced and serenity of mind has to be pursued. Arjuna gives a fitting as well as elaborate reply to Indra's speech. It is particularly significant because Bhāravi's own ideas about poetic diction are reflected here. The famous notion of 'arthagaurava, has been exemplified; in fact, the poet presents his view about heightened poetic language whenever he gets an opportunity to do so. We have already noted this tendency in earlier cantos; it may be found again in the fourteenth canto. Therefore Arjuna's praise of Indra's speech in this canto has to be interpreted as Bhāravi's own opinion about what he calls 'garīyasī gīh.' 'gurvī arthasampad' etc. We can refer to one of his well-known verses about poetic diction which is itself a fine example of 'arthagaurava':

> 'Vivikta-Varṇābharanā Sukhaśrutihprasādayantī hṛdayānyapi dviṣām.
> Pravartate nākṛtapuṇyakarmānām prasannagambhīrapadā sarasvatī'

Arjuna goes on to explain that even a fine speech may prove to be irrelevant if it is used out of context. Therefore the sage's speech (who is actually Indra in disguise) has no relevance to Arjuna since the former does not understand his situation. He says that he has been instructed by Dvaipāyana to take to asceticism to propitiate Indra since the outrageous insult inflicted on the Pāṇḍavas in general and Draupadī in particular must be avenged. Being a self-respecting Kṣatriya, he can take rest only after ensuring the restoration of fortune and honour of his family by destroying the enemies. Then Indra reveals his true identity and disappears after instructing Arjuna to worship Śiva for achieving his end. Thus the epic narrative gains momentum in this canto.

The twelfth canto paves the way for the unfoldment of the final phase of the plot. Arjuna becomes absorbed in very austere penance as a result of which even the great sages residing nearby are unable to endure his splendour. They do not know his identity and hence become apprehensive of the intention of the unknown ascetic. They take refuge of Lord Śiva and express their concern regarding a probable onslaught on the gods and the universe. Śiva allays their fear by disclosing Arjuna's identity; he tells further that the third Pāndava is in fact an incarnation of Nara, the indispensable part of the primeval superman. Both Nara and Nārāyana have assumed human form as Arjuna and Kṛṣṇa respectively to honour the request of Brahmā for protecting the creation by destroying the demons and evil forces. Śiva assures the sages that Arjuna has been practising penance to win His favour since only He can grant such divine weapons with which the suppliant hero can eliminate the wicked Kauravas who were tormenting the entire world. The meta-deity then goes on to describe the forthcoming events which, in fact, takes the steam out of the epic narrative as the readers thereby lose interest in the predetermined sequences in which there is no room for curiosity to follow the progressive development of the subjectmatter. Besides there is enough indication that the epic genre has travelled a long and tortuous way from the world of Kālidāsa. The lack of poetic sensibilities and spontaneity are sought to be compensated by heaps of increasingly extrinsic materials.

Thus Bhāravi zealously introduces mythological materials in his narrative and makes Śiva foretell the events to follow. We are made aware of an impending dramatic moment; a demon named Mūka has assumed the form of a wild boar and at that very instant he was fast approaching towards Arjuna, the incarnation of Nara, with a murderous intent. Śiva declares that He will go there quickly under the guise of a Kirāta chief and kill that boar with an arrow. Arjuna would also shoot it and consequently a quarrel would take place. That incident would bring forth the extraordinary courage and strength of Arjuna. Saying this, Śiva assumes the guise of a Kirāta chief while his attendant Gaṇas transform themselves as Kirāta army and march towards their destination through the forests. When the menacing boar is about to plunge on Arjuna, Śiva intercepts and with this, the canto comes to an end.

The thirteenth canto continues in the predetermined way. Arjuna notices the approaching boar and quickly takes up his bow. At that very instant, Śiva too, gets ready and both shoot at the boar. Śiva's arrow pierces through its body to disappear deep inside the earth. Arjuna comes across a forest ranger near the carcass as he tries to retrieve his arrow. The forest ranger addresses Arjuna politely at first but then rebukes him for trying to get hold of the arrow which allegedly belonged to the Kirāta chief. He demands apology and advises Arjuna to seek friendship with his chief.

The fourteenth canto begins with a fitting reply from enraged Arjuna. He is ireful but nevertheless maintains his cool in replying with much more politeness to the impertinent Kirāta. He firmly declares his intention to claim the arrow and asks the Kirāta to look elsewhere, Arjuna says indignantly that he cannot have any friendly tie with the Kirāta chief who appears to be an envious and wicked person; moreover he does not seem to be a warrior but actually a lowly person with whom neither friendship nor enmity is possible. Hence Arjuna warns the Kirāta that any attempt to claim his arrow would be as disastrous as collecting a gem from the hood of a venomous serpent. Then the Kirāta goes back to Śiva to report what has transpired. At the command of the god, the army of the gaṇas—disguised as the Kirātas—mount an attack on Arjuna who successfully repells it with shower of arrows. Thus this canto abounds in customary heroic spirit.

The fifteenth canto begins with the retreat of the Kirāta army. Skanda, the war god and Śiva's son, then makes a long speech to dissuade them from such unbecoming act and also to instil courage. He rebukes the gaṇas for their show of cowardice and his speech appears to be basically a straightforward lecture to the demoralised soldiers. This only proves the growing tendencies of ossification of epic paraphernalia because the martial episode has been practically stretched over four cantos with elaborate poetic details. Here, in this canto, Śiva himself intervenes and commands his retreating army to regroup; then he prepares to join the battle against Arjuna. The rally of Śiva's army under Skanda's inspiring leadership and the enthralling fight with magic weapons are particularly noteworthy since these have not been derived from the *Mahābhārata*. Bhāravi's innovative genius had added new materials to the ever-renewing creative process of the epic genre. Though the elaborate literary effort and emphasis on the poet's constructive ability as well as his penchant for mythical or magical elements seem to be detrimental for spontaneity and movement of the epic narrative, Bhāravi shone well inspite of his self-imposed limitation.

The sixteenth canto unfolds an absorbing battle between Arjuna and Śiva; being unaware of the true identity of his adversary, Arjuna is bewildered to see the extra-ordinary ability of the Kirāta chief. Though his entire army has fled, the Kirāta chief has not only firmly maintained his ground but he has also compelled Arjuna to use other special weapons since the conventional arrows failed to make any impact. Therefore Arjuna launches two missiles, known as 'Prasvāpana' (sleep-inducing) and āgneya' (fiery), in quick succession but, to his utter dismay and astonishment, Arjuna finds that neither of them can subdue the Kirāta-chief. Thus this canto remains totally engrossed in detailed description of the duel between Arjuna and Śiva.

The seventeenth canto depicts the next stage of the great duel. At the failure of the missiles, Arjuna decides to try arrows once again. Śiva is not only able to intercept these, but He now showers volleys of His own arrows on Arjuna. A flabbergasted Arjuna draws his sword but Śiva smashes it with an arrow. The protagonist faces a desperate situation but nevertheless he can never relinquish a fight. So he continues the battle by hurling stones and uprooted trees on his adversary.

The eighteenth and the final canto depicts the last phase of the duel and its predetermined outcome. Arjuna grasps the feet of the Kirāta chief as the latter springs in the air. Thus unconsciously Arjuna makes a gesture of obeisance to the god for whose favour he has so long practised severe penance. Śiva is finally pleased to witness his devotee's integrity of character and uncommon valour. As he assumes the true form, Arjuna becomes delighted to win the favour of Śiva and after eulogising the god with a hymn, he supplicates for enhancement of strength to ensure victory over the Kauravas. Śiva grants the prayer and as a very special gesture of favour, hands over His own flaming 'raudra' weapon to Arjuna along with the specialised knowledge of archery. Indra also appears there along with other gods and they, too, grant various other weapons to Arjuna. Then Śiva commands Arjuna to go back and be prepared to vanquish the enemy. The epic concludes with Arjuna's confident return to Yudhiṣṭhira as the winning of the divine favour virtually means that the wheel of fortune has turned positively for the Pāṇḍavas.

Bhāravi seems to have chosen the subjectmatter of his epic with great care. The great feud between the Pāndavas and the Kauravas, which occupies the centre-stage of the *Mahābhārata*, has always remained as the immediate perspective of the *Kirātārjunīya*. The poet has attempted a creative reconstruction of an important episode of the great epic in such a way that the essence of its subjectmatter has been effectively concentrated in the thematic scheme of his court epic. He has, in fact, demonstrated one particular method of predominantly elitist reconstruction of the epic tradition; it bespeaks of both a continuum and a renewal. However, like Kālidāsa, Bhāravi could not prove himself to be a harbinger of regeneration of the epic genre since the growing tendencies of ossification in the society have already frozen the creative mind. Nevertheless the poet could successfully display as to where he is at his best. These include the following: delineation of heroic sentiment, rich and poignant descriptions, subtle suggestions about varying complexities of prominent personalities, political insight, theoretical discussion about poetic diction and eloquence, penchant for effective expression etc. Bhāravi's expertise in constructing various figures of speech has been eulogised by many a scholars. Mallinātha observes that three most recurrent figures of speech are as follows: Utprekṣā, Upamā and Arthāntaranyāsa. However, Bhāravi excels in the use of arthāntaranyāsa mainly on which his famous 'arthagaurava' rests. In fact, no other court epic has made such extensive use of this particular figure. For example, the *Kirātārjunīya* has 119 'arthāntaranyāsa's out of 1030 verses while the *Raghuvamśa* has 58 out of 1549 verses, the *Bhattikāvya* has 5 out of 1617 verses, the *Śiśupālavadha* has 84 out of 1645 verses and the *Naisadhīyacarita* has 67 out of 2827 verses.

Bhāravi's epic is not meant for the uninitiated. Mallinātha's observation regarding this is well known:

> 'Nārikelaphalasammitam vaco bhāraveh sapadi tad vibhajyate Svādayantu rasagarbhanirbharam sāramasya rasikā yathepsitam'

Whatever might be its import, nobody can deny the fact that Bhāravi was able to guide the epic genre to a new direction; this is his most important contribution to the Indian epic tradition. The succeeding poets tried to emulate his spirit zealously but by then the time had become increasingly out of joint. Hence, the basic creative fervour was found to be missing. Though Bhāravi himself was a man of elegant genius, he came out to be the father of an abusive school of epic poetry in which the very essence of creative imagination was jeopardised. One example will suffice. Bhāravi could successfully demonstrate his command over the technique of 'citrakāvya' in the fifteenth canto of the *Kirātārjunīya*.[8] But such verbal gymnastics could hardly promote the enhancement of epic poetry; on the contrary, it provided the poets of lesser calibre with convenient masks to hide their hollowness. Inspite of his occasional overenthusiasm, it seems that Bhāravi was aware in his own special way, of certain relation between the creative unconscious and conscious intellectual faculties in the act of composition. But nevertheless, unlike Kālidāsa, he rarely helps us to break through the conventional modes of perception and valuation which are constantly changing to make the readers see the world afresh. Bhāravi sought to make a new beginning in the realm of epic poetry but his successors could not properly understand his art. We may conclude this discussion with the words of Gangā, a poetess of the fourteenth century, who wrote the epic entitled the *Madhurāvijaya*:

'Vimardavyaktasaurabhyābhārātibhāraveh kaveh
Dhatte bakulamāleva vidagdhānām camatkriyām.'[9]

II

Subandhu, the famous author of the prose romance entitled 'Vāsavadattā' (6th Century A.D.), appears to refer to a few lost kāvyas. Though there is now no way to verify whether there were epic poems among such works, it can be reasonably conjectured that the theme of love between Arjuna and Subhadrā, Usā and Aniruddha, Nala and Damayantī, Madālasā and Kuvalayāśva etc. might have inspired the versifiers to fashion epic poems on their romantic adventure. Whatever might have been their literary merit, Subandhu's reference suggests that the epic legacy continued uninterrupted but posterity did not care to preserve them because presumably none of them had distinctive individuality. These assumptions about continuity of the epic tradition is further corroborated by Bhoja's *Śṛngāraprakāśa*. Some of the epics based on the theme, mentioned by Subandhu, have also been referred to by Bhoja. These are as follows: the *Kuvalayāśvacarita*, the *Subhadrāharaṇa* and the *Uṣāharana*.

The popularity of the epic tradition among the elites of the Indian society seems to have inspired the creative personalities to expand the frontiers of the genre to serve some predetermined purpose. It was indeed a difficult task to motivate the epic Muse in relinquishing certain spheres of natural autonomy for accomodating utilitarian and prosaic aims. Therefore it is no ordinary achievement for Bhatti to succeed to a great extent in composing a court epic entitled '*Rāvaṇavadha*' in twenty-two cantos, with covert aim of illustrating the rules of grammar systematically. The epic is usually known as the *Bhattikāvya* after the name of its poet who flourished in the middle of the seventh century A.D. The name of the poet, Bhatti is prākṛta rendering of 'Bhartṛ' because of which he is identified by several traditional scholars with Bhartṛhari, the famous gnomic poet and grammarian. Bhatti is sometimes also mentioned as a son of half-brother of Bhartṛhari. According to many commentators, the poet's name was actually Bhartṛhari and his father was Śrīdharasvāmin. Bhatti is also described as Bhattasvāmin and Bhartṛsvāmin. The poet is sometimes identified with Vatsabhatti of the Mandasor inscription but it does not seem to be tenable. The concluding verse of the epic testifies that it was composed at Valabhī during the reign of Śridharasena. But this testimony also does not seem to be conclusive since Mallinātha did not comment upon it.

Moreover, no less than four kings of the same name viz., Śrīdharasena ruled at Valabhī between 495 A.D. and 641 A.D. According to historical evidence, the city of Valabhī in Saurāṣṭra (i.e. modern Gujarat) was a celebrated seat of learning in that epoch. The fourth Dharasena, who assumed the title of 'cakravartin' i.e. 'emperor' in his inscriptions, seemed to have been the patron of our grammatical poet. Modern scholars have drawn our attention to the interesting fact that this capital city of the Maitraka witnessed the emergence of another grammatical poet designated variously as Bhosa or Vyosa or Vosa or Ghosa or Bhaumaka or Bhatta-bhauma or Bhattabhīma, who composed the epic entitled the *Rāvanārjunīya* or *Arjunarāvanīya* in twenty seven cantos. Thus the unique sub-genre of grammatical epic seems to have been consciously patronised at Valabhī. Kṣemendra typifies it as 'Śāstrakāvya'[10] which prove that the sub-genre did not blush like an unseen flower. On the contrary it was accorded sufficient attention at a remote province even after a couple of centuries, that is, in the eleventh century Kashmir. The sub-genre travelled to the southernmost region as well; that is why, some manuscripts have been found in Kerala. In fine, this only strongly suggests the rapid expansion of the frontiers of the epic legacy to and fro which is obviously impossible without a basic assumption of its continuity. Surely Bhatti played the role of a pioneer by virtue of his unique composition in which poetry is subservient to the burden of grammatical rules that it is made to uphold.

Because of diverse opinions regarding the identity of the poet of the *Bhattikāvya*, several anecdotes cropped up in people's tradition. The commentators were also aware of those floating legends. Thus Bharata, one of the commentators, said: 'Bhartrharināma kavih Śrīrāmakathāśrayam cakāra.' There are different opinions about the poet's patron as well. Those who do not subscribe to the opinion that the expression "Kāvyamidam bihitam mayā valabhyām śrīdharasena-narendrapālitāyām' did not refer to the Srīdharasena IV but to Srīdharasena II, put forward the following arguments. From the internal evidences it seems quite plausible that Bhatti was particularly inclined to Saivism and significantly, Śrīdharasena II was a Saivite. Besides, Bhatti has described his patron with the non-specific epithet 'narendra'i.e. king; Śrīdharasena II has also referred to himself as 'Sāmanta-mahārāja.' Moreover there is no trace of the impact of Buddhism in the *Bhattikāvya*; Buddhism flourished in Valabhī during the reign of Śrīdharasena IV who, as we have already stated, assumed the elevated status of an emperor. Therefore, one can conclude that the *Bhattikāvya* was composed around 570 A.D. during the reign of the Saivite king, Śrīdharasena II who was no less an enthusiastic patron of arts and scholarship.

It is uncertain whether Bhāmaha, who is stated to have lived around second half of the seventh century A.D., referred to a famous expression of the *Bhattikāvya* in the following verse:

> 'Kāvyānyāpi yadīmāni vyākhyā gamyāni 'śāstravat
> Utsavah suddhiyāmalamahodurmedhaso hṛtāh.'

It has been argued that the word 'imāni' actually refers to the subgenre spearheaded by Bhatti's poem. The above verse quoted from the *Kāvyālamkāra* cannot but remined us of the following verses of the *Bhattikāvya*:[11]

> 'Dīpatulyah prabandhoyam śabdalaksaṇacakṣusām
> Hastādarśaivāndhānām bhaved vyākaranādṛte.
> Vyākhyāgamyamidam Kāvyamutswavah sudhiyāmalam
> Hatādurmedhasaścāsmin Vidvatpriyatayā mayā.'

Therefore Bhaṭṭi might be placed in the last quarter of the sixth century A.D. But Bhāmaha's date has not been beyond dispute:; hence Bhaṭṭi's date should be fixed on the basis of other evidences. However the diversities of opinion among the critics make the task difficult. Thus Kane places Bhaṭṭi between Bhāmaha and Daṇḍin while another critic draws the conclusion that the poet appears to have followed

Udbhaṭa's *Alamkārasamgraha* in framing the sequence of figures of speech. As the *Bhaṭṭikāvya* has been referred to by Ruyyaka, Bhaṭṭi is undoubtedly earlier than him. But without going into further details of this crisscross puzzle, we may rely more upon establishing the identity of the poet's patron, about whom our considered opinion has already been put forward.

The 22 cantos of the *Bhaṭṭikāvya* have been arranged in four kāṇḍas or parts, viz., prakīrṇa, prasanna, almkāra and timanta. The epic narrates the entire story of the *Rāmāyaṇa* beginning with the presentation of Rāma as an incarnation of Visnu and concluding with Rāma's coronation at Ayodhyā after his victorious return from Lankā. However the narrative details are of no real concern for the poet since he only intends to illustrate the rules of grammar and rhetoric with examples at the same time. Of the four parts (Kāndas) enumerated above, the first part is constituted with the first five cantos of the epic in order to exemplify the miscellaneous rules of Pānini's grammar. The second section that begins with the sixth canto and ends with the ninth, illustrates the principal rules of Paninian grammar. The third part constitutes of four cantos beginning from the tenth to the thirteenth canto, in which the most prominent figures of speech are illustrated. In the last section (canto xiv-xxii), the variant uses of tenses and moods have been emumerated.

The story of the *Rāmāyaṇa* has not been modified to any recognizable extent though some details were readjusted in some places and occasionally some speeches and conceits as well as fanciful descriptions of seasons and various natural objects were incorporated. But the literary interest being entirely secondary, the epic becomes a compendium of ostentatious grammatical forms. The readers find it extremely unrewarding since, at every step, they have to negotiate with a consciously laboured language. The poet himself seems to have opted for being in chains and whatever creative idea, feeling and thought he had within him were choked by abstruse phraseology. Bhaṭṭi deliberately chose such words and expressions which were frankly conditioned by the exigencies of illustrating grammatical rules. Not even a single stanza is beyond the grammatical scheme, hence the appreciation of the epic narrative is indeed a difficult proposition.

Yet the fact remains that Bhaṭṭi was very much popular with the scholars through the ages since they could find the *Bhaṭṭikāvya* extremely useful as a pleasant-reading manual for illustrating obsolete and quasi-familiar grammatical formation. However no one can possibly deny that the poet could somehow maintain the uninterrupted flow of the epic narrative inspite of lengthy digressions and penchant for syntactical complexities. In fact, this attitude is not entirely new in Sanskrit epic poetry since even Aśvaghoṣa has a canto in each of his epics which illustrates tenses and thus foreshadows Bhaṭṭi's idiosyncratic mode. However Aśvaghoṣa wrote in a creatively fertile period when he had a significant theme to work upon and hence he did not have to take refuge to verbal gymnastics like Bhaṭṭi to conceal inherent barrenness. That is why Aśvaghoṣa's grammatical knowledge does not ever transgress the frontiers of poetic art: these instances fit in well with their contexts. As long as creative imagination remained in the foreground, extrinsic elements could not usurp the sovereignty of poetic inspiration. The balance began to tilt when Bhāravi took command of the epic Muse. Bhaṭṭi has only completed the process of building up a counter-creative legacy within a creative tradition: it was like nourishing a killer parasite that eats into the vitality of the very plant on which it spreads its roots.

Though Bhaṭṭi's epic has been described as 'a great triumph of artifice' over spontaneity of poetic expression, it too has its silver linings. Bhaṭṭi wrote predominantly for the leisure-enjoying elites of a royal court who were well conversant with the narrative of the *Rāmāyaṇa.* Hence Bhaṭṭi could unhesitatingly skip over several episodes of the great epic because he knew that the special category of readers would not expect a mechanical reproduction of Vālmikī's narrative. Rather they would be delighted to patronise his amazingly tireless show of scholasticity; the unusual complexities of involved construction would not vex them as they would be only too willing to participate in strenuous intellectual exercises unleashed in the epic. Therefore Bhaṭṭi's success in quickening the pace of the narrative is noteworthy. Thus, in the beginning of the third canto, we find king Daśaratha's declaration of the solemnisation of Rāma's coronation but the canto ends with Bharata's return to Ayodhyā with Rāma's wooden sandal. However, at some rare moments of poetic exuberance, Bhaṭṭi seems to forget his wearisome task temporarily and slackens the pace of the narrative to a considerable extent in order to watch, for example, the ecstatic advent of autumn in the second canto. There he visualises working cowherdesses imitating the rhythmic movement of dance,[12] undistinguishable white cackling swans among columns of white lotuses[13] as well as many other pictorial details of captivating natural beauty. The phenomena of nature seem to be an extension of human world as even the insects and plants pulsate with delicate feelings and warmth of life. Though there is conscious use of figures of speech, Bhaṭṭi can sometimes draw graceful pen-pictures. For example, there is an instance of Ekāvalī in the second canto:

> 'Na tajjalam Yanna sucārupankajam
> Na pankajam tad Yadalīnaṣaṭpadam
> Na Ṣatpado sau na jugũnja yah kalam
> Na guñjitam tanna jahāra Yanmanah'.[14]

There are commendable examples of the major figure of speech like Upamā, Utprekṣā. Samāsokti etc.[15] In fact, the poet illustrated as many as thirty eight figures of speech belonging to the categories of both Śabdālamkāra and Arthālamkāra. It may be conjectured that Bhatti was follower of the Alamkāra and Guna school. The whole of the eleventh canto may be regarded as an example of Mādhurya guṇa. It may also be noted at the same time that most of the verses of this canto exemplify the Śṛngāra rasa; yet Bhaṭṭi did not put emphasis on 'rasa'; 'alamkāra' and 'guṇa' were more important to him. This bespeaks of the influence of the contemporary rhetoricians; because though both Bhāmaha and Daṇdin accepted 'rasa' as one of the properties of the epic, none of them emphasised on its exclusive prominence.

Bhaṭṭi has narrated the story of the *Rāmāyaṇa* with ease and elegance though his primary allegiance was always towards illustrating the grammatical rules. The *Bhaṭṭikāvya* generally lacks in subtle suggestion, expansive imagination and true emotion evoking imagery.

The verses wherein we find perfect expression of poetic sentiments cannot but be regarded as exceptions. However, in those isolated moments of poetic flourish, Bhaṭṭi is at his best. The pathetic description of Jaṭāyu's death,[16] Bāli's heartrending lament on the verge of death,[17] Bibhīsana's lament over Rāvaṇa's death[18] etc. undoubtedly prove Bhatti's creative ability. Besides the dialogues and prolonged speeches have been depicted convincingly.[19] Bhaṭṭi also excells in the description of Rāvaṇa's court in the twelfth canto in which an interesting debate among Rāvana, Bibhīṣaṇa, Mālyavat and Kumbhakarṇa have been portrayed skilfully. There is no dull monotony here, instead the epic narrative is able to gain certain momentum. Though the *Bhaṭṭikāvya* is comparatively free from decadent tendencies of the post-Bhāravi court epics, at least on one occasion, he, too, fell prey to such devices. For example, the description of the dance of the nymphs for seducing Bharata and his companions.[20]

In comparison to Kālidāsa and Bhāravi, Bhaṭṭi remains far behind in depicting the poetic feelings about human situation as well as in deciphering the truth underneath. When a poet declares that none can understand his poem without the aid of a commentator, we cannot but feel that it is, in fact, a decree for an altogether new order of epic poetry. Therefore we arrive at this inevitable and sad conclusion that the *Bhaṭṭikāvya* practically makes itself an anathema for the connoisseurs of poetry. Bhaṭṭi's decree for a new order of poetry actually initiated the vigorous beginning of a suicidal deviation that sealed the fate of the epic Muse in no time. The amusement of a handful of leisurely elites belonging to the upper strata of society was believed to be the sole aim of epic composition. Poetry was relegated to the status of an ordinary medium for expressing the knowledge of grammar, metrics, poetics etc. The inherent imbalance of the *Bhaṭṭikāvya* has been betrayed to such an extent that the entire poetic texture is vitiated. Thus the poet seems to be totally unmindful of the import of the story as well as the seriousness of a situation; he is only enthusiastic to exhibit gymnastics of language. We may cite the tenth canto as an example. Even when he describes the burning of the pompous city of Lankā, he is more eager to employ the figure of

Śleṣa (pun) throughout the canto. Likewise when Rāma is holding a counsel with his companions at the oceanshore to devise a way for crossing the ocean, the poet does not seem to appreciate that dramatic moment of crisis; instead he has composed the entire thirteenth canto in such a way that it may be read simultaneously as a poem in Sanskrit and Prakrit. There are several instances of poetic ingenuity in which excessive word-play effectively turn the poet into an acrobat. Therefore the *Bhaṭṭikāvya* has no appeal to the sensitive readers whatsoever. Bhaṭṭi, the poet, has absorbed both the intrinsic and extrinsic tendencies of the epic tradition but he could not give it a new lease of life since Bhaṭṭi, the scholar, stood like a colossus on the way. As the role of creative inspiration became obscure, the *Bhaṭṭikāvya* marked the beginning of that phase of laboured craftsmanship from which the epic tradition was only negatively interpreted.

Another grammatical epic, referred to by the critics, is the *Rāvaṇārjunīya* (also known as *Arjunarāvanīya*) by Bhosa about which we have already taken a note earlier. The name of the author has been variously mentioned in different manuscripts. However his where–abouts may be decided with a fair amount of certainty. It is stated in the colophons of the manuscripts found both in Kerala and Kashmir that Bhosa lived in Valabhī whose kings were patrons of scholarly pursuits. Bhosa's *Rāvaṇārjunīya* is a grammatical epic in twenty seven cantos that deals with the story of Arjuna Kārtavīrya and his victory over Rāvaṇa of Lankā. There are several mythic legends about Arjuna Kārtavīrya, who belonged to the Haihaya branch of the Yādava clan, enumerated in the *Viṣṇu Purāṇa* and *Vāyu Purāṇa*. The main source of Bhosa's poem seems to be the Bombay recension of the *Rāmāyaṇa*[21] in which Agastya narrates a more elaborate version of the legend to Rāma after his victorious return to Ayodhyā.

Bhosa's poem adds more details to the legend narrated in the last book of the *Rāmāyaṇa*. It begins with a description of Arjuna Kārtavīrya's learning, his allegiance to orthodox vedic rituals, martial spirit and thousand arms. The march of the army is described in the second canto with all its paraphernalia. In the third canto, king Arjuna kills a wild boar and a lion on the way and then encamps on the bank of the Narmadā. The poet describes watersports, sunset, moonrise, messages of love, drinking in quick succession, that cover the entire fourth, fifth and sixth cantos. Rāvaṇa, the antagonist, is boastful of his earlier martial conquest in the seventh canto. In the company of his ministers at the Hall of the Demons, he grants audience to a spy who reports about Arjuna's prowess. An enraged Rāvaṇa decides to launch an assault; the army of demons marches through the clouds. The king of Lankā sends his minister Śuka with a challenge to Arjuna but by then the protagonist has left his capital. Rāvaṇa marches through the Vindhya and reaches the bank of the Narmadā.

In the ninth and tenth cantos, Rāvana and his army step into the river for taking bath, but its water suddenly sweeps backwards causing much consternation. In the eleventh, Rāvana sends Śuka for investigation who comes back with the report that the stream of the river has been blocked by Arjuna during his watersport. The twelfth canto unfolds how this infuriates Rāvana and he takes the pledge to kill Arjuna and take possession of his kingdom. Śuka is therefore sent again as an emissary to Arjuna to call upon the latter to either surrender or fight. In the thirteenth, the protagonist promises to take up the challenge the next day. The fourteenth depicts Arjuna's counsel with his followers while the fifteenth unfolds the meeting of two armies. In the sixteenth, Mandodarī expresses her serious concern for Rāvaṇa since the reports about the thousand arms of the adversary are alarming. But the antagonist tries to alleviate her anxiety with a laugh and boasts about his ability to kill the enemy. Mandodarī is, however, not consoled and she flies to Pulasti to appraise him of the events. The battle begins at the end of this canto. The seventeenth canto depicts the battle raging till sunset; at dusk, the contending armies encamp on the two banks of the river. This is followed by the customary description of moonrise, sending of messenger for obtaining the news of the fighting young heroes.

The eighteenth canto describes the sunrise and resumption of battle. Arjuna, driving on a chariot, confronts Rāvaṇa in single combat. The demon army is routed and Rāvaṇa loses his horses and the bow. The fight leads us to the nineteenth canto in which Rāvana leaves his disabled chariot and Arjuna, too, in accordance with the established norms of battle, gets down from his chariot. In the twentieth canto, Arjuna and Rāvana confront each other, first with sword, then with maces. The concluding portion of this canto is missing but it seems that there Rāvaṇa may have been knocked out by the protagonist. The beginning of the twenty first canto is also not available; as the narrative resumes, we find that Rāvaṇa has been overpowered by Arjuna. Then the focus is shifted elsewhere; an angry Pulasti tells Mandodarī that her husband has met with a calamity for haughtily abandoning the ways of the wise. In the twenty second canto, Śuka implores Pulasti through a long speech to intervene for securing the release of Rāvana since otherwise he may be killed by Arjuna. Pulasti relents and agrees to go. The twenty third canto depicts as to how Arjuna reaches his capital, the city of Māhismatī, with the prisoner. In the twenty fourth canto, the rush of the women of the capital for having a look at the victorious entry of the king and his army has been described. This is followed by a night of passionate lovemaking. Almost the entire twenty fifth canto is missing; only its concluding portion is available in which Pulasti's arrival at Arjuna's court has been described. The twenty sixth canto unfolds Pulasti's long speech to Arjuna through which he appeals flatteringly to the magnanimity and compassion of the protagonist to release Rāvaṇa though the latter deserves punishment for his animosity to Vedic religion. Arjuna shows his respect to Pulasti and declares that he does not wish to have any ill feeling to the scion of the great sage. Therefore he orders to set Rāvaṇa free and bring him before the sage. In the twenty seventh i.e. the last canto, peace is restored and Rāvaṇa returns to Lankā with Pulastī.

Being a grammatical epic, *Rāvaṇārajunīya* uses the story only as necessary subterfuge i.e. a means to illustrate all the rules (except those related to the Vedic language) enumerated by Pāṇini in his celebrated '*Aṣṭādhyāyī.*' Obviously this called for extra-ordinary ingenuity because the exemplified formations of words have to be accomodated in the continuing narrative. Bhosa's allegiance to the common examples enumerated in the principal commentaries of the *Aṣṭādhyāyī* has also rendered his task more complicated since he has marked preference for stock examples of Pāṇini's rules. While Bhatti had to maintain a much more detailed and complex narrative, Bhosa worked on a simple epic narrative with greater ease and freedom. Besides, Bhaṭṭi chose his own order of grammatical rules and also made his own selection of points for illustration but Bhosa sought to illustrate systematically all the rules of Pānini's grammar. On another plane, the poet of the *Rāvaṇārjunīya* seems to have been more enshrined in the Puranic tradition. In the ultimate analysis, however, as a champion of a unique sub-stratum within the epic genre, Bhaṭṭi was much more nearer to the Muse than Bhosa.

III

Kumāradāsa, the composer of the epic entitled '*Jānakīharaṇa*'. flourished in Ceylon in the second half of the seventh century. Several legends cropped up in Ceylon and India which sought to forge a relationship between Kumāradāsa and Kālidāsa. Thus Jalhana quotes a verse of Rājaśekhara which suggests that the *Jānakīharana* is a unique complement to the *Raghuvamśa*. Actually it means the affirmation of the continuum of the epic legacy and also the dissemination of the genre in general and the Rāma-epos in particular, Kumāradāsa has reproduced the *Rāmāyaṇa*-story faithfully in the *Jānakīharaṇa* where the whole story of the great epic has been presented in outline beginning with birth of Rāma and ending with Rāma's triumphant return to Ayodhyā along with Sītā and others. It is significant that the poet excludes the apocryphal last book, the Uttarakāṇḍa, which cannot but mean that its incorporation in the epic corpus was not yet universally recognised.

Kumāradāsa makes summary of the *Rāmāyaṇa* in 20 cantos and it seems that he expects his readers to be well conversant in the details of the story as well as the characters of the great epic. The poet has narrated the episodes only in brief outlines; this tendency is best evident in the depiction of Rāma's exile. On the other hand, Kumāradāsa shows his fondness for continuing description and long speeches. Though he might have been inspired by the *Raghuvamśa*, the two poets are poles apart from each other in creative method, attitude and worldview. Kumāradāsa's preference for sound play, rhyme and paraphernalia of evolving court epics unmistakably hint at his proximity with a poetic epoch different form Kālidāsa's. This helps us in determining the age of Kumāradāsa who was, it has already been noted, erroneously connected with Kālidāsa through some Sinhalese legends. It has been taken for granted that the poet was a king of Ceylon but this supposition loses credence if Rājaśekhara's testimony regarding the poet being born blind is accepted. Kumāradāsa is identified by some with Kumāradhātusena who reigned during first two decades of the sixth century. But the authoritative *Cūlavamśa* does not make any special reference to the abovementioned king as a literatteur. According to another tradition, Kumāradāsa was a scholarly poet who reigned after Maudgalyāyana I in the early seventh century. But the same tradition describes him as a friend of Kālidāsa and that exposes the vulnerability of such legend.

The colophon of the manuscript preserved in Chennai contains certain personal details about the poet which are supported by Sinhalese Sanna as well. From close analysis of those details, it may be concluded that Kumāradāsā (also known as Kumārabhatta or Bhāta Kumāra) was born around 640 A.D. in the midst of political intrigues, rapid rise and fall of royal fortune and raging civil war. His father Srīmānita, entitled Kumāramani by the then king of Lankā, was murdered by conspirators when the poet was an infant and he was reared up by his maternal uncles viz. Śrīmegha and Agrabodhi. Kumāradāsa's mother might have been a princess, a daughter of king Jyesthatisya; because of uncertainties and lack of security at Ceylon, the poet might have spent a considerable time in exile in Ķāncī. There he seemed to have become conversant with Indian poetics and the epic tradition. The *Jānakīharaṇa* might have been composed in the last quarter of the seventh century; according to modern scholars, substantial portion of the epic was written in India but completed in Ceylon. Though the literary history of Ceylon is dominated by Buddhist texts mainly written in Pāli, the legacy of creative literature in Sanskrit and Prākrit has also inspired the Sinhalese poets through the ages. Therefore Kumāradāsa did not flourish in a vacuum; however no specimen of such literary activity has survived. As a result, the probable impact of such texts on the *Jānakīharaṇa* cannot be measured. We can only observe that Kumāradāsa's epic is another expression of the epic continuum since he is aware of Vālmīki's great narrative and he has consciously modelled the form and spirit of his poem on the two famous court epics of Kālidāsa.

The *Jānakīharana* seems to have been a popular poem and hence its verses are quoted in Sanskrit anthologies prepared around tenth century A.D. This was one of the reasons for which Keith thought that Kumāradāsa might have flourished between the last quarter of the eighth and the first quarter of the ninth century A.D. The Sanskrit text of the epic may have been transcribed from a Sinhalese Sanna or word for word gloss. Though the Madras manuscript mentioned earlier furnishes us with twenty cantos, its text does not seem to be entirely dependable because the Sanna covers first fourteen and part of the fifteenth canto. However it also preserves the colophon and last verse of the twentieth canto with the help of which one can arrive at fairly dependable conclusion about the name of the poet, the title of the work and the range of the narrative.

As we make a scanning of the epic, two facts become obvious. First, the poet did not hesitate to freely borrow ideas and expressions from the continuing epic tradition in general and Kālidāsa in particular. Though some critics have suggested that Kumāradāsa was actually a plagiarist, this might only signify his acute eagerness for imbibing the spirit of high seriousness inherent in the fascinating genre. Secondly, the range of the *Jānakīh araṇa* is co-extensive with the *Bhaṭṭikāvya* which is undoubtedly an interesting coincident. Even if the *Raghuvamśa* was the principal source of inspiration for Kumāradāsa, the poetic vision, schemata of theme and the unique execution was beyond his grasp. Instead he looked for an alternative model for presenting the Rāma-story and got it in the *Bhaṭṭikāvya*. However, he had nothing to do with grammar; therefore he maintained its extrinsic structure and narrated the story of the *Rāmāyaṇa* as far as Rāma's coronation after his victorious return to Ayodhyā. Kumāradāsa's conscious indebtedness to the paraphernalia of the epic tradition is further corroborated by his prolonged and detailed descriptions of various seasons, hermitage, evening, erotic interludes, battles etc. where he closely resembles Bhāravi and Bhatti.

The first canto of the *Jānākīharaṇa* introduces king Daśaratha and gives a customary description of the capital city of Ayodhyā. The poet's adherence to the norms of the court epic has come to the fore time and again. Thus Daśaratha's marriage with Kauśalyā and the physical charm of the queen have been described with gusto in which well-known cliches are in abundance. The poet, however, takes care to reproduce the story of the *Rāmāyaṇa* faithfully. Thus the sadness of the king for being sonless, his hunting expedition near the river Tamasā, the inadvertent killing of the ascetic boy and the resultant curse by the latter's grief-stricken father have been portrayed appropriately. The canto ends with Daśaratha's return to Ayodhyā.

The second canto sheds comprehensive light on the impact of the transition of Rāma as an epic hero to Rāma, the incarnation of Lord Viṣṇu. This also proves that an important phase of the apocryphal incorporation of Puranic materials into the great epic had been complete by then and the deification of Rāma was widely accepted. Thus Kumāradāsa describes how Rāvaṇa was granted a boon of invincibility by Brahmā. The gods were humiliated and went to Viṣṇu for solace; He assured them that He would be born as Rāma to punish Rāvaṇa.

In the third canto, the epic narrative resumes its course once again though the abundance of descriptive details has choked the movement of events altogether. Thus there are customary descriptions of spring, erotic sports of Daśaratha and his queens at a pleasure-garden, water-sport, sunset and night, orgy of drinking etc. The depicition of Daśaratha's wanton drunkenness and his repose in the embraces of beloved queens cannot but startle the readers with its unusually mundane realism. He wakes up the next morning with customary bardic songs and along with him, the epic narrative, too, rises, as it were, from a paralysing stupor. The fourth canto seems to try to compensate for the lack of events in the last canto and thus many incidents take place in quick succession. These include

Daśaratha's sacrifice for obtaining sons, the birth of Rāma and three of his brothers, their childhood, Viśvāmitra's arrival at the court of Daśaratha for seeking protection of sacrificial rituals from the intruding demons. These are followed by Rāma's journey to the hermitage in the company of Viśvāmitra and Laksmaṇa. At the end of the canto, Rāma kills Tāḍakā, a terrible demoness, with his arrow. Here Kumāradāsa faithfully follows the *Rāmāyaṇa* in depicting the relevant episodes and, at the sametime, he is aware of the descriptive details in the *Bhaṭṭikāvya*.

The fifth canto depicts the hermitage of Viśvāmitra in a commendable manner. The prolonged description is followed by the narration of a fierce attack by the demons. In an engrossing battle, Rāma and Lakṣmaṇa completely demolish the host of demons.

The sixth canto is also full of incidents. Viśvāmitra leads Rāma and Lakṣmaṇa to Mithilā, the capital city of Videha, which is described enthusiastically. Rāma breaks Śiva's bow to win Sītā as his wife.

In the seventh canto Sītā's love-lorn conditions i.e. Pūrvarāga has been depicted. The description of her peerless beauty and youthful charm has brought out the imaginative poet in Kumāradāsa. However this also makes us aware of the poet's mechanical assimilation of Kālidāsa's creative devices. The solemnisation of the marriage of Rāma and his brothers after Daśaratha's arrival at Mithilā as well as the ceremonial gaiety have been described in the usual epic style.

The eighth canto unveils a detailed portrayal of the erotic dalliance of Rāma and Sītā, the newly wedded couple, their loving quarrel and then the customary description of sunset, evening, moonrise. After session of love-making, Rāma and Sītā drink in the moonlight from a jewelled goblet. Such a portrayal of the protagonist (i.e. enjoying drinking bout in a mood of romantic orgy) proves unmistakably that inspite of the metamorphosis of Rāma, a basically human epic hero, into an unassailable incarnation of Lord Viṣṇu and hence an epitome of supramundane qualities, human aspects still persist. This means that divinity has not yet overpowered the literary arena with its inevitable consequence in the form of a paralysing stupor under whose impact ethical and religious considerations outweigh the literary sensibility. At any rate, Kumāradāsa makes Rāma describe the evening panorama to his spouse, Sītā; but nevertheless he does not digress too much. Hence, unlike the latter court epics, the perspective of the narrative is never lost sight of.

In the ninth canto, Rāma comes back to Ayodhyā along with his bride. Paraśurāma, the conceited sage who annihilated the Kṣatriyas 21 times, is taught a lesson as he confronts the protagonist on the latter's way from Mithilā to Ayodhyā. Rāma proves his extraordinary powers by debarring Paraśurāma from heaven by shooting an arrow.

The tenth canto has some irrelevant descriptive materials which might have been casually incorporated by Kumāradāsa e.g., the prolonged discussion about frailties of old age, martial principle and characteristics of a perfect minister. Yet this canto has covered much ground rather disproportionately since practically the events of the entire second and third book of the *Rāmāyaṇa* have been summarised here. At the outset, an ageing Daśaratha expresses his intention to consecrate Rāma as his successor and gives a lengthy advice which the latter silently listens to with a feeling of sadness. When the consecration is about to take place, Mantharā intervenes and tells Daśaratha to remember the boons already promised to Kaikeyī in accordance to which Rāma should be exiled for fourteen years. This is obviously a significant departure from the *Rāmāyaṇa*. Rāma starts for the forest sojourn along with Sītā and Lakṣmana. After the death of Daśaratha, Bharata goes to Rāma and implores him to return to Ayodhyā which the latter refuses. Thereafter, there is a series of encounters with the demons in which Virādha is killed. Śūrpanakhā is mutilated, Khara and Dūṣaṇa are wiped out along with their army. Mārīca appears as golden deer and draws Rāma away; Rāvana abducts Sītā in the guise of an ascetic as Lakṣmaṇa goes after Rāma. The canto concludes with Rāvana's boastful declaration of his prowess. It also clearly shows that the *Jānakīharaṇa* has not fallen an easy prey to the elaborate and leisurely manner of description, the most common feature of the post-Bhāravi court epics. Kumāradāsa is always very keen about retaining the interest of the readers to the narrative and therefore, in spite of occasional expressions of his learned refinements, fondness for circumlocution, alliteration and dainty conceits, stock-in-trade descriptions—there is no extravaganza of the later court epics. In this respect, Kumāradāsa seems to offer us the missing link regarding the intermediary phase of epic versification between Kālidāsa and Bhāravi. He was acquainted with the generic features of the court epic and, as we have already noted, Bhāravi influenced him to a considerable extent. But because of his temperament and allegiance to the narrative of the *Rāmāyaṇa*, he was nearer to the earlier phase (i.e. pre-Bhāravi) of the court epic.

The eleventh canto depicts the battle between Jatāyu and Rāvana at the outset. After Rāma and Lakṣmaṇa arrive there in search of Sītā, Jatāyu, the mortally wounded vulture, informs them about Rāvaṇa's abduction and dies. The poet follows the *Rāmāyaṇa*-track as before but leaves out the well-known narrative details. Thus we come across Rāma's encounter with the monster named Kabandha followed by the protagonist's arrival at Kiṣkindhyā. As the narrative moves on swiftly, the friendly tie between Rāma and Sugrīva and then the latter's fight with Vālin take place in no time. The poet, however, makes a brief stop-over, as it were, to present a lengthy but praiseworthy description of the rainy season. Such intercessional depiction of season has been a favourite ploy of the epic poets ever since Vālmīki composed enchanting penpictures of the rainy season and autumn. Kumāradāsa, in fact, affirmed the continuity of traditional motifs yet again. But here the poet is clearly more indebted to Kālidāsa.

The twelfth canto begins with the description of autumn where Kumāradāsa is explicitly influenced by Bhaṭṭi. Rāma draws the attention of Lakṣmaṇa to autumnal beauty and then tells him to remind Sugrīva of his promise regarding finding out the whereabouts of Sītā. According to Rāma's suggestion, Lakṣmaṇa goes to Sugrīva with a thinly veiled threat. Sugrīva puts forward some excuses but nevertheless instructs the monkeys to go out in search of Sītā.

In the thirteenth canto, the events of the *Rāmāyaṇa* are summarised once again. However, the poet has made Sugrīva describe the panoramic view of mountain to Rāma, waiting on its peak for the return of Hanumat. In no time Hanumat descends from the sky to report about Sītā's detention at Lankā. Thereafter Rāma leads his combat-ready monkey army to the coast.

In the fourteenth canto, the epic narrative does not advance much. Their super-human task of building a causeway across the ocean is accomplished.

The fifteenth canto depicts an initiative for truce; Rāma sends Angada to Rāvaṇa with a proposal of peace and friendship with only one condition. That is, immediate release of Sītā. Angada does his best to persuade Rāvana for adopting the right course of action. But Rāvaṇa is too conceited to listen to such words from an ordinary mortal since he has conquered even the mighty gods; therefore, he dismisses the peace negotiation with characteristic haughtiness.

The sixteenth canto breathes in the typical world of court epics. There is a long description of evening, morning and night in Lankā; the Rāksasa youths are engrossed in amorous adventures. The depiction of elaborate preparation for a session of customary love-making cannot but remind us of the post-Bhāravi court epics. The demonesses send messengers to their lovers but ultimately discover with chagrin that their faith has been belied. The demon lovers betray their lack of integrity by being indiscriminately involved in erotic dalliances with other ladies and messengers. In the canto, Kumāradāsa seems to have temporarily lost sight of the narrative and continues with the description of drinking, music and merriment.

The seventeenth canto begins with the performance of ritual by both Rāma and Rāvaṇa before their plunging into battle. Rāvaṇa tries his best to inspire the demons by reminding them of their past glorious victories. But, in the long run, the demons are routed and driven back to Lankā by Rāma's monkey army. Rāvaṇa, therefore, asks his son, Indrajit, to join the battle. This canto is entirely rhymed which undoubtedly proves that the poet was closely acquainted with the contemporary tendencies in the compositional techniques of court epics in particular. The description of battle, which continues to the nineteenth canto, has been modelled on Bhāravi's style.

The eighteenth canto proves that Kumāraḍāsa is no less conversant with the dictum of poetics since he has made use of as many as eleven compositional techniques in narrating the fierce battle.[22] In this canto, Indrajit subdues Rāma and Lakṣmaṇa with his famous missile, the Nāgapāśa; however they are rescued by Garuda. Indrajit is ultimately killed and Rāvaṇa himself joins the battle. This canto provides us with many an editorial difficulties because of unsatisfactory textual readings.

The nineteenth canto depicts the final battle of Rāvaṇa with Rāma. After the death of the antagonist, the poet deals with Mandodarī's pitiful lament and Sītā's fire ordeal. The description of the final assault on Rāvaṇa deserves special mention.[23]

In the twentieth (i.e. concluding) canto, Rāma's aerial journey from Lankā to Ayodhyā has been described. On the way, Rāma draws Sītā's attention to different fascinating sights below. This is obviously influenced by the thirteenth canto of the *Raghuvamśa*. The epic ends with a sketchy narration of Rāma's return to Ayodhyā being closely followed by his coronation. The poet does not forget to note that Rāma was an ideal king who ruled for the welfare of his subjects. As we have already mentioned, Kumāradāsa has left out the last book of the *Rāmāyaṇa* from the orbit of his *Jānakīharaṇa*.

In the ultimate analysis, Kumāradāsa was a skillful craftsman whose creative passions were spent in maintaining the extrinsic epic structure and in making use of conventional materials. The poet had only limited talent and hence he could not chisel out any new path or innovatively rebuild an older path to poetic glory. Moreover, the lingering shadows of old masters like Kālidāsa and Bhāravi did not allow him to rise above the level of poetic mediocrity. Besides, in his fascination for sound effects, Kumāradāsa seems to have taken cue from Aśvaghoṣa though there is dissimilarity between the two particularly because the latter did not use rhyme. Kumāradāsa's metrical skill has been noted by many a critics; like Kālidāsa, he has preference for short musical metres while, at the same time, he also takes care not to venture beyond the metres used by Bhāravi. It is significant that Kumāradāsa is not an exhibitionist like Māgha. He avoids the uncommon and recondite rhythmic forms and tries his best to harmonise the metres with the situation according to subjectmatter and make the compositions pleasing for the readers.

Kumāradāsa has generally adhered to the Vaidarbhī school of style though the long compounds used by him do not augur well with this school.[24] Several examples of grammatical and lexicographical peculiarities can be coined from the *Jānakīharaṇa* some of which are distinctly un-Pāṇinian. The poet has generally made use of the well known figures of speech like Upamā, Rūpaka, Samāsokti, Anuprāsa, Yamaka etc.; he excells in Anuprāsa though their uses are limited. However, his imagery is generally complex and far-fetched.[25] This only confirms our earlier observation about the poet's inherent mediocrity, But, inspite of this limitation, he too had his silver lining. For example, the conversations of different characters in the *Jānakīharana* are straightforward, realistic and forceful. The individuality of Rāvaṇa and Indrajit has been neatly depicted. There are several instances of laboured expressions and genuine poetic sensibility interacting with each other which obviously take away much of his credit . In fact, this also shows that though Kumāradāsa did not try to transgress the frontiers of the *Rāmāyaṇa*, nevertheless he could not resist the temptations of a decadent society and adopted the populist literary methods. Inspiration had little relevance for him and hence he succumbed easily to the exacting demands of artificial poetry. Kālidāsa was never swept away by Puranic myths and knew how to extract symbolic significance out of such materials. Kumāradāsa, on the contrary, allowed his imagination to run riot in epic and used mythological materials almost ad absurdum.[26] Kumāradāsa's achievement may be summarised with the following word: "He is admirable but not excellent, learned but not pedantic, neat but not overdressed, easy but not simple. He has a gift of serviceable rhetoric and smooth prosody, but he is seldom brilliant and outstanding. He has a more than competent skill of pleasant expression, but he lacks the indefinable charm of great poetry."[27]

IV

Māgha, one of the most widely known poets in the realm of post-Bhāravi court epics, appears to have lived in the third quarter of the seventh or in the beginning of the eighth century. A.D. He is said to have been patronised by king Varmalāta who ruled in Śrīmāla in South western Rajasthan. His verses were quoted by Vāmana at the end of the eighth century and a little later ānandavardhana also quoted Māgha's verses in the middle of the ninth century A.D. This undoubtedly proves that Māgha was wellknown to the authors of poetics at least by the third quarter of the eight century. His fame rests on the epic entitled '*Śiśupālavadha*.' based on an episode in the second book of the *Mahābhārata*[28] in which the poet narrates the slaying of Śiśupāla, king of Cedi, by Kṛṣṇa at Indraprastha. It is interesting to note that according to the testimony of popular tradition, Māgha was appreciated essentially for his fanciful observation, melodious diction and, over and above, for his aptitude of a lyric poet. Those, who have preference for intellectual gymnastics, are fascinated by the abundance of grammatical and lexical peculiarities in Māgha's composition. But the poet is seldom objectively appreciated for his achievement as a composer of epic.

Though some words of hyperbolic praises have been haphazardly showered on Māgha, these are not supported by objective assessment and hence can hardly help a modern reader. However some of those statements may be recorded here.

(a) 'Mahākāvyeṣu Māghah kavih Kālidāsah':'Māgha's composition excels in the epic genre while Kālidāsa shines among the poets.'

(b) 'Tāvadhā bhāraverbhāti yāvanmāghasya nodayah':

'Bhāravi's poetic talent shines till Māgha does not rise'....

(c) 'Māghena vighnotsāhā notsāhante padakrame':

'Nobody shows any enthusiasm in composing verses after going through Māgha's poem.'

(d) 'Māghah śīśupālam vidadhat kavimadavadham vidhvatte': 'Māgha has wiped out the pride of all other poets by composing the *Śiśupālavadha.*'

(e) 'Upamā Kālidāsasya Bhāraverarthagauravam
Naisadhe padalālityam Māghe santi trayo gunāh':

'Kālidāsa excels in simile, Bhāravi shines in profundity of thought and Śrīharṣa in lucidity; but Māgha can boast of combining all these qualities in his poem'.

(f) 'Kṛtsnapravodhakṛdvānī bhāraveriva bhāraveh.

Māgheneva ca māghena kampah kasya na jāyate':

'As the rays of the sun illuminate all the objects, likewise Bhāravi's words make us understand the totality of the significance of the objects described. On the other hand, the excellence of Māgha's poem sends shivers to all the prospective poets just as the wintry month of Māgha brings about shivering for everybody.'

(g) 'Navasargagate Māghe navaśabdo na vidyate':

'After going though the first nine cantos of the Śiśupālavadha, no reader can find any 'new' word anywhere.'

Such extravaganza in the guise of criticism actually bespeaks of an extremely mechanistic approach to poetry in an ossified epoch when acrobatic skill was masquerading as creative art. This attitude was best summarised by Bhaṭṭi while he spoke about his poem, to which we have already referred.[29]

But we feel that it could also have been Māgha's own observation since he too believed in imposing extra-literary burden on his poem. In fact Māgha had no escape from the exacting demands of his epoch in which the poets' passage to posterity solely depended on the power elites residing at the alienated ivory towers of a stratified society. Yet our poet was not unaware of the basic tenets of creative sensibility.

This is indicated in the course of his observation about Mount Raivataka.:[30]

> 'Dṛṣto'pi śailah sa muhurmurārerapūrvavadvismaymātatāna
> Kṣaṇe Kṣaṇe yannavatāmupaiti tadevarūpam ramanīyatāyāh'

But this celebrated capacity for renewal of aesthetic feeling has not been properly manifested in the *Śiśupālavadha* itself. On the contrary, Māgha seems to contradict himself by causing serious hindrances to spontaneity of expression. In the name of composing an epic, the poet has actually constructed a huge literary structure with frankly utilitarian aims. Several difficult metrical schemes, tough and ill-executed figures of speech, extremely artificial word-arrangements have been employed unjudiciously. That is why the forward movement of the epic genre was arrested and the positive significance of its ever-renewing tradition was lost. The readers are required to cope with an uninteresting and monotonous mass of verses which lack inner cohesion and have neither fascinating diction nor intricate symmetry of feeling and expression. The subjectmatter is hopelessly lost in the midst of accumulated extrinsic materials and naturally there is absolutely no scope for portraying the development of any character.

The *Śiśupālavadha* is arranged in twenty cantos and the total number of its verses comes to 1625. Atleast half of those verses have no bearing with the theme of the epic. Though such verses are used as descriptive details, most often these seem to digress too much from even the given context. According to an eminent critic, this is the point where Māgha differs substantially from Bhāravi, his source of inspiration. Because, while Bhāravi could manage to let such extrinsic materials retain their umbilical cord with epic narrative, Māgha was indifferent to such an exigency. As a result more than half of the *Śiśupālavadha* has assumed the role of an anthology and the basic epic propensities have become hazy and secondary. Māgha begins his poem when preparations for performing the Rājasūya ritual by Yudhiṣthira are complete. The eldest Pāṇdava is to be ritually consecrated as emperor in order to make his regal status unassailable.

Bhīma has already killed Jarāsandha, the powerful monarch of Magadha as well as the potential arch-rival of the proposed Pāṇdava hegemony. The participation of loyal vassal rulers in the consecration ceremony is ensured by the Pāndavas through their conquest of four directions. But Śiśupāla, the king of Cedi, still remains as the thorn in flesh. Kṛṣṇa participates in the ritual as the major ally of the Pāndavas. The ceremony continues with usual splendour till a crisis develops. Bhīsma advises Yudhiṣṭhira to award the special offering for the most honoured man to Kṛṣṇa. Śiśupāla is infuriated and bitterly objects to this choice and leaves the assembly. Consequently a quarrel ensues in the course of which Śiśupāla insults Bhīsma and accuses Krsna of meanness. After sharp exchange of angry arguments, Kṛṣṇa can no longer endure Śiśupāla's insolence. The protagonist earlier promised to Śiśupāla's mother, who happened to be an aunt of the former, that he would forgive her son at least hundred times. But enough is enough and hence the protagonist feels that he is relieved of that pledge. Hence Kṛṣṇa kills the antagonist with his discus.

Thus Māgha glorifies Kṛṣṇa in a manner which cannot but remind us of Bhāravi who sought to honour Śiva through his epic. Here we can refer to the last of the five interpolated verses on which Vallabhadeva wrote commentaries but which were ignored by Mallinātha. Whatever might be its significance, the aforesaid verse reads thus:

> 'Śrīśabdaramyakṛta sargasamāptilaksma
> .....Lakṣmīpateścaritakīrtanacāru māghah
> Kāvyam Vyadhatta śiśupālavadhābhidhānam.'

Māgha commences his epic with the auspicious word 'Śrī' and, again, at the end of each canto he has used this word. Such usage is known as 'Kavibhāvakṛtacihna' and the *Śiśupālavadha* is described as 'śṛyanka.' This epic is another unique instance of the continuity of epic tradition under whose spell the latter poets try to emulate the idiosyncrasies of their predecessors and thereby attempt a renewal of the old master's creative urge. Thus the *Śiśupālavadha* appears to have been modelled on Bhāravi's *Kirātārjunīya*. Bhāravi, too, commenced his epic with the word 'Śrī' and at the end of each canto, he used the word 'Laksmī' which is a synonym of 'Śrī'.

Bhāravi found the outline of his epic narrative in the Vana Parvan of the *Mahābhārata* but expanded its extent by incorporating a series of descriptive passages; thus a tiny episode of the great epic had undergone a metamorphosis to become a full-length court epic of seventeen cantos. Likewise a small episode in the Sabhā Parvan of the *Mahābhārata* was turned into a full-length court epic of twenty cantos by Māgha. The theme of the *Śiśupālavadha* is comparatively simpler and has less incidents than that of the *Kirātārjunīya*. The processes, through which slenderness of the story was compensated and the initial simplicity was embellished by Māgha, were definitely inspired by Bhāravi. The *Kirātārjunīya* contains several speeches which are fashioned on various branches of human knowledge; likewise Māgha also fully exploited the opportunity to embark in poetic voyages into the realm of politics, ethics, panegyric etc. The erotic passages of the *Śiśūpālavādha* have also been deliberately modelled on Bhāravi's epic. In fact, the close parallelism between these two epics remind us of ānandavardhana's theory about literary imitation about which we have spoken earlier. As we know, he spoke about three types of imitation, viz. ālekhyaprakhya, Prativimbatulya and Tulyadehivat; but praised only the third as the genuine type of creative imitation. Māgha's indebtedness to Bhāravi may be explained with the conception of the above-mentioned type (i.e. Tulyadehivat) of imitation. It means that the *Śīśupālavadha* cannot be regarded as the reflection of the *Kirātārjunīya*. Ānandavardhana was aware of the basic individuality of creative personality; hence he observed:

> 'Samvādāste bhavantyeva vāhulyena sumedhasām
> Naikarūpatayā sarvete mantatā vipasitā.'[31]

This observation is pertinent in our discussion as well.

Even in the structural arrangement of the subjectmatter, Māgha follows Bhāravi faithfully. Nārada's visit to Kṛṣṇa with a message from Indra, urging the protagonist to kill the antagonist immediately, leads us to the epicentre of the *Śiśupālavadha*. This reminds us of Vyāsa's visit to Yudhisthira in *Kirātārjunīya* for inspiring the protagonist, Arjuna, to set out for the Himalayas with a view to propitiating Lord Śiva through penance. There is a council of war in both the epics. In Māgha's epic, Valadeva and Uddhava offer council to Kṛṣṇa in accordance with their own viewpoints while, in Bhāravi's poem, Draupadī and Bhīma confer with Yudhiṣthira. Uddhava's cautious approach bespeaks of his insight regarding statecraft while Bhīma's impetuousness in the *Kirātārjunīya* is dictated by similar pragmatic considerations. After the indication of subjectmatter is made, Bhāravi allowed his narrative to drift apart to digress into a disproportionate mass of descriptive materials which ate up as many as seven cantos. Likewise Māgha also forgot his commitment to the subjectmatter and allowed the narrative to practically remain motionless for no fewer than nine cantos while the poet indulged himself into the luxury of irrelevant descriptions of the mountain which occupy considerable space. Correspondingly in the *Śiśupālavadha*, there is a detailed account of Kṛṣṇa's journey to Indraprastha from Dvārakā in order to attend Yudhiṣthira's consecration and also prolonged description of the mount Raivataka that comes on the way.

Further, the attention of the readers is naturally drawn to the depiction of excessive amorous adventures of the Gandharvas and Apsarasas in Bhāravi's epic. Māgha seems to have become overenthusiastic on this count as he portrayed the almost endless erotic dalliances of the Yādavas with frolicking women. It is interesting to note that Māgha chooses to use the same metres[32] in most of these cantos as Bhāravi does in his epic. While narrating the battle in the fifteenth canto of the *Kirātārjunīya*, Bhāravi exhibits his capacity in verbal gymnastics by employing the ingenious devices known as Ekākṣarapāda,[33] Ekākṣara,[34] Dvyakṣara,[35] Ardhabhramaka,[36] Sarvatobhadra[37] etc. Likewise Māgha also exhibits his skill in literary acrobatics by taking resort to the form of construction known as citravandha in course of depicting the battle-seenes. The abovementioned devices have also been employed by him in the *Śiśupālavadha*. Besides, some details of the battle depicted by Bhāravi (e.g. Śiva's sending of messenger to Arjuna as a provocation, preparation for battle, march and description of actual battle) are also mirrored in Māgha's poem (e.g. Śiśupāla's messenger tries to provoke

Kṛṣṇa, preparations for battle are made, the soldiers set out for the battlefield and the contending armies clash with each other). Both Bhāravi and Māgha have first depicted the confrontation of the two armies and then they narrate the fierce single combat.

It is an indisputable fact that Māgha left no stones unturned to beat Bhāravi in his own game; he seems to have composed the *Śiśupālavadha* more with the intention to prove his excellence in craftsmanship and less out of any geruine creative urge. He sought to eclipse his predecessor and entered eagerly into a competition but his overzealousness proved to be his Achilles' heel. Māgha has quantified his requirements but he has failed to realise the basic fact about the regenerative quality of creative poetry. Thus, as a matter of casual information, we can only note here that Māgha displayed his willingness to surpass Bhāravi in making use of greater number of metres. For example, Māgha employs twenty four types of metres in the fourth canto of the *Śiśupālavadha* while Bhāravi uses sixteen metres in the fifth canto of the *Kirātārjunīya*. Many other details of composition like imagery, poetic diction, figures of speech etc. may also be equally taken into consideration. Māgha is undoubtedly as elegant and conscientious as Bhāravi on most occasions but his overenthusiasm swept him off balance. As a result some of the blemishes and mannerisms of the predecessor were exaggerated by Māgha with gay abandon. Bhāravi initiated elitism in the epic genre but gradually it was completely overshadowed by scholasticism. The contemporary rhetoricians, therefore, sought to standardise those overwhelming tendencies in literature. Bhāmaha said in the *Kāvyālamkāra*:

> 'Na sa śabdo na tad Vācyam na sa nyāyo na sā kalā
> Jāyate yanna Kāvyāngamaho bhāro mahān kaveh'.

Rājaśekhara prepared a syllabus as it were for the poets:[39]

> 'Śruti smrtih Itihāsah purānam pramānavidyā samayavidyā Rājasiddhāntatrayīloko viracanāprakīrnakam ca kāvyārthānām yonayah Ityācāryāh'.

Obviously, Māgha has outsmarted Bhāravi on this score because he could exhibit his scholarship in Veda, Purāṇa, Mīmāmsā, different schools of philosophy including those of the Jainism and the Buddhism, Astrology, Politics, Ethics, Grammar, Medical Science, Rhetorics, Musicology, Martial art etc.

Mallinātha therefore informs us in the introduction of his commentary entitled 'Sarvaṅkasā':

> 'Mallināthamudhīh so'yam mahāmahopādhyāyaśābdabhāk
> Vidhate māghakāvyasya Vyākhyām Sarvamkasābhidhām Ye
> Śabdārtha parīksanapranayino vā ye gunālamkriyā
> Śikṣākautukino vihartumanaso ye ca dhvāneradhvagāh
> Kṣubhyadbhāvatarangite rasasudhāpure mimamsanti ye
> Teṣāmeva kṛte karomi Vivṛtim māghasya sarvamkasām'.

The above statement becomes particularly significant when we understand that Mallinātha preferred not to talk about his scholarship in the commentary of any other poem. But the *Śiśupālavadha* demanded maximum attention from the commentator who, according to the opinion formulated by Rājaśekhara, belonged to the 'tattvābhinibeśi' category of readers. As we know, various contemporary critics sought to discover several points of excellence in Māgha's epic; besides the famous statement- 'Māge santi trayo guṇāh'-we come across the following hyperbolic observation:

> 'Durlabhā khalu kāvyesu ślokā daśagunairyutāh
> Bhaṭṭāveko raghau pañca māghe santi trayodaśa.'

Though it would seem to a modern reader to be an explanatory instance of Pāṇini's caution against talking of 'Śvānam Yuvānam maghavānam' at the same breath, the prevalent norms of criticism in the post-Bhāravi epoch inspired the commentators to search vigorously for the affirmation of the rhetorical dictums. Thus the ten gunas enumerated by Daṇḍin were discovered with satisfaction by a commentator in the *'Śiśupālavadha*: 'Ete gunāh prāyah sarve'pi atra kāvye santi eva'. Likewise Mallinātha also observed while commenting upon a particular verse:[40] 'Ślesah prasādah samatā mādhuryam sukumāratā Arthavyaktirudāratvamojah Kāntisamādhayah itaicāryoktā daśāgunāh prāyenātra sambhavantīti unneyāh.' Besides such adherence to the dictums of poetics, the critics were happy to note that the principal aesthetic experience in the *Śiśupālavadha* was heroic and that the protagonist of the epic was a wellknown personality. It was also observed with satisfaction that the epic exhibited four cardinal aims of life and so forth.

Let us now have a quick resume of the epic. In the first canto, the readers are introduced to the subjectmatter at the very beginning. The very first verse of the epic declares its loyalty to poetics by serving the purpose of 'Vastunirdeśa'. We understand that Krsna, the protagonist, is no ordinary man; he is not only the perfectmost incarnation of lord Viṣṇu, he is clearly stated as the supreme god himself. It means that Māgha flourished in an age when the conception of incarnation as a special feature of the Viṣṇu-Kṛṣṇa hierophany had attained wide approval. In the *Śiśupālavadha*, Kṛṣṇa is therefore totally different from other epic heroes and its indication is given in the opening verse of the epic. He rises above the level of ordinary culture hero and becomes the saviour who fights against the forces of evil. Thus Śiśupāla, the antagonist, is equated with Rāvaṇa and Hiraṇyakasipu. Nārada, the divine sage, arrives at the city of Dvārāvati with a message from Indra to Kṛṣṇa. Thus the poet finds an opportunity to directly plunge into Puranic account under the pretext of narrating the conversation of Kṛṣṇa and Nārada. The sage reminds the protagonist of his earlier incarnations in which various demons were exterminated for saving the tormented worlds. As Śiśupāla is tormenting the entire creation, his menacing presence should now be wiped out. Nārada prays to Kṛṣṇa to act again as the saviour.

The second canto unfolds a human dimension in Kṛṣṇa's divine personality since he is in a fix. As a pragmatic hero, he has to decide whether he should march immediately against Śiśupāla or he should attend the consecration ceremony at Indraprastha in order to honour the invitation by Yudhiṣṭhira. Therefore, he seeks counsel from Uddhava and Balarāma. The situation endows the poet with an opportunity to exhibit his knowledge of ethics and statecraft. Balarāma is drunk and impatient; he impetuously advocates for launching an immediate assault on Śiśupāla. He cites profusely from the science of politics to support his viewpoint. Then Uddhava speaks intelligently and requests for exercising caution for greater interest. He is polite but firm in criticising Balarāma's opinion. According to him, nothing should be done injudiciously at that juncture which might upset the Rājasūya rite. An attack against Śiśupāla would distract his allies from the ceremony and victory might be elusive. On the contrary, all the kings should be persuaded for joining the ritual at Indraprastha where a jealous and quarrelsome Śiśupāla might himself provide an opportunity that Krsna was looking for. Uddhava also exhibits his deep knowledge of statecraft; Krsna approves this plan of action. This canto has a few interesting aphorisms.

In fact, Māgha seems to have maintained a quota of aphorisms and wisecracks for every canto while some of these may be regarded as his idiosyncratic expressions; most often these add unnecessary burden to the already crippled narrative.[41]

Uddhava's speech contains a verse that actually bespeaks of the poet's opinion about good poetry:

> 'Mradīyasīmapi ghanāmanalpa-gunakalpitām
> Prasārayanti Kuśalāścitrām vācam patamiva'[42]

Indeed we cannot but feel that throughout the *Śiśupālavadha*, Māgha has sought to exemplify the abovementioned 'Citrām Vācam'.

In the third canto, Kṛṣṇa set out for Indraprastha along with the Yādava army. The poet has drawn a fascinating verbal picture of Krsna at the outset which is replete with literary cliches and Puranic allusions.[43] This is immediately followed by a customary description of the city of Dvārāvatī[44] and march of the Yādava army.[45] As we have already noted, Māgha shows his expertise in constructing a careful mosaic structure with grandiloquent diction. To use his own words, the exterior of the epic becomes, as it were, 'Prativimvitāngāh Sajīvacitrā iva ratnabhittīh'[46] while the interior is lost sight of.

In the fourth canto, Mount Raivataka is fancifully depicted; in the beginning of the canto, beauty of the mountain is seen through the eyes of the protagonist[47] and then it is described by Dāruka, his charioteer.[48] Nothing else happens, even there is no second object to describe. But Māgha tries to compensate for the lack of matter by resorting to eroticism tirelessly. It is not even the mountain that really matters, the poet needs only a pretext to exhibit his ingenuity. As we have noted elsewhere, Māgha's famous expression about the basic feature of beauty is found here.[49] Besides Māgha's tendency towards constructing far-fetched imagery is also evident in this canto.[50]

But Māgha has won for himself the widely known sobriquet 'Ghantāmāgha' because of his extraordinary fanciful composition of the following verse:

> 'Udayati vitatordhvaraśmi-rajjāvahimarucau himadhāgni yāti cāstam
> Vahati igirayam vilambighaṇṭādvaya-parivārivārita-vāranendralīlām.'[51]

This canto is noteworthy for Māgha's metrical skill as well. It also draws our attention to the fact that the poet has consciously tried to surpass his idol i.e. Bhāravi. Because Bhāravi used nineteen types of metres in the fourth canto of the *Kirātārjunīya* while Māgha has used as many as twenty three metres in the fourth canto (the coincidence may not be accidental) of the *Śiśupālavadha*.

In the fifth canto, Kṛṣṇa decides to camp there and enjoy the beauty of the mountain. Māgha goes on to describe elaborately the moving army with all paraphernalia, the womenfolk of the royal seraglio, the chariots, the elephants, the horses and mares, the cows and bulls, the camels. The soldiers and ladies take bath; afterwards the animals are also washed thoroughly. The poet has added some details pertaining to the Sṛngāra Rasa here and there. In fact, inspite of his allegiance to the dictums of poetics, the poet deserves much credit for his eagerness for realistic details in this canto. Though in some cases the poet may seem to hurt modern taste with inappropriate grotesqueness bordering on perversion, the silver linings in the midst of conventional cliched materials should not be ignored. There are some stray instances of pure humour as well in some of which the Puranic allusions have been given a new lease of life.[52]

In the sixth canto, all the seasons appear simultaneously at Raivataka apparently for Kṛṣṇa's pleasure but actually for the benefit of the poet to enable him to exhibit the extent of his fanciful descriptive power. It is obviously full of cliches associated with monotonous eroticism; warmth of feeling is never to be expected. Likewise the question of relevance with the epic narrative does not arise at all. Moreover, the poet's total lack of self-restraint is evident from the fact that he has repeated the description of different seasons at the end of the canto. Occasionally we come across somewhat off-beat expressions though not wholly distinctive craftsmanship in constructing images.[53]

The seventh canto is practically a poetic feast of overwhelming eroticism that cannot but remind us of Vātsyāyana's *Kāmasūtra*. The Yādava youths indulge in the ecstasy of carnal pleasure in the company of their consorts. The perverse display of extravagant sensuousness in the forest of the Raivataka has nothing to do with Krsna, the protagonist; this is definitely an important departure from Bhāravi's epic where the voluptuousness of the nymphs had at least a semblance of relevance with the protagonist, Arjuna, whose integrity was put to severe test by such eroticism. This also means that Māgha was totally engrossed in depicting conventional materials being completely detached from the epic narrative with the sole aim of catering to the demand of the leisurely power elites. Obviously the womenfolk of that epoch were hopelessly subjected to the whims of dominating male chauvinists. The women are no individual beings; they are physically attractive and ever ready to surrender to the passions of their seducers. No essential difference is discernible among the behaviour-patterns of queens, lady messengers, nameless damsels, harlots, nymphs etc. All of them act like the call girls enumerated in Vātsyāyana's *Kāmasūtra*. The women earlier did have social prestige; their steady descent downhill was first clearly recorded by Bhāravi, while in Māgha's epic, the women seemed to have reached the bottom of the dark inferno.

There does not seem to be any tension in this canto (also in the next four) between what is expressed and how it is expressed. The poet knew well as to how the stereotyped elitist demand for pleasure with elegance, beauty and luxury could be met. The fortunate few at the royal courts have to be amused with the stock-in-trades of the poets repeated ad nauseam. Māgha's limitations were actually the inescapable limitations of his static society under whose relentless pressure he could not ever think of being the poet of the Body and the poet of the Soul at the sametime. In fact, in Indian tradition, love in man has been generally regarded as foible while for woman it is a chattel. It is therefore natural for Māgha to harp on the string of an established notion.[54] In fact five cantos of the *Śiśupālavadha* (i.e. from seventh to eleventh) have presented hardly any new idea: these scarcely describe any situation or emotion which have not been familiarized in Indian literary tradition in general and in the epic tradition in particular. The poet has no other alternative but to exhibit his skill in as many ways as possible. The whole attitude and training of Māgha was such that the notion of using poetry to express his own private feelings, even while depicting love, did not ever occur to him. Hence it is not without reason that a critic has made the well-known comment, 'Sanskrit love-verse are verses about love, not the verses of a lover.' Even that love is also unabashedly physical in which feminine body is the cynosure of poetic description. The erotic extravagances at the forest of the Raivataka (seventh canto) during watersports in lake (eighth), at dusk and evening (ninth), during night (tenth) and in the morning (eleventh) may be referred to. Obviously, these materials are absolutely extrinsic for the epic narrative though the poet shows his skill as a craftsman to his heart's content.

These cantos were favourite hunting grounds for rhetoricians simply because these contained, as it were, descriptive catalogue of epic paraphernalia. These include lovemaking in forest, sketches of various kinds of seducing women, women plucking flowers, chirping birds, humming bees in the midst of creepers and trees (Canto vii); sunset, advancing evening, women engaged in toilet, moonrise, sending of messengers to the lovers, beginning of another session of love-making (canto ix); drinking and wanton love-making at night (Canto x); Dawn, lovers awakening from exhausted slumber with the tune of customary bardic song (Canto xi). Inspite of such display of artifice, occasionally we come across some commendable imagery.[55]

Besides, as an astonishingly refreshing expression, the following verse has something very special about it (particularly in the backdrop of suffocating parade of endless cliches):

> Na vibhāvayatyanisamakṣigatāmapi
> Mām bhavānatisamīpatayā
> Hrdayasthitāmapi punah paritah
> Kathamīkṣate bahirabhīstatamām.[56]

At last, in the twelfth canto, the movement of the epic narrative is resumed as Kṛṣṇa prepares to begin his journey towards Indraprastha along with multitudes of elephants, horses, other beasts of burden and the accompanying women. This canto is full of realistic descriptions some of which are particularly praiseworthy.[57] Though the poet has made use of Puranic allusions to prove his scholarship, the attention of the readers is focused on the detailed description of the march of the Yādava army through the terrains of Mount Raivataka till they reach the bank of the river Yamunā and then cross it by boat. On his way, Kṛṣṇa comes across the women of a village of cowherds. This reminds us of a similar description in the second canto of the *Bhaṭṭikāvya*.

In the thirteenth canto, Kṛṣṇa enters the city of Indraprastha and is received by Yudhisthira and other Pāndavas; Kṛṣṇa's army was equally felicitated by the Pāndava army while the Yādava ladies were greeted by the women of the Pāndava capital. The women of the city become restless after having a look at Kṛṣṇa and the poet gets an opportunity to construct interesting figures of speech.[58] Kṛṣṇa arrives at the royal court of Indraprastha and begins conversation with Yudhisthira after being properly seated. The fantastic architecture of the court is also described in between; incident of humiliation of a bewildered Duryodhana along with its disastrous consequence has been casually referred to. Besides, Purāṇic myths have been extensively used in this canto.

In the beginning of the fourteenth canto, Yudhiṣthira eulogises Kṛṣṇa and seeks his permission to commence the Rājasūya ritual. Kṛṣṇa promises solid support through his speech fraught with political significance. The commencement of the ritual is then described in elaborate details. The poet has made extensive use of mythic allusions throughout the canto. At the end of the ritual, Bhīsma makes speech eulogising Kṛṣṇa and suggests to Yudhisthira that the only person worthy of receiving the special offering is none other than Kṛṣṇa. Bhīsma also alludes to various incarnations of Viṣṇu. The canto comes to an end after Yudhisthira makes the special offering to Kṛṣṇa. Māgha's idiosyncratic expressions are quite frequent here.[59]

The fifteenth canto begins with an ornamental depiction of Śiśupāla's anger.[60] He speaks out to lodge a furious protest against the act of special offering to Kṛṣṇa.[61] In his reply, Bhīsma challenges any one who might dare to oppose the honour shown to Kṛṣṇa.[62] The protagonist however remains unmoved as he is promise-bound to forgive the antagonist at least a hundred times. Māgha then goes on to record the angry reaction of the allies of Śiśupāla.[63] The antagonist makes a ferocious speech inflicting insult on Bhīsma, Kṛṣṇa and the Pāndavas.[64] Then this is followed by customary descriptions of preparation for battle, the warriors taking leave of their spouses (providing the poet with another opportunity to exhibit his erotic obsession) and bad omens.[65]

In the sixteenth canto, Śiśupāla sends a messenger to Kṛṣṇa with arrogant challenge.[66] But the message is an example of extreme artifice since it is throughout ambiguous and, in fact, purposefully worded to carry double meanings at the same time. Thus the envoy's speech may be interpreted as an apologetic and courteous proposal for truce on the one hand and an impudent declaration of war on the other. Though such a parade of ambiguity is indicative of Māgha's mastery over play of words, it is also an unfortunate evidence of his total lack of sensibility and discretion. Being a willing slave to a cut and dried literary convention, he had failed to realise that in the most critical juncture of the story, his indulgence in verbal acrobatics is not only aesthetically incongruous but also signifies irretrievable literary blemish. Māgha has completely ignored the obvious demand of the situation. However, Sātyaki correctly understands the design behind such ambiguous message and, rebuking Śiśupāla for his meanness and arrogance, calls upon the envoy to be specific. He made it clear that otherwise such message would be treated with contempt.[67]

Then the messenger makes a long speech with which this canto comes to its end.[68] He asks Krsna to choose one meaning from the message delivered and haughtily praises his master, Śiśupāla and condemns Kṛṣṇa. His speech is full of cliches, wisecracks, mythical allusions and linguistic stocks-in-trades.

The seventeenth canto begins with the depiction of angry reaction of the allies in Kṛṣṇa's camp at the harsh message of the antagonist delivered through his messenger.[69] It is immediately followed by a large-scale preparation for the impending battle.[70] This includes the description of the Yādava commanders in arms, the spirited combat drill of Kṛṣṇa's army with trumpets, chariots, elephants and horses. The beginning of confrontation between two rival armies is then depicted with exaggerated use of cliches.[71] The poet's obsession for Śrngāra rasa has carried him too far; its undue intrusion in this canto has caused literary blemish.[72]

The eighteenth canto depicts a fierce battle between the two armies with usual exaggerated details. The poet has devoted as many as thirty two verses to describe the role of elephants in that battle.[73] But in the ultimate analysis the describtions have been employed their own sake only because being totally impersonal academic escercise, they do not serve any opuropose in accelerating the pace of the epic narrative. Besides Māgha's unrestrained fascination for overstretched fancy has remained unabated throughout the canto.[74]

In the nineteenth canto, the poet narrates single combats between prominent warriors.[75] Then he goes on to exhibit verbal acrobatics ne plus ultra in which his conscious endeavour to outsmart Bhāravi has been manifested. The fierce battle between the rival infantries, cavalries and particularly the warriors on elephants has been described through several complicated devices.[76] In fact, this canto is known as a typical example of citrakāvya. But due to overemphasis on such devices, the conception of creative poetry has become irrelevant and along with it, the poet has shirked off even his basic responsibility towards the epic narrative.[77]

But it suffices to observe here that such excesses of verbal gymnastics have succeeded only in driving the last nail in the coffin of epic poetry. Māgha's intention becomes clear when we note that he himself has compared some extraordinary verse forms with the formation of an army:

> 'Visamam sarvatobhadracakragomūtrikādibhih
> Ślokairiva mahākāvyam vyuhaistadabhavadvalam.'[78]

Likewise, the poet's obsession for exhibiting his wide range of knowledge has been manifested in his references to grammar.[79]

Kṛṣṇa arrives at the battle when Śiśupāla was showing his prowess to the Yādava army. The poet[80] draws a customary penpicture of Kṛṣṇa's divine personality and then concludes this canto with the conventional elaborate description of the protagonist's unique heroism at the battle.[81]

The twentieth canto marks the end of the epic poem in which the final terrible battle between Kṛṣṇa and Śiśupāla is narrated. The antagonist tries his best to fight with diverse supernatural missiles but all these are effectively countered by the protagonist. When Śiśupāla uses abusive language against Kṛṣṇa,[82] the latter beheads the former with his famous discus, the Sudarśana.[83]

While concluding our discussion about the *Śiśupālavadha*, we cannot say that the episode of the *Mahābhārata* has been creatively renewed by Māgha. It is well-nigh impossible to claim that the undermentioned critical opinion regarding transcreation of traditional materials is applicable to this court epic as well:

> 'Dṛṣṭapūrvā api hyarthāh Kāvye rasaparigrahāt
> Sarve navā ivābhānti madhumāsa ivadrumāh.'[84]

Māgha is indeed the champion of an imitative and reproductive epoch of Sanskrit epic poetry in which there is abundance and variety of efforts in epic composition but nevertheless it is plagued with signs of inescapable exhaustion, recurring dreariness and interminable prolixity.

NOTES

1. *Mahābhārata*. iii. 27-41. (Bombay edition)
2. *Kirātārjunīya*. xviii. 48.
3. *ibid*. ix. 24,61,69.
4. *ibid*. ii. 26; also ii. 27.
5. *ibid*. v. 39.
6. *ibid*. viii. 27.
7. *ibid*. ix. 3, 32.
8. The following verses are widely known:

   i) 'Sa Sāsih Sāsusüh sāso
   Yeyāyeyā-yayāyayah
   lalau līlām lalo'lolah
   Sasisasisusih sasan' (xv. 5)

   ii) 'Na nonanunno nunnono nānā nānānanā nanu
   nunno' nunno nanunneno nānenā nunnanunnanut' (xv. 14)

   iii) 'Nisitāsirato'bhikonyejate' maranārucā
   sārato na virodhi na svābhāso bharavān uta' (xv. 22)

   iv) 'Tanuvārabhaso Bhāsvān adhiro' vinatorasā, cārunā ramate janye ko' bhito rasitāsini' (xv. 23)
9. Madhurāvijaya. i. 9.
10. Suvṛtta-tilaka, iii. 4.
11. Bhaṭṭikāvya, xxii. 33.
12. *ibid*. ii. 16.
13. *ibid*. ii. 18
14. *ibid*. ii. 19
15. *ibid*. i. 6, ii.39, v.18, vi.13, xii.9, xii.46. etc.
16. *ibid*. vi. 43

17. *ibid.* vi. 140
18. *ibid.* canto xviii.
19. *ibid.* iii. 51-56, v. 65.
20. *ibid.* iii. 43
21. *Rāmāyaṇa* (Bombay edition, vii. 31-33)
22. These include the following: Ślesa of various kinds, Ādiyamaka, Dvyakṣarayamaka, Samudrayamaka, Citravandha of various forms (e.g. Gūḍhacaturthaka, Jālaka, cakra, kavināmānkita, cakravākavrta etc.)
23. xix. 19-30.
24. e.g., 'bihaganāthavitīrṇaparabhava-prabhavakopavikam pita cetasah' (xi.4) 'Avamagnasivah Kapālaḍrgvivaraprodgatasadvalah' (iv. 55) etc.
25. e.g. x. 44, 81; xi. 12. etc.
26. e.g. xiv. 16, 46.
27. Dey S.K.: *History of Sanskrit Literature*, Calcutta, 1947, p. 188.
28. *Mahābhārata.* ii (Sabhā parvan). Chap. 33-42.
29. *Bhaṭṭikāvya.* xxii. 34.
30. *Śiśupālavadha.* iv. 17.
31. *Dhvanyāloka* iv. 11.
32. e.g. Praharsinī and Svāgata
33. *Kirātārjunīya.* xv. 5.
34. *ibid.* xv. 14
35. *ibid.* xv.38.
36. *ibid.* xv. 27.
37. *ibid.* xv. 25.
38. *Śiśupālavadha.* xix. 3(Ekākṣarapāda); xix. 114 (Ekākṣara); xix. 66, 84, 86 (Dvyakṣara), xix. 71 (Ardhabhramaka); xix. 27 (Sarvatobhadra)
39. Kāvyamīmāmsā. viii.
40. Sisupālavadha. xi. 19.
41. Some of these aphorisms and wisecracks, probably designed to obviate the monotony of immobile narrative, are certainly memorable; but generally these are pedantic and smack of artificiality and shallow philosophising tendency. An elaborate catalogue of examples may be prepared as follows:

i) 'Mahīyāmsah prakṛtyā mitabhāṣiṇah' (ii. 13).

ii) 'Anyaducchrmkhalam sattvamanyacchāstraniyantritam Sāmānādhikaranyam hi tejastimirayoh kutah' (ii. 62)

iii) 'Ārabhante'lpamevajñah kāmam vyagrābhavanti ca Mahārambhāh krtadhiyastisthanti ca nirākulāh' (ii. 79)

iv) 'Nāvalambate daistikatām na nisīdati pauruṣe/Sabdārthau satkaviriva dvayam vidvānapeksate' (ii. 86)

v) 'Vṛhatsahāyah kāryāntam kṣodīyānapi gacchati Sambhüyāmbhodhimabhyeti mahānadyā nagāpagā' (ii. 100)

vi) 'Anekaśah samstutamapyanalpā /Navam navam prītiraho karoti' (iii. 31)

vii) 'āsāditasya tamasā niyaterniyogād/ākāmksatah punarapakrameṇa na kālam' (iv. 34)

viii) 'Sarvohi nopagatamapyapacīyamānam/Varddhiṣṇumāśrayam-anāgatambhyupaiti' (v. 14)

ix) 'Samharṣiṇā saha gunābhyadhikairdurāsam' (v. 19)

x) 'Mando' pināma na mahānavagṛhya sādhyah' (v. 49)

xi) 'Samaya eva karoti valāvalam pranigadanta itīva śarīriṇām' (vi. 44)

xii) 'Paribhavo' ribhavo hi suduhsahah' (vi. 45)

xiii) 'Upaciteṣu paresvasamarthatām vrajati Kālavaśādvalavānapi' (vi. 63)

xiv) 'Unnatānāmanugamane khalu sampado' gratasthāh' (vii. 27)

xv) 'Kulānyalīnām na paricayo malinātmanām pradhānam' (vii. 61)

xvi) 'śobhāya vipadi sadāśritā bhavanti' (viii. 55)

xvii) 'Pratikülatāmupagate hi bidhau viphalatvameti vahusādhanatā' (ix. 6)

xviii) 'Laghavah prakatībhavanti malināśrayatah' (ix. 23)

xix) 'Bhrāntibhāji bhavati kva vivekah' (x. 5)

xx) 'Niyativiṣayavrtterapyanalpapratāpa-ksata-sakalavipakṣas tejasah sa svabhāvah' (xi. 59)

xxi) 'Madamüdhabuddhisu vivekitā kutah' (xiii. 6)

xxii) 'Mahatīmapi śriyamavāpya vismayah/sujano na vismarati jātu kiñcana' (xiii. 68)

xxiii) 'Aho dayitam janah khalu guṇīti manyate' (xv. 11).

xxiv) 'Satyaniyatavacasam vacasā sujanam janāścalayitum ka īsate' (xv. 40)

xxv) 'Vacanena kim bhavatu sādhyasādhuvā' (xv. 65)

xxvi) 'Sahajāndhadrśah svadurnaye paradose ksanadivyacaksusah. Svagunoccagiro munivratāh paravarnagrahanesvasādhavah' (xvi. 29)

xxvii) 'Anapekṣya guṇāguṇau janah svarucim niścayato' nudhāvati' (xvi. 44)

xxviii) 'Parāṇamī yadapavadanta ātmanah stuvanti ca sthitirasatāmasāviti' (xvii. 19)

42. *ibid.* ii. 74.
43. *ibid.* iii. 2-23
44. *ibid.* iii. 32-64
45. *ibid.* iii. 65-82.
46. *ibid.* iii. 46.
47. *ibid.* iv. 1-17.
48. *ibid.* iv. 19-68
49. *ibid.* iv. 17.
50. *ibid.* iv. 59.
51. *ibid.* iv. 20
52. *ibid.* v. 66.
53. In constructing images, Māgha proves himself to be a craftsman for whom deliberate artifice is more important than spontaneous art; for example:

    a) 'Sphutamivajjvalakāncanakāntibhir-yutamaśokamaśobhata campakaih Virahiṇāmhrdayasyabhidābhṛtah kapisitam pisitam madāgninā' (ibid. vi. 5)

    b) 'Vigatavāridharāvaranāh Kvaciddadrśurullasitāsilatāsitah Kvacidivendragajājinakañcukāh śaradi nīradinīryadavo diśah' (ibid. vi. 51)

54. cf. 'The woman is, indeed, an object of the senses (indriyārtha), an instrument of pleasure—she is merely one among the needs of life, such as a seat, a bed, a vehicle, a house, a corn etc.' G.G. Meyer, *Sexual Life in Ancient India*, London, 1930, p. 531.

55. (a) 'Sthagistāmbarakṣititale paritasTimire janasya dṛśamandhayati Dadhire rasānjanamapūrvamatah Priyavesma vartma sudṛśo dadṛśuh' (ibid. ix. 21)

(b) 'Navacandrikāusumakīmatamah Kavarībhrto malayajāri dramiva dadṛs'e lalatatata-hari/ harer carito mukhe tuhinaraśmidalam' (ibid. ix. 28)

(c) 'Animiṣamavirāmā rāginām sarvarātram
Navanidhuvanalīlah Kautukenātivīkṣya
Idamudavasitānāmasphutalokasampannayana
Miva sanidram ghūrṇate daipamarcih' (ibid. xi. 18)

(d) 'Kumudavanamapaśri śrīmadambhojasandam
Tyajati mudamulūkah prītimāmścakravākah
Udayamahimaraśmiryāti sitāmśurastam
Hatavidhilasitānām hī vicitro vipākah' (ibid. xi. 64)

56. *ibid.* ix. 81.

57. e.g. *ibid.* xii. 5-6.-, 9-10, 21, 25,32,37-42,54,59,73-75.

58. *ibid.* xiii. 22., 38. 61.

In fact, ornamental expressions are interspersed throughout the epic. Thus we come across the following verses.

e.g., xv. 12, 51, 60, 90; xvii. 9, 15, 17, 29, 52, 68; xx. 14, 18, 33, 44, 71, 75.

59. *ibid.* xiv. 3., 7, 46,50,66.

60. *ibid.* xv. 1-12

61. *ibid.* xv. 13-38

62. *ibid.* xv. 44-46.

63. *ibid.* xv. 47-61.

64. *ibid.* xv. 62-66.

65. *ibid.* xv. 72-96.

66. *ibid.* xvi. 2-15.

67. *ibid.* xvi. 17-37.

68. *ibid.* xvi. 39-85.

69. *ibid.* xvii. 2-19.

70. *ibid.* xvii. 20-43.

71. *ibid.* xvii. 44-69.

72. *ibid.* xvii. 25, 43, 48, 66.

    Such intrusion is also evident elsewhere; for example, *ibid.* xviii. 2, 60.

    Even in the midst of depicting a raging battle in the nineteenth canto, Māgha resorts to such eroticiṣm; e.g. xix. 61., 85.

73. *ibid.* xviii. 6,10,24,26-51,56-58.

74. *ibid.* xviii. 8,35,69,72,75.

75. e.g. between Valarāma and Benudārī (xix. 1-6); Unmūka and Druma (*ibid*:8): Rukmī and Pṛthu (*ibid*:9) as well as Pradyumna destroying the enemy (*ibid*: 10-23) including his victory over Bāṇa (*ibid*: 14) and Uttamauja (*ibid*: 16),

76. *ibid.* xix. 25-81.

77. e.g. *ibid.* xix. 3 , 27, 29, 40, 44, 46, 58, 60, 66, 72, 84, 86, 94, 98, 100, 102, 104, 106, 108, 114.

78. *ibid.* xix. 41.

79. *ibid.* xix. 75, 103

80. *ibid.* xix. 83-90

81. *ibid.* xix. 91-120.

82. *ibid.* xx. 77.

83. *ibid.* xx. 78

84. Dhvanyāloka. iv. 4.

6

Epics of Art: The Descent

Bhaṭṭi and Māgha were the sole arbiters of literary taste for the later generations of versifiers. In the name of composing epics, the later poets tirelessly built up some dazzling counterfeits of poetry which had no pretension towards preparing any human document. Under the pretext of composing an inadequate and unsubstantial narrative, the versifiers were only too busy to search for a convenient outlet through which they could pour forth all the tricks in exhibiting scholarly ingenuity and technical skill in producing monotonously repetitive tour de force of rhetorical cunning. Those court epics may therefore be regarded as industrious monuments of verbal gymnastics which accommodated a prodigious amount of pedantry and succeeded in building a curious mosaic of futility and extravaganza. Māgha's successors were deeply entrenched in the quicksand of conventional artifice and pseudo-classicism while they remained completely aloof from the pulsating life around. Its inevitable outcome was the abundant reproduction of laborious trifles in the form of huge epics in which there was no sign of individual talent. In their conscientious efforts to adher to the rigidly fixed rhetorical norms, the versifiers had never developed the conception of progressive unfoldment of a central theme. Likewise the later epic poems had little variation of the general scheme, method, subjectmatter and style. Consequently those poems are storehouses of mannerism in which emphasis is never put on genuine inspiration, judgement based on creative imagination and penetrative spontaneity. S.K. De rightly observed, 'The greatest of them is scarcely a poet at all, but a consummate versifier, who sums up all the traditions of poetic art that can be learned by a clever artisan.'[1]

In spite of occasional flashes and sparks from the accumulated embers of rhetorical extravaganza and intellectual gymnastics, the absence of redeeming poetic imagination sealed the fate of the epic genre. It is interesting to note that various schools of poetics flourished in the eighth and ninth centuries; in fact, in the subsequent centuries, minutest details were incorporated and analysed with reinforced enthusiasm. But, during that period, the epic genre continuously went downhill; nothing could regenerate it anymore. Though various branches of science and philosophy, Smrticodes and theological texts, major and minor Purāṇas as well as architecture, sculpture and music developed, the processes of ossification of the essentially barren feudal society remained unassilable. Literature sought to be faithful to that society which was suffering from the inescapable ailments due to progressive loss of centre and falling apart of values. From tenth century onwards, regional vernaculars were fast assuming linguistic characters of their own and consequently attaining the essential maturity for being fit for the media of creativity. On the other hand, Sanskrit was no longer intelligible to the common people and instead it had already become an exclusively guarded property of the handful power elites. For those top echelons of the decadent society, literature had no meaning if it could not amuse them. Being completely alienated from the pulsating life of the people, they did not care for feeling or imagination; even pretension of intellectual acrobatics was enough to satisfy their ego. Hence the creative fire that sustained the epic genre, through the vales and meadows in its chequered course, was finally extinguished.

The epic versifiers of the post-Māgha epoch lacked in passion and imagination; therefore they tried to compensate by laborious imitation of pedantry, rhetorical details and stereotyped forms. Originality was beyond those ambitious poetasters, even they did not have any courage to experiment. They enjoyed morbid satisfaction, as it were, if they could imitate the literary etiquette established by the old masters of the genre in general and Bhāravi, Bhatti and Māgha in particular. It has been rightly observed. "Marvellous erudition goes hand in hand with marvellous refining of trivialities. The lost art of an earlier generation is thereby not revived, nor is a new art created out of its ashes, but the accumulated resources become the means of parade and dexterity."[2]

II

Rājānaka Ratnākara, also known as 'Vāgīśvara' and 'Vidyāpati, wrote a huge epic entitled the *Haravijaya*, consisting of 50 cantos in the ninth century A.D.[3] Though the poet says that he has imitated Bāna, actually he has exaggeratingly echoed the negative features of Bhāravi and Māgha. However, the influence of the *Śiśupālavadha* is much greater on Ratnākara's prodigal exhibition of ingenuity. The theme of the poem is the killing of the demon, Andhaka, by Siva. The demon is actually a son of Śiva himself who is born blind but later he regains his eyesight through penance and begins tormenting the three worlds. Being unable to bear his torture any more, six seasons appeal to Śiva to restrain the demon. Śiva sends a message to Andhaka for withdrawing from the occupied provinces but the demon haughtily turns down the proposal. Śiva sends his army; a fierce battle takes place and ultimately Andhaka is killed. On the basis of the meagre outlines of such a commonplace and uncomplicated Puranic story, Ratnākara has constructed a huge epic structure of fifty cantos by amassing verses as decorative devices with astonishing assiduity.

The poet seems to have left no stones unturned for incorporating descriptions of different types prescribed by the rhetoricians. Thus we come across practically endless display of erudition; for instance, knowledge of Ethics and Politics has been depicted in ten cantos (from viii-xvi). Besides there are conventional details about Mount Kailāśa. Then the next thirteen cantos (xvii-xxix) are devoted to further customary details which include sunset,evening, moonrise, encampment of the army, erotic dalliances etc. In fact, the twenty ninth canto seems to be replete with illustrations of the points enumerated in the Kāmasūtra. Thereafter the preparations of the army for the impending battle are spread over four cantos. When the army actually arrives, Ratnākara becomes busy in describing Andhaka's kingdom; messages and counter-messages before the commencement of the battle occupy as many as seven cantos. Ultimately the battle takes place; the poet manages to describe it in four cantos. Before Andhaka is killed, a hymn to Goddess Caṇḍī is inserted in the forty seventh canto. The poet does not forget the puerile verse formations as well; hence the forty eighth canto is composed according to the citravandha formation.

The *Haravijaya* is a stupendous exercise in futility; it is indeed one of the most representative poems of the exhausted genre. It is thoroughly conditioned and regulated by the characteristic features of a dissipated scholastic phase of mechanistic and trivial elaboration. Moreover, Ratnākara had little talent though his ambition was enormous; he had neither sensibility nor judgement. As a result, he had laboriously constructed totally disproportionate monument of unrefined verses. There is hardly any trace of oasis in the limitless desert of verbiosity. The monotonously prolonged ornamental descriptions bespeak of Ratnākara's preference for all the negative idiosyncratic traits of the earlier epic compositions. There are exhibitionist attempts of adding burdensome scholasticity while the subjectmatter is totally ignored. Though a recent western scholar has taken up brief in favour of Ratnākara,[4] the laurels are undoubtedly thin and brittle for the *Haravijaya*.

Śivasvāmin, a Buddhist poet, composed the *Kapphinābhyudaya* in the later half of the ninth century A. D. under the patronage of king Avantīvarman. The epic constitutes of 20 cantos to narrate an ordinary proselytizing subject centering around a legend of the *Avadānaśataka* regarding Kapphina, the king of Śrāvastī, who defeated Prsoōenjit, a king of South and converted him to Buddhism. The source of this poem is found in a story of the prose romance entitled *'Avantīsundarīkathā.'* It seems that Śivasvāmin sought to compete with Bhāravi and Māgha in their own sphere. At the very outset, the poem introduces us to the detailed description of the protagonist, the king of Śrāvastī and his capital city, Līlāvatī. A spy arrives with the informations about the prosperity and haughtiness of Prasenjit, the rival king. The direct impact of the *Kirātārjunīya* is quite obvious. A counsel takes place and a messenger is sent to the rival king with an open challenge for battle. These things happen in first four cantos but thereafter further movements of the narrative are suspended. In close imitation of Bhāravi, Māgha and Ratnākara, the poet employs as many as eleven cantos (canto v-xv) to describe the digressive erotic extravaganza. This is perhaps one of the worst examples of total lack of congruity since out of twenty cantos of the poem more than half is eaten up by completely irrelevant materials. The king is compelled to undertake a long voyage under the charm of a Vidyādhara; but obviously this is nothing but a pretext for legitimising the digression. Six seasons appear in the Mount Malaya under the spell of the poet's magic wand as it were; besides the army engages in orgy and erotic dalliances from dawn to dusk. Thus Sivasvāmin has laboriously constructed a weaker replica of Māgha's poem.

In the sixteenth canto, the narrative resumes again when the army marches for battle and ultimately Prasenjit is defeated. But unlike other court epics, he is not killed; he is converted to Buddhism. As we have already stated, Śivasvāmin's competition with Bhāravi and Māgha has been of negative consequence for him. His scholarship cannot be questioned but he had neither imagination nor craftsmanship. He did not even possess the requisite acumen for bearing the torch lit by the earlier poets. The only silver lining in the black clouds is the theme of conversion to Buddhism; it seems that Aśvaghoṣa's innovative contribution is resurrected again, albeit fragmentally, from the limbo of oblivion. In the ultimate analysis, Śivasvāmin remains one of the obscure scribblers of the decadent epic genre since the *Kapphinābhyudaya* is exclusively modelled on those courtepics which never bothered about the nourishing soil of human interest. Therefore it has been, from the very inception and execution of its scheme, sequestered for the alienated elites at the top.

Abhinanda, son of Śatānanda, seems to have attained considerable popularity for composing the *Rāmacarita* presumably in the first half of the ninth century A.D. He has been praised and quoted by Soddhala,[5]

Someśvaradeva,[6] Ujjvaladatta,[7] as well as by two well-known anthologies.[8] Besides Bhoja also quotes profusely from the *Rāmacarita* though he does not refer to the name of the poem. Abhinanda has himself mentioned king Haravarsa Yuvarāja as his patron[9] whose identity has been a matter of dispute among the scholars. At any rate, of all the minor epics, the *Rāmacarita* seems to have been one of those few works which could escape the ignominy of total oblivion.

As it was an epoch of inordinately long ornamental mahākāvyas, Abhinanda too arranged his subjectmatter in forty cantos. However, the last four cantos have two recensions which is obviously another evidence of the epic's popularity. One of these recensions is naturally attributed to Abhinanda but the scholars are not sure about the authenticity of the claim since stylistically this portion is markedly different. On the other hand, the second supplement is written by a poet named Bhīmakavi. Notwithstanding these problems, the *Rāmacarita* faithfully fashions itself on Daṇḍin's famous dictums about court epics. Inspite of the mechanistic adherence to those principles, Abhinanda has furnished enough evidences of his alacrity and independent imagination which are extremely rare among the exponents of the court epics in the post-Māgha epoch. Thus he departs from the original *Rāmāyaṇa* on several occasions to reinterprete the inter-personal relationships and thus remodel the epic personalities like Sugrīva, Angada and Bibhīṣaṇa to restructure certain sequences, to incorporate new details and thus brings about refreshing change to renew the interest of the readers to the age-old narrative.

In fact, the *Rāmacarita* is different from the very beginning because its narrative does not commence conventionally; on the contrary, it has a dramatic beginning. We find Rāma in great anxiety because he is contemplating about the measures to be adopted for rescueing Sītā. However, inspite of occasional variations here and there, the episodic sequences of the *Rāmāyaṇa* are never lost sight of. But the narrative is frequently interrupted by conventional descriptive details viz. city, oceans, mountains, sunrise, moonrise etc. Besides, the characteristic disproportionate arrangement of the narrative is also discernible. Thus, beginning from Rāma's anxiety and Sugrīva's indifference and covering upto the vigorous search for Sītā by the monkeys and Hanumat's acceptances of tokens from Rāma, the narrative conjures up first ten cantos. The narrative moves at a snail's pace from the eleventh to the twentieth canto where Sītā meets Hanumat. It seems that the poet suddenly wakes up from slumber and rushes to narrate the terrible battle in the next sixteen cantos. In the sixteenth, Kumbha and Nikumbha are killed. Hence the last four cantos of doubtful authorship have been contrived to depict the two most important events of the battle, that is, the death of Indrajit and Rāvaṇa.

The *Rāmacarita* has sporadic flashes but it lacks the flush and freshness of natural bloom. Abhinanda deviates from the original track but this does not culminate into innovative expression or any new interpretative unfoldment. Because the genre itself was falling apart due to exhaustion engineered by an immobile society.

Mankha's *Śrīkanthacarita* deserves special mention. The Kashmirian poet composed this epic in twenty five cantos to narrate the mythical story of the demon, Tripura, who was pierced by Śiva's arrow. The epic faithfully follows the conventional paraphernalia of the genre in general and Ratnākara's *Haravijaya* in particular. As it was composed in the first half of the twelfth century, it had the advantage of borrowing freely from the works of the well-known exponents viz., Bhāravi, Māgha, Bhaṭṭi and also Ratnākara. However, Mankha was nothing more than an imitator; hence his attention was limited to only the extrinsic decadent traits.

Therefore, the *Śrīkanthacarita* begins with a prolonged customary benediction as the story is hardly of any importance. Mankha remains exclusively busy in describing the seasons, the sunset, the sunrise, moonlit night, erotic dalliances, pleasure garden, water-sports, Mount Kailāsa and all such details enumerated by the rhetoricians. Only the second and third canto have, to some extent, dealt with new materials because there we come across a philosophical discussion about the difference between good and bad. But it does not cast any impact on the readers due to stylistic incongruity. But from the fourth to the twenty first canto, Mankha indulges in endless descriptions of worn-out details in accordance with the rules of poetics. Significantly indeed, the poet refers to Ruyyaka as his teacher while the latter in his turn quotes from the former's poem in his *Alamkārasarvasva*. It is highly probable that they might have been closely acquainted with each other. At any rate, Mankha goes on monotonously reproducing all the tricks of verbal acrobatics which have been earlier exhibited enthusiastically by his predecessors.

In the twenty second canto, suddenly the poet wakes up from his stupefying slumber to resume his narrative and goes on to depict the march of Śiva's army. It is followed by a conventional description of battle with the demons in which, predictably, the demons are completely routed. Lastly, three cities of the demons are consigned to flames. Mankha has introduced devotional sentiments but these cannot redeem his stereotyped poem plagued with lack of imagination and genuine workmanship. But the twenty fifth (i.e. the concluding) canto unveils an altogether new dimension of the poem in which, practically as an epilogue, the poet has portrayed an unusually lively picture of a learned assembly. Its immense historical importance can never be doubted. We find here a unique realistic account of the royal court of Kashmir in which the poet's brother, Alamkāra, was a minister of King Jayasimha (1127-1150 A. D.). The poet has talked about thirty scholars, poets and officials of that court along with their subjects of specialisation. Though, being practically an epilogue, it has nothing to do with the epic itself, this canto has nevertheless drawn our attention to a very pertinent fact. It is apparent that the composers of court epics remain confined within the predetermined fetters of rhetorical regulations; they can never soar up with the winged words. But if there were any opportunity for them to respond to the call of the ripples and waves of the streaming life with its light and sound around, the epic genre would have acquired an entirely different complexion and character. That is why even a less than mediocre poet like Mankha could come out of the shell in the last canto of the *Śrīkanthacarita*.

In the whole range of post-Māgha epic poetry, Śrīharṣa alone deserves an exclusive treatment in whose *Naiṣadhīyacarita*, marvellous erudition goes hand in hand with refining of trivialities. In the second half of the twelfth century, he did not have any ambition to recreate a decadent form of art out of its embers and disintegrating smoke. Instead he put his total energy to weighty and ingenious elaboration of the formalities with unconcealed zest, laboriousness and learning. As a result we come across a monumental work of twenty two cantos having more than 2,800 verses which bespeak of exaggerated awareness about artifice. Śrīharsa has actually built up a verbal edifice of magnificence in which scholarly ingenuity masquerade under the guise of poetry but nevertheless he was highly rated by the traditional critics. In fact, he was enthusiastically mentioned along with Kālidāsa, Bhāravi and Māgha.[10] The *Naiṣadhīyacarita* is rightly regarded as 'the last master-piece of industry and ingenuity that the Mahākāvya can show' but inspite of stupendous exhibition of verbal skill, it is also a representative of poetic counterfeit. It is an interesting fact that except Ratnākara's *Haravijaya* and Abhinanda's *Rāmacarita*, no other Sanskrit court epic is so much voluminous. Its popularity may be guessed from the prevalence of more than twenty different commentaries on the poem including those of Mallinātha and Caritravardhana. Yet at the same time, its artificialities did not escape notice of the rhetoricians who found illustrations of literary blemishes in this epic.

The *Naisadhīyacarita* is fashioned on the well-known story of Nala and Damayantī enumerated in the *Mahābhārata*. Śrīharṣa has utilized all possible formulations of poetics to build the edifice of a representative ornate court epic. His versatility enabled him to accumulate a pedantic mass of descriptive matters. He has himself spoken of his multilinear talent: 'Yat Kāvyam madhuvarṣi, dharsitaparāstarkeṣu yasyoktayah.'[11] The following catalogue of books, composed by the poet, may be prepared from the references made in several epilogue stanzas of the epic: *Sthairya-vicāraprakaraṇa*,[12] *Śrīvijayapraśasti*,[13] *Khaṇḍanakhaṇḍa-khādya*,[14] *Gaudorvīsakulaprasasti*,[15] *Arnava-varnaṇa*,[16] *Chandahpraśasti*,[17] *Siva Saktisiddhi*[18] and *Navasāhasānkacaritacampū*.[19] Though the authenticity of Śrīharṣa's authorship has not yet been established beyond doubt, at least it is certain that his personlity is marked with the rare combination of a poet and a philosopher. But his wide range of study has proved to be his undoing. In fact, he could cover only upto the less spectacular portion of the story, thus the poem ends with the marriage of Nala and Damayantī. Very significantly indeed, the episodes containing poignant human drama of intrigue, frailty, pangs of separation and the ultimate resurrection were left out of the orbit of the *Naiṣadhīyacarita*. It seems that Śrīharṣa spent all his passions in the periphery of a story otherwise fraught with great aesthetic possibility.

But the time was out of joint for any significant creative endeavour. Therefore Śrīharsa consolidates his attention towards adding new contours occasionally. Notable changes may be detected in the delineation of Nala's character. This is indicative of an attempt to reinterprete traditional materials in accordance with the new attitude to life. In the *Mahābhārata*, the protagonist is a romantic lover but always conscious of duty to the gods; he has surpassed the divinities by keeping the integrity of his human personality intact. But he has his Achilles's heel as well; he cannot resist temptation for the game of dice and loses everything in the process. However, the real Nala comes out when he faces the cruel ordeals of life; his separation from Damayantī in trying circumstances and all the incidents that follow elevate his stature further. Regal dignity never forsakes him; he does not lose control over his passions any more. He accepts the pangs of life with rare fortitude and faces the queer situations squarely. He is perturbed to learn about the second Svayamvara of Damayantī but, even in that darkest hour, he endures the torments of his soul silently. At the end, however, the protagonist regains his paradise as Kali bids final retreat. On the contrary. the protagonist of the *Naiṣadhīyacarita* has no inferno to pass through. Śrīharṣa thrived in a Utopian atmosphere since the power elites at the royal courts recognised no tears, no pangs, no ordeals whatsoever. The poet had to cater to their demands for intellectual feast; hence there was arrangement for nothing but consolidation of their secluded paradise in the epic. Human drama comprising of conflict, tension, abrupt turn of fortune was therefore excluded from the arena of the epic; the poet concentrated on the entertaining story of the romantic love of Nala and Damayantī. Thus, unlike the Nala-episode of the *Mahābhārata*, the *Naiṣadhīyacarita* unfolded an enchanting fairyland of the lotus-eaters since it was an epoch of fantasy, alienation, abstraction and wishfulfillment.

In that stagnant society, the women were relegated to the position of fancy dolls whose existence was solely meant for their masters masquerading as husbands and lovers. In the older strata of the *Mahābhārata*, inspite of certain limitations, the women enjoyed considerable freedom and hence, had individuality of their own. Thus Damayantī, in the Nala-episode, has a personality of her own and can take bold and calculated initiative to regain her husband. In fact, she is unique in fortitude out of fathomless love for Nala. In the *Naiṣadhīyacarita,* however, Damayantī is not an individual with flesh and blood; she is only a type having no genuine feeling. What is worse, she has become one of the many nameless replicas of Vātsyāyana's hetairai who have no utility other than providing perverse sensuous pleasures to their spouses. Śrīharṣa writes a manifesto, as it were, of the perversion of the contemporary decadent society by devoting the entire seventh canto to describe Damayantī's physical beauty limb by limb. Actually such wanton tastelessness is found in the second, sixteenth, eighteenth, nineteenth and twentieth canto as well. The poet was completely swayed by the dictums of poetics and failed to recognise the importance of symmetry. It is the natural consequence of excessive elaboration as we know that less than two hundred verses in the Nala-episode of the *Mahābhārata* have been expanded to almost two thousand eight hundred verses in the *Naiṣadhīyacarita.* It means that Śrīharṣa has, in average, constructed fourteen verses out of every verse in the great epic.

Śrīharṣa is undoubtedly endowed with skill to manipulate diction and metres; but while exhibiting it, he has become oblivious of the subjectmatter and instead totally concentrated on its extrinsic embellishment. He has used nineteen meters quite commendably but the uninspired employment of the complex and monotonously excessive figures of speech can hardly be justified. Particularly his excessive use of Anuprāsa, Śleṣa and Yamaka have caused irreparable damage to the poem. Moreover the innate artificiality of the cliches has proved to be his undoing. He has no less fondness for complex syntactical arrangement; long compounds, forced expressions, rare and obsolete words, unpaninian linguistic mode: these have brought about further complications for the reade s. Besides he has his scholarship to exhibit under any pretext whatsoever.[20] In fact, the poet has boastfully announced the greatness of his poem; according to him, other poets are lifeless stones while his poem is the ocean of milk.[21] The next verse[22] is also equally important since the poet himself declares that his poem is 'granthagranthi' and that it is meant only for the elites, not for ordinary readers:

> 'Granthagranthiriha kvacid kvacidapi nyāsi prayatnānmayā
> Prājnanmanyamanā hathena pathitī māsmin Khalah khelatu
> Śraddhārāddhaguru-ślathīkṛtaḍṛḍhagranthih samāsādaya-
> tvetatkāvyarasormi majjanasukhavyāsajjanam sajjanah.'

Śrīharṣa desired that his creation would be an object of pleasure for the wise;[23] that is why his wide range of philosophical study has furnished the subjectmatter of the entire seventeenth canto. The poet did not bother that it was indeed wholly irrelevant for the theme of his poem. Śrīharṣa's penchant for rhetorical extravaganza is glaringly evident throughout. However, one of the most interesting instances is found in the description of the 'Svayamvara' of Damayantī. In the great epic, this episode has been narrated in a few sentences while Śrīharṣa devotes five long cantos and more than five hundred verses for this.[24] No other description of Svayamvara in Sanskrit literature is more gorgeous and extravagant than that of the *Naisadhīyacarita*. But the most noteworthy aspect of this episode is the introduction of five Nalas (of whom four are disguised deities) to Damayantī. None other than Goddess Sarasvatī undertakes the task and, in her speech, each of the verses has two-fold meanings[25]—one overtly applicable to Nala while another to one of the four gods. Even when the goddess speaks about Nala himself,[26] she manages to put those verses in such a way that each of them becomes applicable to one of the gods. But the ingenuity reaches its extreme when the concluding verse ascribed to the goddess is made to carry five meanings applicable to Nala and the four disguised gods.[27] Nothing can be more irrational than such word-play because the poet indulges in it when the situation does not warrant any ambiguity or uncalled for puzzle. At that most important juncture of her life, what a perplexed Damayantī would least ask for is the help from a commentator. Interestingly, Śrīharṣa himself seems to be aware of such a contingency as he half-jokingly exclaims:

> 'Mā jānīta vidarbhajāmavidūṣīm kīrtim mudah śreyasīm
> Seyam bhadramacīkaran-maghavatā na svamdvitīyām śacīm
> Kah śacyā racayāmcakāra carite kāvyam sa nah kathyatā-
> Metasyāstu Kariṣyate rasadhunīpātre caritre na kaih.'

As it has already been noted, events move at a snail's pace because of the burden of elaborate descriptive details. In the first canto, the poet tells us that Nala and Damayantī are in love with each other. Nala captures a golden swan and then, out of compassion, sets it free. In the second canto, the swan comes back to Nala to express its gratitude and then promises to fly to Damayantī for knowing her mind. Nala gives his consent and the swan starts for Kundinanagara. In the third canto, the swan talks to Damayantī who is equally love-lorn for Nala. It tells her about Nala's feelings and returns. In the fourth canto, Damayantī is in sad plight; her father, Bhīma decides to arrange a Svayamvara. In the fifth canto. Nārada informs Indra, Agni, Varuna and Yama about the proposed Svayamvara. The gods start for Kundinanagara and on the way, comes across Nala. They extract promise of cooperation from the protagonist and sends him to Damayantī as their messenger. In the sixth canto, Nala goes to Damayanṭī being invisible by a boon of Indra. In the seventh, Nala describes the beauty of Damayantī limb by limb. In the eighth, Nala becomes visible and introducing himself as a messenger of the gods, tells Damayantī to choose any one of the four gods. In the ninth. Damayantī says that she does not wish to have any god as her husband and declares that she would die if her love for Nala does not become fruitful. As she sheds tears, Nala cannot restrain himself anymore and discloses his identity. Damayantī requests him to be present in the Svayamavara and Nala agrees. Then he starts for the gods to tell them about his failure in the duty of messenger. Thus, the first nine cantos have some semblance of action; at least, the narrative moves slowly.

But thereafter everything stands still as it were except that the wedding of Nala and Damayantī takes place in the sixteenth canto and Nala returns to his own kingdom. We have already noted that the Svayamvara is described in five cantos followed by elaborate preparations for marriage in the fifteenth canto.[28] Though the seventeenth introduces the intriguing Kali and Dvāpara, it has no relevance to this poem. The conventional erotic extravaganza occupies three cantos closely followed by the bathing sessions of the royal couples, description of dawn etc. As usual nothing happens and the epic draws to its close as Nala and Damayantī enjoy the tender night, describing with great poetic flourish, the queen Moon at her best splendour.

Though the *Naiṣadhīyacarita* has been consistently sitgmatised as a 'Perfect masterpiece of bad taste and bad style', it too has its silver linings in the form of witty and animated expressions as well as quite a few notable epigrams. Some examples may be cited below:

(i) 'Tyajantyasūn sarma ca mānino varam Tyajanti na tvekamayācitavratam.'[29]

(ii) 'Svata evastām parārthatā grahaṇānām hi yathā yathārthatā.'[30]

(iii) 'Vidherapisvārasikah prayāsah parasparam yogyasamāgamāya.'[31]

(iv) 'Niviśate yati sukaśikhā pade srjati sā kiyatīmiva na vyathām.'[32]

(v) 'Rūpasya śilpe vayasā ca vedhā nirjīyate, sa smarakinkareṇa.'[33]

(vi) 'Satām mohāt sammukhadhāvi pauruṣam.'[34]

Śrīharṣa's obsession for continuous affectation of diction has been criticised by many; he has been taken to task for display of 'fatiguing ornateness of overworked diction.' At any rate, no one can deny that he knows varied tricks of expression; though he makes his diction deliberately difficult, his verbal proficiency makes him distinct from other obscure scribblers of that epoch. He may not be an imaginative poet but his fancy is definitely indicative of a cultivated and sophisticated mind. Even in his limited sphere, Śrīharsa has been able to develop his own system of idioms and phraseology, set of ideas and conceits. Some of his expressions are interestingly smart and breathe in an air of uniqueness.[35]

Though, at the first glance, Śrīharṣa seems worlds apart from even Bhāravi, Māgha, Bhatti (and also Śūdraka and Bānabhatta)- not to speak of Kālidāsa- actually our poet has built his massive palace of artifice on a strong foundation of past legacy. At the sametime he has borrowed his materials in an exceptionally shrewd manner; he took the cues from the old masters and then proceeded to discover and stretch the circles of penumbra so long concealed in poetic language. But, as we have emphasised earlier, he was basically not an innovative poet; yet none other than Śrīharṣa could so much motivate fancy without the guiding presence of inspiration. Though the impact of Bhāravi, Māgha and Bhatti can be detected in the *Naiṣadhīyacarita*, the poet has travelled a long way from the earlier epoch when the umbilical cord with the life around was stretched to the limits of endurance but, definitely, it was not severed. Kālidāsa was undoubtedly a perennial source of inspiration for the scholarly poet but Śrīharṣa could not properly interprete the meaning of his art. The penetrating vision of the great poets provoked the thirst of Tantalus in him. Hence he concentrated on chiselling out a few clues to verbal magic from the invaluable repertory of Kālidāsa.[36]

In fine, Śrīharṣa is the foremost poet in the second rank of the epic genre who is memorable but not adorable. He demands attention from the readers as the best representative of the prodigal workmanship of ingenuity at a time when regional vernaculars have been eroding the inconvertible soil on which the litterateurs stood unsuspectingly. The patronage of the feudal lords was still continuing, but the disintegrating medieval society could no longer replenish nor readjust the frontiers of the old genre and give it a new lease of life once again.

IV

A few Jaina epics have been composed in that period which are remarkable for the proselytizing zeal. But due to the decadent traits of the exhausted genre, those works lack the universality of appeal and spontaneity of refined craftsmanship. Jinasena's *Pārśvābhyudaya* is one of the first Jaina epics composed in ninth century A.D. The poet seems to have ambitious approach to poetry since he has sought to use Kālidāsa's *Meghadūta* in a unique manner. Each verse of the *Meghadūta* has been reinterpreted by Jinasena as a puzzle and then he has offered its answer. The biography of Pārśvanātha, a famous Jaina saint, can be construed if those answers are arranged together. Obviously it is an example of unique ingenuity and great labour; besides, the poet has tried his best to endow his effort with literary embellishment. It is of course not an easy task and hence, Jinasena can deserve credit for it; but except this, the *Pārśvābhyudaya* has no other merit.

Haricandra, another Jaina poet, composed the *Dharmaśarmābhyudaya* in twenty one cantos with a view to narrating the pious life of Dharmanātha, the fifteenth Tīrthamkara. On the one hand, Haricandra models his epic on Māgha's *Śiśupālavadha* while, on the other, he closely follows Vākpatirāja's *Gaudavaha.*

Sarvānanda, a Jaina poet of the fourteenth century, wrote the '*Gagaducarita*' in seven cantos in which he narrated the philanthropic services rendered by a compassionate man during the difficult days of famine in Gujarat (1256-1258). Supernatural elements abound in this poem but its unique theme was not supported by adequate imagination and craftsmanship. Caritrasundaraganī wrote an epic entitled the *Mṛgavatīcarita*, having fourteen cantos, in the fifteenth century. He had written another epic named *Mahīpālacarita* which is valuable only for sociocultural history.

Two other works are referred to by the scholars. Amaracandra, a pupil of Jinadattasūri, is said to have composed an epic entitled

Padmānanda in nineteen cantos with a view to narrating the biography of Ṛṣabha, the first Jina, in typical Mahākāvya-style. The same poet composed another work known as '*Caturviṃśatijinendrasaṃksiptacaritānī*' in order to briefly describe the biographies of twenty four Ginas. Amaracandra seems to have modelled his poem entirely on Hemacandra's work. However, in its conception and execution, it is actually farthest from the epic genre.

The flourish of the various schools of poetics, from ninth century onwards, may have inspired a good number of poetasters to wield their pen in the realm of court epics and other variant subgenres. But acceleration of number of composition did not help much. Except limited recognition in the history of literature, those poems could not secure their passage to posterity. On the contrary, such poems receded further from common life and realities; having no redeeming feature, these proved to be exclusive products of artificial and erudite fancy. Śatānanda's *Rāmacarita* is such an epic that deals with Sītā's abduction and never rises above the level of the commonplace. Likewise Vāsudeva wrote the *Yudhiṣṭhiravijava* and also its sequel, the *Dhātukāvya* in the ninth century. Both these poems attempt to retell the great episodes of the *Mahābhārata* in an unpoetic manner. According to a recent opinion, Vāsudeva also composed two other poems entitled the *Tripuradahana* and the *Śaurīkathodaya* but is expected to promote religious purposes. This is what we have earlier come across in the Jaina epics. In the concluding decades of the eleventh century, Lolimbarāja composed the *Harivilāsa* in five cantos with this purpose. He is said to have been a contemporary of king Bhoja and particularly enjoyed the patronage of king Harihara of South India. However, the affinity of the poem with the epic genre is limited to superfluous level and it has little notable features. There are customary descriptions of one season while the legend of Kṛṣṇa, eulogised here as the supreme God, is dealt with in a casual manner. Kavirāja Sūri wrote the *Pārijātaharaṇa* to retell an episode of the *Mahābhārata*. Though it may remind us of Vāsudeva's epics discussed above, Kavirāja Sūri is somewhat different since he clearly aimed at composing a poem with emphasis on devotional feelings on the one hand and a pleasant lovestory on the other. The poet presents his subjectmatter with conventional ornamentation but nevertheless he lacks both in imagination and genuine inspiration.

Rājānaka Jayaratha, a Kashmirian poet of the twelfth century, wrote a religious epic entitled *Haracaritacintāmaṇi*. Though it has little literary value as a poem, it is replete with all the myths and legends of the Kashmira school of Saivism, its teachings, theological details and rituals. Hence, historical value of such a compendium cannot be ignored.

V

The supreme charm of the highest poetry was out of question; even soft richness of fancy or the expertise of a clever artisan capable of refining the stereotyped themes was not to be found anymore. In that fossilised socio-cultural milieu, the shallow streams of poetic fancy could not quench thirst any more; these only gave rise to a few marsh-lands of hollow sub-genres. This is proved in the emergence of Śleṣa-Kāvyas (i.e. poems with double or more meanings). Thus, in the concluding decades of the eleventh century A.D., Sandhyākara Nandī of Bengal composed the *Rāmapālacar*ita in the epic style with a view to narrating the glorious career of Rāmapāla (1084-1130 A.D.), the renowned Pāla king. It has quite faithfully followed the historical events. The poet has depicted Rāmapāla as a great warrior and strategist who salvaged the prestige of his family by defeating Bhīma, a rival king, in battle. The protagonist reinstated himself as the king of Bengal and then directed a martial expedition against Mithilā to annex it under his domain. On another plane, the poem narrates the story of the *Rāmāyaṇa*. That is why each verse of the *Rāmapālacarita* has been constructed in such a manner that each carries double meaning one of which is relevant to Rāma while another to Rāmapāla. Obviously, this calls for a laborious fancy parade of artificiality and ingenuity resulting into complexities ne plus ultra. Rāma and Rāmapāla are protagonists of entirely different dimensions and epochs. Sandhyākara Nandī had no other alternative but to choose his words and prepare their syntactical structure with greatest possible caution. Consequently no connoisseur of poetic sensibility can find anything fascinating in it. Possibly the poet was not quite confident regarding his acceptability to contemporary readers and also passage to posterity by composing a simple panegyric about a regional king; hence he was constrained to search for greater number of readers. Ultimately, however, this method of constructing double meanings got standardised and a few other similar works came into existence.

Dhanañjaya (also known as Śrutakīrti), who belonged to the Digambara Jaina sect, wrote the *Rāghava-Pāṇḍavīya* between 1123 and 1140 A.D. It is also known as the *Dvisandhānakāvya* (i.e. a poem with double meanings) because each verse may be interpreted as related to the story of the *Rāmāyaṇa* and the *Mahābhārata* at the sametime. Likewise another poet named Mādhavabhaṭṭa (also known as Kavirāja sūri or Kavirājapaṇḍita) composed a poem with the same name (i.e. *Rāghava-Pāṇḍavīya*) under the patronage of Kāmadeva of the Kādamba dynasty (1182-1197 A.D.). The poet declares boastfully that none other than Bāṇa and Subandhu can be at par with him in use of Vakrokti. Actually both Dhanañjaya and Mādhavabhaṭṭa have, as it were, sought to deconstruct the linguistic habits of the readers with amazing dexterity. In order to make puns they have stretched words and syntactical structures ad arbitrium. Thus they have ignored the principles of compounds, sandhis, prepositions and postpositions at will. The syntactical systems have been done away with to construct new types of sentences according to their choice. Obviously such wanton play with words can hardly promote any poetic aim. Hence the sub-genre was condemned to the quicksand of time at its very inception.

Haradatta Sūri, whose data cannot be ascertained, wrote a similar work entitled *Rāghavanaiṣadhīya* with a view to narrating the stories of Rāma and Nala simultaneously.

Venkatādhavarin's *Yādava-rāghavīya* (Seventeenth century A.D.) apparently narrates Rāma's career but it has sought to incorporate further ingenuity by arranging to furnish Kṛṣṇa's story in a different way. When it is read backwards, the second meaning comes to the fore.

Vidyāmādhava composed the *Pārvatīrukminīya* under the patronage of king Somadeva (1126-1138 A.D.) of the Cālukya dynasty. It deals with the love and marriage of Śiva and Pārvatī on the one hand and that of Kṛṣṇa and Rukmiṇī on the other. Thus it is somewhat different from other works of the subgenre but otherwise it does not show any individuality of treatment.

However, such worksmanship is stretched ad absurdum in Cidambara's *Rāghava-Pāṇḍava-yādavīya* (late sixteenth century) in which each verse carries the burden of triple meanings related to the *Rāmāyaṇa*, the *Mahābhārata* and the *Bhāgavata Purāṇa.*

There is yet another poem that transgresses all permissible limits of endurance. It is known as the *Nala-Yādava-Rāghava-Pāṇḍavīya* which attempts to present four different stories simultaneously.

Though such specimens of pseudo-literary pursuits never express any dissatisfaction with the fetters and limitations that these create for themselves, the last remnants of the decayed epic genre have been silently but unequivocally laid to rest by those pallbearers.

VI

We come across a few miscellaneous subgenres as well which are off-shoots of the continuing epic tradition but nevertheless considerably remote from their source. Among them, there are a group of poems which are actually abridgement of great epics or some other famous works. In the ninth century, Abhinanda, son of Jayanta Bhaṭṭa, a resident of Kashmir, wrote the *Kādambarīkathāsāra* in epic style. But it has no merit of its own. Kṣemendra, the famous Kashmirian polymath, wrote two poems of this type entitled *Bhāratamañjarī* and *Rāmāyana Mañjarī* in the first half of the eleventh century. According to the critics, both these poems try their best to conform to the standard epic norms but ultimately these remain poetical exercises for a litterateur in the making. Kṣemendra is said to have written another work of the same category, viz. the *Padyakādambarī.*

Amaracandra Sūri (composer of the epic entitled *Padmānanda* referred to earlier), attempted a close adaptation of the entire

Mahābhārata in his *Bālabhārata* consisting of nineteen cantos. He wrote under the patronage of Viśāladeva of Gujrat in the first half of the thirteenth century A.D. It is a fairly intelligent work that keeps its awareness for the dictums of the rhetoricians in tact on the one hand while on the other it does not deviate from the narrative of the great epic. Amaracandra could handle different metres with notable alacrity.

Besides, there are a few Yamaka-kāvyas as well. Vāsudeva (composer of the *Yudhiṣṭhira-vijaya* referred to earlier) wrote the *Nalodaya* in the ninth century A.D. as a Yamakakāvya. Nītivarman, who flourished in the tenth century, wrote the *Kīcakavadha* as a Yamakakāvya to narrate the famous episode of the *Mahābhārata* about Bhīma's killing of Kīcaka. Venkaṭeśa, son of Śrīnivāsa, wrote the *Rāmyamakārṇava* consisting of thirty cantos, in 1656 A.D. Except that these poems may be regarded as the evidences of the ever-extending frontiers of the peerless epic tradition, these do not have any other intrinsic value.

Several other miscellaneous works were modelled on the various facets of the epic genre. These include Śākalyamalla's (also known as Mallācārya or Kavimalla) highly artificial work, the *Udāra-rāghava*, Venkateśvara's *Citrabandha-Rāmāyaṇa* in the form of sword, cross, wheel etc. and Venkateśa's *Rāmacandrodaya*, consisting of thirty cantos and written in 1635 A.D.

Vastupāla's *Naranārāyaṇānanda*, written in the first half of the thirteenth century, depicts the friendship of Kṛṣṇa and Arjuna along with the latter's marriage with Subhadrā. The poem constitutes of sixteen cantos.

As we have already noted, the romantic story of Nala and Damayantī have been used by the litterateurs time and again. Thus Kṛṣṇānanda, who flourished in the court of a king of Puri before fourteenth century A.D., wrote the *Sahrdayānanda* in fifteen cantos. Unlike Śrīharṣa, Kṛṣṇānanda has dealt with the entire story of Nala. We also have the *Nalābhyudaya*, consisting of eight cantos, written by Vāmanabhaṭṭa Bāṇa in the last decades of the fourteenth or the first decades of the fifteenth century A.D. under the patronage of Reddi prince, Vema of Kondavīdu.

We can also speak of an epic entitled *Suratotsava* written by Someśvardeva (1179-1262) in fifteen cantos, that dealt with completely mythological subjectmatter. At the end of the poem, Someśvaradeva has furnished us with some autobiographical details; besides some informations about his patron, Vastupāla, have also been given. These are of considerable historical importance though the poem as such has little merit.

For an interesting historical reason, we can refer to Śrīvara's *Kathākautuka*, composed in the fifteenth century. It is otherwise an ordinary epic of negligible merit; but it is memorable because it is a free adaptation from the Persian poem about the romantic love of Yusuf and Zuleikha. It was originally written by Dsachami in the reign of Muhammad Shah. It begins with a glorification of the original patron and, presumably to counteract the Mohammedan association, the last canto is entirely devoted to the glorification of Śiva.

In the seventeenth century, Nīlakantha Dīksita, a Saiva devotee, wrote the *Gangāvatarana* in eight cantos. Special mention may be made of Madhuravānī, a court-poetess of king Raghunātha of Tanjore in the seventeenth century, who wrote the *Rāmāyanasāra*. In the long history of epic poetry, we come across only two poetesses wielding their pens (the other is Gangā, composer of the historical Mahākāvya, *Madhurāvijaya*) in the exclusively male-dominated arena.

NOTES

1. S.K. De, *History of Sanskrit Literature*, Calcuta, 1947, p. 304.
2. *ibid.* p. 311.
3. Ratnākara himself informs that the work was composed in Kashmir under the patronage of king Cippada Jayapida (832-844 A.D.). According to the testimony of Kalhana, Ratnākara enjoyed the patronage of king Avantīvarman as well whose reign began in 855 A.D.
4. David Smith, *Ratnākara's Harvijaya*, Oxford University Press, 1985.
5. Soddhala, *Udayasundarīkathā*:
   'Srstam tadārta yuvarāja-nareśvarena
   Yad duskaram kimapi Yena girah Śriyaśca

Pratyayanam sphutamakāri nije Kavīndram
Ekāsane samupaveśayatabhinandam'

6. Someśvaradeva, *Kīrtikaumudī.*
'Na māghah ślāghyate Kaiścinnabhinando'bhinandyate Nisphalahkālidāso'pi yaśovīrasya sannidhau'
7. Ujjvaladatta, *Unādi-sūtra-vṛtti*: 1,2,4,48, iv. 117 quote the following verses from the *Rāmacarita* respectively: xiii. 86, x. 2; xviii. 85.
8. *Sadūkti-karṇāmṛta* (ii. 748, v. 100) quotes the following verses from the *Rāmacarita*: xi. 84 and xv. 67 while *Sūktimuktāvalī* (141) quotes the following: *Rāmacarita*. iii. 98-99.
9. *Rāmacarita*, xxxvi. 86.
10. cf, 'Upamā Kālidāsasya bhāreverarthagauravam Naisadhe padalālityam māghe santi trayo gunāh.'
11. *Naisadhīyacarita*. xxii. 155.
12. *ibid.* iv. 123.
13. *ibid.* v. 138.
14. *ibid.* vi. 113.
15. *ibid.* vii. 110.
16. *ibid.* ix. 160.
17. *ibid.* xvii. 222.
18. *ibid.* xviii. 154.
19. *ibid.* xxii. 151.
20. An interesting catalogue of different branches of knowledge can be prepared with the help of references in the following verses: i. 4, i.17-18, ii. 40,65,95,125; iv, 116. x. 76,80,81,82,85,88, xx. 35. Besides there are several allusions to Purāṇic legends.
21. 'Diśi diśi girigrāvāṇah svām vamantu sarasvatīm/Tulayayatu mithastāmāpatasphuraddhvani dambarām/sa paramaparah Ksīrodanvān yadīyamudīyate/Mathituramrtam Khedachhedi pramodanamodanam' (xxii. 151)
22. *ibid.* xxii. 152.
23. 'Maduktiścadantarmadayati sudhībhūya sudhiyah' (xxii. 150)
24. Cantos x-xiv.
25. Canto xiii.

26. *ibid.* xiii. 28-31.
27. *ibid.* xiii. 34.
28. *ibid.* xv. 86.
29. *ibid.* I. 50.
30. *ibid.* ii. 61.
31. *ibid.* iii. 48.
32. *ibid.* iv. 11.
33. *ibid.* x. 131.
34. *ibid.* xii. 8.
35. *ibid.* i. 41; vi. 103; vii. 22, 41, 72; viii. 38; ix. 26,56,109; x. 103,133; xi. 2,52; xii. 28,66; xv. 49, 78, 82; xix. 8, 39.
36. cf. *Raguvamśa.* ii. 19; iv. 42; xii. 2.
    Meghadūta. Pūrvamegha. 2

7

Historical Epics

The historical mahākāvyas constitute another interesting subgenre of the Indian epic tradition which flourished during the first half of the second millennium A.D. (that is from eleventh to fifteenth centuries). Like many other subjects, 'history' has been regarded as another subject to deal with. Indians have their own interpretation about the concept of history which does not quite agree with the western concept. When we consider the fact that even the best composition in Indian historical tradition (i.e. Kalhana's *Rājataranginī*) is treated basically as a poem, the typical Indian approach to history becomes clearly evident. Besides, it also means that for Indian mind no subject matter was alien for creative poetry. In fact, it appears that the Indians had unfaltering conviction about the omnidirectional potency of imagination with which creative experiments could be conducted over any subjectmatter. Unlike the western world, the Indians had not worked out any clear line of demarcation between myth and fact or fiction and history. That is why, Indians not only allowed them to coexist but also wove a myriorama of sorts by allowing those apparently contradictory elements to interpenetrate and interact with each other. The western literary historians took note as to how historical facts were wrapped in panegyrical fiction and poetic embellishments, Keith, for example, had observed: 'In view of the antiquity and developed character of Indian civilization, it would be ridiculous to expect to find Indians destitute of historical sense, but what is really essential is the fact that despite abundance of its literature, history is so miserably represented and that in the whole of the great period of Sanskrit literature, there is not even one writer who can be seriously regarded as a critical historian.'

In this context we can recollect the following well-known definition of history which enjoyed wide approval in ancient India:

> 'Dharmārtha-Kāmamokṣāṇām-upadeśasamanvitam
> Pūrvavṛttakathāyuktamitihāsam pracakṣate'.

In this overtly metaphysical and utilitarian conception of history, the essence of the transcendentalist worldview of Indian power elites has been neatly summed up. Its foundation is deeply entrenched in the belief about an unbreakable continuity of the cycle of life which constitutes of both here and hereafter. Naturally it has prejudiced the creative minds to such an extent that there is practically no clearly worked out watershed between history and legend. Consequently Indian mind was never bothered with any contradiction between imaginative poem and historical chronicle. So long the established rhetorical norms and prescriptions were faithfully followed, it really did not matter as to what the subjectmatter was. Moreover, poetry (particularly in the post-Kālidāsa epoch) was seldom considered as an end in itself; it was rather a golden wing for the privileged few by dint of which a leisurely voyage could be made to a predetermined destination. The subgenre under discussion i.e. the historical epic also justifies this observation in which various facets of tradition were assimilated in an interesting way. Let us now make a brief survey of the works which belong to the sub-genre of historical epic.

The *Navasāhasāṅkacarita* was composed by Parimala Padmagupta between the last quarter of the tenth and the beginning of the eleventh century A.D. On the basis of the undermentioned verses of the work, we can surmise that the poet was patronised by Vākpatirājadeva and his successor, Sindhurāja who were the scions of the Paramāra dynasty of Gujarat:

'Sarasvatīkalpalataikakandam vandāmahe vākpatirājadevam Yasya prasādādvayamapy-nanyakavīndracīrne pathi sancarāmah.
Divam Yiyāsurmama vācimudrāmadatta yo vākpatirājadevah Tasyānujanmā kavi bāndhavasya bhinatti tām, samprati sindhurājah.'[2]

According to the testimony of Merutunga's *Prabandhacintāmaṇi,* which is also supported by several grants and inscriptions, Vākpatirāja was captured in a battle and then executed between 994 and 998 A.D. while Sindhurāja was killed by enemy in 1010 A.D. It seems that Parimala Padmagupta composed the poem around 1005 A.D. to narrate the winning of Śaśiprabhā, a princess of the Nāga dynasty, by Sindhurāja Navasāhasānka. The poet has sought to glorify his patron by a poetical depiction of the protagonist's uncommon valour. Sindhurāja, the younger brother of Vākpatirāja II, kills Vajrānkuśa and brings the golden lotus from the latter's pond to fulfill the promise set by Śaśiprabhā's father and then marries her.

Padmagupta's epic constitutes of eighteen cantos each of which bears a special name and is of moderate length. Thus the shortest canto has sixty eight verses while the longest has one hundred twenty one verses. An analysis of the content of those cantos shows that the poet is keenly aware of the varying facets of Indian cultural legacy in general and the epic tradition in particular.

Thus there are customary descriptions of both real city (Ujjayinī: Canto I) and imaginary city (Bhogavatī: Canto viii); the hero and the heroine as well as their love at first encounter in which all frontiers between the materials pertaining to reality and legend have been removed. In this epic, human beings co-exist with the mythical beings like the Nāgas, demons, Gandharvas and Vidyādharas. There are cliches endeared by the rhetoricians through the ages; viz., the use of deer and swan as the preliminary agents towards making liason between the hero and the heroine, female attendant of the heroine helping the protagonist to reach his heloved, the pitiable love-lorn condition of the lovers strictly according to the pūrvarāga formulation. As we have noted already, there are many supernatural events in the poem; viz., the disappearance of Śaśiprabhā, the heroine, by the magical trick of demon: the metamorphic changes of a lion into a tree, a monkey into a man named Śaśikhanda (due to the curse of a sage), a deer into human form but which flies in the sky; the disappearance of an elephant; the river Narmadā assuming the appearance of a lady advise the protagonist about his future course of action and then disappearing; a cursed parrot acting as the messenger of love only to be relieved of its curse; an underground as well as an aerial journey etc. Besides there are counsel, hunting in forest, night and daybreak, hermitage, proposal of alliance, ministerial activity and finally the events immediately preceding the terrible battle between Sindhurāja, the protagonist and Vajrānkuśa, the demon. The demon is slain by Sindhurāja whose victory is celebrated with much enthusiasm. The protagonist weds the heroine amid gay abandon.

From a close perusal of the *Navasāhasānkacarita*, we can make an estimate of Padmagupta as an epic versifier. The angīrasa i.e. the principal sentiment of the poem is śṛngāra while the sentiments of heroism, wonder etc. are subordinate to it. The poet has commendable merit in describing both the tender aspects of nature and touching moments of life.[3] Even within his limitations, the poet can sometimes scale the heights of creative imagination. e.g.

(i) 'Arkānsuglapitairebhirato' pylikhitairiva.
Rāja-jambūnikunjesu paśya pumskokilaih sthitam'[4]

(ii) 'Amūni puspāni mahīruhānām ābhānti līnabhramarodarānī ·
Vidyādharī vibhramadarsanārtham uttānitānīva vilocanāni'[5]

or sometimes he can exhibit his skill of craftsmanship. Thus he has shown awareness about elegance and the appropriateness of diction. Undoubtedly he had both control and refinement of style; 'lālitya' may easily be regarded as his forte. His dexterity in the arrangement of words is discernible in the following expression:

'Nibaddhabhīmabhrukutirvilokayan
Dṛśā tadolkākapiśogratārayā

Sa tīvrakopasphuritādharo vadat.
Vaco mamākṣipyekrtānateriti.'[6]

Padmagupta has used as many as nineteen metres of which almost all have been extensively used by the Sanskrit poets. The prominent figures of speech like Upamā, Rūpaka, Utprekṣā, Dīpaka Arthāntaranyāsa. Virodhābhāsa, Anuprāsa and Śleṣa are found in his poem. The impact of the epic tradition is discernible not only in the conventional use of poetic materials but also in the poet's frequent allusion to various anecdotes of two great epics and the Purānas.

However such allusions are never overdone and hence the extreme exhibition of scholasticity (that jeopardises the onward movement of the narrative in the post-Kālidāsa court epics) is not found here. However due to the unrestrained use of the fanciful and mythic materials, the meagre historical basis has neither relevance nor significance. Consequently Sindhurāja, the protagonist of the poem, could not be presented as a historical personality with flesh and blood. Comparing him with the famous mythical kings like Yayāti, Māndhātā and Bharata,[7] the poet has eulogised his patron but the supernatural feats of the protagonist do not sufficiently elevate his personality.

Padmagupta had the rare opportunity to fashion his poem on the eye-witness's account of historical events and thus add a totally new dimension to the epic genre. But instead he chose to ignore the mundane reality of his time and depended on the wornout materials of literary convention only because he was in search of a variegated mask of heroic personality. An established image of an ideal protagonist was considered more important and safe than the real person. That is why, Padmagupta was busy in depicting Sindhurāja as an epitome of the combined traits of the dhīrodātta and dhīralalita type of protagonists. The protagonist of this poem, has earned the coveted epithet of 'Navasāhasānka' because he has to his credit no less than hundreds of daring deeds:

'Anena vihitānyatra yat sāhasaśatānyatah
Navīnasāhasānko'yam vīragoṣthīsu gīyate.'[8]

He is handsome, jovial, romantic, polite, generous and sober on the one hand while, on the other, he is brave, courageous and daring. He is also a good administrator and statesman. Likewise Śaśiprabhā, the heroine of the poem, has been portrayed in accordance with the traditional principles. As a Nāga-princess, she does not even have the semblance of historical reality. Expectedly she has peerless beauty:

> 'Upodhalāvanya tarangabhangyā sarāgabimbosthagata pravālayā.'[9]

She is bashful but romantic; such a jewel among women can only be won by undertaking a difficult task. Thus the protagonist had to procure the golden lotus by killing Vajrānkuśa, the terrible demon.

However the poet failed to raise Śaśiprabhā from the level of an abstract type of a love-lorn heroine.

After going through this historical epic, one cannot but be aware of the importance of reconstructing the perspective of the medieval past. Being conditioned by a stagnant society, a poet like Padmagupta learnt only to respond to the system of conventions. Artistic expression usually involved a subordination of the creator's personality to the needs of his patron. The idiosyncratic style of the subgenre, as expressed in the *Navasāhasānkacarita* is a feature of the age that produced it; it is brought with its own virtues and limitations, potentialities and tensions.

Bilhana composed *Vikramānkadevacarita* in the last quarter of the eleventh century A.D. with a view to glorifying his patron, Vikramāditya Tribhuvanamalla of Cālukya dynasty who reigned from 1076 to 1127 A.D. The work is effectively a panegyric in eighteen cantos written basically to reciprocate the conferment of honorific title of 'Vidyāpati' on Bilhana by the king. It celebrates certain prominent incidents of Tribhuvanamalla's life though it also deals with the general outlines of the history of the Cālukyas. Bilhana shows his awareness of historical facts to a considerable extent but nevertheless he makes us feel time and again that he is primarily a fanciful poet, not a chronicler. Indeed the very fact that the composer of the

Vikramānkadevacarita has also written the intensely passionate lyric poem entitled the *Caurapañcāśikā* is a clear evidence of his versatility, craftsmanship and plurality of imagination.

The poet has dealt with the historical facts conscientiously but the poet in him was able to maintain a delicate balance between fact and fiction. Moreover, his primary aim was to wield his pen as an imaginative poet; history is not more than a swinging door for him. The readers have an inkling of Bilhana's mental make up when he praises the vaidarbhī style in the beginning of the poem:

> 'Anabhravistih Śravanāmrtasya sarasvatīvibhramajan mabhūmih
> Vaidarbharītih krtināmudeti saubhāgyalābhapratibhūh padānām'[10]

His poetic urge is reflected in the attempts towards embellishment of expressions on the one hand and in the delineation of sentiments as well as in the employment of various descriptive details on the other. From a close perusal of the *Vikramānkadevacarita*, it becomes clear that the poet is a skilful craftsman since he has presented his subject-matter neatly and elegantly. The poet is loyal to historical events pertaining to the bright career of king āhavamalla and the martial exploits of Vikramānka, the protagonist. But nevertheless, in accordance with the true epic-Puranic tradition, the poet also traces the lineage of the Cālukyas in the domain of myth in which Brahmā and Indra have their share. Besides the epic begins with a customary benediction to Krsna. True to this logic Āhavamalla is blessed with three sons by the grace of Śiva. The protagonist is described as specially empowered by the divine favour.

On another plane, the paraphernalia of court epics have been carefully imbibed by Bilhana. There are descriptions of a good number of battles and political intrigues; besides there are march of the army, spring, summer, rainy season, autumn, Svayamvara ceremony, messenger with invitation, wedding, newly married royal couple in the pleasure garden, setting sun, moonlight, drinking bout, water-sports, hunting etc. The poet has also described various cities, rivers, mountains, oceans, clouds, rainbows along with flora and fauna around. There are conventional descriptions of the ladies of the capital city of Kalyāna rushing to have a look at the protagonist as he arrives with the newly wedded bride, Candralekhā; of women suffering from pangs of separation since their spouses are far away. Thus, on the basis of carefully remodelled historical facts, Bilhana has sought to compose a court epic of sorts of moderate length always keeping the legacy of the predecessors in view. Hence Vikramānka is more a 'Dhirodātta' type of protagonist than merely a historical figure. He is a great warrior but free from selfconceit; he is chivalrous but grave and unruffled; he is noble, generous and forgiving but unrelenting to the mischievous. Inspite of the predominance of heroic sentiment in the poem, the erotic too has considerable prominence. Undoubtedly vikramānka acts like a typical epic protagonist when he is fascinated by the charming beauty of Candralekhā, and being lovelorn, remains engrossed in her thoughts and finally like his prototypes, he enjoys love-sports with her after marriage. Notwithstanding Bilhana's unflinching devotion to his patron and eagerness to celebrate the latter's heroic deeds, the poem has been planned and executed according to the well-established conventions of the epic genre. Even when the poet modestly says:

> 'girām pravṛttirmamanīrasāpi mānyābhavitrī nṛpateścartraih ke vāna śuskām mṛdamabhrasindhu-sambandhinīm mūrdhani dhārayanti'[11]

We cannot but note that such expression is typical of a poet with creative sensibility, not of a chronicler with matter of fact attitude to historical events.

This is further corroborated by the poet's remarkable use of figures of speech like Upamā, Rūpaka, Utpreksā, Atiśayokti, Dṛṣṭānta, Bhrāntimān, vyatireka, Samāsokti, Vyājastuti, Arthāntaranyāsa, Virodhābhāsa etc. Likewise no less than eighteen types of metres have been used in this poem. In accordance with the dictum of rhetorics, the poet has generally used one metre predominantly in one canto while in composing the concluding verses of each canto, he has made use of a different metre. However, there are variations as well since the poet has employed different metres in a single canto also. These bespeak of a poet thoroughly entrenched in creative tradition. In fact, Bilhana's awareness of the ever-renewing impact of Indian cultural legacy is proved in his several allusions to the important episodes of the *Rāmāyaṇa*, the *Mahābhārata* and the Purānas. Besides there are instances of pithy and epigrammatic sayings in this poem which seem to be remote echoes of Bhāravi's witty expressions impregnated with profundity of thought. A few examples are cited below:

(i) 'Phalam hi pātra pratipādanamsriya;'[12]

(ii) 'Nakaiśçidapi labhyante niskampāh sukhasampadah'[13]

(iii) 'Ucitācaraṇe Keṣām notsāhacaturam manah'[14]

(iv) 'Mahātmanāmamārgena na bhavanti pravṛkṣyah'[15]

(v) 'Eṣā bhagavatī kena bhajyate bhavitavyatā'[16]

(vi) 'Rājyagrahagrhītānām ko mantrah kim ca bheṣajam.'[17]

(vii) 'Dūṣaṇam hi mukharatvamarthiṇām.'[18]

Kalhaṇa's *Rājatarangiṇī* is regarded by many a critics as the jewel in the crown of the sub-genre of historical court epics. The work was composed in twelfth century A.D. and arranged in eight tarangas with a view to narrating the history of various dynasties which ruled Kashmir till that date. As we have noted earlier, the Indian conception of time has determined the attitude to history. As the temporal age is only a tiny phase of eternity, legendary fiction and historical fact are regarded as interconnected phenomena in the timeless continuum. Hence, the first three tarangas of the *Rājatarangiṇī* narrate legendary events yet these are accepted as part of the whole historical scheme. However, due to the abundance of historical materials, the work has found favour with wide sections of readers. Obviously those who emphasise on poetic qualities, are vexed with the problem as to whether the work should be included in the study of epic genre.

The *Rājatarangiṇī* undoubtedly deserves special mention as an invaluable socio-cultural document. But Kalhana does not seem to have thought about relinquishing his special role as a creative poet. That is why, in the beginning of his work, he has significantly referred to the qualities of a good poet.[19] He seems to believe in the efficacy to creative reconstruction of age-old materials; therefore he informs us that he has sought to give a new lease of life by rearranging the older materials borrowed from the works of the predecessors. Kalhana impresses the readers with his genuine independent spirit, rationality, keen observation, penetration into human mind and intricacies of personality and, above all, with excellent capacity of narration. The traits of realism are plenty in the *Rājataranginī*; it is no ordinary achievement that unlike majority of the Sanskrit epic poets, Kalhana has been able to create individuals with flesh and blood rather than abstract types. His descriptive power is evident in the depiction of struggles, battles, siege, intrigues, murders and deaths etc which, inspite of their inherent realism, remind us of court epics. In the manner of the composers of court epics, Kalhana too exhibits his range of knowledge whenever he gets an opportunity. He seems to have been conversant in rhetorics, grammar, astronomy, a few schools of philosophy and religion, puranic myths, the *Rāmāyaṇa*, the *Mahābhārata* and of course, various branches of literature.

Though Kalhana is a champion of simplicity of narration and generally his style has less diversity and sophistication, he has occasionally made use of ornate style. The poet has depicted pathos with admirable skill; he has also shown his ability in portraying dramatic moments. Kalhana has introduced brief dialogues appropriately which brings about refreshing respite as it were from the dreary monotony of lengthy descriptions. Here we may refer to a critical comment about Kalhana's proximity with the style of court epics: 'More than once, digression is made for the sake of highly florid descriptions of a conventional type.'[20] In fact, he echoes the older poets on many occasions. His consciousness about the continuing tradition has been manifested in simplicity and elegance of diction on the one hand (there he is nearer to Vālmīki, Aśvaghoṣa and Kālidāsa) and in deliberate obscuration of diction by employing rare words, maxims, proverbs etc. on the other (there he has kinship with Bhaṭṭi, Māgha etc.).

Besides, in the disproportionate arrangement of the verses in different tarangas, Kalhana reminds us of the post-Kālidāsa court epics. As the poem consists of as many as 7826 verses, its bulk is quite big indeed which is not properly distributed in 8 tarangas. The poet has discarded the division into cantos but it has not resulted into any improvement. Because the length of these tarangas has not been maintained proportionately; for example, the second taranga constitutes of only 171 verses while the eighth has 3449 verses. In fact, the seventh and eighth tarangas are inordinately big while the remaining six tarangas are of ordinary length. It may be debated whether this means total lack of cohesive poetic scheme as well as any formalistic discipline whatsoever simply because composition continued through several phases as more materials poured in. Understandably the necessity of scheme was felt much later and along with it workable generic regulations were agreed upon. But, by then, the bulk of verses became so unwieldy that Kalhana could not make any better arrangement. However, it is significant that the poet chose the epic as the most appropriate genre for casting his anchor.

The critics have noted that the predominant sentiment of the *Rājataranginī* is Śānta while the otherwise prominent sentiments like śrngāra, Karuna, Raudra etc. are subordinate to it. Kalhana has mostly used the uncomplicated Sloka metre though occasionally we come across a few variations also particulary at the end of the tarangas. The figures of speech like simile, Antithesis, pun etc, are used few and far between; it seems that these add variety to the monotonous flow of the narrative. In fine, the *Rājataranginī* is basically an object of delight for the historical analyists since the orthodox connoisseurs of epic poetry may find it difficult to reconcile with the absence of prominent characteristic features of the genre.

Jayānaka composed the *Pṛthvīrājavijaya* in the beginning of the last decade of the twelfth century A.D. with a view to celebrating the gallant victory of Pṛthvīrāja Cauhān over Muhammad Gauri. Unfortunately its manuscript was discovered in a mutilated condition and it was broken off towards the close of the twelfth canto. Hence we can follow the narrative as far as the coronation of Pṛthvīrāja and the narration of his most important achievement (i.e. his conquest over Muhammad) is lost for ever. Therefore, no opinion can be formulated about the central motif of the epic narrative. As we are to reconcile ourselves with the fragmentary condition of the poem, our study remains confined within the framework of twelve available cantos. At the same time we are not in a position to even determine the total number of cantos of this poem.

The *Pṛthvīrājavijaya* furnishes us with valuable historical accounts; but it also shows its conscious allegiance to the epic tradition. Jayānaka seems to have been well-conversant with the epic paraphernalia; therefore narration of historical events is interspersed with commendable descriptions of towns and cities,[21] lakes and oceans,[22] hunting,[23] counsel,[24] Marches of armies.[25] Besides there are glamourous descriptions of weddings, birth of princes, festivities, sending of messenger, battles etc. There is also conscious display of the poet's wide-ranging scholarship encompassing the following: Śrautasūtras, Gṛhyasūtras, Nyāya and other schools of philosophy, Grammar, the *Rāmāyaṇa*, the *Mahābhārata*, Purāṇas, Painting, Astronomy. Astrology, Moreover Jayānaka has been influenced by the following illustrious predecessors: Kālidāsa, Bhāravi, Māgha, Bilhana. While Kālidāsa's impact is discernible in the use of figures of speech, Bhāravi's influence is more straightforward. Jayānaka clearly resembles Bhāravi while attempting verbal jugglery as follows:[26]

'Nitāntamunnatimato netumānatimātatām
Tene tena natānnetumunnatim māninā matih'
'Natenatetena tena tena tena natena te
Nate nate tena tena te nate na nate nate'

However, it is heartening to note that the poet has not succumbed to such puerile acrobatics of language. Hence the *Pṛthvīrājavijaya* does not vex the readers with suffocating artificiality.

There are some pithy and epigrammatic saying in the poem which may remind the readers of Bhāravi and Māgha. A couple of examples are cited below:

(i) 'Sādhuh pramādāttyajati svabhāvam
Khalastu nārohati sādhubhāvam
Nirgandhatāmeti hi candanādi
Na saurabham samghatate rasone.'[27]

(ii) 'Śilālamkaraṇam rūpam tyāgālamkaranam dhanam
Śrutālamkaraṇam meghā yatra puṇyāni śamsati.'[28]

According to the critics, Jayānaka's style closely resembles that of Bilhana. Here we may note that the invocation and the criticism of other poets in the beginning of the *Pṛthvīrājavijaya* seems to be modelled on the *Vikramānkadevacarita*. Jayānaka deserves credit for employing appropriate diction in accordance with the situation; his language is generally less complicated, compact and reflective. The poet has made use of three different formats of style viz. lātī[29] pāñcālī[30] and Gauḍī.[31] Except the eleventh canto where he uses several metres, the poet has generally employed one single metre in each canto. However, for the sake of variation, he has occasionally made use of different metres as well. Thus Jayānaka has, interestingly, employed twenty three types of metres as well as same numbers of figures of speech in his poem most of which bespeak of his skill. Inspite of his sound knowledge of grammar, Jayānaka has tended to use, albeit occasionally, a few peculiar word-formations which may have been inspired by Bhaṭṭi's idiosyncratic epic.

Like court epic, the arrangement of verses in a couple of cantos of the *Pṛthvīrājavijaya*, has not been proportionate. Because its third canto constitutes of only 38 verses while the fifth has 139 verses. In fact, Jayānaka's affinity with the genre is further evident in the conception of Pṛthvīrāja as a protagonist belonging to the Dhīrodātta category. The principal sentiment is of course heroic while the last two cantos depict the erotic; besides the sentiments of abominable, terrible and pathetic act as the customary angarasas. Jayānaka's use of the Kulakas, Yugalakas, and viśeṣakas may also be noted here. Likewise the frank use of supernatural elements even in a poem with historical theme makes it clear that the poet is deeply entrenched in the epic tradition. Thus Cāhamāna, the founder of the Cauhāna clan of the Rājputs, is stated to have descended from the orb of the sun (canto ii). The poet tries to mystify it further by furnishing different identification for the light that emanated from the sun. It is the oblations offered to Indra in the fire but now coming back. Otherwise it is the ocean incarnate requesting the Ganges flowing on earth as it were through anger or it is Candra entreating suṣumnā ray on the new-moon-day or Kāma's descent on earth or Dhanvantarī leaving the orb of the sun to cure the earth from ailments or descent of the son of the earth to exterminate the mlecchas etc. Even the very name of Cāhamāna is the outcome of such tendencies of mystification.[32] Further, in the manner of the *Mārkaṇḍeya Purāṇa,* the poet describes that several deities have contributed their essence to form his character. In the Puranic accounts. Viṣṇu assumes human form to punish the wicked and establish righteousness. But, in the *Pṛthvīrājavijaya*, Viṣṇu sends Cāhamāna to earth in the form of a sūtradhāra to destroy the Mlecchas. Then, in the fourth canto, there is a mythical account of the origin of salt-lake belonging to Goddess śākambharī; that lake is gifted to Vāsudeva, the first king of the Cauhān dynasty, by a Vīdyādhara with whom the former develops acquaintance. In the ultimate analysis, however, historical details far outweigh such conventional embellishments; but the poet in Jayānaka takes command whenever there is an opportunity either to look beyond or within. On the one hand, he seeks to extend the horizon of temporal history and interpret it in the perspective of eternity while, on the other, he aspires to take up the challenge of reorienting history as a specially designed swinging door for the expansive epic genre.

II

Hemacandra Sūri wrote his *Dvyāśrayamahākāvya* during the fifth and sixth decades of the twelfth century A.D. The title of the poem suggests that it has not been composed to satisfy any creative urge; on the contrary it has a definite purpose to serve history and grammar at the same time. In fact, it is regarded as more a grammatical work than a historical epic. Hemacandra intends to teach Sanskrit and Prākrit grammar and also relate the history of the Cālukya kings of Anahilapattana of Gujarat at the same time. The *Dvyāśraya* consists of 28 cantos of which the first 20 cantos, having 2439 verses, are composed in Sanskrit and illustrate its grammatical rules; the remaining 8 cantos, having 742 verses, are in Prakrit and illustrate its grammatical rules. It may be noted here that Hemacandra wrote the *Siddhahemaśabdānuśāsana*, regarded by Keilhorn as the best grammatical treatise of medieval India, at the request of his patron, Jayasimha Siddharāja. In arranging the illustrative verses of Sanskrit portion of the *Dvyāśraya*, Hemacandra follows the order of rules enumerated in his own treatise. However, he has taken care to maintain the flow of the historical narrative, that is, to eulogise his patrons and their ancestors. Likewise, in the Prakrit portion, he has narrated the achievements of Kumārapāla, the protagonist, because of which it is named as *Kumārapālacarita*.

The critics are unanimous about Hemacandra's encyclopaedic eruditions. They speak about his unique personality which is a combination of scholar, devotee and historian but significantly there is no reference to his poetic aptitude. However, owing to his close acquaintance with the norms of poetics, Hemacandra has been able to invest the narrative with dignity. As the *Dvyāśraya* belongs to the subgenre entitled 'Śāstrakāvya,' it has its inherent limitations; but nevertheless, Hemacandra has adhered to classical literary style. Since the whole poem is exceptionally terse with the abundance of obsolete words, grammatical similes, tough analogy and various other forms of verbal ingenuity, the style is said to be Gauḍhī. The scheme of the portion in Sanskrit (i.e. first twenty cantos) is particularly interesting because it has no single protagonist; rather, the dynasty of the Cālukyas is the collective 'hero'. This cannot but remind us of the *Raghuvamśa* though artistically they are worlds apart. The royal personalities portrayed by Hemacandra are epitomes of all virtues; for example, Mūlarāja, the first king of the dynasty, is a brave warrior, Cāmuṇḍarāja is learned and clever; Durlabharāja is courageous and able administrator; Jayasimha Siddharāja is pious, brave and charitable while Kumārapāla is religious. In the Prakrit portion, Kumārapāla is depicted as a great conqueror but, more importantly, he is a wise and philosopher king.

Hemacandra has attached prominence to the Vīrarasa; but he has occasionally delineated with other sentiments also viz. Śṛngāra, Karuṇa and Śānta. Particularly in the Prākrit portion, Śānta is the most prominent sentiment. Hemacandra may not be an ambitious creative poet; but nevertheless he was not oblivious of the features of Sanskrit court epics. Though he is primarily in search of adequate opportunity for grammatical illustration, he makes it a point to describe objects in their minutest details. But due to his commitment to grammar, the jugglery of words attains prominence and poetic expressions are choked. An eminent critic has therefore commented: 'Pedantic, tediously descriptive, never profound, it (the *Dvyāśraya*) accepted compilation as a substitute for scholarship:' Yet even a bird's eye-view of such descriptions makes us aware of Hemacandra's kinship with the court epics since these include the following: the city of Anahilapātaka, gardens with different trees, the Sarasvatī river (canto I), Śiva appearing in dream, the royal court, march of army (canto II), preparation for battle, autumn, harvest, festival, music session, religious ceremony, march of army (canto III), encampment, sending of messenger, preparation for battle (iv); clash of two rival armies, single combat, pilgrimage of the victor (v), birth of son, counsel in royal court, march of army, battle, appointment of the heir-apparent, renouncement (vi), pilgrimage, renouncement, Svayamvara, marriage, battle (vii) etc. In fact, such descriptions recur till the end of the poem which also include gardens, seasons, mountains, moonrise, night etc. That Hemacandra has devoted the entire seventeenth canto to describe night, is undoubtedly a significant fact. Equally noteworthy is his frequent allusions to the great epics, Puranic myths and legends, Smṛti texts etc. However, all these factors combined together have sealed the fate of the *Dvayāśraya* as a creative literature; hence one normally can only expect intellectual gymnastics in which lucidity, naturalness and warmth of human feeling are considered as anathema.

Hemacandra has used no fewer than twenty four types of metres in the Sanskrit portion. His figures of speech are only a few in numbers but generally these are marked with unsophisticated simplicity. It seems that the poet's overt purpose of composing a Śāstrakāvya did not allow him to extend his craftsmanship to that sphere where fancy reigns supreme. Thus Hemacandra made use of the epic tradition upto a predetermined area since to him, poetry was only a mundane and expendable means to achieve a more important end.

III

Someśvaradeva composed the *Kīrtikaumudī* around 1229 A.D. with a view to eulogising Vastupāla, his patron and the minister of King Lāvanyaprasāda and Virādhavala. The poem constitutes of nine cantos of moderate length through which the subjectmatter has been skilfully dealt with. Apart from its great historical importance, the readers can appreciate some graceful poetic flashes as well. In the very beginning of the poem, Someśvara displays his keen awareness of the literary legacy in general and the epic tradition in particular. After paying his obeisance to Viṣṇu, Śiva, Sarasvatī and the dual divinites like Śiva and Pārvatī, Śiva and Kesava—he has paid his tributes to the older poets in general. Then he offers rich compliments to the widely acclaimed poets like Vālmīki, Vyāsa, Kālidāsa, Bhāravi, Māgha and Bāṇa. Next he speaks of some lesser known poets. This catalogue of names suggests that Someśvara is thoroughly embedded in literary tradition and he has defintely a wide range of study. His admiration for Kālidāsa and the *Raghuvamśa* is particularly noteworthy:

> 'Kālidāsah Kavirjātah Śrīrāmacaritasya yat
>
> Sa eṣa śarkarāyogah payasah sampadyata'[33]

Each canto of the *Kīrtikaumudī* has assumed a sub-title in accordance with the subjectmatter it unfolds. For example, the first canto is known as 'nagaravarṇana' since it depicts the city of Anahillapura while the second canto is entitled as 'narendravamśavarnana' and so forth. Each canto hints at the subject matter of the next canto towards its end. From a close perusal of the poem we can guess that its various descriptive details are fashioned on the model of court epics. Thus Someśvara has made use of the oft repeated details like invocation, splendours of city along with its gardens, palaces, lakes, temples, sacrificial session and bardic songs, coronations, battles, dream, sending of messenger, festivities, music, summer, autumn, sunset, night, moonrise, dawn, pilgrimage etc; at least some of these are nicely executed and deserve praise. The impact of the predecessors on such descriptive details is easily discernibile. On some occasions he has exhibited genuine warmth of feeling and expertise in craftsmanship; the following instances may be cited here: Virādhavala's dream in the second canto; description of evening in the seventh, morning in the eighth and seasons in the sixth and eighth cantos. According to the prevalent method of composition, he also alludes to several myths, legends and anecdotes of the great epics, Purāṇas and different schools of philosophy.

Someśvara is undoubtedly bestowed with both poetic vision and expertise of a craftsman to a considerable extent. He may not be a poet of very high order but he is not easily swayed by the corrupting tendencies of a decadent epoch. When the classic model itself degenerated hopelessly, he could not suggest any viable alternative but nevertheless he did neither forsake taste nor stooped low to drift with the exhausted mariners in their aimless pseudo-literary voyage. It is true that he could not remain entirely unaffected by contemporary trends of degenerative imitation of the older poets. He, too, tried to exhibit his skill in verbal acrobatics by resorting to artificial play with words as well as alliteration and pun of different varieties. But generally his figures of speech are pleasant reading; at least twelve varieties of figures are found in it. His metres are indeed very simple; in fact, there is predominance of 'anuṣṭup' to which 'upajāti' comes a distant second. Eleven other metrical types have been used intermittently. Perhaps one can detect Bhāravi's impact on a few epigrammatical sayings of the poem; for example-

(i) 'Utpattiruttamānām hi, riktapūranahetave.'[34]
(ii) 'Parakaṣṭe Vinaṣṭe hi, Satām prītih pracīyate'[35]
(iii) 'Loke hi Kāraneṇaiva gauravam gunināmapi.'[36]

Vastupāla, the protagonist, has been portrayed as the roof and crown of beings. This has been done according to the well-established norms of the epic tradition. In the introductory section of the poem,[37] Someśvara goes on to declare that 'his (Vastupāla's) personal appearance is splendid (since he is the scion of a noble family) his conduct is excellent, his charity is accompanied by courtesy; his elevated status automatically subdues the enemies, his talents even outshine those of Bṛhaspati, his compassion obliterates all seeds of fear, his fame is an ornament of the world and his administration is always regulated by justice.' Later on the poet observes that the protagonist is also a champion of the ideals of self-restraint; he is not only free from the desire of appropriating the wealth of the people, he can even rise above the temptation of praise. Thus Someśvara has not only remained faithful to his patron and contemporary events, he has sought to make history his lyre to invoke the Epic muse.

Arisimha wrote the *Sukrtasamkīrtana* in 1229 A.D. to eulogise his patron who is none other than Vastupāla, whom we already know as a minister of king Virādhavala and also of his son, Visāladeva of Dholkā. Thus along with Someśvaradeva's *Kīrtikaumudī* and Bālacandra Sūri's *Vasantavilāsa*, the *Sukrtasamkīrtana* also deals with the same subjectmatter. Arisimha begins his narrative with the account of two dynasties of Gujarat; viz., the Cāpotkatas and the Vāghelas and then proceeds to depict the achievements of Vastupāla, the protagonist. However, it is not a replica of the other historical Mahākāvyas stated above since it has furnished many a new details of those events which are mentioned briefly by others; besides he has added some new incidents as well. The *Sukṛtasamkīrtana* consists of eleven cantos having 553 verses in all. It is interesting to note that a poet named Amarapandita has appended five verses at the end of each canto which are not directly related to the text of the poem.

Unlike other works of the subgenre, it does not begin with any invocation; rather it plunges straight into the narrative and takes up the description of the dynasty of the Cāpotkatas. At any rate Arisimha is not unaware of the mechanistic dictums of the rhetoricians, hence he goes on to record the customary details of the city of anahillavada temples, the Raivataka mountain, six seasons, sunrise, conquest, pilgrimage, festivities etc. The sixth and ninth canto are particularly noteworthy since these are devoted exclusively to the descriptions of sunrise and six seasons respectively. This bespeaks of Arisimha's adherence to the epic paraphernalia. Though the poet seldom rises above the level of the mediocre, occasionally we come across delightful expressions as well. The depiction of the appearance of the soul in Bhīma's dream is particularly fascinating. The poet uses only a few figures of speech of which the figures belonging to the category of Sabdālamkāra (i.e. Anuprāsa, Yamaka and Punaruktavadābhāsa) are somewhat plentier than the figures of othe category (i.e. Utpreksā, Atiśayokti and Virodhābhāsa). He shows his fondness for long compounds and highsounding words; thus his style has the features of Gaudī school. Arisimha has used sixteen types of metres quite creditably; on another plane, like many other composers of court epics, he shows his close acquaintance with the *Mahābhārata* and the Puranic legends.

Like its counterpart, the *Kīrtikaumudī*, each canto of the *Śukṛtasamkīr tana* has a different subtitle in accordance with the subject matter it unfolds. Thus, the sub-titles of its first two cantos viz. 'Cāpotkatānvyavarnana' and 'Cālukyānvayavarṇana' contain sufficient indication of their respective subjectmatter. Besides customarily, the concluding verses of almost each canto hint at the subjectmatter of the following canto. Inspite of his primary commitment to the composition of a panegyric on the strong foundation to historical facts, the poet seems to have been aware that the variegated mask of poetry has to be maintained with care. Therefore he portrays Vastupāla, the protagonist, according to the established norms of the court epics as far as practicable. He is depicted as the champion of Caturvarga i.e. four cardinal principles of life. The poet is also careful about the delineation of sentiments; thus the sentiment of quietitude (i.e. Śānta rasa) predominates in the poem while the heroic sentiment (i.e. Vīra rasa) has also considerable prominence. The presence of erotic sentiment (i.e. Śṛñgāra rasa) is a part of the epic convention; therefore it is also not left out. But, in the ultimate analysis, the *Sukrtasamkīrtana* remains plagued with all the usual limitations of the hybrid sub-genre.

Bālacandra Sūri's *Vasantavilāsa* is the latest poem in the series, that is, the historical Mahākāvyas as based on the career of the illustrious minister, Vastupāla. According to the testimony of the poet himself, the work was composed to please Jaitrasimha, Vastupāla's son; it indicates that the poet wielded his pen at the end of the thirteenth or in the beginning of the fourteenth century A.D. It is different from its counterparts because it has unfolded very little historical events; instead it has sought to fill up the resultant vacuum with heaps of conventional but irrelevant descriptive details. The *Vasantavilāsa*, constituting of fourteen cantos, is however valuable because it furnishes us with the date of Vastupāla's death though, inexplicably, he fails to narrate the later life of the protagonist. But he makes it a point to give a detailed account of his own life in the first canto which may therefore be regarded as introduction to the actual epic narrative. In fact, according to the prevalent practice, the poet calls the first canto as 'prastāvanā.' Likewise the second canto describes the capital city and consequently it is entitled as 'Rājadhānivarṇana.'

It has already been noted than the *Vasantavilāsa* abounds in the conventional descriptive details which include invocation, city, temples, palaces, consecration, battle, conquest, appearance of deity in dream, counsel, march of army, six seasons, moon-rise, sun-rise, pleasuregarden, water-sports, drinking bout, pilgrimage etc. No less than three cantos are completely devoted to the depiction of totally extrinsic conventional details. But these also provided the poet with an opportunity to express his skill in craftsmanship. In fact, the descriptions of the city of anahillapura, the seasons with blooming flowers and top floors of the palaces at night are particularly beautiful. An example is given below:

'Yatrānurātrakilaniskalamkāh sucāru candropalacandraśālāh
Pratisphalaccandrakalamka bhītibhṛtorudantivagalajjalaughaih.'[38]

The descriptions of the marches of the armies and battles are also noteworthy. The poet has generally adhered to the Vaidarbhī school of style though he has not hesitated to make use of the Gauḍī school on certain occasions. We find that Bālacandra has constructed nine types of figures of speech and employed fifteen types of metres which bespeak of his allegiance to the continuing epic tradition. Besides, in accordance with the existing practice, the poet makes frequent references to the *Rāmāyaṇa*, the *Mahābhārata*, the Purāṇas and various schools of philosophy, viz., Sāmkhya, Nyāya, Vaiśeṣika, Yoga, Mīmāmsā, Jainism and Buddhism.

Like its counterparts, the *Vasantavilāsa*, too, presents the sentiment of quietitude (i.e.Śānta) as predominant (i.e. Angīrasa) while the heroic (i.e. Vīra) and the erotic (i.e. Śṛngāra) sentiments are also depicted customarily. Vastupāla, the protagonist, has in the mean time become thoroughly standardised; hence Bālacandra Sūri faithfully follows his older contemporaries only to add more lustre to the already established more-than-life image of his protagonist.

Nayacandra Sūri composed the *Hammīramahākāvya* in the last decades of the fifteenth century A.D. with a view to narrating the glorious deeds of the cauhān kings in general and king Hammīra in particular. It is a poem of moderate length whose subjectmatter is arranged in fourteen cantos. The verses in each canto are generally arranged proportionately. But there is exception as well; because the twelfth canto constitutes of 225 verses while the fourteenth has only 46 verses. Each canto has a sub-title of its own signifying its content; thus the first two cantos are entitled as 'pūrvajavarṇana' while the third and fourth are named as 'pṛthvīrājasamgrāmavarnana' and 'tajjanmavarṇana' respectively and so on. This is obviously done in accordance with the usual practice of the sub-genre. The poet makes use of the conventional genealogical accounts that remind us of Jayānaka's *Pṛthvīrājavijaya*. But from a close persual of Nayacandra's poem, it becomes obvious that there are substantial differences between the two.

In the opening verse of the epic, the poet has invoked paramajyoti, the divine flame, which is considered sacred by both the Hindus and the Jainas. In the following benedictory verses, the poet manages to address the Hindu deities and Jaina Tīrthamkaras simultaneously, viz. Brahmā and Ṛṣabhadeva, Viṣṇu and Pārśvanātha, Śiva and Mahāvīra, Sūrya and Śānti, Candra and Neminātha. Such tendencies of ingenuity are obviously modelled on the popular trends of the court epics. As usual there is abundance of descriptive details which include palaces and dwelling houses,[39] lakes, [40] birth of prince,[41] political counsel,[42] espionage,[43] march of armies and battles,[44] hunting[45] and also night, dawn, spring season, beautiful damsels in royal seraglio, watersports etc. The characteristic asymmetrical arrangement of subjectmatter is also found in three consecutive cantos (i.e.v-vii) which are entirely devoted to the description of the seasonal beauty of spring, watersports and other frivolities. Likewise there is conventional exhibition of scholarship; the poet makes frequent references to the Vedas, the great epics, the Gṛhyasūtras, the Dharmasūtras and various schools of philosophy. Besides the poet depicts Hammīra as a Dhīrodātta type of protagonist. In order to emphasise on his excellence, the poet also customarily compares him to various legendary personalities:

> 'Māndhātṛsītāpatikamsamukhyāh Kṣitau Kṣitīndrā Kati nāmanyāsan Tesu stavārhah parameśā sattvaguṇena hammīra mahībhṛdekah.'[46]

The predominant sentiment of the *Hammīramahākāvya* is heroic though, on some occasions, the customary erotic sentiment is present as an 'angarasa.' The poet seems to follow the principles of the Vaidarbhī school of style; hence his composition is marked with lucidity, clarity, sweetness and perspicuity. Nayacandra has been substantially influenced by his illustrious predecessors. A few examples may suffice here:

(a) Kālidāsa's lingering presence may be detected in the following verse:

> 'Ranesu yena svakarāmbujena prollāsyamānāsilatā cakāse
>
> Antahsphuratkrodhakṛśānujāta dhūmmeva sākṣādbahirull asantī.'[47]

(b) Bhāravi's impact is discernible in the following witty and epigrammatic expressions:

> (i) 'Sarvahko'piparasya paśyati janodosam na ca svasya.'[48]
>
> (ii) 'Mūle Chhinne hi sugrāham Phalādyuccaistarovapi.'[49]
>
> (iii) 'Veśyānām ca nṛpānām ca dravyadohi sadāpriyah'[50]

(iv) 'Mūlādvinaste Kārye hi Kim Kuryād balavānapi'[51]

(v) 'Kurvannapi' hitam mūrkhohitāyaiva pragalbhate.'[52]

(c) Bhaṭṭi's influence may be detected in the following expressions where grammatical skill has been consciously exhibited:

(i) 'Śastrāsāstri Sarāsari Kuntā kunti gadāgadi dandādandi Dantādanti bhujābhuji virāh ke'pi pare Vidadhū ranalīlah.'[53]

(ii) 'Kecinmamluh kepijagluh pare ca tresurnesuh kecana melcchapāśah

Hāhārāvam cakrire Kepi Kecijjīvami trātum prāviśan gupta deśam'[54]

(iii) 'Kim Kurvīmahi kim bruvīmahi vibhum Kam cānurundhīmahi Vyācakṣīmahi kim svaduhkhasamam kam vābhāsemahi Yanniṣkāruṇa dārunena vidhinā tādṛggunakākaram

Hammīram haratām ajasā hṛtamaho sarvasvamevāvaneh'[55]

(iv) 'Edhantām prabalairbalaih Svabirudānadhyāpayamtām janān Gāhamtām nayavartma madhyamasamam sphitām vahamtām bhudam

Bādhmitām yudhi bāhujesa nikarān praudhi majamtamtamām Ekasmimstvayi vīra nākamayite Svairam varākāh Śakāh'[56]

Nayacandra uses sixteen types of figures of speech and fifteen types of metres in the poem in which he conforms to the established standard of epic versification. However, it may be noted that he mostly depends on different. arthālamkāras on the one hand while on the other he makes predominant use of 'upajāti' metre in five cantos and 'Anuṣtup' in three. Apart from such allegiance to rhetorical formalities, the *Hammīramahākāvya* is interesting for its treatment of historical subjectmatter. It agrees with the account of the *Pṛthvīrājavijaya* to a good extent that includes Pṛthvīrāja's valliant fight with Sahabuddin culminating in the former's execution in capitivity. Likewise, Hammīra's battle with Alauddin ending in the former's glorious death has been narrated with uncommon sagacity. The protagonists of the Sanskrit epics are generally unputdownable and always victorious. But Nayacandra could not alter the sad fact of history even for the sake of fanciful wishfulfillment nor could he, like Jayānaka, stop abruptly at an opportune moment to avoid the tryst with destiny. Indeed the historical epic is a specially conceived sub-genre which can serve two masters (i.e. history and rhetorics) only upto a certain point. The *Hammīramahākāvya* unmistakably shows that, in the event of a conflict between those Two, it cannot but accept the dictates of the former.

IV

Of the ιwo epics that deal with the famous southern kingdom of Vijayanagar, Gangādevī's *Madhurāvijaya* (also known as Vīrakamparāyacarita) comes first. This epic, consisting of eight cantos, was composed in the last quarter of the fourteenth century by the queen of prince Kamparāya of Kampana who wrested Srirangam and the kingdom of Madhura in 1371 A.D, from the mohammedan rulers.That the epic is composed by a woman is a very significant fact for different reasons. The literary arena is totally dominated by the males because in an exclusively patriarchal society, the women had to live a life of abject servitude and seclusion in the dark corners of inner apartments. After the age of the Brāhmanas, education was made inaccessible to them except only the hetairai.[57] In the subsequent ages, the hapless women existed only to satisfy the whims of the pleasure-hunting males. While the hetairai provided variety for leisurely hours, the women at home ensured the continuation of family to the next generations. Naturally Manu, the great arbiter of Indian society declared,[58] that, for the women, marriage was equal to the investiture ceremony (upanayana), rendering of daily service to husband was equal to the study of the Vedas while living in the family of husband was equal to the stay in the house of preceptor. However, as time rolled on, some families of the power elites tended to lift the embargo when, after a millennium, the old and worn-out Brahmanic model of conservatism was showing signs of wear and tear on the one hand while on the other, new cross-currents of thought emanating from varied cultural milieu could not be ignored any longer. In the medieval principalities of South India, the position of women seems to have been better than anywhere else. Therefore the highly educated queen could cultivate her creative impulse and wield her pen to compose an epic.

That the poetess is well-versed in the works of earlier masters, is clearly evident from her references to the great poets and litterateurs of earlier epoch. viz., Vālmīki, Vyāsa, Kālidāsa, Bhāravi, Bānabhatta, Daṇḍin and Bhavabhūti and also some lesser known predecessors, viz. Karnāmrtakakavi, Tikkaya, Agastya, Gangādhara and Viśvanātha.[59]

This bespeaks of the poetesses' awareness of tradition.

In fact, she goes on to confirm her indebtedness to Kālidāsa:[60]

> 'Dāsatām Kālidāsasya kavayah ke na bibhrati
> Idānīmapi tasyārthānupajīvantyamī yatah.'

This has been actually demonstrated in her poem about which two examples are cited below:

(a) Gangādevī writes:

> 'Mukhena tanvī sarapāndurena vimuktaratnābharaṇā vireje
> Vilūna rājīvavanā dinānta chhāyā śaśānkena śarannadīva,[61]

which reminds us of Kālidāsa's following expression:

> 'śōarīṛasādādasamagrabhūṣaṇāmukhena sālakṣyata lodhrapānduta̅
> Tanuprakāsena viceyatārakāprabhātakalpā śaśineva śarvarī.'[62]

(b) Gangādevi depicts a pregnant woman as follows:

> 'Tāmambugarbhāmiva meghamālām
> Velāmivābhyantaralīnacandrām
> Antahstharatnāmivasūktirekhā
> Māpannasatvām prabhurabhyanandat'[63]

whose source may be traced in the following verse of Kālidāsa:

'Nidhānagarbhāmiva sāgarāmbarām
Śamīmivābhyantara-līna-pāvakam
Nadīmivāntahsalilām sarasvatīm,
Nṛpah sasatvām mahiṣīmamanyata'[64]

The impact of the great poet may also be felt in her graceful exposition of the Vaidarbhī style in which diction is generally easy and simple. What is most noteworthy, it is generally free from laboured expression, pedantry, puns, alliterations, artificial rhymes and long compounds. Though her wide range of learning is evident from the occasional references to *Atharvaveda*, legends and heroes of great epics and Purāṇas, rites prescribed by Smrti—these do not vex the readers. Her preference for various prominent arthālamkāras has never transgressed the frontiers of sensibility.

Gangādevī is well aware of extrinsic requirements of a court epic; hence she furnishes the prescribed descriptive details while dealing with the historical data regarding the career of her husband, prince Kampana. It is indeed no small credit for her that some descriptions are undoubtedly fascinating. Those details include invocation of Ganeśa, Pārvatī and Parameśvara, Sarasvatī and Kriyāśakti[65] (the Kulaguru of the royal family); the city of Vijayanagar;[66] lakes and oceans;[67] spring;[68] winter;[69] march of army;[70] battle;[71] hunting;[72] espionage;[73] water-sports;[74] drinking;[75] sun-set;[76] birth of son etc.

Simile and metaphor seem to be the forte of the poetess though she uses them with rare discretion. A few examples are given below:

(i) 'Sahasrasastumgaturangavīcavomadadvipadvīpavise sitāntarāh/Bhavantamugrāyudhanakrarājayo bhajanti nityam bahulā balābodhayah'[77]

(ii) 'Himabhararvihatah kamalākaro mṛditakāntirabhūmr galānchanah Vadanameva narendranatabhruvāmabhajataśriy amapratiśāsanah'[78]

(iii) 'Pratibimbaparamparāmbudhau
pavanīddhūtatarangasanginī
nabhaso' vatarisyatokhermani-
sopānadhiyam vyabhāvayat'[79]

Moreover, a subtle and distinctive feminine touch may also be felt in some expressions; for example:

(i) 'Saubhāgyagandhadvipadānalekhā
Rarāja tasyā navaromarājih
Tejonidhi garbhatale nigūdham
Kāloragī raksitumāgateva.'[80]

(ii) 'Śaśimaṇḍalaśankhapetakā-.
davakṛśa kṣapayā samarpitam
Kumudacchavi Kaumudīmayam
Dadhatī Kṣaumamabhād digaganā'[81]

The *Madhurāvijaya* does not digress much from its avowed purpose; after introducing king Bukka with all his splendour and greatness in the first canto, the poetess narrates the birth of Kampana in the second canto and plunges straight into the mainstream of the epic narrative. The following six cantos depict the exploits of Kampana, the protagonist; however, it should also be noted that the sixth and the seventh canto are more out of convention than necessity. The seventh canto is interesting because here the poetess introduces herself. But the canto does not seem to be complete while, in the eighth, the manuscript breaks off abruptly. Thus the *Madhurāvijaya* may not have been available to us in its full form. But, the extant form is sufficient for us to form opinion about the epic and its poetess. Gangādevī is, as we have already noted, generally a conformist but nevertheless she does not overdo her allegiance to the epic tradition. Thus, at the end of almost each canto, the subject-matter of the next canto is customarily hinted at. The stature of Kampana, as a Dhīrodātta type of protagonist has been built up commendably. Different sorts of details have been conjured up for the purpose; the poetess is never swayed by her subjective feelings though the protagonist is her husband whom she idolised. In fact, medieval beliefs and superstitions remain unassailable; that is why the protagonist is accosted by an unknown lady in a strange manner who presents a divine sword to him with which he has won the final battle. The predominant sentiment is predictably heroic while the erotic is subordinate to it.

Sometimes Gangādevī has taken resort to the Kulaka[82] and Kalāpaka[83] types of composition which prove that she has absorbed the influence of the typical trends in post-Bhāravi court epics. Even, on some rare occasion, she has shown her awareness about the idiosyncrasies of grammatical epics (i.e. Śāstrakāvya). The poetess has used twelve types of metres with credit. Lastly, a couple of pithy sayings may also be detected in the poem that reminds us of the popular trend set by Bhāravi and Māgha:

(i) 'Na madah kasya vikāra kāraṇam'.[84]

(ii) 'Hṛdayam Kah khalu vetti rāginām'[85]

In fine, Gangādevī has attained considerable success though she has to operate under the aegis of conventionalized formulas derived from and coexistent with habitual patterns of language.

Rājanātha Dindima wrote the '*Śāluvābhyudaya*' in thirteen cantos to celebrate the career of Narasimha, the protagonist. It is held that it was written before 1486 A.D. The protagonist is said to have been only a commander of the army of Vijayanagar under Mallikārjuna and his successor; but the wheel of fortune turned in his favour when no scion was left in the samgama dynasty. He, therefore, proclaimed himself as the founder of ths Sāluva dynasty in 1456. A.D. and thus began his career as a king. In the poem, the protagonist is projected as a champion of four cardinal principles of life. He is a peerless warrior and an excellent administrator with all other expected qualities.

Rājanātha is as usual a versatile scholar, keenly aware of all the requisite paraphernalia of the court epic including descriptive details, different types of allusion, figures of speech, metrrical scheme, grammatical peculiarities etc. Yet the *Śāluvābhyudaya* never rises above the level of the commonplace; the poet employs the Vaidarbhī, Gaudī and lāṭī styles but he can hardly be regarded as a fanciful poet.

However, inspite of such limitations, Rājanātha is equally alive to the lessons of the epic tradition. Particularly he borrows from Kālidāsa's depiction of Queen Sudakṣiṇā;[86] while describing queen Mallāmbikā;[87] he is similarly indebted to Kālidāsa's description of Raghu's conquest,[88] which is the model for his depiction of Narasimha's martial expedition in the south.[89]

Likewise Rājanātha borrows from Bhāravi on a few occasions.[90] In the ultimate analysis, the *Śāluvābhyudaya* cannot be regarded as a significant work even in the limited sphere of this subgenre.

Some other works are also mentioned by critics. These include the *Somapālacarita* written by Jalhana, a Kashmirian poet of the late eleventh century as a panegyric of king Somapāla of Rājapurī who was later defeated by Sussala. As Kalhana has dealt with this small episode in the history of Kashmir in a much more interesting way, Jalhana's poem sank into oblivion in no time. Besides, the poem did not have any intrinsic merit of its own.

Besides we are told about epic entitled *Bhuvanābhyudaya* written by Śankuka, probably in the eighth century A.D., which describes the fratricidal feud of Mankha and Utpala.

In the thirteenth century, Jinaharsa wrote *Vastupālacarita* to praise the versatility of the famous minister, Vastupāla. In the second half of the fourteenth century, sarvānanda wrote the *Jagadūcarita* in typical ornate style; it is actually biography of a simple merchant of Gujrat in seven cantos.

In the sixteenth century, Rudrakavi wrote the *Rāṣṭraudhavamśakāvya* in twenty cantos to narrate the history of Bāgulas of Mayūragiri. The narrative begins with the account of the Rāstraudha dynasty, and ends with the activity of the poet's patron, Nārāyaṇasāha.

Raghunātha wrote the *Rasikamaraṇa,* consisting of eighteen cantos in the same century with a view to describing the biographical details of Durvāsas, a Vaiṣṇava preacher. In the seventeenth century, Rāmabhadrāmbā, another poetess, wrote the *Raghunāthābhyudaya* in twelve cantos with a view to praising certain events in the life of Raghunātha of Tanjore. In the same period, Mādhava wrote the Vīrabhānūdayakāvya in twelve cantos in which scanty historical materials are interwoven with legendary details.

The phenomenal popularity of the *Rājataranginī* induced some ambitious versifiers into writing a couple of insignificant sequels. In the first half of the fifteenth century, Jonarāja wrote a historical poem about Kashmirian princes covering upto his own time, that is, the reign of Sultan Zainulabidin. He was ambitious enough to entitle it as *Rājataranginī.* Śrīvara, his disciple, was equally enthusiastic and wrote the *Jainarājataranginī* in four chapters that encompassed the events taking place between 1459 and 1486 A.D. He was, in fact, a slavish imitator of Kalhana; like his preceptor, he too exercised in futility.

V

Indeed most of the works composed in the post-Māgha epoch suffer the inevitable ailments peculiar to an immobile society. They could not afford to look optimistically forward to a strange and unidentifiable posterity since beyond the periphery of the administrative unit of their respective patrons, everything seemed hazy and insecure. They learned only to sing pleasing lullaby to the lotus-eaters, as it were, in the form of Narcissistic panegyrics while the society around was fast disintegrating. As the courtpoets of their patrons, they had to invent truth and manufacture details to make these subservient to an established tradition. These priests of temporality went on masquerading as poets so long lucrative rewards pampered them. But it took a heavy toll as the genre was further impoverished and in no time completely invalidated. Their stagnant style is the typical reflection of the elitist attitude born of alienation from the living streams of the greater society. Inspite of minor readjustments within the subgenre, there was no major innovation. Because, like linguistic changes, stylistic changes occur only if the means of human expression are continuously adapted to the needs of a changing cultural environment. It cannot be denied that each literary epoch achieves for itself not only an appropriate language for its requirements, but also varied but definite verbal patterns through which it may unfold its own social conventions and communicate its opinions and feelings. The compositions belonging to the exhausted epic genre, discussed in this chapter, demonstrate albeit negatively the rationale of the above statement.

We have discussed elsewhere about a consciously promoted intimacy and interdependence between different genres of art and literature including the epic. When intellectual and artistic activities were cultivated vigorously, the epic genre too reached its heights. Particularly, the Gupta period is renowned for an unparalleled flowering of literature, music, sculpture, architecture and philosophy with all the characteristic refinement, stylisation, idealisation as well as conception of purity of form and harmony of proportion. But slowly, in the post-Gupta epochs, these began to degenerate and beneath the surface of apparent cohesion, paradoxes and contrasts came in the offing. With the gradual ossification of Indian society, the basic strength of tradition tended to be misinterpreted and taste for rules and regulations degenerated into rigid straitjackets. Interestingly, the artistic and literary genres interacted positively with each other solong the social dynamic remained undisturbed. The penchant for regulation was manifested in the creation of a vocabulary of gestures, as it were, in all the creative genres. In the court epics, this was expressed through the cultivation of ornamentation and formulaic descriptive details. We have already discussed as to how canonical texts set down aesthetic and iconographical rules which ultimately became sacrosanct. Instead of providing the artists and litterateurs with set of continuously renewing aesthetic code from which they could draw an inexhaustible supply of modes of expression, these tended to paralyse their creative impulse itself.

As long as syncretic tendencies remained valid as social experiences, the poets and artists could add a new accent to old accents and a new direction to the older forms of articulation. Their imagination could freely create many a variations of a few cardinal themes; an effective balance was maintained between creative thought and the norms defined by the treatises of the rhetoricians. But the gradual extinction of creative fire brought about a steady decline in all art forms including literary genres, since according to Indian world-view there was an all-comprehensive totality in basic artistic sensibility inspite of apparent distinctiveness. Indian mind believed in the impossibility of practising one artform without any knowledge of the other. The royal families as well as the aristocracy patronised various genres. As a result the interdependence of one art-form upon another can always be recognised. Thus the reliefs and paintings seem to be the faithful reproduction of literary episodes with all their attitudes and emotions. Likewise, various descriptive details employed in the court epics reproduce a repertoire of stylisation endeared by the exponents of sculpture and painting. Like any other creative personality, an epic poet equally plunges his roots below into the soil of experience and sensation; on the other hand, he exhibits his thoughts and sensibilities in the transmuted but ramified forms of foliage. But when the soil dries up, the roots are inevitably weakened and consequently the process of degeneration sets in.

When tendentious feigning of life took over the artforms, the epic poets also could not escape it any more. There was no way to salvage the exhausted genre since at the close of the first millennium, the mastery of composition in the sister genres was gradually degenerating and ultimately series of stereotypes were proliferated. The manifestations of perfection of form, confident craftsmanship and brilliant innovation in the dignified works of art at Ajantā, Illorā. Bāgh, Elephantā, Māmallapuram undoubtedly indicate great flourish. But, at the same time, these also bespeak of an overriding concern for conforming to the established canons. As long as the artists maintained technical accomplishment along with their creative impulse, the sparkle and spontaneity remained intact. In the next couple of centuries, however, the works of different genres tended to become increasingly heavy, dry and mannered. Though due to the emergence of different dynasties, the artists and craftsmen enjoyed unprecedented patronage, acute sociocultural uncertainties resulting from constantly changing political equilibrium brought about a contrastive change. The creative minds succumbed to the pressure of easy success by conforming to rigid norms of stylisation; soon these became imitative and shallow. The works of art of the subsequent period seem to have been executed in a lifeless manner; the flame has been finally extinguished. Therefore decorative pieces have been accumulated under royal and aristocratic patronage which are marked with mechanical artifice, ornamentation, naivety of conception and poverty of composition. In this perspective, our detailed account of the exhausted epic genre becomes particularly significant because this proves that as there is mutual illumination of arts, likewise, there is contrarily the process of mutual disillumination as well.

Kalhana, one of the representative poets of the post-māgha epoch, however, show that the traditional conception about a poet's exclusive and honourable status in the social hierarchy is still popular. He says:

> 'Konyah Kālamatikrāntam netum pratyaksatāmkṣamah
> Kaviprajāpatimstyaktvā ramyanirmānasālinah'[91]
>
> and
>
> 'Ślāghyam sa eva gunavānrāgadvesa bahiṣkṛtāh
> Bhūtārthakathane yasya stheyasyeva sarasvatī.'[92]

Whatever might be Kalhana's claim, we have already noted that in spite of his emphasis on factuality, the poet's closer approximation to history hardly yielded the desired result. The poets were sadly conditioned by their temporal and immediate situation. They chose to write about historical personalities and events not because they sought to improve our knowledge of history but because they intended to immortalise their patrons by extracting fiction out of history. At any rate they failed to serve two masters i.e., art and history or fiction and fact with equal dexterity. But, on the other hand, the epic poets of the earlier creative epoch did not have to base their poems on immediate reality. In fact, their poetic microcosms are more real than that of Bilhana or Kalhana or Jayānaka, and consequently enough powerful themselves. Those 'superreal' worlds weave their webs around us and sufficiently exist for themselves. In fact, the epic genre, being one of the finest flowers of time, cannot restrict itself in description of external phenomena; it blossoms best when it transforms and recreates. Precisely here, the post-Māgha epics, lacking in intensity of imagination, fail to make their mark.

Let us conclude with the following significant words of Niccolio Tommaseo (1802-1874), a nineteenth century Italian poet:

> 'Not the radiating image
> Nor the hidden idea.
> Nor the rhythmical harmony,
> Nor love create.
>
> Idea, rhythm, image, air
> of fecund love
> Merge into one form from which
> the verse, the flower, the world come out.'[93]

NOTES

1. Keith, A.B. *History of Sanskrit Literature*, Oxford University Press, 1973, p. 144.
2. *Navasāhasānkacarita*. i. 7-8.
3. *ibid.* xii. 16,26,32,33,55.
4. *ibid.* ii. 61.
5. *ibid.* xiv. 35.
6. *ibid.* xii. 54.
7. *ibid.* xi. 99.
8. *ibid.* xi. 102.
9. ibid. vii. 2.
10. *Vikramānkadevacarita*. i.9.
11. *ibid.* i. 28.
12. *ibid.* ii. 26.
13. *ibid.* iv. 46.
14. *ibid.* iv. 61.
15. *ibid.* iv. 95.

16. *ibid.* iv. 97.
17. *ibid.* iv. 115.
18. *ibid.* v. 13.
19. *Rājataranginī.* i. 7.
20. Stein, ed. *Rājataranginī*, vol. i, Introduction, p. 23.
21. *Prthvīrājavijaya.* iv. 72-73; v. 53, 140, 169, 177; viii. 63-71; ix. 75, 82.
22. *ibid.* iv. 80-88; v.1-3.
23. *ibid.* i. 27.
24. *ibid.* xi. 3-5.
25. *ibid.* v. 52; vi. 1-20; x. 9-29.
26. *ibid.* v. 9-10.
27. *ibid.* i. 23.
28. *ibid.* v. 163.
29. *ibid.* i. 66.
30. *ibid.* i.75-77.
31. *ibid.* ii. 1.
32. *ibid.* ii. 44: Cāhamāna is so called because he possesses cāpa (bow) in his hand. Hari in his mind, Māna (pride) in strength and Naya (statesmanship).
33. *Kīrtikaumudī* i. 12.
34. *ibid.* iv. 25.
35. *ibid.* viii. 2.
36. *ibid.* viii. 15.
37. *ibid.* i. 44-47.
38. *Vasantavilāsa.* ii. 28.
39. *Hammīramahākāvya.* xi. 27, 31, 33.
40. *ibid.* xi. 35.
41. *ibid.* iv. 139.
42. *ibid.* iv. 21.
43. *ibid.* iii. 23.
44. *ibid.* i. 27-31; iii. 50, 79; iv. 84; ix. 119.
45. *ibid.* iv. 48.

46. *ibid.* i. 8.
47. *ibid.* ii. 68.
48. *ibid.* i. 101.
49. *ibid.* iv. 105.
50. *ibid.* ix. 169.
51. *ibid.* ix. 177.
52. *ibid.* xiii. 138.
53. *ibid.* x. 51.
54. *ibid.* x. 58.
55. *ibid.* xiv. 7.
56. *ibid.* xiv. 10.
57. In fact the *Tattirīya Āraṇyaka* is very sarcastic about the educated ladies: 'Striyah satīh u ye purmsah Āhuh' (i. 11. 4.)
58. *Manusamhitā.* ii. 67.
59. *Madhurāvijaya.* i. 6-16.
60. *ibid.* i. 7.
61. *ibid.* ii. 2.
62. *Raghuvamśa.* iii. 2.
63. *Madhurāvijaya.* ii. 12.
64. *Raghuvamśa.* iii. 9.
65. *Madhurāvijaya.* i. 4.
66. *ibid.* i. 55-59; v. 36; viii. 10.
67. *ibid.* i. 50,60; iii. 40; viii. 4.
68. *ibid.* v. 42.
69. *ibid.* vii. 42.
70. *ibid.* iv. 35.
71. *ibid.* iv. 69-73.
72. *ibid.* ii. 6; v. 14.
73. *ibid.* v. 4.
74. *ibid.* v. 16; vi. 62.
75. *ibid.* viii. 32.
76. *ibid.* vii. 8.

77. *ibid.* iii. 40.
78. *ibid.* v. 16.
79. *ibid.* vii. 8.
80. *ibid.* ii. 10.
81. *ibid.* vii. 46.
82. *ibid.* i. 43-54.
83. *ibid.* viii. 18-21.
84. *ibid.* vii. 5.
85. *ibid.* vii. 6.
86. *Raghuvamśa.* iii. 5, 15.
87. *Śāluvābhyudaya.* ii. 65, 75.
88. *Raghuvamśa.* v. 44-50.
89. *Śāluvābhyudaya.* v. 1.
90. *ibid,* v. 20 and *Kirātārjunīya.* iv. 62; also ibid. iii. 18; v. 18 etc.
91. *Rājataranginī.* i. 4.
92. *ibid.* i. 7.
93. The original Italian version is as follows:
    Non la ragginate immagine,
    non la riposta idea.
    non l' armonia de' numeri.
    none i' amor che crea.

    Idea, concento, immagine.
    aura d' amor facondo,
    formansi in uno, e n' escono
    il verso, il fiore, il mondo.

SECTION –II

8

Perspective of Nineteenth Century Bengal

From Forced Amnesia to Revival of Legacy

The genesis of the Bengali epic genre in the middle of the nineteenth century is concomitant with the final breach with the nagging hang-overs of the residues of the medieval Bengali literature. In the opening decades of the nineteenth century, the old order in the society was fast disintegrating yet the new world was powerless to be born. The transition from the dark abyss of feudal epoch to the illuminated realm of a rational modern age had commenced under the yoke of colonial rule; but initially its impact on the literary arena was minimal. The inherent limitations of an enormously superstitious society could not be easily overcome; the fetters were too numerous and imposing. Since the eighteenth century, the masters of the feudal society were the champions of decadent cultural syndrome. Several poetasters were patronised for providing vulgar amusement according to the debauched taste of their leisure-enjoying masters. It was also the opportune hour for the compraedors to help the British to consolidate their colonial power in Bengal. In the late eighteenth century, those compraedors wielded enough wealth and power in that society; it was then their turn to participate in the syndrome of decadence. As there was no alternative model, they sought to emulate the existing pattern. But the changing socio-historical reality gave rise to a hybrid generation popularly known as 'Bābu' (i.e. 'gentleman'—but its subtle nuances are not exactly translatable in English). Their activities sounded the death-knell of the prevalent cultural habits.

But external stimuli were necessary for heralding a new dawn after centuries of darkly night. For their own colonial interest, the British ushered in a new era; they introduced a modern system of education and gradually established a new structure of civil administration. These brought about a completely metamorphic change, or rather unleashed chain of transformations in the social, economic, political and cultural environments. The cumulative impact of the colonial rule, bourgeois economy and western culture gave birth to an altogether new awareness about life and culture among the educated strata of the Bengali society. This awareness is commonly regarded as symptomatic of the 'renaissance'; thus many a critics have sought to identify fifteenth century Florence with nineteenth century Calcutta.[1] Sir Jadunath Sarkar, an eminent historian, observed: 'The dry bones of a stationary oriental society began to stir under the wand of heaven-sent magician. It was truly a renaissance, wider, deeper and more revolutionary than that of Europe after the fall of Constantionople.'[2] This is an exaggeration ne plus ultra and it is based on a false analogy. Even if Florence is equated with Calcutta, Bengal cannot be compared to Italy. Because the great impact of the Italian renaissance shook the European civilization with a great dazzle in all spheres of human activities. Anthropocentric worldview gave a new lease of life to various artistic and literary genres throughout Europe; actually an entirely new world was born bringing in its train fundamental changes in the conceptions of life. Nothing of such magnitude happened in Bengal; in fact, the dazzling aura of awakening was meant exclusively for the chosen few belonging to the upper strata of the inhabitants of Calcutta. The new ray of awareness could not pierce through the perpetuating darkness that existed for many centuries even in the periphery of that city in the making. Florence had its fellow-travellers in Venice and Rome and Naples while Calcutta had none. In fine, unlike the Italian renaissance, only a handful of elites became aware of a new essence of life.

But the most important difference between fifteenth century Italy and nineteenth century Bengal lies in the latter's status as the part of a British colony. The newly acquired western education made the elites only vaguely aware of the bondage since, notwithstanding such awareness, their class interests were inseparable with the perpetuation of the colonial rule. Hence it was natural for many of them to frankly side with the British; those who could not reconcile themselves to the humilitation, tried to trace its cause in the not-so-remote past. This led to a self-deceiving process of witchhunting; the middle age was branded as 'Muslim age' and the Muslim invaders were held responsible for the present humiliation. We will see in a later chapter as to how such witchhunting was reflected in the Bengali epics. The British rulers were generally given the benefit of doubt and instead the medieval age was made an easy and safe target which ultimately paved the way for religious revivalism and a consequential communalisation of literature. Along with the dismissal of the medieval age as insignificant as well as positively detrimental to the promotion of national glory, there is a strong pleading for revival of India's glorious past which is actually thoroughly idealised and tailored as imaginative compensation for the disagreeable present.

In the first phase of the contact with the western ideas, the young Calcuttans were completely won over. The Hindu College was the famous breeding ground for a group of young rebels popularly known as 'Young Bengal'. Kishorichand Mitra, an eminent person of that turbulent time, observed almost as a self-estimate: 'The youthful band of reformers who had been educated at the Hindu College, like the tops of Kanchanjunga, were the first to catch and reflect the dawn.'[3] No other social group has generated so much controversy in its own time. The memory of those pupils of the Hindu College is inseparably connected with its most famous teacher, Henry Louis Vivian Derozio (1809-1831), son of Portuguese merchant and an English woman, who inculcated the spirit of radicalism, patriotism and rationalism with passionate fervour. He was successful in igniting the minds of his pupils with the vision of a brave new world emerging out of chaos. He left no stones unturned to impress upon his students that the call of the hour was to prepare for sacrificing everything to direct a crusade against the colossal social vices of superstition, pretension and ignorance. Derozio inspired them to live and die for nothing but truth, to consider independent thinking as a sacred duty and to shun the worn-out legacies of a habitual past at any cost. Naturally such revolutionary concepts were branded as blasphemous by the vindictive conservative society and Derozio was eventually dismissed from the college. But the panicky reaction of the orthodox society failed to break the morale of the enthusiastic young rebels.

The untimely death of Derozio was indeed a crushing blow to the Young Bengal; but already Derozianism had become an act of faith for them. Hence the guiding spirit of Derozio crystallized into a strong elitist movement which continued under the collective leadership of Derozio's pupils. From 1828 to 1843, their activities were confined to the formation of associations[4] and promotion of radical views through their journals,[5] viz., *The Enquirer* (founded in 1831), the *Jnananvesan* (1831), the *Parthenon* (1830), the *Hindu Pioneer* (1830) and the *Bengal Spectator* (1842). Whatever might be the outcome of their endeavours, it cannot be denied that the Young Bengal group was the harbinger of a new socio-political consciousness. However they suffered from inherent contradiction from the very beginning since their ideology contained the inevitable characteristic ideological features found in the colonial countries: duality, indecision and inconsistency. Because the Young Bengal movement had genuine concern for promoting the spirit of freedom but they could not think of snapping ties with 'albion's' distant shore. Actually they wanted that the feeling of being in chains might at least be notionally allayed while the cage should remain undisturbed. Thus, in the inaugural meeting of the Bengal British India Society in 1843, Ramgopal Ghosh declared that he wished 'nothing more sincerely than the perpetuity of the British sway in this country.' It only shows that the British colonialists were successful to a considerable extent in creating a stratum of intellectuals that might be the mediators between the British and the millions of Indians under their rule. It was intended that those elites would be Indian in blood and colour of skin only but English in tastes, views and attitude.

Ramgopal's declaration is, in fact, a reconfirmation of what was exclaimed by none other than Rammohan Roy in 1823 while making an appeal to the king against the Press regulations: 'Your dutiful subjects consequently have not viewed the English as a body of conquerors but rather as deliverers, and look up to your Majesty not only as a ruler, but also as a father and protector.'[6] Such an one-sided attitude to the British developed in the late eighteenth and early nineteenth century because the enlightened section of the Bengali society saw that the British had done away with the fragmentation of perpetually alienated village community; instead, the establishment of road and railway communications as well as law and order has buttressed an unprecedented period of progress and material development. It has brought about a fundamental change in their own life-styles; hence, they were not in a position to recognise the imperialist design. Moreover the act of permanent settlement of land (1793) gave rise to a new aristocracy of wealth who filled up the vacuum caused by the fading out of the erstwhile feudal lords. Naturally these neoelites and their scions became the power base of the British. Therefore, in the initial phase of the encounter with the enlightenment provided by the British, they were overwelmed by a feeling of gratitude and went unhesitatingly to the extent of glorification of bondage. This is evident in the following comment: 'If ever any conquest proved a blessing to the conquered, it was the empire of Great Britain in India....The kind and wise dispensations of God must be acknowledged by the improved Hindoo in timely sending a civilized, and in every respect a clever people *to give light where there was darkness*, to elevate what was low, to improve what was mean and to reform what was corrupt.'[7]

In order to consolidate and perpetuate their economic and political dominance, the British colonialists took their offensive in the ideological front for enslaving their subjects spiritually. The old world was ruined and the new world was never built[8]; the introduction of western education was meant for installing subterfuges in Indian society and also for ensuring the provision of faithful personnel at the back and call of the colonial administration. In order to obviate possibility of mental resistance, the British sought to further consolidate the gain by winning over the neoelites with various forms of ideological stimuli. This reminds us of a famous comment by Jean Paul Sartre: 'The European elites undertook to manufacture a native elite. They picked out promising adolescents; they branded them, as with a red-hot iron, with the principles of western culture; they stuffed their mouths full with high-sounding phrases, grand glutinous words that stuck to the teeth.'[9] Indeed the emergence and growth of the petty-bourgeoise intellectuals in nineteenth century Bengal are the unique contribution of British colonialism. When the days of feudal patrons were finally over, all intellectual and literary activities were sponsored by the newly emerging middle class though till the sixties, some benevolent rajas (mostly beneficiary of the permanent settlement of land) continued to patronise literary pursuits. But the new age had already dawned whose strewardship was no longer in their hands. The inherent ambivalence of the petty-bourgeoise intelligentsia was reflected in the chequered development of various literary genres as well as in the complexities of sociocultural activities.

Under the influence of Derozio, the students of the Hindu College drew their inspiration from Bacon, Hume and Tom Paine; particularly Paine's *Age of Reason* became the Holiest book for the Derozians. But we have already noted that the orthodox society branded them as blashphemous because they scrapped the traditional manners and customs and openly challenged religious obscurantism. They affiliated themselves with the latest model of bourgeoise liberalism since, being colonial elites, they had no second choice. In spite of their declaration of allegiance to the colonial rule (as we have already stated) their courageous rebellion had positive historical significance. But opinions about the Derozians have remained polarized ever since the 'Oriental Magazine' made sarcastic remarks about 'cutting their ways through ham and beef, and wading to liberalism through tumblers of beer.' Their anarchic and iconoclastic activities alienated them further but, like true crusaders, they refused to budge. *The Enquirer* depicted the wounded but angry reaction of the Young Bengal: 'persecution is high for we have deserted the shrine of Hinduism. The bigots are violent because we obey not the calls of superstition. Our conscience is satisfied, we are right; we must persevere in our career. If opposition is violent and insurmountable, let us rather aspire to martyrdom than desert a single inch of the ground we have possessed.... A people can never be reformed without noise and confusion; the absurd prejudices of the Hindus can never be eradicated without violent persecution against the reformers. We have undertaken this task. And shall fear, the quality of the coward and the attribute of the guilty, be our guide?...Blessed are we, that we are to reform the Hindu nation'.[10]

Yet, in spite of such unquestionable sincerity, zeal and indomitable energy, the alienated Young Bengal spent all their passions in raising the battlecry. They looked at the peaks of the society but never thought of looking below; moreover they looked around through a predetermined prism that presented the historical problem with wrong colours.[11] At any rate, the inherent contradictions were impossible to overcome; hence after three decades of storm and quakes, the Young Bengal movement gradually not only calmed down but also went a few steps backward. Hence there cannot be any uniform assessment of the sociocultural perspective of the nineteenth century Bengal. Sushobhan Sarkar, an eminent historian, rightly said about the role of the Young Bengal: 'Its most memorable positive aspects are a fearless rationalism and a candid appreciation of the regenerating new thought from the west. Much of this was drowned in the current of traditionalism, mysticism, religiosity and revivalism fashionable in the later part of the century.[12] The changed attitude is best reflected in an article written by Kristodas Pal in the mid-fifties. There he not only sounds apologetic but there is also an admission that the wheel has indeed come full circle by then. He says: 'The Young Bengal is neither a wholesale condemner of Hindu manners and customs nor a sworn enemy to everything that is Hindu.... He is characterised by boldness and freedom. He is a hard-working man in the field of literature. He loves those habits and tastes of the English which are free from blame.... The educated native has not been denationalised by imbibing English thoughts and communing with English feelings.... The tide of patriotism has now run so high that it is hard to stay its course...Some time ago, it was a fashion to cry down the language of our country... Men run so mad with English that they counted it a degradation and a waste of time to apply themselves to the study of the Vernacular. But happily those men that cherished this strange disposition have now altered their creed of literature, reformed their tastes. The blood that boiled within them when, in the May-flush of Youth, having become cool, they have sobered themselves down in their literary habits. They are now the zealous advocates of Bengali.'[13]

This is undoubtedly a very important statement which bespeaks of an intense yearning for the roots. Thus in the greater historical perspective, the earlier phase of Young Bengal movement seems to have presented an inverted mirror for the discovery of self-identity and honour. There is no use denying the fact that the Young Bengal do not have a single face and that they have their historically conditioned limitations.They have been, in fact, constrained to collectively assume the role of Tantalus, the famous mythical hero of Greece, whose thirst can never be quenched. The Young Bengal dreamt of bringing about an abrupt metamorphic change in the value system of the Hindu society but they failed to realise that mere dreaming and declaration of revolt were not enough to obliterate the past altogether. When the phase of initial extrovert overreaction was over, the Young Bengal graduated to the stage of maturity and they applied their mind in searching for alternative routes to as well as modules for regaining the lost paradise. As we have already stated, the immediate past was repudiated; moreover, the contemporary time has to be set on the path of glorious transcendence. Initially, the escape from the present had no significance other than violent self-negation but, in course of time, it led to the fortified Utopia of remote antiquity. The next generation of the elites took resort to the collective pride about a glorious heritage; unlike the disagreeable middle age, the ancient period had a distinct advantage. It could be rebuilt with imagination and a hope of regeneration could be gathered there. Like Prometheus, the second generation of Young Bengal collected compensatory light to illuminate the dark corners of their desperate existence. The seeds of self-expression were thus sown though the harvest could be reaped only later. Here we may refer to the following thought-provoking words of Rabindranath Tagore: 'There are some who are exclusively modern, who believe that the past is the bankrupt time, leaving no assets for us, but only a legacy of debts. They refuse to believe that the army, which is marching forward, can be fed from the rear. It is well to remind such persons that the great ages of renaissance in history were those in which men suddenly discovered the seeds of thought in the granary of the past.'[14]

III

The sense of continuity with past is very important particularly when a nation is searching for its true identity. The elites in the fifties and sixties of the nineteenth century Bengal found themselves confronted with the Herculean task of combining the enduring indigenous tradition with the desirable elements of English civilization. The basic problem is to combine the diametrically opposite cultural ingredients in a harmonious way so that an entirely new world order comes out and yet the regenerated and idealised past is established as a symbol of eternity. That way the present bondage becomes an illusory fact in the limitless continuum of time. Hegel put this elevating notion in his famous pun: 'wesen ist was gewesen ist', that is, 'our essence is what have been.' In the nineteenth century Bengal, the rediscovery of that 'essence' was a complicated process since it had to encounter several historical paradoxes. Before coming in contact with western education sponsored by the colonialists, the concept of any 'have been' never occurred to the last remnants of the feudal elites. Being engrossed in stupefying slumber for many generations, they did not bother to look beyond; there was neither past nor future to fall back upon. They were happy to maintain the status quo within their isolated and fortified settlements.

When they were exposed to the existence of the greater world outside, the shells were shattered and the present offered no consolation. Therefore the search began for an honourable past where the self-sustaining 'essence' could be located. It was believed to be located somewhere beyond the reach of the irritating historical account. The idea of an inferno of middle age was therefore cultivated by the new elites for whom the past was split into two segments. On the one hand, there was a more recent past, stretching like a gulf of time between the present and the past that really mattered. On the other hand, there was an elevating past what was both precious and remote. It was infinitely worth recovering but it could only be recovered or recreated now since it had ceased to exist long ago. The catastrophic great divide was thought to be the handiwork of the Muslim invaders. It was believed that due to the decline and fall of the glorious ancient India, the Bengali Hindus of the nineteenth century have also been subjected to suffering and humiliation. Therefore without resurrecting the ancient glory, they cannot improve their social position substantially. The ushering in of the intervening middle age devoid of all merits, had brought about the destruction of the great ancient Indian civilization. In the middle of the nineteenth century, the inevitability of a renaissance was conceptually established and the inheritance of the glorious past was vigorously cultivated.

It presupposed the chiselling out of a brilliant idealised image of Indian antiquity through a continuous process of creative blending of fact and imagination, history and myth, achievement and aspiration. Such image was clearly formulated to justify the newly evolved concept of renaissance in nineteenth century Bengal in which the past was completely disentangled from the present and in a position to actively impose its own forms and attitudes on the Bengali elites. Thus the ideal situation for the emergence of the epic genre was launched; the epic was by and large the symbolic representation and outcome of the turmoils of the time. Along with the medieval phase of history, the intelligentsia equally repudiated the worn out genres of mangalkāvyas, ballads, Vaiṣṇava and Śākta lyrics as irrelevant. But we shall come to that later on. Here we may note that the making of an idealised image of ancient India was also the outcome of the renaissance of interest and enthusiasm for the language. Philosophy, arts and literature of ancient India which began as largely academic pursuit of the European indologists in the late eighteeenth century. Actually even during the crazy days of conscious westernization, many a scholars were busy in rediscovering the Indian heritage. That is why we have noted earlier that the nineteenth century did not have a single facet nor was it free from consequent complexities.

The rediscovery and regeneration of a golden age in ancient India may be regarded as the most significant ideological contribution of the European orientalists. The conception of a polarity between dark age and golden age helped the Bengali intelligentsia to regain and cultivate the national self-respect and revitalize their cultural perspective. Moreover, a reliable storehouse of heritage was made available to them from which guidelines for the transitional society could be borrowed. It contributed substantially to the emergence of nationalism in the later half of the nineteenth century; then the Bengali elites intensified their quest for an ideal model of civilization within heritage. The scholarly models furnished by the European orientalists was appropriated to infuse these with heightened feelings of national pride. Hence, when the blatant colonialist policies wounded that newly acquired pride, one of the leading elites of Calcutta in the sixties, recollected the activities of the pioneer orientalists with nostalgic feelings: 'There are those among us who look upon this state of things (the growing feeling of Anglo-Saxon racial superiority among the British) with surprise. They call to mind the generation of Englishmen who, in past years, walked among our fathers without betraying the least symptoms of hatred...they call to mind Jones, Colebrooke, Wilson and ask how it is that the successors of such men be so unsympathetic?

As regards Indian literature...history, antiquities, the present race of Anglo-Indian (the British in India)...are lamentably ignorant...Jones, Colebrooke, Wilson...respected our fathers and looked upon us hopefully at least with melancholy interest, as you would look on the heir of a ruined noble. But to the great unwashed abroad today, we are simply niggers without a past; perhaps without a future. They do not choose to know us.'[15]

Actually, the promotion of Indological research in the late eighteenth and early nineteenth century and the apathy to it thereafter are two facets of colonial policy dictated by nothing but the exigencies of situation. The cultural policy of the British was integrally connected with their colonial interests. Hence Warren Hastings's orientalist cultural policy and Lord Bentinck's anti-orientalist attitude are, in fact, two sides of the same coin. It is entirely incomprehensible that the colonial masters or their agents would do anything without any shrewd calculation regarding their long-term political and economic gains. In the phase of the East India Company, the British plunderers were short-sighted and had no other interest but to extract maximum wealth from the hapless Indian people in minimum time. They did not, at the first instance, try to dispense with the decadent feudal structure; on the contrary they became feudal lords themselves. But the dominant bourgeoise in England soon realised that the direct plunder of the merchants-turned-into-administrators could not be beneficial for a long time to come. This realisation came in the wake of a thorough readjustment in the British society in transition. The nascent British bourgeoise were searching for nourishment and India was obviously the easy bet. At that time, the rapacious Company servants, who stayed in Bengal between 1757 and 1770, ravaged the fertile land unabashedly in search of quick fortune. Their atrocious activities culminated into the worst famine of history during 1769 and 1770, which destroyed the old feudal aristocracy and enfeebled the peasantry in Bengal. None other than Horace Walpole, therefore, admonished his countrymen with these words: 'We have outdone the Spaniards in Peru. They were at least butchers on a religious principle, however diabolical their zeal. We have murdered, deposed, plundered, usurped nay, what think you of the famine in Bengal in which three millions perished being caused by a monopoly of the servants of the East India Company?'[16] If we now have a look at the career of Hastings, we would find that he did not fare any better. He had first arrived in 1759 at the age of seventeen, as simple clerk of the Company earning a meagre sum of five pounds annually. But he left India in 1764 with a staggering wealth of thirty thousand pounds. It is self-explanatory.

The British colonialists recognised Hastings' talent and sent him back to Bengal in 1772 as an empire-builder. The British policy about India had, in the meantime, undergone a basic change; they had decided to gradually turn India into an agrarian and raw-materials appendage—first, as a market for their manufactured goods and later into a source of high-yielding raw materials and foodstuffs. In this background, Hastings's cultural policy should be interpreted; he aimed at creating a new generation of civil service elites who would be proficient in Indian languages and responsive to Oriental tradition. At the same time, he was extremely busy in playing the role of an imperialist swashbuckler to perfection by annexing new territories by dubious means and also conspiring to send Maharaja Nandakumar to the gallows. Therefore, the following romanticised account of Hastings's contribution to the 'revitalization' of India's old heritage cannot but be regarded as simplistic: 'Sitting in a remote Bengali town, with ample leisure for reflection, Hastings wondered at the vastness of the country, its richness and variety, and above all the antiquity and splendour of its civilization.'[17] Likewise, the much-publicised opinion of an English historician that Hastings sought 'to understand Indian culture as a basis for sound Indian administration[18] is equally untenable.' Moreover, the following comment of an American analyst is wholly unacceptable: 'Behind the expediencies of his policy lay a fund of understanding of and *benevolence toward the* Indian masses.'[19] However he hastens to add that 'In his relations with Indian potentates, Hastings was not above using Machiavellian means to extend British power and influence on the subcontinent.[20] He talks about Hastings' 'love' and 'respect' to the Indian people and concludes: 'His basic convictions became the credo of the orientalist movement; to rule effectively, one must love India; to love India, one must communicate with her people, and to communicate with her people, one must learn her languages.'[21]

Therefore, any opinion about Hastings's policy of so-called 'Indianization' should be viewed with caution. In fact, he worked for establishing a semblance of rapport between the exploiter and the exploited; it is quite natural for an intelligent alien administrator. Education and culture are no separable items; these are integrally connected with the basic colonialist policy. Actually the issue is clinched if we look at the letter written by none other than Hastings himself to

N. Smith on 4th October, 1784: 'Every accumulation of knowledge and especially such as is obtained by social communications with people over whom we exercise a dominion founded, on the right of conquest, *is useful to the state.*'[22] Therefore, being a shrewd ruler, Hastings put exclusive emphasis on promoting and accelerating the processes of learning various Indian languages. Generous grants were sanctioned for the purpose which continued even when Lord Cornwallis was in charge. But, besides those who learned Indian languages for filling their purses quickly by taking up translations of such works that might be helpful for the administration, there were some talented persons who made use of the new cultural policy to foster their academic interest. They were more competent as well as enthusiastic to a new phase of curiosity for Indian literature and dissemination of new-found awareness.

IV

Among the pioneers of oriental studies, Charles Wilkins arrived first in 1770. Within a couple of years, Nathaniel Halhed and Jonathan Duncan came to Bengal. But it is the arrival of William Jones, the first president of the Asitatic Society and the high priest of India's 'golden age', that set the wheel of zealous cultivation of ancient Indian literature into motion. Henry T. Colebrooke, an eminent Indologist came in 1783. Wilkins' one of the memorable contribution was the completion of a set of Bengali fonts and establishment of the first vernacular printing press in India in 1778. This single event marked the beginning of the transition in the realm of literature from the patron-oriented medieval age to the diffusive modern age. Within the span of a few years, another epoch-making event took place in 1784 when the Asiatic Society of Bengal was founded. The stage was now set for western and Indian scholars to engage in the studies of Sanskrit language and the literary, mythological and philosophical works contained therein. Wilkins translated the *Bhagavad Gītā* in 1783 and studied inscriptions to prepare the history of the Pāla dynasty of Bengal. Wilkins, Jones and Colebrooke had really built the foundation on which the regenerated image of ancient India was firmly erected in no time. The persons like S. Davis, F. Wilford, William Hunter, James Prinsep and particularly, H.H. Wilson had also contributed to a considerable extent in the studies of various facets of ancient Indian culture. Of course, some of their works were more out of amateurish enthusiasm than of systematic study. But, nevertheless, these had psycho-social impact of their own. However, the opportunists like John B. Gilchrist, an unscrupulous indigo-planter-turned-linguist continued to have their shares in the lucrative fun. It is, in fact, Jones who had applied himself to the developing studies with perfect seriousness and earnestness. Among other things he rediscovered Kālidāsa as one of the greatest poets in the literary firmament. His translation of the *Abhijñānaśākuntala* gained popularity among the European scholars. He was a scholar with varied interest; hence his curiosity was renewed with every new finding and discussion about mythology, philosophy, fine arts, literature, ethics and social codes. Therefore, in 1786, Jones was first to slowly build up the conceptual framework of a golden age in ancient India. Besides, it was he who suggested about the existence of common patrimony for the vanquisher and the vanquished in India, that is, the family of Indo-European languages.

Jones' famous 'Third Annual Discourse' about ancient Indians 'with a fertile and inventive genius' took the successive generations of the educated Bengali in the late eighteenth and almost the entire nineteenth century by storm. He observed: 'The Sanskrit language, whatever be its antiquity, is of a wonderful structure, more perfect than the Greek, more copious than the Latin, and more exquisitely refined than either, yet bearing to both of them a stronger affinity both in the roots of verbs and in the form of grammar, than could possibly have been produced by accident.'[23] Indeed, for several decades his words continued to cast spell on the various strata of Indian elites searching frantically for a heritage to bank upon. Particularly when the appreciatory remarks were from one of the power elites, these had tremendous psychological impact. The evolving Bengali intelligentsia were grateful to Jones since he had also initiated the morale-boosting concept of a golden age. In that discourse mentioned above, Jones also exclaimed: '... how degenerate and abased so ever the Hindus may now appear, that in some early age they were splendid in arts and arms, happy in government; wise in legislation, and eminent in various knowledge.' This was the best solace for the then Bengali elites who accepted Jones' observation as the authoritative manifesto of the resplendent 'Aryan genius.' Now, it was possible for them to assume a honourable position, at least notionally, at par with the British conquerors. It also called for reanimation of India's glorious past. The Indological researches stimulated the emergence and crystallization of a new ideology of cultural encounter between traditional India, exceptionally rich in heritage, and modernist Europe, well advanced in material wealth. This new awareness spread its roots steadily for a couple of decades and in spite of penchant for westernisation and extrinsic denial of the seemingly worn out tradition in the stormy days of the Young Bengal. It bore fruit in the realm of Bengali literature when the soil was fertilised with heterogeneous seeds.

Notwithstanding their colonial background and inherent limitations therefrom, the historical role of the first tillers for the later harvest has to be recognised. Besides Jones, as we have already pointed out, there was Colerbrooke too who emphasised on the West's 'debt of gratitude' to the civilizations of the East in the spheres of arts and sciences and declared 'civilization had its origin in Asia.'[24] This was also a tremendous morale booster for the Bengali elites. Max Muller has in fact, compared Jones to a 'dashing and impatient general who tries to take every fortress by bombardment and storm.'[25] But nevertheless observed that while Jones 'explored a few fields' only, Colebrooke went much farther. He dealt with 'the really difficult works, the grammatical treatises and the commentaries, the philosophic systems, and before all, the immense literature of the Vedic period.[26] By virtue of his sustained research on Vedic India, he had built up a new composite image of golden age in ancient India. Besides, Colebrooke's discovery of the monotheistic tradition in ancient India and enumeration of several discrepancies between ancient ethical, philosophical and ritualistic treatise and contemporary degenerated practices further consolidated the thesis of polarity between the illuminating past and the dark present. This tradition of indological research continued unabated in spite of the reversal in the British policy; it actually reached its peak in the last quarter of the nineteenth century as a result of the sustained effort of a good number of European scholars, viz., Friedrich Schlegel, Alexander Hamilton, A.Z. Chezy, Franz Bopp, Eugene Burnouf, Rudolph Roth, Christian Lassen, Albrecht Weber, A. Bergaigne, A. Barth, H. Oldenberg, H. Bloomfield, Ludurg von Schroder, M. Winternitz, F. Max Muller and a host of others. Their extensive studies had manifold impact on Indian psyche in general and the receptive Bengali mind in particular. As long as it was creatively assimilated, it nourished the imaginative poets and litterateurs; but in the concluding decades of the nineteenth century, the euphoria turned into the launching pedestal for religious revivalism.

V

As we once again look back to the eighteenth century, we find that its concluding year is particularly remarkable. Lord Wellesley's proclamation about the formation of a college at Fort William on 10th July, 1800 was of far-reaching consequence; it 'gave such an impetus to Bengali learning, as was never given by any other institution since the establishment of British rule.' However. Wellesley had his own colonialist justification for the promotion of orientalism. He had steadily expanded the British domination in India through annexation of more territories and other means; but yet he was apprehensive of a possible French offensive. Therefore, he thought of counteracting the doctrines of the French Revolution by encouraging and allowing the rapid diffusion of enchantment for a glorious past. Thus Wellesley seemed to have calculatingly initiated the formulation of counter-ideology; he had himself clarified his intention somewhat bluntly: 'It cannot be denied that during the convulsions with which the doctrines of the French Revolution have agitated the continent of Europe, erroneous principles of the same dangerous tendency had reached the minds of some individuals in the civil and military service of the Company in India...to fix and establish, sound and correct principles of religion and government in their minds at an early period of life was the best security which could be provided for the stability of the British power in India.'[27] However the colonial design seems to have met with only partial success since history does not move in a linear pattern; rather it usually follows a zigzag path and, in spite of pre-determined designs of persons like Hastings and Wellesley, circular movements occur continually. That is why, notwithstanding the initial response received by the British policy makers to their game plan, the great possibilities inherent in the newly curved out academic discipline did not remain unnoticed for long. Within a couple of decades a vigorous search for national identity began in right earnest; instead of being a counter-ideology, the new-found enthusiasm tended to wrest the initial advantage from the colonial masters. Thereafter, the colonial administrators were compelled to review the entire situation; the ascending confidence of the Bengali elites had to be countered by stemming the tide in the oriental studies.

This criss-cross pattern in British cultural policy had only sharpened the contradictions and paradoxes inherent in the historically conditioned situation of the sensitive Bengali intelligentsia. The dichotomy between their collective and individual existence came to the fore in which their frailties and high seriousness constantly interacted with each other. There was a strong conviction about the continuum of heritage yet there was the inescapable feeling of void and irrelevance. In the relam of creativity, only a few new genres could withstand so much burden; these were fashioned out of the necessity of forging a synthesis between the inclinations of the ostentatious present and the sobering as well as introspective voyage to the past. But, before we deal with it in details, the great importance of the Fort William college in the history of modern Bengali literature should be emphasised. Besides H.T. Colebrooke, there was another pioneer named William Carey who is reasonably hailed as the 'father of modern Bengali prose.' This clergyman had amazing linguistic ability; apart from his missionary zeal, he had interest for publication as well, purely mundane aptitude was reflected in his management of indigo factory.

However, his tenure at the Fort William College proved to be most eventful. His visits to the centres of traditional learning only enthused him further to work for the upliftment of Bengali language and literature. The presence of the Sanskritist scholars like Mrityunjay

Vidyalamkar, Ramnath Vidyavacaspati, Sripati Mukhopadhyay and Rajiblochan Mukhopadhyay in the Bengali department of the college set a trend in building the much-felt bridge between the ancient repertory of Sanskrit and its scion, Bengali, which is modern but even then in the making and trying to come to terms with its futuristic aspirations. Undoubtedly the college was meant for the covenanted servants of the Company but it had developed into the epicentre of the fusion of two worlds under the exigencies of history.

In the meantime, the missionaries at Serampore had developed the best Sanskrit press of that period. This press worked in unison with the Asiatic Society and the Fort William College to promote the studies in old classics. After the arrival of H.H. Wilson, John Leyden and Thomas Roebucke—the Indological research went from strength to strength; the scholars of the later generations were entranced with their new-found interest for its own sake.With the assemblage of European and Indian scholars and maintenance of a fine library of old manuscripts along with facilities of publication the Fort William College became an ideal centre of academic pursuits. John Gilchrist's optimistic wishes, as expressed in the preface of the 'Oriental Fabulist' (1803), therefore, does not seem unjustified: 'A prophet is not required to predict that in a few years more, the orient gleam of learning in the days of Hastings and Jones will be totally eclipsed by that precious dawn in the Eastern lore apparent now, and which will then break forth with meridian splendour, to promote and confirm the happiness and prosperity of British India.' The concluding part of the statement just quoted is to be expected since, as we have argued earlier, the crux of the colonial cultural policy is indicated there. However, due to a substantial change in the British policy in 1807, the European curriculum was removed from the college as a result of which the institution became more responsive to the requirements of the Hindu elites in the rapidly growing city of Calcutta. But translations of old classics, studies in various aspects of ancient culture and linguistic experiments continued in the college till 1813 because the best students flocked to it in good numbers. Besides, under the indefatigable inspiration of the college, some enlightened families in Calcutta took to patronising traditional scholarship, which in its turn crystallized into a few peripheral and satellite institutions. The establishment of printing presses was definitely necessitated by the zealous academic activities in the college. Hence what Lord Minto said in February, 1808, was correct: 'It may be hoped that the introduction of the art of printing among the Hindoos, which has been thus begun by the institution of a Sanscrit press, will promote the general diffusion of knowledge among this numerous and very ancient people at the same time that it becomes the means of preserving the classic remains of their literature and sciences.'[28]

Actually the phenomenal impact of printing press on the explorative Indological studies in general and the budding modern Bengali literature in particular is discernible from the very beginning of the nineteenth century. As a result of the steady growth of new printing establishments, more works in Sanskrit and Bengali became accessible for which the fast-expanding readers were eagerly waiting. The trend was firmly and definitely set. But, when the newly groomed cultural intermediaries in the Bengali Society tended to manifest unmistakable signs of maturity and independence, their increasing aspirations for revitalized national identity became an object of concern for the colonial masters. The unique experiment with the orientalist cultural policy had by then outlived its necessity. Under the compulsion of new reality, a bluntly aggressive policy of cultural imperialism was therefore promoted by Lord Bentinck. His new educational policy was officially announced on 4th May, 1830 and, just after a year, he dissolved the college council on Ist March, 1831. Carey's desperate proposal for continuing Indological studies in Serampore College was bluntly refused. During 1841-1843, Major George T. Marshall made a last attempt to revive the college with the assistance of Iswar Chandra Vidyasagar. The college was finally dissolved with an official announcement by Governor General Dalhousie on 24th Janaury, 1854. But, in spite of the emergence of the Young Bengal in the intervening years with all din and bustle associated with the denial of heritage and extreme orientation towards westernisation—the search for the roots quietly continued.

The possibility of a renaissance of ancient Indian civilization and culture was first explored by the appreciating European scholars. The Fort William College initiated the process of a literary and cultural revival by its sustained emphasis on Indological studies. The British policy of supporting the activities of the college remained unchanged till the tenure of Lord Amherst (1828). The early students of the college argued that it was the primary responsibility of the British policymakers to help the Indians rediscover the lost sources of their own civilization 'hitherto lain smothered under the despondency of neglect.' W.P. Eliot went to the extent of observing that any attempt to anglicize a people with superior culture of their own could not but be an exercise in futility. According to him: 'Learning and science flourished in higher perfection in the East in some branches, probably to a greater degree of excellence than has ever been since attained.' In fact, the Sanskritic tradition was praised highly in that period and generous grants were available for translations would also go a long way in countering the current superstitions and prejudices among the Hindu due to ignorance about as well as erroneous interpretation of ancient texts. William B. Martin wrote: 'The Asiaticks had climbed the heights of science before the Greeks had learned their alphabet,...Literature, taste and science originated in Asia and by a general diffusion, in the course of time spread themselves over Greece and Italy. Such then having been once the state of the sciences and arts among the Asiaticks, it cannot be unreasonable to suppose, that *their ability still remains unhurt and vigorous; and that those sparks of genius hitherto smothered or enfeebled by the noxious climate of oppression, might under the congenial influence of a milder government and more favourable laws, again be fanned into a flame.*'[30]

It can be easily guessed that such almost hyperbolic appreciating words from a European power elite must have cast a spell on the slowly crystallizing Bengali elites. With a newly acquired sense of pride and confidence, they tried to reorganise their perspective of life. But, as we have already indicated, the contradictions among the nascent English bourgeoise were influencing the policies of the Court of Directors in London. Lord Wellesley's bitter opposition to the monopoly of the shipping trade of the Company actually strengthened a coterie who had nothing but short-sighted mercantile mentality as well as a typical imperialist attitude. In the long run, this coterie became successful champions of a confrontationist policy of cultural imperialism. They openly proclaimed their aversion to pluralism of culture and promoted the policy of evangelization of India. They firmly believed that the permanence of British domination in India was impossible if the indigenous people were not converted to Christianity and the education policy should therefore be reoriented. They also did not forget to add that such policy would ensure the formation of market for the British manufacturers. However, during the rule of Lord Moira, better known as Marquess Hastings (1813-1822), the Evangelical triumph was not reflected in practice.[31] On the contrary, the college continued with its policy of restoration of the positive elements of the Sanskritic tradition. Lord Moira had also strong inclination for vernacular mass education. He had his own idea about cultural reformation. He observed: 'To be the source of blessings to the immense population of India is an ambition worthy of our country. In proportion as we have found intellect sterile here, the obligation is stronger on us to cultivate it. The field is noble; may we till it worthily.'[32]

During his tenure the enthusiastic elites of the Fort William College extended their active cooperation in forming the following institutions: The Hindu College (1816), the Calcutta School Book Society (1817) and the Calcutta School Society (1818).

In that predominantly elitist atmosphere, the missionaires at Serampore seemed to have first become aware of the necessity of popularising the programmes of cultural regeneration. They did not oppose the attempts for reconstructing an ancient golden age but nevertheless launched virulent attack against Indian religious heritage. The publication of Joshua Marshman's *Hints Relative to Native Schools* in 1816 has considerable historical significance. Because it propagates the dawn of a new age in Bengal reminiscent of European renaissance. Secondly it puts emphasis on the development of varnaculars instead of the revival of classical learning. Therefore, it advocates for integration of useful modern knowledge in the vernaculars so that the common people is able to express various aspects of the new enlightenment in the 'colloquial social intercourse.' The missionaries of Serampore published a periodical entitled 'Dig Darsan' in April, 1818 through which they sought to develop their concept of renaissance. Just at that time, the first Bengali newspaper entitled 'Samachar Darpan' was published in Serampore. These progressive activities were supplemented further by the establishment of a college at Serampore. On the other hand, the number of printing press multiplied rapidly; the increasing demands for reading materials in the twenties (due to proliferation of primary schools under the stewardship of the Calcutta School Society) could not be met adequately. Thus the stage was set for the flourish of the Derozians. In fact, at least three of them were definitely reared up through such primary schools that planted the first seeds of curiosity about the newly emerging frontiers of human wisdom.

VI

The old world was disintegrating all around while the new one was yet powerless to be born. The orientalist environment was slowly but decisively receding; however, the extrinsic manifestation of the continuing search for roots was becoming redundant only to inspire a more intense and deeper quest within. Its intrinsic nature can be realised in the phase of a creative resurrection and hence it proves to be more fundamental and of far-reaching consequence. But the quest is also symptomatic of the paradox caused by the seemingly unreconciliable conflict raging in nineteenth century Bengal as the inevitable concomitant of two sharply polarised facets of colonial policy. In spite of expansion of the horizons of Indological research in the twenties and thirties, the dazzling presence of the Derozians described earlier has taken the steam out of the traditionalists. The newly found psychic mobility was no longer used for building the past anew but for preparing a wish-fulfilling modernist future. The Hindu College was the symbol of new reality which survived the initial fear of extinction due to the able leadership of David Hare and H. H. Wilson. After the Sanskrit College came into existence in 1827, the Hindu College gradually became the centre of secular Western culture. Initially it was to provide stimulus for transforming the worn-out Indian culture from within but the clear emphasis on the cultivation of European literature and science instead of ancient theology and metaphysics made all the difference. Besides, the class-orientation behind the management of the college should also be taken into account. The scions of the compraedor bourgeoise—the power elites of the rapidly growing urban Calcutta—were at the helm of affairs. As they could attain their material splendour as a result of close and profitable collaboration with the colonial masters, they tried to promote nothing but European form of education for consolidating their social positions. The orientalists had no role to play in the territory of the sycophants.

When the policy of cultural imperialism was manifested most arrogantly in the widely known Minute (1835) of Thomas Babington Macaulay, the wheel seemed to have come full circle. In the meantime, Derozio's revolutionary concept of liberalism and perfect freedom of intellect had swerved from the intended track. The Young Bengal movement got further confused by the sweeping generalizations of Macaulay. The crude aggressiveness underneath the following observations is not only indicative of obnoxious English chauvinism and insensitive rigidity, it also marks a decisive shift in British policy—shrewdly calculated to obviate the possibilities of nationalist upsurge among the educated Indians in general and the Bengali intelligentsia in particular: 'A single shelf of a good European library was worth the whole native literature of India and Arabia...It is I believe no exaggeration to say, that all the historical information which has been collected to form all the books written in the Sanskrit language is less valuable than that what may be found in the most paltry abridgements used as preparatory schools in England.' In the face of such an obstinate display of malignant cultural imperialism through sound and fury, the academicians in quest of Indian heritage had to retreat and concede the educational leadership to the anglicists but definitely they were not defeated. Particularly the castle of confidence built in the meantime through sustained efforts in accelerating the pace of progress in the realm of Bengali language and literature was impregnable. Therefore, in spite of the one-sided over-reaction of the Young Bengal as the trumpets of Macaulism, the dust settled down within two decades. Besides, the course of history is seldom linear, hence in their mature years, the Young Bengal applied themselves to the pathetic absurdity and innate ambivalence caused by their historical position. In the long run, they could overcome the adolescent fervour and cultivated their mother tongue vigorously; they tried to absorb the best humanistic trends of European thought since they could not afford to lose the modernist worldview. But at the same time they struggled desperately to return to the solace of being rich in the repertory of ancient culture.

VII

As we have referred to earlier, the British colonialists sought to enslave the Indian people spiritually as well. Besides the programme of anglicisation, they deputed the missionaries to spread Christianity as their principal ideological weapon with a view to consolidating and perpetuating the political dominance. Enormous sums of money were spent for the purpose and the network was spread through establishing schools, hospitals, orphanages, printing presses and various societies. But the 'spiritual stick' policy of the colonialists and their ideological offensive ran into stubborn resistance from the very beginning. Almost all the strata of the society—except the beneficiary landlords, compraedor merchants and native colonial officials—resisted the pernicious colonial conspiracy. Swami Dayananda Sarasvati of Gujarat, Syed Ahmad Khan of North India, Annie Besant (Theosophical Society), Swami Vivekananda were, in fact, the prominent representatives of the various facets of ideological struggle. But the resistance gained momentum with the inception and gradual evolution of the Brāhma movement. Rammohun Roy, according to Romain Rolland, was a 'gigantic personality' who 'forced his plough deep into the soil of India', founded a society for religious reform entitled the 'Brahma Samaj' in 1828. That Rammohun viewed religion from a rational stand point is evident from the following comment:

'I regret to say that the present system of religion adhercd to by the Hindus is not well calculated to promote their political interest.'[33] In order to counter the ideological weapon of the British, he took up the task of religious reformation. That is why he opposed idol worship and caste system in articles, public speeches, pamphlets etc. On the other hand, he opposed the activities of the missionaries for spreading Christianity. His Brahma Samaj was open to all persons regardless of any difference in caste, colour, creed etc. The members of the samaj actively supported the movement for abolition of the 'Suttee' or 'widow immolation rite.' Their activities cemented the unity of the nascent progressive forces and also raised the cultural standard of the people by launching a struggle for eliminating the caste system. Rammohun was supported by Dwarakanath Tagore in these endeavours; his son, Debendrantath, joined the Brahma Samaj in 1842.

However, Debendranath soon initiated a new phase in the ideological movement. Along with Akshaya Kumar Datta, he criticised Rammohun's 'westernism' and his inclinations towards christian ethics. It only shows that the apathy towards cultural imperialism had become stronger by then; that is why, even the concept of fusion with western thought was considered detrimental to the interest of Indian awakening. The founding of the *Tattva-bodhini Sabha* and the *Tattva-bodhini Patrika* (1839) fostered the new school of thought to a great extent. Akshaya Kumar Datta clearly advocated for combating the British policy of spiritual conquest; he lamented: 'We no longer rely on ourselves in anything. We are subject to foreign power, receive education in a foreign language and suffer from foreign oppression, while the Christian religion assumes an influence that makes one wonder if it is the national religion of this country. That is why we must at present teach where we can in our own language and instruct in full agreement with the spirit of our religion, or else in the near future we shall not differ from the English in any way: their language will be our national language and their religion, the national religion of this country. My heart breaks when I think that the word 'Hindu' may be forgotten and we shall be called by a foreign name.' However, it cannot be denied that the nascent bourgeoisie in India was politically dependent on the colonial powers; yet they had to accommodate the yearning for national identity. They were tormented at every step with the developing intensity in the crisis of identity; being dependent on the very force whose cultural aggressiveness they detested, their ideologues viewed religion as the only form of expression of national awareness. Hence their thoughts of enlightenment and demands for social transformation were half-hearted and inconsistent. The ideological pursuits developed in religious and theological form. In the forties, a good number of young intellectuals flocked around Debendranath's Brahma Samaj. It was indeed historically imperative for them because the proselytizing zeal of Alexander Duff, a Scottish missionary, had been regarded as dangerous for the integrity of the society. He was successful in converting some of the brilliant youth of that time, viz. Krishna Mohan Banerji, Mahes Chandra Ghose, Gopinath Nandi and others. But thereby he accentuated the polarity between aggressive west and tradition bound India; naturally, a strong resistance developed in no time. Its manifestation is found in the regrouping of the Indian orientalists at the academic level and in the crystallization of the Brahma movement at a more popular level.

Keshab Chandra Sen, one of the most prominent figures of the Brahma movement, joined the Samaj after the Sepoy Mutiny and within a couple of years, became the leader of the younger generation of the Brahmas. Debendranath clung to old rituals though he did not believe in the infallibility of the Vedas; actually, he did not like to snap the umbilical cord with the mother community. Keshab Chandra's radicalism made a split in the Brahma Society inevitable hence in 1866 the Brahma Samaj of India came into existence to which younger elites were attracted in large numbers. There were energetic men of letters like Sivanath Sastri, Durgamohan Das, Dwarakanath Ganguli and Anand Mohan Bose; they began to outshine Keshab Chandra in progressive thinking in no time. It seems to be an irony of history that the younger Brahmas raised allegation of highhandedness against Keshabchandra; they were unhappy about his public demeanour which appeared to contradict and dilute the Brahma ethos. But the discontentment snowballed into a storm when they found the evidence of serious breach of integrity in their leader. Another split occurred soon after Keshabchandra arranged the marriage of his own minor daughter with the prince of Coochbehar; moreover, the marriage was solemnised in accordance with the old rites. Such open defiance of Brahma convention switched on the revolt; the younger Brahmas left him in the lurch and set up the Sadharan Brahma Samaj in 1878. They had patriotic zeal and hence, they participated wholeheartedly in different movements related to socio-political awareness.

But, there was another facet of Bengali intelligentsia as well. Those who were conservative in their basic approach to the new awakening sponsored mainly by the orientalists, tried to preserve all the cultural traits indiscriminately. The first phase of their defensive mechanism was manifested in the formation of the Dharma Sabha in 1831. The crisis of identity about which we have spoken earlier was an equally vexing problem for the neo-orthodoxy. With the rapid transformations in the society, they too could not afford to hide their pangs, contradictions and bewilderments like the perplexed camels in the midst of desert storm. With the onslaught of Macaulayism, they were compelled to go through a process of strategic retreat before regrouping again in the seventies. H.H.Wilson and his close allies were trying to keep the flame of ancient India ablaze during the difficult days. Rajendra Lal Mitra, Ram Camul Sen and others were busy in finding many a missing links not only in vaguely defined antiquity but also in more assured realms of archaeology as well as in Buddhist, Puranic and Medieval periods. These explorative studies paved the way for romantic escapism. It had a great impact in the realm of creative literature in general and in the crystallizing processes of newly emerging genres in particular. But we will deal with it later.

The growing popularity of the Brahma movement among the young elites seemed to have been the immediate impetus for the conservative section of the Bengali Hindus to regroup and revitalize themselves. For them, the revelation of a glorious past was one of the strongest foundations on which a new Indian nationalism might be built. Neither the Brahma reformism nor the western rationalism was acceptable to them. In the name of discovering the purple patches of glory in the ancient and medieval history, they were guided exclusively by a psychological necessity of having imaginative compensation for what they sadly lack in the uncertain present. The cumulative effect of several historically conditioned factors was thus expressed through a clarion call of 'back to Hinduism.' In fact, after the mutiny, Rajnarayan Bose prepared its initial stepping stones though for some time he was associated with the Brahma movement. In 1861, he founded a society for the promotion of national glory at Midnapur and prepared a prospectus as well for stimulating the awareness for nationalism. Incidentally, in the same year, Michael Madhusudan Datta (who was Rajnarayan's intimate friends) published his epoch-making epic, the *Meghanādvadha.* The word 'national' seemed to have become a fetishistic cult-word. Hence Nabagopal Mitra started a national school, a national press, a national paper and a national gymnasium because of which he was half-jokingly mentioned as 'national Mitra.' In association with Rajnarayan Bose and Jyotirindranath Tagore, he founded the Patriots' Association in 1865. However, the most notable event was the holding of the 'Hindu Mela', an annual fair on the last day of the Bengali year. It continued to be an annual community gathering for several years which inspired the contemporary litterateurs to compose patriotic poems and songs. Besides the fair arranged lectures, detailed reviews of the prevalent social, political, economic and religious conditions in India as well as exhibitions of indigenous arts and crafts and performance of physical exercises.

There was pervasive spirit of Hindu revivalism; it went from strength to strength with the passage of time. In such an atmosphere Ramkrishna Paramahamsa appeared with his magnetic influence through subjective, sincere, deeply personal and homely approach to religion. His impact was unputdownable; hence many a young elites flocked around him of whom Swami Vivekananda was the most noteworthy. Ramakrishna taught the sanctity of all faiths and thus absorbed the fury of the militant protestants on the one hand and, on the other, gave a new ease of life to the revivalists. Vivekananda's successful participation in the world religious conference at Chicago literally fired the passion of the Indian youth. The academicians had so long only discovered and interpreted the ancient glory but there was one who had spiritually conquered the colonial masters in their own land. The renaissance had thus notionally blossomed with its complete hues and fragrance; obviously it was nothing but a 'Hindu renaissance.' Bipin Chandra Pal, one of the prominent personalities of late nineteenth century, wrote: 'At the back of this reaction and revival there was undoubtedly a new national self-consciousness and a new pride of race which commenced to openly repudiate the pretensions of European thought and culture to superiority over Hindu thought and life. This social reaction and religious revival possessed the Hindu mind all over India, and offered an effective check, for a time to our religious and social reform movements...The motive force behind it was more a determination on the part of our people to assert themselves against the imposition of imported European thoughts and ideals, on the one hand, as it was, on the other, an organised expression of the deep anti-British feeling that had overcome every class and section of the educated community.'[34]

viii

The encounter between the Bengali elites and the European scholars is thus very complex and multilinear. In two different phases of colonial cultural policy, the quest for identity as well as the model for cultural values and adaptation thereto could not but be different. There is no unified stream in the nineteenth century Bengal; on the contrary, there are several eddying cross-currents. When the western scholars brought the light of glorious past to the darkened territories of colonial Bengal, it was regarded as the Promethean heat and the act of rediscovery became symptomatic of notional deliverance from bondage. We have already noted that it had its persisting dialectics of impact and response, continuity and breach, tradition and modernity. In the mature phase, the urge for regeneration culminated in creative syncretic schemes in which traditional and alien elements could be meaningfully accommodated and blended to bring about a metamorphic change. We have also noted that even in the face of the aggressive westernization, the Bengali intelligentsia could soon overcome the initial stupefying effect; they did not entirely relinquish their quest. Rather it seemed to have renewed itself with reinforced vigour. Various forms of syncretism gave rise to an altogether new worldview which emphasised on the participation in a modern expansive world but cared to retain and also reinterprete the ancient modes of thought. Because of the ambivalence inherent in their historical position, the Bengali elites could not but be stirred in the depths of their being, with the clash as well as interpenetration of contradictory thoughts. As colonial intelligentsia, they could not afford to assume uncompromising attitude to the contemporary life, society and cultural miscegenation. They were constrained to admit and even succumb to the co-existence of logically opposed ideas; at any rate, the quest for the purgatory continued though a series of conscious and unconscious trials about the validity of eccletic combination of diverse models.

In fine, this is the perspective in nineteenth century Bengal in which no worn-out genre could have adequately expressed the dialectics of life. Hence a new genre has to manifest itself in which both form and content would be innovatively readjusted to be tuned to the dialectics of tradition and modernity. As we look back at the beginning of the nineteenth century, we find that the prevalent situation in Bengali literature was disheartening. When Bharatchandra Roy Gunakar, the composer of the *Annadamangal* died in 1760, the sun finally set in the horizon of medieval Bengali literature. The literary works of this period had inherent weakness that retarded their growth and, therefore, with the passage of time, these tended to fade out. Medieval literature is crippled with monotony of subjectmatter and limitation of form; its microcosm is basically dehumanised because life is seldom valued for its own sake. The mundane existence is considered only a brief stop-over in the voyage to eternity; most often it is a tryst with unmitigated evil which can only be overcome by virtue of unquestioning surrender to a cultic deity who frightens and destroys only to extract compulsive worship from hapless men and women. Even such persons enact some predetermined roles, as it were, since they are ultimately proved as some sort of divine characters going through stints of curse.

The genre of Mangalkāvya flourished in the hierarchical medieval society which seldom demanded anything more than a fixed pattern. As vernacular Purāṇas, the mangalkāvyas, definitely quenched the thirst for interesting narratives but, at the same time, these were deeply entrenched in religious ethos. These simultaneously provided the eagerly waiting community with amusement and enlightenment; several generations participated in their progressive crystallization while some more equipped bards used to give the final touch. The mangalkāvyas may also rightly be regarded as the scions of the Indian epic tradition which, due to limitations of the static medieval epoch, are nevertheless devoid of stirring incidents and living characters who dynamically interact with the polarities of life around. There is little scope for elevating imagination, astounding fancy or any genuine intensity that might hurry away the soul. In the microcosms of these mangalkāvyas, almost everything is homogeneous and tiresome; the expecting mind of a reader consequently sinks into a state of aching torpidity. Actually the ancient genre was resurrected after denuding it of literary contention and natural growth was arrested by way of subordinating it to the excruciating demands of a barren and stagnant society. Bharatchandra gave the genre a new lease of life only temporarily. When the feudal society was disintegrating and the British colonial power was gradually consolidating its grip, the genre of the Mangalkāvyas as well as other literary forms had become totally irrelevant. A new epoch always brings in its train new innovative thoughts, new motifs, new themes and new genres. The complexities and aspirations, paradoxes and tensions of nineteenth century Bengal had to be creatively interpreted; but no worn-out genre could have borne such an enormous responsibility. Hence, the time-honoured epic genre was resurrected in the later half of the oneiric as well as omnivorous nineteenth century.

From the cold world of deities and their ever-obliging worshippers, the Bengali literature graduated into the pulsating human world and gradually the Bengali language also matured to be the appropriate vehicle for new humanism. The budding poets had to make a choice from amongst the conflicting values; Iswar Chandra Gupta could not solve the dilemmas which he had to confront. He could not understand the beckoning of time and chose to extend the life-span of the exhausted old school. But this could not satisfy the new generation of Bengali elites about whom we have already spoken at length. The rediscovery of national heritage inspired the creative personalities to give vent to their newly acquired high seriousness through the reoriented epic genres. The poets looked backward to their ancestral treasure-house to study the secret of its infinite mutations and also to learn their own odyssey. In that juncture of time, the rejuvenated epic form came into being to cater to the high promise and experiences in the new social and ideological milieu. It also necessitated the remodelling of subjectmatter and poetic diction since the nagging effect of sterility and bankruptcy of older literature had to be overcome. The budding poets were required to have great circumspection in blending form, content and meaning with one another. The success and failure of the epic poets of nineteenth century Bengal entirely depended on their ability to forge an affinity between form and content and also on their insight in adding deeper meanings to the mere frame of explicit story. Moreover, the thematic range of those epic poets may be regarded as the catalogue of their typical reactions to specific socio-historical situation in which life had cast them.

In fine, the emergence of the epic form in the nineteenth century Bengal was an unavoidable historical necessity. A new value system was in the offing as a result of strife, tension, contradiction, situational paradox and above all an unprecedented quest for human truth. The epic was not only an adequate but also a correct medium for the values built anew. Here we may refer to a pertinent comment: 'In the case of emerging national literatures, authors may seek in form or ideology that which they can adopt or transmute for their own consciousness, time and nation.... Literary influence appears to be most frequent and most fruitful at the times of emergence of national literature and of radical change of direction of a particular literary tradition in a given literature. In addition, it may accompany or follow social or political movements or especially upheavals.'[35] When the Bengali poets tried to come to terms with their innermost urge, they had to fall back upon the rich ancestral heritage in general and the epic-Purnaic tradition in particular. It has also been proved that when the quest for roots and identity is more intense, the creative harvest is invariably more rich and far-reaching. We are also led to conclude that when a truly innovative form is created, it exists and lives its own life; that is why, when the stream of humanistic consciousness was lost in the quicksand of regressive revivalistic trends, the Bengali epic genre was also choked to death.

NOTES

1. Binoy Ghosh, *Vidyasagar or Bangali Samaj,* Orient Longman Ltd., Calcutta, 1973, pp 373-374.
2. Sir Jadunath Sarkar, *Fall of the Mughal Empire,* vol. IV, Orient Longman Ltd, Calcutta, 1972, p. 347.
3. Kishori Chand Mitra, 'The Presidency College', *The Bengal Magazine,* vol. II, pp 132-133.
4. cf. Tarashankar Banerjee: '*The Young Bengal: general estimate,*' in *Renascent Bengal*, Asiatic Society, Calcutta, 1972, pp. 60-61.
5. *Ibid.*
6. Rammohan Roy, 'Appeal to the King in Council, petition against the Press Regulations, 1823', in *Rammohan Rachanabali,* Haraf Prakashani, Calcutta, 1973. p. 509.
7. 'British Empire in India', Reprinted from The *Enquirer*, in *The India Gazette,* Dt. 10.2. 1832.
8. cf. Sushobhan Sarkar, *On the Bengal Renaissance*, Papyrus, Calcutta, 1979, p. 13.
9. Jean Paul Sartre, *Preface* in the *Wretched of Earth,* by Frantz Fanon, Penguin, 1980, p.7.
10. *The Enquirer* quoted by Binay Ghosh in *'Bidrohi Derozio.'* Ayan Prakashani, Calcutta, 1980, p. 105.
11. cf. Amalesh Tripathi: *Vidyasagar: The Traditional Modernizer,* Orient Longman, Calcutta 1974, pp. 86-87.
12. Sushobhan Sarkar, *'On the Bengal Renaissance' op. cit*, p.111.
13. Kristodas Pal, *The Young Bengal Vindicated,* Calcutta, 1856, p. 12.
14. Rabindranath Tagore, *Nationalism*, Macmillan, London, 1917, p. 273.
15. Girish Ch. Ghosh, 'They hate us youth', in *Selection from the Writings*

of Girish Ch. Ghosh ed, M.M. Ghosh, India Daily News Press, Calcutta, 1912, p 434.

16. Speech of Horace Walpole, in *Cambridge History of India*, Vol. V, Cambridge University Press, 1929, p. 187.
17. V.B. Kulkarni, *British Statesman in India,* Orient Longman, Calcutta, 1961, pp 28-29.
18. P. Spear, ed *Oxford History of India*, 1958, p. 513.
19. David Kopf, *British Orientalism and the Bengal Renaissance,* Firma K. L. Mukhopadhyaya, Calcutta, 1969, p. 20.
20. *Ibid*, p. 21
21. *Ibid.*
22. Quoted by Rajani Kanta Das in *Bangla Gadya Sahityer Itihas*, Mitralaya, Calcutta, 1963, p. 52.
23. Willaim Jones, 'Third Annual Discourse', *Asiatick Researches* I (1788), pp 422-423.
24. H.T. Colebrooke, 'Discourse at the Royal Asiatic society of Great Britain and Ireland,' Miscellaneous Essays, William H. Allen & cd. London, 1837, vol, I p. 3
25. F. Max Muller, *Biographical Essays,* Longmans Green and Co, London, 1884, p. 271.
26. F. Max Muller, *ibid,* p. 262.
27. Minute on the foundation of a college at Fort William, July 10, 1800, Reprinted in the Despatches, Minutes and correspondence of the Marquess Wellesley, K.G., during his administration in India, ed. M. Martin, W.H. Allen, London, 1837, Vol II, p. 346.
28. Lord Minto's speech, in, Public disputations of the students of the college of Fort William, Hindoostanee Press, Calcutta, 1808, p. 23.
29. W.P. Eliot, 'On the advantages to expected from an academical Institution in India, in *Essays by the Students of the College of Fort William in Bengal*, 1802, p.22.
30. W. B. Martin, 'On the character and capacity of the Asiaticks and Particularly of the natives of Hindoostan', *Essays by the Students of the College of Fort William in Bengal*, 1802, p. 115.
31. cf. David Kopf, *British Orientalism and the Bengal Renaissance op. cit*, pp. 145-166.

32. Minute of the Governor General in Council on the administration of justice in Bengal, Dt. Oct 11, 1815, quoted in J.C. Marshman, Vol. II, p.117.
33. Letter to John Digby, Dt. January 18, 1828, in *Rammohan Rachanabali,* ed. Ajit Kr. Ghosh, Haraf Prakashani, Calcutta, 1973, p. 462.
34. Bipin Ch. Paul: Memories of My life and Times, Bipin Ch. Paul Institute, Calcutta, 1973, pp. 411-412.
35. J.T. Shaw, 'Literary indebtedness and comparative literary studies' in, *Comparative Literature, Method and Perspective,* ed. by Newton P. Stallknecht and Horst Frenz, revised edition, Southern Illinois university Press, 1971, pp. 92-93.

9

The Bengali Epic Genre

Mount of Sisyphus: Colonial Elites Write Back

The epic form became the aesthetic manifestation of the innermost zeal, aspiration, dream and pangs of the poets having new sensitivity. Here we may also note that no literary genre becomes mature until appropriate form, diction and style evolve for it with a distinctive character. The emergence of the epic genre in nineteenth century Bengal is neither abrupt nor coincidental; it has sprouted partly accepting the greater Indian epic tradition and partly in opposition to it. It has sought to absorb some prominent traits of the newly experienced western epic tradition. Yet basically the Bengali epic genre is the scion of the Indian epics in relation to which the spheres of continuum, contrast and assimilation are more discernible. The Bengali poets cultivated their ancient heritage and the newly discovered western literary firmament with equal enthusiasm. Their epic poems are the outcome of that unprecedented process of acceptance and renewal and reflect the commitment of the representative modern minds of nineteenth century to create new and living forms. For them, the epic was an ancient but continuously renovated form—symbolically representative of the urge of regeneration inherent in that age; that symbolic form was fraught with artistic possibilities, ready to assume meanings and express ideas which had no appropriate medium before.

The Bengali epics composed in the nineteenth century clearly prove that whatever might be the themes chosen by the poets, these had to be substantially transformed to cater to the hopes and aspirations of the enlightened section of the society. This transformation was linked to the vital urge for ushering in a new era of national consciousness; it helped the poets to a considerable extent in rendering the old and frequently repeated themes acceptable and fascinating to the contemporary readers. We find that the poets like Rangalal Bandyopadhyaya (1826-1887), Michael Madhusudan Dutta (1824-1873), Hemachandra Bandyopadhyay (1838-1903) and Nabin Chandra Sen (1847-1909) derived their inspiration from the heroic episodes of the annals of the country or from the Great Epics or from the Purāṇas. The spirit of the age revealed itself in two-fold ways: first, in the choice of themes and secondly in the reorientation of the whole theme to conform to the demands of the age. The epic genre is thus associated with an intensely felt purposefulness of life and a new conception about human nobility. The Bengali poets were in search of an appropriate literary model that would ideally suit and adequately express the yearnings of their souls. The imposing European models were impossible to ignore but the Sanskrit epic tradition had to be cultivated as the primary source of inspiration. The contact with the western worldview reinforced faith in human dignity but nevertheless the poetic imagination was kindled by a keen awareness of heritage; the poets were absorbed in introspection and also in infusing life into the traditional materials.

The creative personalities in nineteenth century Bengal looked back to a mythical past but they could not remain satisfied with the not-so-encouraging status of imitator. They aimed at doing something better by synthesising the traditional and modern knowledge to arrive at the most truthful philosophy of life and best literary form. They reexamined the materials derived from the cultural heritage in general and the epic legacy in particular; they retained only what was genuinely unalienable from the continuum and what could even then be utilised to meet the challenge of the time. The burden of modernisation was also to be borne by the thoroughly renovated genre. The poets attempted a new grasp on the fact of human existence, an anthropocentric world had to be firmly established. Unlike the vernacular Purāṇas (i.e. the mangalkāvyas) of the earlier epoch, man was set at the centre of life without any subservience to god. The realisation of being different from the preceding ages gave nineteenth century Bengal a vantage-point from which the past could be surveyed and interpreted. At the sametime, the importance of creating significant literary expressions for posterity was genuinely felt.

II

Rangalal Bandyopadhyay

One of the reasons which prompted Rangalal Bandyopadhyay to compose poems was the impulse to kindle patriotism in the Bengali society. He made a statement in an article read on 13th May, 1852 at the Bethune Society against the extreme disparagement of Bengali poetry; he gave vent to the doubt simmering in the enlightened minds about the possibilities of poetic achievement by a nation under prolonged foreign dominance. The *Padmini Upakhyan* was composed and published in 1858 to support his contention in the above mentioned article. The poem was based on an episode taken from Tod's *Annals of Rajasthan*. Rangalal himself claims in the preface that his poem is an 'abhinava Kāvya' i.e. a 'new poem' fashioned on the glorious history of the Rajputs. He feels that it is desirable to feed the contemporary enlightened young men with such inspiring stories about patriotic heroes.

Rangalal has significantly remarked that the literary arena should first be freed from heaps of 'shameless and ugly' poems (Vrīḍāśunya Kadarya Kavitā-Kalāp) with the help of new pleasures derived from the study of English literature.[1] This attitude is quite natural in an atmosphere ensnared by new-found dazzling treasures of the western world. But when the creative minds applied themselves to erect a new image of spiritual regeneration based on national honour, they had no other alternative but to fall back upon the lost horizons of the national past comprising of fact and fiction, history and myth, legends and the epic-puranic legacy. Rangalal has initiated the search for an appropriate medium; hence, he has only paved the way for a true epic to flourish but stopped before reaching the gateway to the genre. Yet the *Padmini Upakhyan* is to be studied in the context of the emergence of the Bengali epic genre since it has reflected several features of the epic tradition. In spite of the poet's explicit preference for 'pure English model' (Viśuddha Englaṇḍīya Praṇālī), his poem is thoroughly steeped in the Indian cultural heritage that includes the Sanskrit court epics in general and the historical epics in particular.

Rangalal wrote two other poems within the span of ten years, viz. the *Karmadevi* (1862) and the *Surasundari* (1868). After a lapse of another decade, he wrote the *Kancikaveri* (1879) but none of these three poems came anywhere near the periphery of the Bengali epic genre, already standardised by Michael Madhusudan Datta through his *Meghanadvadh* (1861). Yes, not even the *Padmini Upakhyan* is a regular epic but it is somewhat closer to the mark because of its spirit and use of certain materials.

III

Michael Madhusudan Datta

It was Michael Madhusudan Datta, the prodigal genius of nineteenth century Bengal, who has unfolded a glittering splendour of striking form. His is a frenzied genius in an overwhelming vertiginious avalanche of creativeness. Madhusudan has indeed perfectly realised that the first requirement for the epic genre is a straightforwardness of attitude, loftiness of execution and high seriousness of conception. In the brief period of his self-induced apprenticeship, he deduced the interesting story of Tilottamā, the celestial nymph with ravishing beauty, from the *Mahābhārata* and worked it into what he called 'The first blank verse epic in the language'. It was apparent that the *Tilottamāsambhava* (1860) was a departure from the prevalent norms of workmanship and that it was a mosaic work. The materials were freely taken from diverse sources which included the epics of Vyāsa and Kālidāsa. It is difficult to apportion its various elements because the harmonising chiselling of the poet has rendered it into a homogeneous creation.

Madhusudan himself had no illusion about this 'epicling' of four cantos since he was aware that it was only an experiment and a preparatory foregrounding for greater things to follow. He wrote in a letter to his friend, Rajnarayan Bose: 'You must not, my dear fellow, judge of the work as a regular 'heroic poem'. I never meant it as such. It is a story, a tale, rather heroically told.[2] But even with its limitations, it has relegated *Padmini Upakhyan* far behind.

The *Meghanadvadh* (1861), consisting of nine cantos, is the roof and crown of the Bengali epic genre in which Madhusudan's creative talent was best exhibited. The boldly innovative reinterpretation of the story of the *Rāmāyaṇa* took the readers by storm. Madhusudan felt that nothing but the epic can appropriately express the tune and rhythm of that turbulent time; it must communicate of what it was like to be alive at that time. An episode of the great epic was chosen not for its unique story alone; it had attained a deeper significance for the poet. It was only then and neither earlier nor later, vitalised with a symbolic meaning. It had brought in its train new values, new forms, new diction and new stylistic presentation. It proves once again that the manifestation of the grand style is conditioned by the inception of an awakened spirituality. Madhusudan's eccentric preferences for western modes of life and his peerless scholarship in European literatures tempt us to conclude that the *Meghanadvadh* is basically a replica of western epic. The poet is himself no less responsible for strengthening such opinion as he has expressed in a letter: 'Remember that I am writing for that portion of my countrymen who think as I think, whose minds have been more or less imbued with western ideas and modes of thinking and that is my intention to throw off fetters forged for us by a servile admiration of everything Sanskrit.'[3]

But as we carefully scan the above statement before jumping at a conclusion, a deeper nuance comes to the fore. In the context of our discussion in the foregoing pages of this chapter, Madhusudan has only confirmed the conscious process of modernisation inspired by the contact with the west. Besides, the reference to the 'fetters' of 'servile admiration' is to be interpreted as a caution against blind adherence to the materials of the past. The futuristic vision of the poet is based on the process of creative resurrection since the denial is only aimed at 'servile admiration'. (This may remind us of a famous

Sanskrit saying 'Tātasya Jalayamiti Vruvāṇāh Kṣāram jalam Kāpuruṣāh pivanti'). Moreover Madhusudan has himself declared in one of his letters: 'In matters literary, old boy, I am too proud to stand before the world, in borrowed clothes. I may borrow a necktie, or even a waistcoat, but not the whole suit.'[4] He is in favour of a creative blending which is, in fact, the forte of all great poets. In a famous essay, T. S. Eliot has expressed such an opinion: 'Surely the great poet is, among other things, one who not merely restores a tradition which has been in abeyance but one who in his poetry retwines as many straying of tradition as possible.'[5]

Rajnarayan Bose counselled Madhusudan to choose some other subject for his magnum opus and suggested the conquest of Ceylon as a fitting theme. He said that an epic poem was expected to infuse patriotic zeal and warlike spirit into the breasts of our degenerate countrymen.' Madhusudan's reply to his friend is particularly noteworthy: 'The subject you propose for a national epic is good - very good indeed. But I don't think I have as yet acquired a sufficient mastery over the 'Art of Poetry' to do it justice. So you must wait a few years more. In the mean time, I am going to celebrate the death of my favourite Indrajit. Do not be frightened, my dear fellow, I won't trouble my readers with Viraras. Let me write a few Epiclings and thus acquire a pucca fist.'[6]

Though Madhusudan thought himself only as a poetic apprentice while composing the *Meghanadvadh*, it remains the best flower in the garden of Bengali epics. It is now useless to speculate whether he would have turned again to the epic composition if life had spared him enough time to serve the coveted Muse. But, in spite of his expressed wish to write a few 'epiclings', the above-mentioned letter itself suggests that he did not maintain any objective remoteness with the epic form. He has, on the contrary, a mysterious sense of subjective correspondence with the objects to be depicted; that is why the death of Indrajit costs him 'many a tears'. He becomes passionately involved with the fate of his chosen anti-hero, Rāvaṇa, and perhaps half knowingly, he takes side. That means, the *Meghanadvadh*, unlike all other Bengali epics, has a life of its own and it has become the incarnation of some aspects of both the poet's internal drama as well as the raging undercurrents of the Bengali society. Obviously, such poetic moments cannot be prolonged. Therefore, even while composing the poem, Madhusudan expressed the opinion that he was going to bid adieu to the epic genre after the *Meghanadvadh* because a fresh attempt would be in the nature of a repetition. Moreover, he realised that he had a tendency in the 'lyrical way'.

But the idea of sinking into the level of a versifier of occasional sonnets and lyrics was too preposterous for him. Hence he wrote in a letter to Rajnarayan Basu: 'Give me the 'Simhala'—old boy, I like a subject with oceanic and mountain scenery, with sea-voyages, battles and love-adventures. It gives a fellow's invention such a wide scope'.[7] But his restless spirit did not allow any new poetic scheme to materialise. He talked of acquiring 'a pucca fist' but a creative spectacle like the *Meghanadvadh* can hardly be repeated. The fragments of poetic attempts (viz. the *Draupadīsvayamvara*, *Subhadrāharaṇ*, *Pāṇḍavavijaya*, *Simhalavijaya*) only doubly confirm that Madhusudan's poetic passion has completely spent itself within a brief span of few years. The poet wrote to Rajnarayan Basu in the early moments of exuberance: 'I am smit with the love of sacred song. There never was a fellow more madly after the Muses than your poor friend. Night and day I am at them'.[8] That is why, he could produce with creative fury such varied works within no time. It was a rare and unique phase of artistic renewal of tradition in which the epic mode was entirely reconstructed to suit the particular demands of his time. The epic Muse continued to smile upon him when the poet attempted a creative reinterpretation of Ovid's Heroic Epistles in terms of famous Puranic and epic heroines. The *Bīrānganākāvya* is unique both in conception and execution and it is a distant descendent of the epic genre. Nevertheless we exclude the poem from the purview of our discussion since its generic features are distinctively different. However the *Vīrāngāna* also sheds illuminating light on the process of creative assimilation of the genius of the west with the sensibilities of the East.

After carefully going through these poetic endeavours of Madhusudan and weighing his contribution to the development of the epic genre, one cannot but conclude that the masterpieces of Sanskrit and western epic tradition had powerful influence on his feeling evoking vital interest, poetic associations and varying emotions. His three principal poems in general and the *Meghanadvadh* in particular are intrinsically linked with the great flowers of unfading epic imagination. His works have new artistic values yet there are old elements in each of them; thus the law of literary heredity is most discernible in Madhusudan's poetic microcosm. However, the struggle between old and new has not been consigned to oblivion by the poet. His works only reconfirm the importance of understanding the continuity of aesthetic phenomena as well as the interaction of tradition and innovation. Madhusudan's new epic art, nevertheless, cannot be interpreted as something inherent in the old repertoire of Sanskrit epic firmament or an expansion of the ancient mode. His was a giant leap forward that involved a basic readjustment in poetic structure itself. A thoroughly new worldview emerges and asserts itself in the *Meghanadvadh*, perfecting and deepening its content.

Though the Bengal Renaissance left many things to be desired, it was the logical outcome of historically conditioned economic, political and cultural development. Undoubtedly the Renaissance poetry did not simply evolve out of medieval culture; on the contrary, it marked a fundamental break with the previous epoch and its prevailing ideas. There were Rangalal and Hemchandra, but Madhusudan was the true harbinger of the new spirit. In spite of its limitations, the Renaissance humanism rang up the curtain on a new dawn, it was the embryo and beginning of contemporary literary flourish. Having thrown off the spiritual yoke of the feudal world outlook, its theocentricism and the monotonous Mangalkāvyas—the new age showed the litterateurs like Madhusudan the way towards the beauty of real life, of the real human being. Despite the complexities of the aesthetic phenomena and ideological varieties of humanism, the epic genre became the true symbol of Renaissance creativity and finally overcome the stereotyped medieval forms of literary consciousness. What Bankimchandra and

Dinabandhu Mitra did in the genres of novel and drama respectively, Madhusudan did in epic poetry; he was instrumental in renovating the ideological foundation of poetry, asserting a freedom of thought and spirit of humanism. That is why altogether new Rāvaṇa, Meghanād, Sītā and Pramilā came about while Rāma and Lakṣmaṇa sank into a dark pit. Madhusudan's unique discovery of the cultural legacy overturned all the fetters of prevalent notions and inhibitions of medieval legacy imposed by the spiritual dictatorship of the orthodoxy.

IV

Hemchandra Bandyopadhyay

A deeper view of nineteenth century Bengal reveals conflicts and controversies due to contradictory points of view. Thus what appears at first sight as a unified stream untimately breaks up into eddying cross-currents caused by preference for either westernism or orientalism. But there were half-unconscious attempts to accommodate both the new literary modes as well. The poets of post-mutiny Bengal were becoming increasingly aglow with patriotic feelings. Consequently the literary firmament was radiant with fresh hopes and aspirations; the poets were enthusiastically exploring the new horizons of creative possibilities. This awareness inspired the litterateurs to rediscover the epics and Puraṇas in the context of contemporary time. Hemchandra belonged to the newly awakened strata of Bengali society; he, too, found that there was an ideal of human life in antiquity by dint of which he might deduce both moral and intellectual profit to a great extent. Though his imagination was not of very high order, nevertheless he was absorbed in retrospection and in infusing life into the dead past. For a considerable time, Hemchandra enjoyed enviable popularity among the educated middle class; indeed, he was rated as a better poet than even Madhusudan.

Bipin Chandra Pal writes in his memoir: 'Hemchandra however was our special favourite. The intense patriotic passion that breathed through his poems captured our youthful minds in a way which no other Bengali poems had done. The new generation of English-educated Bengalis had already commenced to provoke a conflict in the country.

Hemchandra was, in a special sense, the poet of this new conflict and of the new racial self-respect and sensitive patriotism, born of it.'[9] This 'new conflict' and 'new racial selfrespect' found expression in Hemchandra's fanciful poem, the *Vīravāhu* (1864). The poet has chosen an imaginary theme to delineate his militant patriotism. The poem has poor aesthetic quality; it is nothing but an imaginative compensation for the sad plight of the Indians under foreign subjugation. It reminds us of the minor epics of this period in which the Yavanas i.e. the Muslims are portrayed as the antagonist. Thus Hemchandra played an important role in communalising the Bengali literature in the name of promoting nationalist fervour. History has been rendered subservient to fancy; communal considerations have completely overshadowed reality as well as the scale of time. It is interesting to note that Hemchandra's tryst with poetry began in 1861', that is, the year in which the epochmaking *Meghanadvadh* was published. But the *Cintātaranginī* decisively proves that Hemchandra was absolutely unmoved by the May-flush of exuberant youth in contemporary poetry. On the contrary, he seems to have been deeply embedded in the worn-out legacy of Bharatchandra, Iswar Gupta and Rangalal. The *Vīravāhu* was published after three years but it seems that the tide of time does not move in Hemchandra's microcosm. The poet tried to rewrite history but it failed to add any new dimension to his poetic art because he did not seriously ponder over the possibility of following the emerging epic genre. However, in spite of its total failure as a poetic endeavour, we are including it for two-fold historical reasons. First, it has paved the way for its mighty successor, the *Vṛtrasamhāra*; secondly it is the prototype of several minor epics which were churned out by ambitious poetasters.

The *Vṛtrasamhāra* was published in two volumes; the first volume came out in 1875 while the second in 1877. Hemchandra was fortunate to have an exceptionally patronising review written by none other than Bankimchandra Chattopadhyaya as soon as the first volume came out. It had a tremendous impact on the general readers and the poet was elevated to such a status which he did not actually deserve. In fact, extra-literary considerations far outweighed the poetic merit in the critique prepared by Bankimchandra. The theme of the *Vṛtrasamhāra* fascinated the contemporary readers with its emphasis on philanthropic ideal. Dadhīci's unique self-sacrifice for the cause of deliverance from bondage i.e. the regaining of lost paradise from the yoke of a tyrant demon had indeed captivated the attention of the readers since, in the context of humiliating colonial experience, nothing seemed to be nobler than this. Hence any critical analysis of the validity of poetic conception and propriety of execution was hardly attempted; poetry was not regarded as an end in itself. Ethics and pseudo-metaphysics took command while poetry gradually receded in the background. With a view to propagating the high seriousness demanded by his time, Hemchandra undoubtedly thought of a befitting subject matter. But he failed to realise that no lofty subjectmatter can automatically ensure its artistic elevation into the coveted status of an epic. When a specially equipped creative mind can conceptualise the innermost yearnings of an epoch, the subjectmatter goes through a process of reorientation and attains a hitherto unknown symbolic meaning. This is what has happened with the *Meghanadvadh* but the same is not true about the *Vṛtrasamhāra.*

Hemchandra has undoubtedly visited the granary of the past but his approach to tradition was rather mechanical. The famous Puranic myth of Vṛtra was extended in a modernist frame but nevertheless the creative enrichment is lacking. Albeit unknowingly Hemchandra has lumped together the accidental and the necessary, the essential and superficial, the important and trivial. Unlike the *Meghanādvadh*, the *Vṛtrasamhāra* is rarely fed by the juices of life and it does not seem to have grown up in living soil. Likewise Hemchandra does not also have a wide range of choice which is an unfailing hallmark of a creative poet. It may be noted here that while relying on previous cultural experiences in general and literary tradition in particular, only the true poets can give us something of their own. The poet of the *Vṛtrasamhāra* has not sufficiently appreciated the fact that all aspects of the traditional past cannot retain their validity in later ages. The nineteenth century Bengal was basically a complex and transitional period; the living elements had to be separated from the irrelevant habits when an exceptional genre, like epic, was taking shape. Hemchandra ignored this vital task and it seems that even the unique example of the *Meghanādvadh* could not stir his soul to the desirable extent. The *Vṛtrasamhāra* cannot claim to have scaled the zenith of Bengali epic poetry because its events have not grown out of the thematic scheme like a plant from a seed and consequently it is peopled by abstractions rather than living characters. But surely the uniqueness of Madhusudan's epic poem depends not in its external form, nor in its sequence of accidental events but in the poet's intention, in the characters, the nuances and fusions of human moods; in short, in the creative conception itself. This essential difference between these two epic poems reflects different attitudes and worldviews of the two poets along with their altogether different responses to, as well as interpretations of the continuum of tradition.

The *Vṛtrasamhāra* conforms more closely to the form of the lesser known Sanskrit epics in length in which it surpasses all previous attempts. We have already noted that it has an appropriate theme for the solemn atmosphere intended by the poet; besides its diction is tense and sombre. Hemchandra has sought to compose a modern epic with the help of a language of the past. He could not overcome the doubt and confusion that silently consumed his very being; the poetic diction employed by him is not exactly the seismograph of his strife and tension, paradox and contradiction. It lacks both subtlety and depth without which no poetry of high order can be created. Moreover Vṛtra, the protagonist, is not the true representative of the poet's own time; he remains the titanic demon of the Puranic antiquity. He represents the brute physical force who has not been able to book his passage to the domain of great spiritual elevation characteristic of the renaissance humanism. Unlike Rāvaṇa whose idea kindled Madhusudan's imagination, Hemchandra's Vṛtra can only frighten and cause much ado about nothing; the latter does not elevate the readers' feelings since he can never be loved and sympathised.

V

Nabinchandra Sen

It is argued that the renaissance inspires the revolt of the awakened man against the despotism of creeds, dead legacies and arbitrary authority. The Bengal renaissance had its limitations—inevitable in a colonial society—but nevertheless the poets tried to make up by giving vent to their newly discovered idealism. Nabinchandra composed works in different poetic genres—lyrics, ballads and epics. Of these, the two ballads entitled *Palashir Yuddha* (1875) and *Rangamati* (1880) bear evidence of the impact of Byron and Scott respectively. The *Palashir Yuddha* is complete in five cantos while the *Rangamati* in six. However, notwithstanding their arrangement in cantos, these are remote from the mainstream of renaissance poetry. The creative minds of Bengal were busy at that crucial juncture of time in deciphering the joy of awakening. Besides working for the rebirth of classical antiquity, they were interpreting the new consciousness in a larger sense to mean an entire renewal of life in all its branches. Nabinchandra was undoubtedly stirred by such inspiring idealism but he was groping for an adequate poetic form that would best suit his temperament. There are some critics who ventured to describe the *Palashir Yuddha* as an epic; probably they were overwhelmed by the instantaneous popularity of the poem. But, in actuality, it is more closely allied to the English verse-tales or romances in verse. Nabinchandra showed his mental alertness by choosing a theme from not-so-remote history, and sought to interprete the events in terms of new poetic mode. Yet his success is limited because even sincere portrayal of the externalities of life and mere imitation of established generic forms or pure formal quests cannot produce desired effects in the arena of creative literature.

The spirit manifested in the *Palashir Yuddha* was very dear to the nationalists but its enthusiastic readers were strongly inclined to reduce the function of the Muse to preparing evidences for history. Nabinchandra was a fanciful poet but he did not seem to have penetrating imagination. It is argued that creative investigation of the world presupposes not only exceptional sensitivity to what is going on within it but also a determination by the poet to penetrate into the depths of existence beneath mere appearance. For a creative poet, history is not merely a mechanistic chronicle of past events; he does not intend to reproduce it without revealing the real essence of things and recreating them in the light of the representative genre of the epoch. But, in the *Palashir Yuddha*, our poet remains too engrossed in the temporal frame; the Epic Muse maintains cool distance. However, Nabinchandra proposed a fitting theme with immense possibilities of depth and expansiveness in his trilogy consisting of the *Raivataka* (1886), *Kurukṣetra* (1893) and *Prabhāsa* (1896). In fact, this claim for inclusion in the galaxy of the epic poets is based on this trilogy also known as 'the Mahābhārata of the nineteenth century Bengal.' This epic cycle describes the career of Kṛṣṇa systematically from his youth to the end; the poet has interpreted Indian history in a new light and explained various philosophical ideas throughout. The idea of national degradation, its causes and cure have been brought out and discussed in details.

Even at a cursory glance, it seems that the magnitude of the trilogy is indeed peerless. The problem related to the racial and cultural miscegenation of the Aryans and the non-Aryans forms the background and also lends seriousness to the epic composition. One of the contemporary critics wrote patronisingly: 'one vast Indian Empire, a realised universal human brotherhood, embracing Aryan and non-Aryan in bonds of religious, social and political unity, a grand design, scenic pomp, an antique as well as modern significance like this what national epic can show?'[10] There cannot be any doubt about Nabinchandra's sincere idealism; but it is disputable whether he could effectively unfold any significant inner cohesion in the trilogy while absorbing the traits of ancient tradition in terms of changing social perspective. The poet also does not seem to have maintained proportionate and integral embodiment of ideas and formal devices. If we are aware of the perspective of the last quarter of the nineteenth century Bengal, it would be clear to us that Nabinchandra reacted to the historical situation in his own way and his creative output was based only on those themes and problems that attracted his attention. But, when we remember that a truly innovative poetic work is always an invention in form and a discovery in content, it seems that the trilogy has many a frailties and also lacks systematic unity. In spite of the poet's ambitious goal of creating a completely reinvigorated

Mahābhārata with an all-pervasive design to clothe new thematic and ideological structure, the poet has himself ignored the importance of maintaining dynamic unity as well as functional correlation between different components of his works.

Nabinchandra's awareness of cultural heritage in general and the continuum of epic tradition in particular cannot be denied. But somehow he did not adequately realise the operative methods of the interpenetrative aesthetic categories like 'tradition' and 'innovation'. If we take into account the chequered history of the evolution of the epic genre (from the Sanskrit to the Bengali epics), it may be confidently concluded that the essence of the law of literary continuity has been throughout manifested in the complex and contradictory correlation of tradition and creative innovation which assumes different forms and character in every succeeding age. This correlation brings about a unique enrichment of aesthetic categories in both form and content. New poetic values do not depreciate the aesthetic values of the past.

A poet with new sensibilities is required to simultaneously resolve the tricky problem of modernisation and archaisation of the aesthetic heritage. But Nabinchandra does not seem to be particularly aware of the necessity of progressive enrichment of both form and content in his trilogy. Rather, we confront with an onesided orientation on archaic stereotypes of a vaguely defined past and hollow stylisations; besides, there is a subjective misinterpretation of the epic heritage in modern terms. However, our experience about Nabinchandra's adherence to the epic tradition confirms once again that it is imperative for an innovative poet to correctly understand the complex features of the formation and development of the poetic heritage. Otherwise, in spite of best intentions, the poet might lose the vital link with the dialectical progress of the genre. Nabinchandra's progress from the *Raivataka* to the *Prabhasa* unfolds the sad fact of dilution of poetic scheme and loss of the context of heritage. Nevertheless it proves that irrespective of creative success or failure, the Bengali epic genre is correlated with the greater context of Indian epic tradition either in a positive or a negative manner.

NOTES

1. Rangalal Bandyopadhyaya, 'Bhumika' (introduction) *Padmini Upakhyan,* Rangalal Granthabali, Basumati Sahitya Mandir, Calcutta, p. 68.
2. Letter to Rajnarayan Bose, Letter No. 60, undated ed. Kshetra Gupta, *Kabi Madhusudan Otnar patrabali,* Granthanilay, Calcutta, 1370. (B.E.)/ p. 137.
3. Letter to Gourdas Basak, Letter No. 52, *Kabi Madhusudan Otnar Patrabali*, Granthanilaya, Calcutta, 1370 (B.E.) p. 124.
4. *Ibid.*
5. T.S. Eliot: *The Use of Poetry and the Use of Criticism,* Faber and Faber, London, 1945, p 85.
6. Letter to Rajnarayan Bose, Letter No. 56, Dt. 24th April 1860, *Ibid,* p. 129.
7. *Ibid*, Letter No 73, Dt. 29th August 1861, p. 156.
8. *Ibid*, letter No 59, Dt. 14 th July 1860, p. 135.
9. Bipin Ch. Paul, *Memories of My Life and Times,* Bipin Ch. Paul Institute, Calcutta, 1973, p.185.
10. Brojendra Nath Seal, *New Essays in Criticism*, quoted by Asit Kr. Bandyopadhyaya, 'Bhumika' (Introduction) in *'Raivatak Kurukshetra Prabhas,* Bookland Pvt Ltd, Calcutta, 1966, p. 28.

10

The Withering of Epic Flower: The Final Count Down

In the realm of nineteenth century Bengali literature, there were several poetasters as well who aspired to twinkle as stars in the vicinity of the shining galaxy of the epic genre dominated by Madhusudan, Hemchandra and Nabinchandra. But it is a pity that hardly any of them rose above the level of mediocrity; it is perhaps a futile exercise to trace epic qualities in their works which are, in fact, the specimen of the ambitious crop of ephemeral 'pseudo' epics. We may refer to these poetic endeavours only to satisfy our curiosity about the frontiers of the Bengali epic genre beyond which the expansive epic tradition could not sustain its any longer. Hence, those are, for all practical purposes, apologies for epic poetry having absolutely no literary value. The creative fire ignited by Madhusudan demanded constant nourishment but its heat proved to be inbearable for the lesser beings. Hence it extinguished in no time leaving only embers for his ambitious successors. The poetasters with little or no calibre were attracted by the dazzle of the genre but they could not afford to share the inevitable agony and ecstasy associated with it. Yet they could not resist the temptation of joining the selected band of 'elite' poets; hence they took to composing 'epics' because the very act of epic composition was heavily loaded with symbolic propensities.

Being unable to decipher the true import of the epic genre, these poetasters blindly followed the extraneous structure of the Sanskrit epics mostly on the basis of a few well-known Puraṇic and epic episodes. They had neither any vision nor any message for the society whose changing facets were beyond their comprehesion. They had vague understanding about the rapidly changing social reality and the values underneath. They were not in a position to critically assess the mounting pressures on creative sensibility anc interprete the epic genre as the inevitable response to the demands as well as artistic possibilities of exploring time-tested literary tradition. They also did not realise that the possibilities inherent in language were also opened up by the pressures in times of cultural and psychological crisis when all the past legacies were being chaotically subjected to iconoclastic scrutiny. Unlike the major poets of the genre, these ambitious poetasters were busy only in grafting some cliched subject, without any restructuring or reinterpretation, from the readily available storehouse of the Sanskrit epics and Purāṇas. They neither pursued nor recognized the importance of new thresholds and new anatomies of poetry. They seem to have missed the fact that they were confronting with a new dynamic genre artistically which was perfectly tuned with the demands and complexities of nineteenth century Bengal.

These pseudo-epics are peripheral to the mainstream of Bengali epic poetry; we do not notice any shift of psychic direction and the axes of aesthetic sensibility in those works. Hardly any one of these can be accepted as a work of art which is improvised to hold, however precariously, some sort of equilibrium or balance against disorder, especially against its own disharmony and incongruities. These poetasters tried to imitate the idiosyncratic energy and character of Madhusudan and Hemchandra on the one hand while, they sought to imbibe the general stock of ideas from the post-Kālidāsa Sanskrit court epics. But the volatile richness of contemporary awareness was sadly beyond their reach. It is generally accepted that the successful poems depend for their vitality neither on continuous narration nor on developed argument but on a progression of specific qualities and intensities of emotionally and sensuously charged awareness. It is, however, imperative that the mechanical regularity should not be confounded with organic form. The form employed in the minor epics is mechanical since a predetermined form has been imposed on stereotyped materials. The true significance of the genre being lost to the poetasters, the form remained wholly extrinsic and did not arise out of the properties of the materials. The high seriousness and zealous activities manifested in the early nineteenth century having waned with time, the epic Muse climbed down from her lofty pinnacle of glory only to be stuck into the marshiland of shallow poetic endeavours.

The hectic activities in the contemporary society and the consequent strife and tension deeply stirred the minds of these poetasters. But due to lack of talent, they were unable to translate their innate urge into successful epics. They tried to compensate for their lack of imagination and poetic inspiration by mechanically clinging to the norms of epic versification envisaged in the decadent court epic of Sanskrit literature. It is evident that the flourish of the Bengali epic genre was possible because its prominent exponents affirmed the continuum of Indian epic tradition yet did not compromise their independent position as creative personalities. But the poetasters with insufficient talent did not seem to have any awareness of the inevitability of creative renewal; hence their laborious works are plagued with interminable prolixity and endless dreariness. Monotonous repetitiveness sucked up the vitality of the genre, which had already exhausted itself; as well as the ability to salvage the sinking genre and to return to the earlier heyday of the pioneers. The mechanical and fossilised form and subjectmatter taken resort to by the minor poets connote stagnation of the worst kind in which the shallow streams of elementary poetic fancy respond more sluggishly to make several ripples of untruth in the process. They took Bhāravi, Māgha and Śrīharṣa as their models for imitative and laborious literary exercises. They adhered to conventionality in order to make up for what was lacking in passion and poetic inspiration. Like their counterparts in post-Bhāravi Sanskrit epic poetry, the Bengali poetasters too spent their passion in imitating the earlier poets mechanically and showed no hesitation in constructing their artifices tenaciously on the basis of the most worn-out and commonplace subjects.

Besides, the negative influence of the tenets of Sanskrit poetics on these pseudo-epics is also not negligible. In these works, we notice a willing and unquestionable subservience to modes and models prescribed by the theoreticians. The poetasters are, therefore, more enthusiastic about well-regulated craftsmanship rather than idiosyncratic manifestation of false creative urge; more eager to learn the tricks of the trade and exhibit marked preference for extrinsic techniques and conventionality rather than display free exercise of poetic imagination and individuality in treatment. All these pseudo-epics are fashioned in accordance with the same pattern and hence these seem too much alike; their subjects have too little variety and their treatment is fundamentally the same. These works draw their subjectmatter from well-known epic-Purāṇic sources which are too slender to support a lofty and extensive structure. Besides, there is no awareness of any urgency to unfold the central narrative and steer it to its natural conclusion nor is there any regularity in the arrangement of various episodes and depiction of the poetic personality. In fine, these poems lack the essential sinew for a convincing human drama and remain satisfied with cheap romance and fantasy.

As the prodigality of loosely connected descriptive dissertations is wearisomely similar in every pseudo-epic which hampers, interrupts and buries under its load the inadequate and attenuated narrative. In these works, not only the subject is of little importance but the treatment is also narrowly conditioned. These poems make use of stock situations, familiar motifs, tiresome cliches and thus prove themselves to be colossal wastage caused by misdirected literary endeavour. In the last quarter of the nineteenth century, the trends of anthropocentricism and the urge for freedom from chains of superstition were swallowed by the quicksand of Hindu revivalism. Consequently the protestant attitude of the earlier decades gradually faded out and preference for status quo became the credo of the colonial elites. The creative renewal of tradition no longer remained relevant; the poets with lesser calibre sought to compensate for their lack of vision by taking resort to laborious constructionalism with emphasis on imaginary redemption and conquest of Utopia. As the frailties, doubts, paradoxes and progressive loss of centre became increasingly apparent in the sociocultural perspective of contemporary Bengal while the colonial intelligentsia were hopelessly alienated from the eddying time—the poetasters went on composing a good number of so-called epic poems to voice forth their pseudo-patriotism and shallow religious ehtics. These works have presented either yavanas (i.e. Muslims) or demons as the easily targetable antagonists. Thus these minor Bengali epics have contributed a great deal in the process of communalisation of Bengali literature.

According to their subjectmatter, these pseudo-epics may be classified in six principal categories, viz., (i) the poems based on the *Rāmāyaṇa;* (ii) The poems based on the *Mahābhārata;* (ii) the poems based on the Puranic episodes related to the mother-goddess; (iv) the poems based on the Puranic episodes related to Kṛṣṇa; (v) the poems of miscellaneous origin; and (vi) the poems based on the episodes derived from foreign sources. After a close scrutiny of the poems included in these categories, we find that their generic features are often indistinct; some of those may seem to be long narrative poems masquerading as epics having disarrayed structure. Yet these are classified according to the categories enumerated above because these bear unmistakable signs of their common patrinomy. Besides, all such poems emerge from the same regressive sociocultural tendencies. As we have already noted, in order to escape from the ignominious reality of colonial subjugation, the emerging ideologues of the Bengali petti bourgeoise class were engrossed in searching for scapegoats in communalised medieval history on the one hand and constructing a wish-fulfilling image of golden age with the idealised ingredients chosen sparingly from ancient India. The pseudoepics mentioned above sought to exploit shallow patriotic sentiments and vague religious thoughts; these totally lacked poetic insight and had neither preparation nor capacity to interprete the inherent aspirations and frustrations of contemporary society. Though these works have very little literary value, these seem to have some historical significance as the records of the poverty and infirmity of thought which had infested the world-view of many a Bengali Hindu elites in that period. By making use of a famous Kalidasian expression, these poetasters may be described are the examples of 'mandakavih Yasahprārthī' i.e. 'bad poets hankering after fame.'

II

(a) Among the poems based on the *Rāmāyaṇa,* we find the following, Rasbihari Mukhopadhyaya's *Sitar Vanabas* (Dacca 1868), Jadabananda Roy's *Sita-nirvasan* (Dacca 1870); Ramkamal Bandyopadhyaya's *Lavanavadhakavya* (Beharampur 1870), Upendranarayan Roy Choudhury's *Ramvanavas Kavya* (Murshidabad 1872); Anath Bandhu Roy's *Vaidehivaidhavya* (Dacca 1873); Girish Chandra Basu's *Balivadhakavya* (1876), Aghornath Mukhopadhyaya's *Ravanavadhakavya* (1877); Gopal Chandra Chakrabarty's *Bhargavavijayakavya* (1877); Harimohan Mukhopadhyaya's *Mukutauddhara* (1881); Sashibhushan Mazumdar's *Dasasyasamharakavya* (1883) and Krishnendra Roy's *Sitacarita* (1884).

(b) Among the poems based on the *Mahābhārata,* we find the following: Harishchandra Mitra's *Kicakavadhakavya* (Dacca 1861), Bholanath Chakrabarty's *Savitricarita Kavya* (1868); Prafulla Chandra Bandyopadhyaya's *Damayantibilapakavya* (1868); Aghornath Bandyopadhyaya's *Abhimanyuvadha* (1868); Mahesh Chandra Chakrabarty's *Nibatakavacavadha* (1869); Prafulla Chandra Bandyopadhyaya's *Sambaranavijayakavya* (1869); Naranarayan Roy's *Srivatsacarita* (Jasohar 1870); Bhubanmohan Ghosh's *Gandharibilapa* (1870); Haricharan Chakrabarty's *Bhadrodvaha Kaya* (1871); Kirshorilal Roy's *Naladamayantikavya* (1872); Rukminikanta Thakur's *Uttara-bilapakavya* (1874); Baladeb Palit's *Karnarjunakavya* (1875); Bhubanmohan Roychaudhury's *Pandavacaritakavya* (1877); Anonymous poet's *Yadavanandinikavya* (1880); Jibankrishna Ghosh's *Duryodhanavadhakavya* (1886); Haripada Konar's *Pandavabilapa-kavya* (1888) and Dinesh Charan Basu's *Mahaprasthana Kavya* (1894).

(c) The poems based on the *Mārkaṇḍeya Purāṇa, Devībhāgavata* etc. are as follows:

Bharatchandra Sarkar's *Madanabhasma* (1866); Biharilal Bandyopadhyaya's *Saktisambhavakayva* (1870); Ramchandra Mukhopadhyaya's *Danavadalanakavya* (1873); Srinath Kundu's *Tadakavadhakavya* (1875); Ramgati Chattopadhyaya's *Surarivadha* (1875), Lalitmohan Mukhopadhyaya's *Apurvapranaya* or *Dakṣavadha* (1877); Akshoy Kumar Sarkar's *Taraka samhara* (1888); Sasadhar Roy's *Tridivavijaya* (1896) and Saraccandra Choudhury's *Deviyuddha* (1900).

(iv) The poems based on the *Bhāgavata Purāṇa, Viṣṇu Purāṇa* and *Harivamśa* are as follows:

Dinanath Dhar's *Kamsavinasa* (1861); Banoarilal Roy's *Dvarakakelikaumudi* (1863); Haricharan Chakrabarty's *Bhadrodvaha* (1871) and Harilal Goswami's *Narakasamhara* (1896).

(v) There are some poems of miscellaneous origin of which some pretend to have relationship with the Puranic world but in actuality these deviate from the Purāṇas to a great extent. There are some others which are fashioned on historical episodes. Among such poems, we find the following:

Banoarilal Roy's *Yojanagandha* (1858); Banamali Ghoshal's *Padmagandha Upakhyana* (1864); Banoarilal Roy's *Jayavati.* (Howrah 1865); Chandrasekhar Bandyopadhyaya's *Bharatabhramanakavya* (1865); Jagacchandra Debsarkar Chaudhury's *Abjodvaha* (1867); Ishanchandra Basu's *Cittavinodanakavya* (Barddhaman 1868); Brajanath Mitra's *Kadambarikavya* (1869); Baladeb Palit's *Bhartṛharikavya* (1872), Ananda Chandra Mitra's *Mitrakavya* (Dacca 1874 and 1877); Durga Chandra Sanyal's *Mahamogal Kavya* (Aurangzeb Parvan 1875; Sivaji Parvan 1876, Joysimha Parvan 1877); Shyama Charan Shrimani's *Simhalavijaya* (1876); Dinanath

Gangopadhyaya's *Kamalakalikakavya* (1876); Nabinchandra Das's *Kalidaser Vidyalabha Kavya* (1876); Upendranarayan Roy Chaudhury's *Viravalikavya* (1877); Dhirendra Nath Paul's *Yaminiprabhata* (1879); Harimohan Mukhopadhyaya's *Adṛṣṭavijaya* (1881) and Yogendranath Ghosh's *Vanger Viraputra* (1884).

(vi) A couple of poems are based on non-Indian sources; e.g., Girish Chandra Basu's *Svargabharasta kavya* (1869) and Ananda Chandra Mitra's *Helenakavya* (Mymensingh 1876 and Dacca 1877).

Besides, a few translation works were also undertaken seemingly to popularise Kālidāsa's epics among the Bengali readers. Sometimes, instead of taking up the whole epic, the translators confined their attention within the limited periphery of certain interesting episodes only. These attempts may be deciphered as extra-evidences of the continuum of Sanskrit epic tradition in the paradox-ridden arena of nineteenth century Bengal. A few works of this category are named hereunder:

Harimohan Karmakar's *Kumarasambhava* (1857); Pyarimohan Sengupta's *Kumarasambhava* (1861); Sibchandra Bhattacharya's *Ajabilapa* (1867); and Radharaman Adhikari's *Dagdhamadana* (1877).

After going through these pseudo-epics, the following conclusions may be arrived at:

(a) These poetic adventures generally imitate the extrinsic structure and demeanours of the Purāṇas and post-Bhāravi Sanskrit court epics.

(b) These ambitious endeavours may be described as disarrayed and montonously prolonged collections of unimaginative and disorganised non-prosaic expressions in which poetic traits are little more than nothing.

(c) Whatever might be conscious intention of the poetasters named above, it is a pity that even the barest minimum preconditions of creativity have been seldom adhered to. There is hardly any regularity in regards to the treatment of subjectmatter.

(d) Neither the narrative nor the arrangement of cantos and neither the characterisation nor the poetic diction could reflect any positive affinity with the Sanskrit epic tradition. These bear only the negative impact of that tradition because of imperfect understanding of the significance of the epic genre as well as lack of creative imagination and skill of craftsmanship.

(e) Very few works among the pseudo-epics bear any print of contemporary strife and tension. When migthy storms have been raging in the then Bengali society, the poetasters seem to have assumed the role of desert camels trying to protect their utopian isolation from the torments of change. They chose to bury themselves in the sands of directionless past under the pretext of codifying and falsely emulating traditions.

(f) These works are interesting examples of much ado about nothing because these seek to invoke not only totally irrelevant values but also establish counter-ideologies at a time when the entire Bengali society was going through a process of traumatic transformation.

(g) Being unable to cultivate the true import of new awakening and the demands of contemporary society, the poetasters took resort to escapism. They tried to build up wish-fulfilling utopian ivory towers by collecting ingredients at random from some vaguely defined Puranic past or episodes of imaginary history or children's fantasy or illusory folk-tales.

(h) Being the beneficiaries of the British rule, the poetasters who belonged to the emerging middle class intelligentsia—found in the colonial masters their heaven-sent saviours from the Yavanas i.e. Muslims. Like the proverbial one-eyed deer, they fell prey to the snares of increasing tendencies of communalisation of history. As the renaissance humanism faded out gradually to yield place to the imposing demands of religious revivalism, no subjectmatter remained valid for constructing the appropriate microcosm expected in the epic genre.

(i) Men and women pulsating with flesh and blood are very rarely found in these pseudo-epics because these are crowded with gods and demons, other imaginary beings and folk deities. Gods and goddesses of the Great and Little tradition cohabit without any hesitation; the poetasters are never sure about the roles to be assigned to them in the epic narrative.

(j) Almost all such works put emphasis on the religious and ethical principles of life. The epic personae have been designed as the mouth-pieces of those principles but their relevance to the contemporary social reality have been seldom taken into consideration. Hence there is hardly any scope for characterisation; instead, the ambitious attempts to portray a few characters have invariably produced chaotic, dull and shadowy abstractions which lack human warmth, structure and conflict. They talk endlessly but seldom act.

(k) The language of these pseudo-epics has been irretrievably inspired by the abundant use of long compounds, obsolete words, grotesque usage, verbiosity, forced metaphors and similes, obscure puns and alliterations. Obviously the Bengali minor epics derived their modes of expression, figures of speech, meters etc. from the post-Bhāravi Sanskrit court epics. Consequently the forward movement of the meagre narrative has been rendered impossible and this immobility culminated in making these poems unredeemingly monotonous and extremely affected.

(l) Many a poems of this category describes the heaven of Śiva, Viṣṇu and Brahman as well as the torments of hell in accordance with the various Purāṇic texts. The victory of the virtuous and fall of the sinners are depicted with much enthusiasm.

(m) In order to follow the dicta of poetics faithfully, these poetasters have sought to portray different varieties of sentiments or 'rasa's of which the heroic (Vīra), love (Śṛngāra) and pathetic (Karuṇa) are generally employed as the principal sentiment (Angīrasa) while the remaining sentiments are treated as auxiliary (Angarasa).

(n) The poetasters seem to have been generally inspired by the phenomenal popularity of the great triad of the Bengali epic genre, viz. Madhusudan, Hemchandra and Nabinchandra.

However, Hemchandra seems to have inspired the poetasters most; hence the model of the *Vṛtrasamhāra* has been zealously imitated time and again. Besides, Rangalal has also cast his spell over some of these minor epic poets. But the poetasters lacked the talent of their great predecessors; hence their ambitious endeavours remained exercises in futility.

III

It is indeed unnecessary to discuss all such works here. We may, therefore, briefly analyse only those which deserve no better than birds' eye-view since there is absolutely nothing in those to appreciate. But the brief comments noted hereafter would indicate to what extent to Bengali pseudo-epics nullified the positive impact of the profoundly rich epic tradition fraught with immense creative possibilities.

Among the poems based on the episodes of the *Rāmāyaṇa.* let us first take up Girish Chandra Basu's *Vālivadha* (1876). It constitutes of seven cantos but the poet could nowhere show his skill in arranging the subjectmatter. He merely narrates the events mechanically and succeeds in making his work hopelessly monotonous. It is evident that the poet is totally devoid of imagination and as a result the narrative is built very haphazardly. The chaotic structure of the poem reminds us of the post-Bhāravi Sanskrit court epics. Because, in the third canto itself, Vali is vanquished and wounded; but even after that his prolonged lamentation has been depicted injudiciously. Though Vali dies in this canto, the narrative limps on and thus the poem stretches most unnecessarily to four more cantos. The personalities of the great epic have been casually introduced; the poet has failed to infuse life into the theme.

Gopal Chandra Chakrabarty's *Bhargava-vijaya* (1877) constitutes of sixteen cantos which depict Paraśurāma's humiliating defeat at the hands of Rāma. The subjectmatter lacks both expanse and depth; whatever meagre materials the poet has derived from the repertory of tradition, the fails to control even that. The shades of the Sanskrit court epics loom large over this poem. It seems that the poetaster has adhered to the literal meaning of the 'mahākāvya', that is, 'a big poem.' That is why even after the depiction of the defeat of Bhārgava (Paraśurāma) five more cantos have been incorporated by the author to describe various natural scenes as well as record some data about himself and contemporary Bengali poets. There he has eulogised his mothertongue as well. Gopalchandra has attained little success in portraying the epic personae. Thus Bhārgava i.e. Paraśurāma, the central figure of the poem, has not been delineated properly. He lacks both Puranic dignity and epic propriety; his infatuations for Sitā seem to have been conceived as innovative addition but instead this has caused serious damage to the important figure by transgressing all permissible limits. Rāma is a dignifid figure but due to the mechanistic approach of the poet, he remains sketchy and unconvincing. Sitā is little more than a name. Laksmaṇa is portrayed as a short-tempered man while Daśaratha is shown as a weak and timid person. Gopalchandra seems to have derived the clues for these two characters from Vālmiki's great epic itself.

Harimohan Mukhopadhyaya's *Mukuta-Uddhara* (1881) is an interesting specimen of wild fancy where the episodes of the *Rāmāyaṇa* have been transformed into chaotic mass of incongruous materials. In fact, its subject-matter is the product of Harimohan's ill-directed fancy which remains tempestuous throughout the fourteen Ucchvasas of the poem. In the first Ucchvasa, queen Kauśalyā laments at her sad lot and the sun god sends his charioteer to console her. In the second, we find a joyous preparation for the coronation of Mandodarī to the throne of Lankā. Even Śacī is brought to wait upon Mandodarī; Brahman, Śiva and Vīrabhadra are introduced along with Bhāvanī and Maya. Except their nomenclature, such deities retain no trace of the original Puranic character.

In the third Ucchvasa (i.e. canto), mannerisms of the ornate epics and nostalgic feelings are used alternately. Rāma is depicted as invested with the divine strength of Soudamini (a fictitious goddess) and Cāmundā; he is entrusted with the noble task of rescuing the motherland from the clutches of demons. In the fourth, a pensive Rāma confornts with symbolic natural calamities and divine beings. He takes an oath to kill the demons and returns home to take leave of his wife, who is interestingly a different woman. Because, in this poem, Sītā is depicted as the presiding deity of Aryan fortune; she is totally unrelated to Rāma. The canto comes to an end with Rāma's preparation for battle. In the fifth Ucchvasa, Brahman delivers Bhāvani's message to the lamenting Kauśalyā and Śaci predicts Daśaratha's deliverance by Kāma. Indeed the poem has opened the chaotic pandora's box, as it were, by completely reversing or changing at will the well-known roles of the Puranic deities as well as the prominent personalities of the great epic.

In the sixth, the hectic activities in the city of Lanka are depicted after the alarm of impending battle is sounded there. In fierce encounter, Indrajit is defeated by Rāma. In the seventh, Kauśalyā asks Rāma not to go out for battle anymore; however, he manages to persuade Kauśalyā and, in the next encounter, Indrajit is severely wounded. An enraged Rāvaṇa plunges into the battle and kills Rāma. In the eighth Ucchvasa, the sun-god tries to inspire the gods to join in the battle against the rāksasa. Sitā (the goddess of fortune for the Aryans) arrives there with the information of Rāma's death and expresses her despair. When the gods prepare for battle, Niyati (i.e. the goddess of destiny) dissuades them by preparing a vision of India's glorious future and the extermination of the demons. This is clearly indicative of the contemporary tendency towards wish-fulfillment since the colonial intelligentsia always preferred to assume the disguise of such simplified metaphor. They could not afford to point out the accusing finger to the immediately available colonial rulers because the advantages enjoyed at the level of material existence would then be at stake. At any rate, Indra is entrusted with the responsibility of soliciting advice from Kali. As Sitā returns to her prison, Indra starts for Kali.

In the ninth canto, Kali first pretends not to recognise Indra and orders to throw him to a fire pit. However, he agrees to extend his help to the gods. In the tenth canto, Kali advises Vibhīṣaṇa to desert his kins. Initially Vibhiṣaṇa reacts adversely but afterwards he agrees and, with the help of his wife, Sarama, frees Daśaratha from the prison. In the eleventh, we find Sarala, Rāma's wife, engrossed in grief; she seeks permission from Daśaratha to join the battle. But Daśaratha himself sets out for the battlefield. In the twelfth, the sprinkling of nectar restores life in Rāma's corpse. A fierce fight ensues between Rāma and Indrajit on the one hand and Daśaratha and Ravana on the other. Indrajit is killed and Rāvaṇa takes to his heels. In the thirteenth, Rāvaṇa prepares for battle once again; a divine message implores him to return Jānaki, the presiding deity of Aryan fortune. At the bidding of his ministers, Rāvaṇadecides to concede the request but Mandodarī intervenes and instigates him to plunge into the battle instead. In the fourteenth ucchvasa, Daśaratha fights with Rāvaṇa while the gods too join the battle. Bibhīṣaṇa advises Daśaratha to use the indomitable Brahmāstra i.e. the mighty missile of Brahman and eventually Rāvaṇa is killed. India's lost glory is restored thereafter.

Thus the *Mukuta-uddhāra* is a typical wish-fulfillment of the paradox-rideen, self-deceiving, escapist attitude of the colonial elites of the nineteenth century Bengal who could not afford to displease the rulers nor could they entirely ignore their increasing anxiety, frustration and dismay at the perpetuation of the British sway. Those who possessed poetic ambition but had little imagination and skill, were fascinated by the contemporary popularity of Madhusudan and Hemchandra in particular. The models of the *Meghanadvadha,* the *Vīrabahu* and the *Vṛtrasamhāra* were imperfectly understood and mechanically imitated by several poetasters of whom Harimohan Mukhopadhyaya was one. His *Mukuṭa-uddhāra* is sadly devoid of any redeeming feature; though it seeks to present patriotism as its theme, its significance is unfortunately lost in the midst of a totally chaotic arrangement of the subjectmatter. The anarchic mismanagement of the narrative and its absurd incongruities might have been the outcome of the author's allegiance to the methods of the Sanskrit court epics. Whatever might be his ambitious intention, his unbridled fancy has failed to imprint any lasting impression. The poem has obviously nothing to do with the *Rāmāyaṇa* from which only some names have been collected at random. They are completely new individuals and have little to do with the Rāmāyaṇa. The author is never very keen to systematically portray them as distinctive individuals; he is eager only to fashion them as promoters of certain ethical and spiritual values. Most of them voice forth patriotic spirit.

In the ultimate analysis, the *Mukuta-uddhāra* may be regarded as a unique specimen of the outcome of negative interpretation of the epic-Purāṇic tradition.

Sashibhushan Mazumdar's *Daśāsya-samhāra* (1883) narrates the event beginning from the mutilation of Surpanakha's nose and ears and ending in Rāvaṇa's death. It constitutes of fourteen cantos and, in the manner of the campus, it is composed both in prose and verse. In the prose portion, we find the following: Surpaṇakha's arrival, Rāvaṇa's instruction to Marica and the episode of golden deer, Sitā's abduction, Jatāyu's fight with Rāvaṇa, Rāma's search for Sitā, his friendship with Sugriva followed by Vāli's death: Hanumat's aerial journey to Lankā, his meeting with Sitā followed by the burning of Lankā, Hanumat's return and report to Rāma regarding the whereabouts of Sita.

In the verse-portion, we find the following events: Rāma's preparation for the battle, the construction of bridge across ocean, siege of Lankā, Bibhīṣaṇa's futile attempts to persuade Ravana for truce leading to his insult, Bibhīṣana's desertion and his acceptance in Rāma's camp, terrible battle, death of Ravana's several sons, Kumbhakarna's death, Meghanāda's death, Rāvaṇa's missile strike at Laksmaṇa and the latter's life at stake, Hanumat's bringing of the uprooted Gandhamādan mountain and restoration of Laksmaṇa's life, Rāvaṇa's death and the funeral rites.

Except the unsuccessful attempt to add novelty by initiating the Campu genre of Sanskrit literature, the author has achieved nothing in this work. He is faithful to the narrative of the *Rāmāyaṇa* but lacks genuine innovative spirit. The epic personae have been casually introduced and there is no attempt whatsoever to portray them appropriately.

Krishnendra Roy's *Sitācarita* (1884) has been composed with a didactic purpose and is complete in four cantos, each of which is subdivided into several sopanas. This arrangement may have been made to add novelty to the work. The first canto has fifteen, the second thirteen, the third six and the fourth three sopanas; thus there are thirty seven sopanas in the four cantos of the poem. Krishnendra has tried his best to faithfully follow the *Rāmāyaṇa* in portraying the complete life of Sita that begins with her miraculous birth and ends in her disappearance in the furrows of earth. The poet owes his allegiance to both Vālmiki and Kṛttibāsa but nevertheless his work totally lacks the epic spirit and seldom rises above the level of a crude folk narrative.

IV

Among the poems based on the episodes of the *Mahābhārata,* we may first note the *Kīcakavadhakāvya* (Dacca 1861). Interestingly it was published in the most significant year since in the same year, the *Meghanādvadh* was published that took all the connoissseurs by storm. Harishchandra Mitra, the author of the *Kīcakavadhakavya* was a prolific writer because he wrote several poetic pieces, plays etc and was involved with the publication of a few monthly and weekly journals. Harishchandra's acquaintance with the Sanskrit literature in general and two great epics in particular is evident from the publication of his '*Janakinataka*', '*Jayadratha Vadha*', '*Prahladanataka*' and translation of the first book of the *Rāmāyaṇa.* He seems to have been substantially inspired to wield his pen by Madhusudan's instantaneous popularity though he is unfortuantely as remote from the latter as Hyperion to Satyr. At any rate, the second edition of *Kicakavadha* was published in 1878.

Bholanath Chakraborty's *Savitricarita* (1868) narrates the famous story of Savitri and Satyavat in seven cantos. This episode of the vanaparvan is replete with poetic expressions but Bholanath could not retain the splendour of the original; instead he has presented the subject matter in an unembellished manner. On the one hand, the work limps with the burden of prosaic statements while on the other, the progress of the narrative is seriously hampered by the manifestation of his inclination towards hyperbolic expression. The famous myth of Savitri is full with poetic possibilities; but Bholanath has failed to grasp its significance and hence could not properly explore it. Therefore, the figures of both Savitri and Satyavat have become flat and uninteresting. The figure of Yama has been drawn in accordance with the epic-Puranic legacy but it does not connote any new dimension.

Maheshchandra Tarkachudhamani's *Nibātakavacavadha* was first published in 1869 and its second enlarged edition came out in 1883 in which four more cantos have been added to the poem to accommodate the episode of Urvasi's curse to Arjuna. In the preface (Vijnapana) of his work, the poet himself speaks of his allegiance to the norms of epic versification standardised in Sanskrit literature. Maheshchandra has derived his subjectmatter from an episode of the Vanaparvan of the *Mahābhārata.* The poem begins with Indra's invitation to Arjuna to visit the heaven and concludes after Arjuna kills the terrible demons who are collectively known as the Nibātakavacas. The poet's fondness for extravagant verbiosity under the pretext of description and exhibition of hollow pedantry cannot but remind us of the post-Kālidāsa Sanskrit court epics. The circuitous movement of the narrative bears close resemblance with the methods followed by Bhāravi, Māgha, Ratnākara and Śrīharṣa whom Maheshchandra imitates faithfully. But, in sptie of his adherence to the Sanskrit epic tradition, his lack of originality proved to be his undoing

The *Nibātakavacavadha* was comparatively well received by the contemporary critics who belived in the efficacy of uninterrupted continuum of ancient literary and cultural heritage. Faithful reconstruction of age-old edifices was given priority over innovative creation; the conformists of the then Bengali society did not like to be too deeply involved with the disagreeable present. It is but natural that they were in favour of unquestioning reaffirmation of time-tested concepts and values. They preferred to remain firm in the faith and consequent acceptance of ancient authority; they were suspicious of the non-conformists. Being positively uneasy with the transnational tendencies of the exponents of the new epic genre, they tried to counteract by revalidating those elements, which they believed to be truly 'national.' In no time, these enthusiastic 'nationalists', with little insight and talent, took over control from those who had opted for adventurous voyages into the brave new world. Maheshchandra was one of those conformists who interpreted tradition mechanistically and through an idealised prism.

It is therefore expected that the *Nibatakavacavadha* exhibits scholarship and indulges in verbal gymnastics. The poem remains stale and monotonous, the portrayal of various epic personae also indicates the poet's adherence to the epic-puranic legacy. The gods and titans are replica of their respective archetypes and no new dimension has been added to them.

Jibankrishna Ghosh's *Duryodhanavadha* (1886) is complete in seven cantos and deals with the incidents beginning with Sakuni's death and concludes with the description of Duryodhana breathing his last. The poet seems to have before him the instance of Māgha's *Sisupālavadha* under whose impact an episode of the *Mahābhārata* has been presented with elaborate epic paraphernalia. Though Jibankrishna has arranged the events creditably, his limitations are quite obvious. Due to lack of creative imagination, his apparent allegiance to the narrative of the great epic on the one hand and the formalism of the court epics on the other has not sufficiently elevated the status of his work. It remains, on the whole, dull and unattractive.

But it has its silver lining too in the formulation of various poetic personae. Thus it introduces a thoroughly new Duryodhana to us who is a conscientious person and suffers from remorse. He is obstinate but nevertheless this does not counterbalance the milk of human kindness in him. His relationship with Bhanumati, the devoted queen, as well as parents bespeaks of his loving and sensitive nature. As a truly living human figure, Duryodhana pulsates with life and naturally he is depicted as having several complexities that flesh is heir to. He is, therefore, a unique example of creative reconstruction of the ingredients of epic tradition; obviously such instances are indeed very rare among the minor epics. It seems that while depicting the figure of Bhanumati the poet has been substantially influenced by Hemchandra Bandyopadhyay's Indubala. Both these figures are exceptionally tender-hearted; like Indubala, Bhanumati also does not like the ferocity of battle and prefers to live a tranquil life with her husband. Dhṛtarāṣṭra has been depicted as a cowardly but cunning man who has no filial affection for Duryodhana.

This is an interesting departure from the version of the *Mahābhārata* which once again makes us aware of the poet's inclination towards creative renewal of traditional materials. Unlike his counterpart in the great epic, here Dhṛtarāṣtra blames his son for bringing about the destruction of his clan and ascribes everything to the cruelty of destiny. Gandhari is depicted as usual as a pious and dutiful lady suffering silently for what is happening around. Likewise, Yudhiṣthira's moral excellence, Bhima's seriousness of purpose and heroism, Kṛṣṇa's statesmanship and presence of mind, Arjuna's nobility etc. have been portrayed commendably.

Dinesh Charan Basu's *Mahaprasthāna* (1887) consists of twenty one cantos; it begins with Abhimanyu's ceremonial installation as the commander of the Pāṇdava army and ends with the Pāṇdava's ascent to heaven. The narrative is quite often loaded with extravagant descriptions and emotional outbursts. Dinesh Charan has tried to improve upon the materials of the *Mahābhārata* but he does not seem convincing and hence met with limited success. Moreover, the under-currents of Hindu revivalism have sometimes carried the poet too far away from the mainstream of the epic narrative. He seems to be obsessed with the idea of reinstatement of the Aryan glory. The narrative of the greet epic has thereby assumed metaphorical significance; in fact, sometimes Dineshcharan overstretches the story with a view to extracting his own predetermined meaning. He posts a clear signal of his intention, fed fat by contemporary revivalism, while invoking poetic imagination in the very beginning of the poem. In the concluding section of the poem, the author again expresses his optimism towards a bright future for the revitalized 'Aryan' nation. It clearly indicates the subservience of the creative epic tradition to chauvinistic tendencies of the age.

Naturally the famous epic personae of the *Mahābhārata* have been somewhat remodelled in this poem but the outcome of such re-orientation has not been quite encouraging. Often the famous characters of the great epic are caught between the Scylla and Charybdis of the original import and the new intention. However, occasionally they too have their own silver linings, some of them are on the whole quite interesting. Kṛṣṇa, Arjuna, Yudhiṣthira, Duryodhana, Subhadrā and Bhānumatī deserve special mention because they are endowed with some distinctive trait of personality. In fine, Dineshcharan's interaction with the epic tradition could not arrest the process of dedadence that had set in the Bengali epic genre and trigger off any new phase only because the poet himself divested the epic Muse of its essential freedom at the very outset.

V

Among the poems based on the Puranic stories about the mother goddess which include the episodes related to the birth of Kārttikeya, the commander of divine army, the following may be discussed.

Ramgati Chattopadhyaya's *Surarivadha* (1875) is fashioned on the outlines of the famous episode of the *Candi* that narrates the killing of two demons, viz., Sumbha and Nisumbha by the mother goddess. Throughout its eight cantos, the progress of the central narrative has often been temporarily suspended. The poet has inflated the bulk of the poem by incorporating several common Puranic motifs and maintaining the paraphernalia of the post-Bhāravi Sanskrit court epics to a considerable extent. There is, however, absolutely no scope for characterisation in the midst of abundant mythic materials. It remains throughout a poem about the superhuman beings, that is, gods and titans who summarily exclude living mortals from their august company.

Lalitmohan Mukhopadhyay's *Apurva Praṇaya* or *Dakṣavadha* (1877) constitutes of six cantos which mechanically record Dakṣa's sacrifice, Sati's death, Śiva's wrath, beheading of Dakṣa, restoration of his life, creation of fifty one holy pithas and Śiva's meditation. There is scope for neither mundane details nor any living characters in it.

Aksay Kumar Sarkar's *Tārakasamhāra* (1888) has nine cantos through which the slaying of Tāraka by Kārttikeya has been delineated. This work has absorbed only the secondary influence of the Sanskrit epics since the impact of Hemchandra Bandyopadhyay's *Vṛtrasamhāra* is more pronounced in it. In the first canto, the gods quarrel in their assembly; in the second, Śaci's sad plight is described exactly in the manner of the *Vṛtrasamhāra.* The third canto introduces Taraka and his queen, Surasā to us. Her craving for Rati's service cannot but remind us of similar situation in Hemchandra's poem. In the fourth canto, the prominent gods wait upon Brahman and the latter manifests his devastating anger just as Śiva does in the *Vṛtrasamhāra*. Along with Brahman, the gods go to Viṣṇu; they are told that the slaying of Tāraka by Kārttikeya is foreordained. In the fifth, a reluctant Madana is entrusted with the task of disturbing Śiva's penance. In the sixth, the haughtiness of Tāraka and Surasā on the one hand and Śacī's generosity on the other are portrayed. In the seventh, Madana is reduced to ashes but life is restored to him by Śiva after the latter's marriage is proposed; a grief-stricken Rati is also dissuaded from giving up her life. In the eighth, Kārttikeya is borne of Śiva's seed; he is a child prodigy and assumes the command of the divine army. In the ninth, Taraka is killed by Kārttikeya with Śiva's trident. Surasā jumps into ocean and commits suicide.

The simultaneous influences of both the Sanskrit and the Bengali epic tradition in general and the *Kumārasambhava* and the *Vṛtrasamhāra* in particular are clearly evident in this poem. But nevertheless such influences have not been absorbed in a meaningful way; besides, the poet lacks both imagination and craftsmanship. Moreover unnecessary details have considerably retarded the progress of the narrative; it is needless to mention here that it is an ailment equally shared by the latter poets in both the Sanskrit and Bengali epic tradition.

While depicting different characters, Akshay Kumar has faithfully imitated the model of character portrayal as envisaged in Hemchandra's *Vṛtrasamhāra;* comparatively, the influence of the *Kumārasambhava* is peripheral and distant. The epic personae in the *Tārakasamhāra* have been designed as the spokesmen of patriotic feeling which has added new dimension to them. The poet's range is obviously limited; yet, even in that limited sphere, he has drawn the two important figures i.e. the protagonist (Kārttikeya) and the antagonsist (Tāraka) quite admirably. Tāraka and Surasā, however, resemble Vṛtra and Aindrilā of the *Vṛtrasamhāra* in more ways than one. On the other hand, Aksaykumar's Indra has considerably come down from the pedestal of Puranic glory because he does not seem to possess the characteristic grandeur expected from the lord of gods. Instead, he appears to be somewhat fickleminded, light-hearted and shallow. His consort, Śaci, is comparatively an attractive figure though she has little activity and very limited sphere to move. The figure of Brahman in this poem reminds us of Śiva is the *Vṛtrasamhāra.* Besides, Agni, Yama, Pavana, Varuṇa, Kāma, Rati and Capalā are also modelled according to their counterparts in Hemchandra's pantheon. However unlike the *Vṛtrasamhāra,* here Rati refuses to serve the queen of demons, it has been incorporated in the poem to give vent to the ideal of devotionalism. This figure seems to have been drawn on the basis of readily available ingredients of the epic-Puranic tradition.

Saśadhar Roy's *Tridivavijaya* (1896) constitutes of eight cantos and narrates the slaying of Tāraka. The narative has often been supplemented by theological details of the Hindu religion. The poet has tried to incorporate a good number of new details but these could not help the work much which remains basically an instance of miserable artistic failure. The author is explicitly 'traditional' but the true import of the epic tradition is obviously beyond his grasp. He, too, follows the *Vṛtrasamhāra* very closely in regards to characterisation though sometimes he tries his best to be different by attempting to fabricate fresh nuances to some of the characters.

Sasadhar depicts the figures of Kārttikeya, Indra, Śiva, Kuvera, Gaurī, Kāma, Rati, Mahāmāyā, Viśvakarman, Nandi etc. It seems that the poet has blended the Purāṇic and non-Purāṇic materials unscrupulously. Moreover, his tendency towards cheap philosophisation has also proved to be another stumbling block. For example, Mahāmāyā has, for all practical purposes, assumed the role of a professor of philosophy. Some of her words remind us of the famous Nāsadīya hymn of the *Ṛgveda* and the *Kena Upaniṣad.* Even Viśvakarman, the divine engineer, usurps the role of a philosopher and talks of lofty ideals to Kārttikeya in the fifth canto where the echoes of the *Gītā* and the impact of Nabinchandra's triad are discernible.

Interestingly, the frivolous nature of Kāma has also been transformed to some extent. The ethical overtone of the poem has manifested itself whenever there is an opportunity. The use of folk myths of Bengal is another feature that deserves mention. The figures of Himālaya and Menakā in the fourth canto have clearly been grafted from the typical cultural tradition of Bengal, more particularly from the repertory of śākta lyrics. It is better not to trace their origin in the first canto of the *Kumārasambhava* because they are totally divested of the characteristic Puranic lustre in the *Tridivavijaya.*

In this category of minor epics, the *Śaktisambhavakāvya* (1870) of Biharilal Bandyopadhyaya may be mentioned separately. The famous episode pertaining to the slaying of the mighty buffalo-demon (Mahiṣāsura) by the mother goddess is presented in this work, consisting of eight Skandhas. But in spite of all sound and fury associated with the epic structure, it signifies nothing and remains an example of colossal wastage of literary labour. Being unable to register proper direction and channelise creative imagination, the edifice has floundered and consequently the whole poem sounds like a ridiculous verbiage. Like the poets of post-Bhāravi court epics of Sanskrit literature, Biharilal has also tried to exhibit his scholarship while both the progress of the narrative and the portrayal of the poetic personae suffered terribly. Confusion prevails everywhere as the Purāṇic and non-Purāṇic materials have been blended injudiciously. In his anxiety to show the range of scholarship, the poet has referred to obsolete Purāṇic details, Upanishadic doctrines and Bengali folk-myths at random. As a result, the narrative has been diluted neplus ultra.

Throughout the poem, Śiva, Indra, Varuṇa, Kārttikaya, Śacī and Nārada appear and disappear alternately. For no sufficient reason, the tottering narrative has been stretched to a wearisome length. The *Saktisambhavakayva* has failed to imbibe the legacy of the Sanskrit court epics on the one hand while on the other hand its explicit intention to imitate Madhusudan's style has landed it in a topsy turvy situation.

Saraccandra Choudhury's *Deviyuddha* (1900) is a poem with eleven cantos that deserves our special attention. It deals with the episode of slaying of Sumbha and Nisumbha by the Mother goddess. Obivously, it is taken from that portion of the *Mārkaṇdeya Purāṇa* which is famous as the *Caṇdī.* The poet has handled this subject in such a way that the *Devīyuddha* contains strong suggestions of an allegorical work that sustains on intense patriotic feelings. There are ethical and religious overtones as well which, as we know, may be regarded as the hallmark of the worldview of the sociocultural milieu in the last quarter of nineteenth century Bengal. In this poem, the gods have been portrayed as home-internee who seek advice from Bṛhaspati and in the process are indoctrinated with the ideal of nationalism. They set out to achieve their goal but different vices put their integrity to test. They become disillusioned and cannot retain their enthusiasm any longer. Instead, they reconcile themselves to the 'reality' of colonial bondage with a view to achieving only their selfish ends for which everything has to be made subservient to the maintenance of status quo. Bṛhaspati fails to bring the gods back to the path of duty and plunges into meditation for the well-being of the three worlds.

After sometime, the gods practise penance to propitiate the mother goddess since she is the fundamental source of strength and energy of all beings. The goddess appears and advises the gods about the means of conquering the three worlds in course of which the concept of political independence comes to the fore. However, she takes initiative to kill the demon brothers rather belatedly. After going through this poem, we get the impression that the poet has followed the *Caṇdī* only to prepare a broad outline of his intended text. He seems always very eager to add new details from contemporary experiences and discover metaphorical import in the Puranic details. In fact, the Puranic narrative furnished Saraccandra merely with an outward structure in which he has woven new textures derived from newly awakened spirit of patriotism and national glory. The *Deviyuddha* may therefore be regarded as a unique product of the ninetenth century Bengali epic genre. Being a colonial elite, Saraccandra was not in a position to express his dismay, frustration and anger in a straightforward manner; nevertheless, unlike other authors of the minor epics, he was not ready to conceal his attention altogether under some insignificant Puranic exterior. Though the thematic design deduced from the cosmic struggle between gods and demons has become hackneyed by then, Saraccandra appears to be very keen to avoid cliched materials and discover new dimensions in that cosmic drama in such a way that these might be interpreted as archetypes having validity in contemporary life. At any rate, the message against colonial domination is loud and clear, which was noted by the British rulers as well. Hence, their wrath came down upon the book and it was proscribed. That is indeed a rare honour for a poem which is never included among the elites of the genre.

Indeed patriotic spirit is not simply one among many ingredients nor can it be regarded as a passing phase of poetic ecstasy because it permeats the entire microcosm of the *Deviyuddha*. The unmistakable traits of reality can be detected easily beneath the thin mythic mask. No one can miss the unconcealed feelings of the poet when, under the pretext of describing the self-criticism of the unenterprising gods, he actually takes his fellow countrymen to task for their indifference, lethargy and reluctant attitude. This is again evident in the poet's emphasis on the necessity of unity of dedication and self-sacrifice. He has also come down heavily upon the tendency of inaction, compromise and timidity emanating from total lack of self-confidence and immobility in the contemporary society. It is therefore natural that the Purāṇic deities will be thoroughly transformed and retain very few divine traits. However, due to the emphasis on allegorical nuances of the theme, they are never complete individuals with human essence. Thus Bṛhaspati, Śiva, Kārttikeya etc. have been suitably remodelled as the interpreters of the thoughts and ideas predominant in the last quarter of the nineteenth century Bengal. Even Caṇḍa and Muṇḍa, two insignificant demon characters, are practically spokesmen of peoples' rights whose words are astonishingly close to cardinal socialistic conception. Likewise Śumbha and Niśumbha are not merely two mightly demons of the *Mārkaṇḍeya Purāṇa* while Vīrabhadra has some affinity with Indubala of the *Vṛtrasamhāra.* Interestingly, the demon characters are livelier than their divine counterparts and display sincerity, strength, cruelty and straightforwardness with equal vigour.

The *Deviyuddha* thrives on the contemporary political awareness blossoming into yearning for a sustained struggle for freedom. The loss of paradise has been a convenient metaphor for the Bengali poets right from the time of Hemchandra Bandyopadhyaya; they went on repeating the description of its reconquest tirelessly. As we have already noted elsewhere, this signifies an imaginative compensation for the lack of enterprise in reality as well as a national wish-fulfillment. But Saraccandra went a few steps forward; hence the old metaphor was animated once again. It was revitalized albeit temporarily in such a manner that it could accept the burden of the exigencies of socio-political reality and did not crumble down. The mythic paradigm was built anew in this poem; interestingly the poet made use of old and new ingredients with equal dexterity. Thus the image of the mother-goddess in the *Deviyuddha* seems to have been substantially inspired by Bankimchandra's famous conception of the icon of mother India in his epoch-making novel, the *Anandamatha.* Besides those already mentioned earlier, the figures of Pavana, Raktavīja, Mahāmāya are also noteworthy. The description of the heaven of Brahman has not remained confined within the set limits of Puranic model; it has clear metaphysical undertones. But Saraccandra fascinates us by his sincere efforts towards creative renewal of traditional materials so that these might be adequately tuned to the new rhythms and aspirations of the contemporary society.

VI

Among the poems based on the episodės of Kṛṣṇa's life, only a couple may be mentioned here. Dinanath Dhar's *Kamsavināśa* (1861) is an incomplete poem having four cantos. It deals with the episodes of the early childhood of Kṛṣṇa. Dinanath published it as the first volume but no other volume came out. It is significant that such an instance of futile literary labour could be found in an epoch-making year in the history of Bengali epic genre (that is the year of publication of the *Meghanādvadha.*). It means that the mechanical continuum of the epic tradition is by no means enough; a process of creative renewal is imperative if a new case of life is to be given. There is nothing noteworthy in the subjectmatter, formal device, characterisation of the *Kamsavināśa.* Dinanath seems to have been influenced by the *Harivamśa* but he blends the Puranic and non-Puranic elements together. That is why we find Arādhanā and Bhakti along with Viṣṇu, Śiva, Devakī, Vasudeva, Pārvatī etc. It is quite probable that Madhusudan's pantheon may have cast its spell here. However, the unnecessary intrusion of the folk myths from the legacy of the mangal kāvyas has further weakened the work. The demons like Sakaṭāsura Vikaṭāsura, Pūtanā and of course, Kamsa himself, have emerged from the childrens' world of magic and fantasy.

Haricharan Chakraborty's *Bhadrovdvāha* (1870) is an incomplete poem of three cantos which is described as the first volume; but no other volume was ever published. It deals with the story of king Śrīvatsa, queen Cintā and the wrathful Śani. It may be taken as another instance of sheer wastage of literary labour and symptomatic of non-creative pursuit of vaguely understood tradition.

Harilal Goswami's *Narakasamhāra* (1896) is a vast poem of twenty one cantos but his plot is weak and the structure is totally inadequate. He is often carried away too far because of his fondness for unnecessary details. This is an indication of the negative impact of the post-Bhāravi court epics. Harilal is keen to exhibit his scholarship; occasionally he refers to contemporary situation as well. Quite expectedly, he derives inspiration from the great triad of the Bengali epic genre. But, in spite of his explicit intentions to follow the method of the older poets, Harilal actually landed him in a mess. Because merely mechanical reproduction of established formulae does not make an epic poem. Hence, the abundant presence of cosmogonic and Puranic myths and repetition of the catalogue of cliches like the loss of paradise, the torment of demon Naraka, the incarnation of Kṛṣṇa, the heavens of Brahman and Śiva, the wailing of the Earth etc. could not elevate the *Narakasamhāra.* Likewise, the cohabitation of the Puranic and non-Puranic deities has improved nothing.

VII

Among the poems based on subjectmatter of miscellaneous origin, we may discuss the following:

Jagaccandra Dev Sarkar Choudhury's *Abjodvaha* (1867) deals with Daṇḍin's marriage with Abjā, the daughter of Śukra, in seven cantos. There is absolute anarchy both in the spheres of arrangement of the subjectmatter and in characterisation. Jagaccandra has not bothered to maintain even workable logic.

Brajanath Mitra's *Kādambarī* (1869) narrates the marriage of Kādambarī, daughter of Varuṇa, with Kali and the latter's downfall in three cantos. Like other contemporary poetasters, Brajanath too had a message to deliver through his work, viz., the habit of drinking alcohol spells disaster. But the haphazard presentation of the subjectmatter has totally frustrated whatever purpose he had and instead unmitigated chaos has held sway. Hence there seems to be not even the faintest trace of textual planning. We come across heaven and hell, gods and demons, Kali and Dvāpara in which these Puranic details appear perfunctorily. It is another instance of literary anarchy which, under the pretext of adherence to tradition, destroys its very roots.

Prafulla Chandra Bandyopadhyaya's *Sambaraṇavijaya* (1869), consisting of six cantos, was declared as the first volume of a proposed work whose second volume was never brought to light. In fact, such a detail seemed to have become customary in the sixties and seventies of nineteenth century; it actually signifies that the ambition to be an epic poet had percolated far and wide after the meteoric rise of Madhusudan. Consequently there was a tendency among the neo-elites of that period to jump into the frey to book seemingly easy passage to immortality. Under the spell of a sudden May-flush of youthful exuberance, the first volume used to be announced enthusiastically. But it was soon realised that the Epic Muse could not be propitiated so easily. Therefore, those poetasters used to call off their ambitious projects unceremoniously. Prafullachandra's *Sambaraṇavijaya* was one of those misdirected literary adventures. It deals with the Puranic story of king Sambaraṇa whose kingdom suffered owing to Indra's wrath. Unnecessary details have jammed the progress of the poem quite often. It is totally devoid of poetic merit. Besides Indra and Sambaraṇa, it introduces Vasiṣṭha, Pṛthvī, Kali, Śiva and Nārāyaṇa; but these figures remain hollow throughout.

Harimohan Mukhopadhyaya's *Adṛṣtavijaya* (1881) constitutes of ten cantos. As usual, this was declared as the first volume whose sequel never came out. Some Puranic ingredients have been used indiscriminately. The author seems to have no definite scheme and structure; moroever the subjectmatter is imaginary. There is a customary message underneath but it has not been presented convincingly. In the ultimate analysis, in spite of Harimohan's explicit allegiance to the Sanskrit court epics, the *Adṛṣtavijaya* remains a wastage of efforts. The poet has made use of mythic and quasi-mythic materials, viz., Indra's intrigues, Varuṇa's assistance, the invasion of heaven by Kali, the activities of Laksmī, Nārāyana, Māyā and Satyavrata. But, due to lack of cohesiveness, the work remains a literary failure.

VIII

A few poems were fashioned on some historical episodes which were substantially reshaped by poetic fancy. Their main points of emphasis were patriotism and restoration of national honour. Most of these poets were directly indebted to the prominent poets of the Bengali epic genre while their dependence on the Sanskrit epic tradition was only secondary. Among such poems, we have the following:

Banoarilal Roys' *Jayabātī* (1865) closely resembles the *Padmini Upakhyana* of Rangalal Bandyopadhyaya. The poet has chosen an imaginary story about the Rajputs as his subjectmatter but tried to endow it with an appearance of historicity. We have already noted in earlier chapter that the Sanskrit historical epics thrived on such blending of imaginary details with historical facts. Hence the works like the *Jayābatī* has their antecedents in epic tradition. The author seems to have mechanically followed the dictum of Sanskrit poetics in adding many descriptive details but it could not rescue his work from being artistically irrelevant.

Shyamacharan Shrimani's *Simhalavijaya* (1875) owes its subject matter to the famous Pali text, the *Mahavamśa.* The poet has freely mixed supernatural and historical elements and thus produced a queer mixture of conflicting details. The intervention of the gods in the narrative, having claims of historicity, has given rise to a paradoxical situation. It also hints at the poet's inadequate understanding of the true import of the epic genre on the one hand and his own role in interpreting the changing reality of his time on the other. Shyamacharan has freely drawn his materials from the decadent court epics, the mangalkāvyas, the *Meghanādvadha* etc. The poem constitutes of four cantos in which Vijayasimha's conquest of Lankā, his marriage with Kubeni, intrigues and battles have been described. The *Simhalavijaya* is crowded with supernatural elements, however, patriotic spirit has also been displayed in abundance. But, as we have already noted, the sumtotal of these contradictory details has not culminated into an epic poem. The poet's explicit awareness of various legacies of the past could not stir up his creative sensibilities sufficiently and hence, the outcome of his mechanical adherence to tradition is far from encouraging.

Durga Chandra Sanyal's *Mahāmogala* has three volumes, the first of which is known as the *Aurongzeb Parva* (1875). It is followed by *Sivaji Parva* (1876) while the third volume is known as the *Jayasimha Parva* (1877). The poet seems to have tried to arrive at a workable compromise between the norms of Sanskrit and western epics. In the preface of the *Aurongzeb Parva,* Durga Chandra speaks of his indebtedness to Madhusudan, Hemchandra, Nabinchandra and Milton. Though he did not particularly mention the Sanskrit epics, the penumbral extension of the legacy of the Sanskrit historical epics is discernible in the *Mahamogal.* The poet shows his eagerness to make the best use of the available historical data but, in the manner of the Sanskrit historical epics, he has relied more on imagination and some pre-determined stock-in-trade. Consequently the work throughout remains merely descriptive and the progress of the narrative is suspended. The *Sivaji Parva* (i.e. the second volume) has clearly been influenced by Ramesh Chandra Dutta's famous historical novel, the *Mahāraṣtra-jiban-prabhat.* The *Jayasimha Parva* is also the result of free blending of historical facts with imaginary events. Due to the impact of the Sanskrit epic tradition on the general structure and descriptive details, each volume of the *Mahamogal Kavya* is marked with immobility, incongruity and confusion.

Dhirendranath Paul's *Yamini-Prabhat* (1879) has ten cantos in which the author has not even cared to maintain his pretension of historicity. Because, imaginary events have completely overshadowed the historical elements; even the gods have their roles to play. In fact, the poetic personae are histoircal in names only. The spirit of Hindu revivalism has completely taken over the reins of the poem. The creative facets of the tradition are no longer traceable.

Yogendranath Ghosh's *Vanger Viraputra* (1884) forms the first volume of an intended epic whose second volume, as usual, was never published. It deals with the mythicised history of the Bengali warrior-king, Pratapaditya, in seven cantos. It contains the spirit of patriotism in abundance though some Puranic motifs have also found their way in the narrative. Yogendranath seems to have idolised Hemchandra and searched for a golden mean between the fading epic and the rising novel. He did neither have the courage to ring out the old nor could he aspire to ring in the new.

The poems based on non-Indian sources, viz., Girish Chandra Basu's *Svargabhrasta Kavya* (1869) and Ananda Chandra Mitra's *Helena Kavya* (Mymensingh 1876 and Dacca 1877).

In the ultimate analysis, these minor Bengali epics have failed to attain the pinnacle of artistic glory only because their authors could not exercise the requisite control over the method of seeing and conceptualizing reality. They could not feel the pulse-beat of tradition—old yet renewing itself constantly—and consequently they failed to arrest the degeneration of the epic genre and infuse new life into it any more.

The wheel of epic genre thus came in full circle during the initial onslaught of colonial subjugation. The epic Muse arrived with a bang but ended with a whimper.

Index

■■■